NEWS

NE

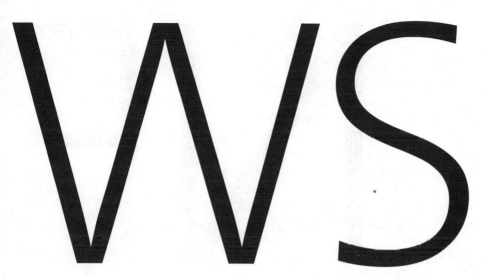

THE POLITICS OF ILLUSION

TENTH EDITION

W. LANCE BENNETT

THE UNIVERSITY OF CHICAGO PRESS

Chicago and London

W. Lance Bennett is professor of political science
and the Ruddick C. Lawrence Professor of
Communication at the University of Washington.

The University of Chicago Press, Chicago 60637
The University of Chicago Press, Ltd., London
© 2016 by The University of Chicago
All rights reserved. Published 2016.
Printed in the United States of America

25 24 23 22 21 20 19 18 17 16   1 2 3 4 5

ISBN-13: 978-0-226-34486-7 (paper)
ISBN-13: 978-0-226-34505-5 (e-book)
DOI: 10.7208/chicago/9780226345055.001.0001

Earlier editions of this book were previously published by Pearson
Education Inc. Any questions concerning permissions should be directed
to Permissions Department, The University of Chicago Press, Chicago, IL.

Library of Congress Cataloging-in-Publication Data
Names: Bennett, W. Lance, author.
Title: News : the politics of illusion / W. Lance Bennett.
Description: Tenth edition. | Chicago ; London : The University of Chicago Press, 2016. |
Includes bibliographical references and index.
Identifiers: LCCN 2016002843 | ISBN 9780226344867 (pbk. : alk. paper) |
ISBN 9780226345055 (e-book)
Subjects: LCSH: Journalism—Political aspects—United States. | Press and politics—United
States. | Mass media—Political aspects—United States. | Digital media—Political aspects—
United States. | Online journalism—Political aspects—United States.
Classification: LCC PN4888.P6 B46 2016 | DDC 302.230973—dc23
LC record available at http://lccn.loc.gov/2016002843

♾ This paper meets the requirements of ANSI/NISO Z39.48-1992
(Permanence of Paper).

CONTENTS

PREFACE

This edition of *News: The Politics of Illusion* might be termed the "great transformation" edition, as the focus is on American press-politics in transition. Many observers are now referring to conventional news organizations as the *legacy press*, signaling both their past glory and the effects of disruptive competition from *native digital* upstarts. These new-generation information companies have only existed online, with platforms, business models, and content creation systems aimed at engaging so-called digital natives who came of age in a participatory social media environment. As a result, familiar news brands such as the *New York Times, USA Today*, and CNN are operating in a fragmenting and expanding mediaverse that resembles a big bang of proliferating online competitors that are stealing audiences and ad revenues and challenging the very definition of news itself. The legacy press is struggling to reinvent itself while maintaining, as best it can, journalism standards developed in the last century: balance and objectivity, timeliness, credibility, and relevance, to name a few. Those standards are being disrupted on different fronts. For example, audience-powered sites such as *Huffington Post*, BuzzFeed, *Vox*, and *Vice* blend some (more or less) conventional political reporting with opinion blogs, swimsuit models, celebrity gossip, cat videos, and other ephemera aimed at getting clicks, likes, and shares. While BuzzFeed does have a "news" tab, other content can be sorted in terms of LOL, OMG, WTF, and a curious category named WIN that at one time revealed a feature on "photos of hot men and cats." A different challenge to legacy journalism comes from other parts of this expanding mediaverse with the rise of serious investigative organizations such as ProPublica, InvestigateWest, and *The Intercept*, among others. Seeking to reinvent watchdog journalism that holds government accountable to public interest standards, members of these organizations often find the legacy press too dependent on government officials for daily information handouts, and too timid or resource poor to investigate and expose deceptions beyond the spin.

Thinking back over the previous nine editions that have bridged these changes is a bit dizzying. When the first edition of this book was published in the early 1980s, the American press was embedded within a mass media system that transmitted much the same information each day to a mass public that has been termed "captive" because the information channels were so few and the differences among them so small. Information in the news media tended to be packaged around cues from prominent authorities (public officials, business executives, and leaders of social organizations). Those cues shaped opinions and channeled participation in politics. The daily news was a primary conduit through which those opinion-shaping messages traveled. The press distilled competing points of view for public consumption and filtered out voices deemed less prominent or less credible. Those functions of the press were called "gatekeeping." While this process often made journalists dependent on those in power, there was a greater sense among the public that those in power cared more about the public interest.

For their part, news organizations were able to invest in reporters, investigative units, and large numbers of domestic and international bureaus because they faced only moderate pressures from owners and investors to steer clear of controversy and maximize profits. TV news was not expected to produce the revenue levels of entertainment programming. Newspapers generated enough ad revenues to reinvest in the quality of the news product and still return profits to owners. Until the mid-1980s, there was relatively strong commitment in broadcast and print media to investigative reporting, as many news organizations were still invigorated by the role of the press in exposing the crimes of the Nixon administration in the Watergate scandal just a decade before, and the government deceptions that led to the Vietnam War a decade before that. In this era of the mass media, neither the press nor the political system were perfect—far from it—but they operated very differently than they do today.

Flash forward to this tenth edition, and much of this has changed. The media system has fragmented into broadcast and cable channels, online platforms, and social media. The bonds of common social belonging in parties, clubs, unions, churches, public schools, and other institutions of civic life have dissolved or weakened. The result has been a shift from a mass society stitched together by federations of clubs and organizations to a networked society in which individuals are more responsible for constructing their own social support systems and selecting the information that gives their lives meaning. In this era of The Daily Me, personalized communication technologies are key to making society and politics work. Meanwhile, most of what we still recognize as news is produced by legacy news organizations. But those news organizations have been bought and sold, merged and divested, and squeezed for profits at the expense of quality journalism. More importantly, the emerging business models and audience engagement logic of digital media have transformed how content is produced, sold, and distributed.

It remains an open question whether the legacy press could have better adapted to the participatory spirit of the digital age had it not been so wounded by its economic struggles. One of the interesting stories running through this edition is how various legacy news organizations are trying to adapt. The even bigger story—as told in several sections of the book, including a completely revised chapter 7 on the economics of the news business—is what kinds of news will emerge from all of this, and what role will remain for the legacy press. The participatory culture of the digital age invites audiences to join in the creation and sharing of content in ways that conflict with the standards of legacy journalism. The traditional journalism authority of telling people "that's the way it is" no longer works, as public information habits change and people want to be more involved in the information process. The proliferation of so many alternative channels of information offers people greater choice over what to believe, how to share it with others, and what actions to take. Because of the increasing tendency of people to select the information they want, the effects of news exposure are not as clear as in earlier times. The kinds of media effects associated with the current era involve reinforcing, rather than challenging and changing, prior beliefs and biases.

How will these competing forces play out to reshape the forms and roles of news in the American democracy? This edition of *News: The Politics of Illusion* explains the mix of old and new and points to possible outcomes. Where areas of change are clearly established, key concepts from earlier editions have been revised. For example, the nature of information biases in the legacy press has evolved over the arc of ten editions. Three of the four biases—*personalization, dramatization,* and *fragmentation*—have remained relatively constant features of news stories over this period. However, the bias that most commonly drives news plots has changed. Early editions discussed the bias of normalization. Some news organizations even instructed journalists to frame stories in terms of "Is my world safe?" and how things are being worked out. As partisan conflict in Washington grew more intense in the 1990s, reporting shifted to a bias I referred to as a tension between "authority and disorder." Politicians did not seem as often to be in control or as able to restore the security and safety of everyday life. Authorities seemed to be permanently in conflict, and many problems seemed to be too big, too global, and perhaps too captured by inside interests to solve. During this time, disorder often replaced the normalization of reassuring authority from an earlier era. The present era comes across in the news as one of strategic posturing on the part of many officials, which the press often frames as a game, reflecting the growing role of punditry and commentary in contemporary journalism. Journalists now routinely interview other journalists as news sources, posturing as political insiders providing color commentary on the posturing of politicians and parties. The posturing and cynicism of both politicians and journalists has turned off many citizens, who feel that Washington is out of touch with the people and that the news does a poor job of explaining why this has happened. This *game-framing bias* only captures part of the reality of contemporary politics. The news surrounding these dramatic and personalized political games is offered up as fragmented episodes that seldom explain why breakdowns in cooperation and concern for the public interest occur, or what can be done to fix them. Indeed, news articles report on the political winners and losers inside the Beltway, but seldom talk about the winners and losers among the interests and broader publics affected by the outcomes of political games. It is not surprising that in this imagined media community called America, the Beltway has become a symbolic border separating Washington from the rest of the country.

At the same time, there are many interesting and hopeful developments in press politics to report. Recent years have witnessed a number of investigative journalism startups dedicated to holding public officials and business elites accountable to democratic values. These accountability news organizations promise a new era of watchdog journalism aimed at restoring transparency and trust in government. This edition of *News* charts the rise of such organizations as ProPublica and *The Intercept* and various hybrids such as Wikileaks that have invigorated political reporting with blockbuster stories about the wars in Iraq and Afghanistan and the US government spying on its own citizens, among other topics. The growing divide between the legacy press and this new investigative journalism runs through the discussions in chapter 5 on political reporting and in chapter 6 on the role of objectivity in the journalism profession.

All along the way in this tenth edition, there are new case studies, updates on old favorites, and lots of new material on how the new media system and new kinds of information engagement affect our politics. Many older examples are gone, along with unnecessary verbiage. Thanks to a shorter length, the publisher has generously agreed to increase the font size, which should ease the strain on tired eyes. However, the big news about the tenth edition of *News* is that the whole book has been reframed to look at the tensions between the legacy press and emerging native digital media—tensions magnified by changing audience and citizen information habits. In addition to understanding how these different systems with their different communication logics interact, the book aims to illuminate how they interface with our national politics.

Not since the formation of the legacy press during the early twentieth century have such forces of change been present in society, technology, and politics. Chapter 6 tells the story of the origins of the last press system and draws a lesson that applies to the current era as well: there was no grand discussion and no master plan to fit the press system to the needs of democracy. There were, of course, adjustments, reforms, and political debates from time to time. It may be comforting to think that the next system will emerge from more rational processes. However, as shown in the new case study in chapter 6, the legacy press is struggling to find answers for many of its current professional dilemmas. Meanwhile, as explained in chapter 7, the rise of native digital formats with new business models and audience engagement technologies seems to be creating a kind of news system that bears little similarity to the old one. How will this emerging information system fit democracy? It is not clear that there is much consideration of this question during the present era of change either. Perhaps the news should contain a consumer warning.

> **WARNING**
> **The news has no democratic warranty.**

Recognizing that there is no guarantee that the news will suit the needs of democracy raises a disturbing question: Why is there so little focused public (and formal government) debate aimed at defining and improving this most important product in order to better supply the information needs of democracy? Indeed, much of the public debate that we have is focused on precisely the wrong issues: the alleged liberal political biases of reporters or calls for more balanced or objective reporting. As we will see, these concerns are not only impossible to fix, but they miss more important underlying problems.

Meaningful change requires people to better understand some of the underlying defects in the current communication system. In particular, change requires thinking more critically about how to inform people in ways that bring them together around programs of political action that might actually solve problems in society and government. We will return to consider the possibilities for improving communication infrastructure and technologies to better suit the needs of contemporary democracy at the close of the book. If such reforms are possible, however, it is important to build a basis for thinking sensibly about what they are and how to implement them. Above all, a better understanding of how the communication system operates might enable journalism schools, news organizations, government representatives, and citizens to convert disillusionment into constructive responses.

The goal of this book is to challenge comfortable myths by introducing evidence that invites new ways of thinking about our political information system. To stimulate the reader's thinking, the book provides a perspective that is critical of both the news and politics—a perspective intended to provoke thought and reaction. I have chosen to present a broad, alternative point of view for a simple reason: there would be little gained by going over the story of the free press in America yet another time. Most Americans, and many readers abroad, already know the saga of a free press and a free people. True, you may have forgotten a few characters or some of the episodes. Nevertheless, memorizing those missing facts once again would not change the plot about how the enduring struggle for freedom of speech and information has created the foundation for democracy in America. Because you know this story already, you should use it in thinking about the argument in this book. Don't feel that you must accept either the story of the free press or the perspective in this book in its entirety. Use the two perspectives to challenge each other and help you draw your own conclusions. After all, the capacity to think independently, without fear or insecurity, is the foundation on which our political freedom rests.

1

NEWS IN A CHANGING
INFORMATION SYSTEM

Over the past two decades, economic, cultural, political and
technological changes have challenged the stability of the existing
media regime . . . raising questions such as the relative merits of
Saturday Night Live, *CBS Evening News*, Fox News, Twitter, Facebook,
the *Huffington Post*, and the *New York Times* as sources of political
information.
                            —Bruce A. Williams and Michael X. Delli Carpini[1]

I don't know anything about the newspaper business. . . . I went
through a few gates before deciding to buy The [Washington] Post.
Is it hopeless? I didn't want to do it if it was. The Internet has radically
disrupted traditional newspapers. The world is completely changed.
                            —Jeff Bezos[2]

Around the time the first web browsers sparked the Inter-
net boom of the 1990s, Nicholas Negroponte envisioned the coming of a vir-
tual news experience that he termed The Daily Me.[3] As the name implies,
such an information system delivers what each of us wants to know about,
when, where, and how we like it. Negroponte, a founder of the MIT Media
Lab, called the old mass media system The Daily Us because it brought
people in society together around pretty much the same reporting of common problems, threats, and triumphs (and still does when something really
big happens). We now live with both media systems in play. People born
after 1980 have been termed "digital natives"[4] because they have or will
come of age in a highly personalized digital media environment. These
digital generations are more likely to experience The Daily Me, as they get
information through Facebook and Twitter and by surfing the web. Many
other citizens live comfortably within both information systems, combining
personalized online sources with what we now call "legacy" news sources
such as TV, radio, and daily papers. Meanwhile, another segment of citizens
(primarily those over 55) live mainly with The Daily Us of newspapers and
broadcast news—but the size of that "us" is shrinking, as the legacy media

generation grows older. While we are not likely to see the legacy news media disappear, the dominance of that system is being challenged by new forms of content production and distribution that involve more audience participation and even bypass traditional journalism in content creation. A source of friction at the interface of these two systems is that much of the serious news that continues to circulate through the digital sphere is produced by legacy news organizations that are having trouble generating revenues as advertising money follows prime younger demographics online.

As these changes play out, the emerging information order still retains some echoes of what we once thought of as news: *important information delivered in timely fashion to people who want to know it.* Yet more information is automated, digested by machines, and delivered through highly personalized channels. Consider, for example, how the reader of this book may encounter important local news in the not too distant future:

> Jan is in her self-driving car on her way to a meeting in a city nearby, when a severe thunderstorm hits her hometown, spawning a small tornado. Jan's smartwatch issues a storm warning, then alerts her that her daughter's school is in lockdown. The smartwatch asks Jan if she wants more details. "Yes, neighborhood news," Jan replies. "Car display." . . . Real-time posts from her neighborhood appear with details of damage and with photos. Jan's house sends a message that the power is out. A request for a map of her town shows the path and real-time location of the tornado. It also shows which neighborhoods have power and which schools are locked down. Road closures and traffic jams appear as red lines.[5]

The information in this scenario seems intuitively like news, in that it is timely and important. However, this information is produced and distributed largely by machines, not journalists and news organizations. Even in this simple weather scenario, it is not clear how people would learn what public officials are doing or whether their response seems adequate. Many local news organizations that would report such political information are struggling to stay in business as audiences migrate to an array of digital information sources. The advertising dollars that once supported local news media are flowing to digital platforms such as Google that target consumers in more refined and personalized ways.

As journalism organizations struggle to find stable niches within this complex information environment, many critics worry that the quality of reporting is deteriorating, contributing to the growing numbers of citizens who have stopped following news produced by conventional journalism organizations.[6] Among those who continue to use legacy news sources, the average time spent each day on those sources declines dramatically across each generation from retirees to young adults.[7] As the balance tips toward The Daily Me, social media sites are increasingly popular as news feeds, with some 30 percent of the public getting news from Facebook. Compared to people who go directly to an online news site, those referred by Facebook spend only one-quarter as much time on each story, while encountering just one-sixth as many total stories. Entertainment is the most popular type of news on Facebook, favored by 73 percent of the site's news seekers. National political news comes in fourth, regularly encountered by 55 percent of the Facebook news audience, while international news comes in ninth at 39 percent.[8] In addition to providing a sketchy impression of the day's events, social media news feeds enable people to select their own versions of just the topics that interest them, resulting in scattered public attention mixed with polarization of views on critical problems.[9]

Will publics in this mixed information environment be less in the know, more polarized, and less able to come together to decide what to do about important issues? Motivated by these concerns, many communication scholars and journalists lament the decline of *traditional news based on investigations by journalists and distributed by news organizations as what citizens need to know about their world*. Meanwhile, others argue that the legacy news media have seldom lived up to the watchdog journalism ideal of holding officials accountable. Besides, there is so much information available online that it is easy to become informed if one really cares. But how do we establish the accuracy of much of what passes for political information online? Or, is The Daily Me based on what people want to believe, making facts and evidence less important?

No matter where one falls in these controversies, one thing is clear: we will not return to anything like the mass media news system and its large "captive audience" of the last century.[10] The legacy news organizations that anchored that system have suffered a number of shocks that include competition from an explosion of mobile apps and specialized online platforms that growing numbers of people find more in tune with their lifestyles. When people share the information that pulses through their devices, they often edit and add commentary to help it travel over particular social networks. This involvement of audiences in producing and distributing information changes the neat *one-to-many* communication logic that defined the mass media era. Social media employ a *many-to-many* logic that involves people more interactively in the communication process. Jay

Rosen has argued that this shift is so significant that we need a new terminology for "the people formerly known as the audience." He even published a mythical manifesto from them telling the mass media people:

> You don't own the eyeballs. You don't own the press, which is now divided into pro and amateur zones. You don't control production on the new platform, which isn't one-way. There's a new balance of power between you and us.
>
> The people formerly known as the audience are simply *the public* made realer, less fictional, more able, less predictable. You should welcome that, media people. But whether you do or not, we want you to know we're here.[11]

During such a time of change, it is best to resist defining news as only that content produced by journalists and formal news organizations. Bruce Williams and Michael Delli Carpini propose a set of grounding questions that point us beyond the changing world of journalism in thinking about the political role of information media: "Do the media provide us with the kinds of information that helps individual and collective decision-making? Do media provide us with enough of this information? Do we trust the information provided by the media?"[12] The answers to these questions given by ordinary citizens do not bode well for the legacy media. For example, roughly one-third of people surveyed have dropped a legacy news source because of declining quality.[13] Public confidence in print and television news is hovering around 20 percent, with surprisingly little difference across age, education, or gender.[14] Some of this discontent is surely due to an overriding discouragement with the mean tone of politics today—a tone that inevitably saturates conventional news reporting. Beyond the negativity of politics and the tendency of journalists to get caught up in it, there are many other factors affecting the quality of our political information system today. Let's begin with why so many observers argue for finding ways to save or reinvent journalism.

Why Journalism Matters

The struggles of the legacy press system may not worry most people because there appear to be so many outlets for information that it is hard to keep up with them. One only need enter a topic in a search engine to find hundreds or thousands of sites with information about it. Yet many of the blogs, webzines, and online news organizations are merely recycling the shrinking journalism content produced by increasingly threatened news organizations. Consider a revealing study of one news microcosm: the "news ecosystem" of the city of Baltimore. The Pew Project for Excellence in Journalism conducted a study of where information about politics, government, and public life came from in that city.[15] The study looked at various media, from newspaper, radio, and television to blogs and other online sites. Although this information system seemed rich and diverse, with some 53 different outlets for news, tracking the origins of actual news items showed that 95 percent of the stories containing original information "came from traditional media—most of them from the newspaper." Even more distressing was a look back in time showing that the sole surviving paper, the *Baltimore Sun*, reported 32 percent fewer stories between 1999 and 2009, and 73 percent fewer than in 1991.

In his sweeping look at the creation (and demise) of the modern media, Paul Starr argued that if these trends continue, the growing ignorance of the citizenry and the diminished public accountability of officials will surely be accompanied by a great wave of public corruption.[16] Indeed, many citizens already see corruption in government as a major problem. For example, a 2008 poll on the roots of the financial crisis showed that 62 percent strongly agreed with the statement that political corruption played a major role in the crisis, and another 19 percent agreed "somewhat" with that statement.[17] By 2013, 76 percent of Americans felt that the political parties were the most corrupt institutions and that the problem was growing worse.[18]

Despite evidence that problems with accountability or watchdog journalism began long before news organizations encountered financial problems or lost audiences, many proposals focus on improving the financial health of existing journalism organizations. While remedies such as putting up paywalls for access to online information may work for specialized publications such as the *Wall Street Journal*, they do not seem destined to save journalism in general. The immediate problem is that as long as there are free news outlets, those charging for the same information will not likely attract many paying customers. Whether or not there is truth to the popular Internet mantra that "information wants to be free,"[19] it is also equally true that those who produce quality, independent information want to be paid.

Despite these perceived limitations, a strong case can still be made that independent journalism is the only hope for regular and reliable information about what those in power are doing.[20] Without it, say proponents of this view, the lights go out on democracy, meaning that government is left to police itself while promoting its own activities through public relations, propaganda, or spin.[21]

Can the News Be Fixed?

In the view of scholars like Thomas Patterson, the answer is for journalism organizations to return to their core values of informing the public with timely and accurate information about government and public life. He notes that studies of what kinds of news Americans follow most closely put topics like wars, economic problems, and policy issues at the top (along with bad weather and natural disasters), while scandals and the lives of celebrities are at the bottom.[22] The problem, according to Patterson, is that even when journalists try to cover important issues, they often get caught in tedious battles between politicians that shift the focus from the underlying issues to power struggles and spin. Since controversy and fights are thought to be good for drawing audiences, news organizations often amp up the political drama at the expense of more useful information.

However, before we decide that fixing the news is a simple matter of returning to core values, we must address a serious problem that stands in the way: a commercial media system that has been in a downward spiral of declining audiences, revenues, and product quality for several decades. News organizations in modern America were unusual businesses in the sense that they produced a public good (the news) through commercial transactions involving selling audiences to advertisers.[23] Until fairly recently, the ethics of professional journalism maintained something of a "firewall" between the journalism and the advertising sides of the business, with the result that advertisers had minimal direct control over what the news side did. At the same time, advertisers generally cared little about whether their money helped support a news bureau in Berlin or paid for reporting a story about the effects of climate change in Bolivia. There were, of course, times when commercial sponsors clashed with reporting decisions, as we will see in chapter 7. However, the current system has become bent on finding content that delivers desired consumers to advertisers, often to little avail. Online information sites can deliver advertising images in far more personalized ways to each individual, so that different people see different ads in the same article, and even different articles on a site. When the Internet suddenly offered cheaper and more precise means of targeting both ads and content to audiences, advertisers and audiences began to drift away from conventional media formats, leaving the news itself as an odd piece out in the media picture. Who would pay to produce that story on climate change? Who would pay to watch it? Most other democracies (including America in earlier times) have better understood the benefit of protecting such a valuable public good by figuring out how to support it through public subsidies, much in the way defense, public safety, education, and health care have been variously supported or subsidized as public goods.

In response to these fundamental problems with the legacy press, scholars such as Robert McChesney and John Nichols offer a variety of public subsidy models for the press that they argue have precedents in the American past.[24] However, in today's antigovernment political environment favoring privatization and market solutions, public subsidies for the press seem unlikely to be met with the reasoned debate necessary for such sweeping changes to occur. Even if new ways to support the press are developed (and there have been interesting experiments in recent years as discussed in chapter 7), citizens still must want the kind of information found in newspapers and broadcast programs.

Despite surveys showing that people say they would consume higher-quality news reporting, many people under 30 cannot imagine making appointments to watch the nightly news or sit in front of shouting pundits as their parents or grandparents do. News reports emphasizing the game of politics and fighting between the parties put many people off. And delivering those reports through clunky newspapers or scheduled broadcasts often clashes with how people seek information in mobile lifestyles. Younger citizens would rather search for topics of interest or follow links to YouTube videos sent by trusted friends on Facebook. Watching reports directly from other citizens who upload cell phone videos on YouTube may seem more authentic than having reporters interpret the same events. Indeed, in many cases, it is hard to distinguish reporters from ordinary people in technology-equipped crowds at the scene of events. One journalist observed such confusion during the public protests against the government in Turkey in 2013: "With everyone carrying cellphones and various digital gear, police had trouble distinguishing actual journalists from protesters."[25]

In short, economic problems are not the only challenges to "saving" the legacy press system. The public, particularly younger citizens, increasingly prefer different forms of information than engaging with the lumpy collections of content delivered in newspapers or television newscasts. As digital media scholar Clay Shirky put it, consumers "are not interested in single omnibus publications." Even more challenging, according to Shirky, is the fact that content flows through social networks according to a very different audience logic than defines the mass media: "the audience for news is now being assembled not by the paper but by other members of the audience."[26]

The Citizen Gap: Who Follows the News?

As more people get their information online from Facebook and Twitter or Google News, Yahoo News, and the *Huffington Post*, fewer are consuming conventional news formats. As noted earlier, this often means seeing fewer stories and spending less time per story than citizens who go directly to general news sites with the aim of following a broad scope of daily events. Studies claiming that large and growing populations of young online news consumers exist have produced a debate about whether the glass is half-empty or half-full. The Pew report *State of the News Media 2013* claimed that 60 percent of those under the age of 30 "got some form of digital news yesterday."[27] Critics such as Thomas Patterson contend that those reports may be counting people who report seeing a few headlines as they pass through their Internet portals en route to Facebook, fan sites, or games.[28] Other studies claim that younger citizens are meaningfully engaged with politics online but simply do not go in depth in following stories the way older citizens do.[29] Whether there is an encouraging upswing in online news consumption or a far more scattered exposure to isolated stories via Internet portals and social media platforms remains an important question. Part of the answer involves the changing definitions of what people think of as news when they report their information habits. Another piece of this puzzle is the selective exposure to news that is personally interesting. Younger people are more likely to absorb news about selected issues such as gay and lesbian rights and immigration than about other issues such as oil drilling or partisan debates about shrinking the government.

These trends suggest a sea change in information habits. The dispersal of attention is greatest for young citizens faced with rising education costs, unstable job situations, and a far richer media environment than past generations. Casual observers often assume that the news deficit just has to do with being young and that it will change as young people grow up and take on more adult responsibilities, such as starting careers and settling down. Here again, the evidence does not seem optimistic. Martin Wattenberg's careful look at comparable generations of news consumers going back as far as data permit (nearly a century in the case of newspapers) shows that news consumption has dropped substantially in each generation of young people over the past 40 years. For example, 70 percent of Americans born in the 1930s read newspapers on a daily basis by the time they turned 20, compared with just 20 percent of those born in the early 1980s. Equally steep declines mark parallel age groups with respect to TV news consumption in later decades. These trends are not unique to America. Most of the advanced democracies report similar declines in news consumption across the age range of their citizens.[30]

Why does following the news matter? Not surprisingly, there is a connection between scattered engagement with the news and not knowing what is going on in the world of politics. Wattenberg also analyzed correlations between age and political information among Americans at different points in time. In the 1940s, 1950s, and 1960s, for example, citizens under 30 were about as well informed as older age groups. After the 1970s, each decade saw younger generations become increasingly less informed and less likely to follow political issues and events (with a few notable exceptions such as 9/11). These trends are also true for most other democracies. He concludes that "today's young adults are the least politically knowledgeable generation ever in the history of survey research."[31] However, more recent studies suggest that political knowledge among citizens under 30 is less an across-the-board problem and based more on self-selective exposure to particular topics and interests. For example, a Pew survey showed that citizens under 30 lagged significantly behind older age groups in the ability to identify various contemporary politicians and historical figures. They were also lower in knowledge about issues such as which party favored shrinking the federal government, taxing different income groups, and oil drilling in wilderness areas. However, the under 30s were far and away the most knowledgeable demographic about party positions on immigration and gay and lesbian rights.[32]

Recent trends suggesting that younger citizens are getting information about issues that matter to them seem to be good news. However, there is also an interesting shift away from the earlier mass media model in which most Americans were something of a captive audience watching more or less the same newscasts about the same issues. This common exposure to an agenda of the nation's issues surely created a different sense of who we are and what we have in common in contrast to today's scattered exposure to issues of selective interest to different fragments of the public.[33] It is hard to sort out which came first, the fragmentation of society into warring political interests or the fragmentation of the media that produces different information flows in so many different media outlets. It makes sense to think that both of these changes interact to produce publics that are harder to reach, find less in common, and view politics and participation in very different ways. All of which makes it harder for various media to find and keep their audiences. All of this raises a big question: As audiences become harder to reach, more polarized, and selectively informed, what is the role of news in creating the link between citizens and officials that is so important to governing in a democracy?

Governing with the News

Political communication scholar Timothy Cook described the processes through which politicians and journalists have become inseparable as "governing with the news."[34] Politicians need to get their positions into the news to establish themselves as movers and shakers in the Washington image game and to signal to their backers and voters that they are visible and active leaders. Observing the rise of news management in governance, former CNN pollster and pundit William Schneider described Washington as a town of individual political entrepreneurs whose success and power often depend on their media images. Those images can be boosted when they are associated with the popularity of other visible politicians, like a winning president, or with popular developments, such as economic booms or successful wars.[35] When presidents appear to be losers, other politicians are less eager to be associated with them or their programs. For example, in the 2014 elections which proved disastrous for the Democrats, President Obama's popularity was well below 50 percent among voters in many contested House and Senate races, so Democratic candidates did not invite him to campaign for them. In states such as Kentucky where Obama's approval was extremely low, the ever popular ex-president Bill Clinton stepped in to campaign against scare and hate messages that he said were "keeping the people so torn up and upset that they can't think anymore."[36]

Journalists in this system receive a fresh and economical daily supply of news, along with insider status and professional respect when they land the big interviews and inside scoops. Journalist Marvin Kalb described these perverse developments in "press-politics": "There isn't a single major and sometimes minor decision reached at the White House, reached up on the Hill, reached at the State Department or the Pentagon, that does not have the press in mind. The way in which this is going to be sold to the American people is a function of the way in which the press first understands it, and then accepts it, and then is prepared to propagate a certain vision to the American people."[37]

What is ironic in this process is that despite the often fierce competition for these inside tidbits, the overall results display relatively little variation in stories across the mainstream media. Even organizations with a political point of view, such as Fox News or MSNBC, start with much the same topics but favor the spin from one end of the political spectrum over the other. Cook concluded that the similarity of approaches to covering the news and the homogeneity of content across the thousands of mainstream news organizations support the idea that the news media (despite the plurality of the term "media") operate as a single political institution, covering much the same territory with much the same often sensationalistic results. He described this as "the abiding paradox of newsmaking: News professes to be fresh, novel, and unexpected, but is actually remarkably patterned across news outlets and over time. Rather than providing an unpredictable and startling array of happenings, the content of news is similar from day to day, not only in featuring familiar personages and familiar locales, but also in the kinds of stories set forth and the morals these stories are supposed to tell."[38] The mutual dependency of journalists and officials in the production of news means that this institution of the press—even though protected in its freedom and independence by the Constitution—in fact amounts to a fourth, and not so independent, branch of government.

The ability or inability of officials to make and control the news is an important part of the power to govern, as reflected in the capacity of news to (a) shape public opinion among those citizens still paying attention, (b) sway different political factions to join or oppose political initiatives, such as going to war or addressing climate change, (c) hold officials more or less accountable for those initiatives, and (d) simply inform citizens about what the government is doing. At the forefront of information politics is the struggle over influencing or *spinning* journalists and news organizations to report versions of events that favor particular political sides.

As more and more citizens defect from this system, politicians increasingly find direct ways to reach them such as through Facebook and Twitter or by placing campaign ads inside video games. However, an important part of the governing process is creating images that other politicians react to, making much of what goes on in the press rather insulated and inside the Beltway of Washington, DC. Yet, even as citizens defect from this system, and even as the press suffers as a result, the dance of politics between politicians and the press goes on.

Politicians and the Media: A Symbiotic Relationship

From the standpoint of the politicians, businesses, and interest organizations that largely define politics in America, it has long been clear that power and influence depend on the control and strategic use of information. Despite growing public skepticism, newsmaking continues to be the most important way to get issues on the public agenda. The idea of *agenda setting* involves using the news to influence what the public regards as important for them to think about in society and politics.[39] Because of the importance of newsmaking for public relations, politicians from presidents and members of Congress to abortion activists, environmentalists, and antitax groups all have learned to go *public* by finding ways to take their political messages into the news.[40] An irony of mediated politics is that being well informed about the issues on the public agenda often means taking cues from familiar sources using the news to *frame* stories around their partisan viewpoints.[41] When this influence process works, the news not only tells people what to think about; it can also tell them what to think.[42]

Desperation to reach audiences (who are often running away from this kind of communication) has led many politicians to poison the well of politics through negative campaigning and railing against government as the root of most evils. Having warned citizens about people like themselves, politicians who then get into office are forced to hire communication consultants to sell themselves and their ideas back to increasingly wary and weary publics. These staged political performances often appear forced and artificial to media-savvy audiences—and young citizens are among the most savvy media consumers. Indeed, reality TV and political comedy often seem more authentic than the political performances made for news.[43] News that resembles entertainment has earned the name "infotainment" from communication scholars. The difference is that the characters in political programming often seem less sympathetic and emotionally accessible than the young and vulnerable characters starring in reality programs.

A case in point is the long-running national health care debate that has continued for years after passage of the Affordable Care Act in 2010, running through the elections of 2010, 2012, and 2014, fueling the government shutdown of 2013, and filling thousands of hours of talk shows and news in between. Republican opponents quickly dubbed the legislation "Obamacare." The Obama administration neglected to brand or market the new program and eventually embraced the Obamacare brand to defuse its negativity. The lengthy news battle was amped up by PR and hype to reach elusive audiences. One memorable episode began with a press release by then House minority leader (later House Speaker) John Boehner claiming that a provision in the proposed legislation would lead the country down the road to government-encouraged euthanasia.[44] The talk radio echo chamber, blogosphere, email lists, and YouTube videos[45] soon turned this into chants that Obamacare would "kill your grandma." Talk radio personality Rush Limbaugh likened Obama's plan to Hitler and the Nazis,[46] which provoked Republican columnist David Brooks on NBC's *Meet the Press* to call the attacks "insane."[47] Yet the shock rhetoric continued to be delivered by prominent Republicans from members of Congress to Sarah Palin, who talked about "death panels" on her Facebook page and tweeted: "R death panels back in?"[48] And so the "kill yer granny" messages cycled through the mainstream news media, as they were too tempting too resist for news organizations seeking cheap sensationalism. The death panel rhetoric earned the 2009 Lie of the Year award from the fact-checking organization PolitiFact. The hysteria continued for years, as the Republicans deemed it their best political issue. Problems with the government launch of public sign-up websites in 2013 added to the frenzy, and Obamacare was chosen as the central campaign issue in the 2014 elections. A national ad produced by the Republican National Committee warned that Obamacare would "cost our economy 2.5 million jobs." Other ads warned of soaring costs of prescription drugs and loss of current health coverage.[49] Such campaign ad themes were recycled in the news, magnifying their effects for better or worse. The attacks continued into the 2016 Republican primaries, with Florida senator Marco Rubio claiming he had done the most to undermine the national health care program, although not mentioning that he had signed his own family up through one of the programs created by the Affordable Care Act.

This mutually dependent relationship enabling politicians to spin the press explains how the news helped the Bush administration sell the war in Iraq. Do you remember the Iraq War, which officially ended in an American troop withdrawal in 2011? According to many observers, most Americans have tried to forget it, in the words of one scholar, as "a very bad memory."[50] A report authored by some 30 scholars and policy experts issued in 2013 on the 10th anniversary of the US invasion noted, among other things, a cost of nearly 500,000 mostly Iraqi civilian lives; around 2 million Iraqi refugees, and some 2 million more displaced inside the country; a financial cost to US taxpayers possibly as high as between $4 and $6 trillion, depending on the interest rates on the war debt; and a legacy of social destruction, political corruption, and instability in Iraq afterward.[51] In 2015 the United States sent a small number of troops back into Iraq to help train an inept Iraqi army in its efforts to regain territory lost to ISIS. How did this unfortunate situation get started?

Within a year of the attacks of September 11, 2001, the Bush administration rolled out a well-designed marketing campaign to link the attacks of 9/11 to Iraq.[52] The United States was already waging a far more credible war with broad international support in Afghanistan. The fight there was against a government that supported al-Qaeda and Osama bin Laden, who were clearly linked to the attacks on America. There was little evidence that Iraq was similarly involved. Nonetheless, the president and other high administration officials began a public relations offensive to create the impression that there was a link between Iraq and that terrible day when airliners full of passengers were hijacked and flown into the World Trade Center towers and the Pentagon, and a plane intended for another target in Washington crashed in a Pennsylvania field after passengers struggled to overpower the hijackers. The news following these events was enriched with allegations that Iraq possessed weapons of mass destruction. Officials appeared on Sunday news interview programs and punctuated their arguments with images of mushroom clouds. Those erroneous claims would later become material for late-night comedians, who joked about "weapons of mass deception."

The Iraq War stands as an iconic episode in the modern history of spin. Selling the war to the media and, in turn, to other politicians and to the American people stands as an example of how governing with the news when PR is deceptive can lead to bad outcomes for public faith in both government and the news. Beyond the loose facts and the foggy justification for the war, one thing became clear afterward: the battle for control of news images was the most important factor in shaping support both for the war and for the Bush administration's capacity to govern effectively for several more years after the invasion. The first media victory was predictably inside the Beltway, among elected officials, where opinion matters most. As the government dominated the media imagery, opponents shrank from challenging the war. The few who spoke out were relegated to the back news pages, if reported at all. From the viewpoint of the mainstream press, they were minority voices on the losing side of a policy decision. The second line of symbolic victory was over the American public, who grew increasingly attentive to an issue as big as waging war against an alleged terrorist nation.

With so few opposition voices in the news, who and what were the American people to believe? When administration dominance of news was at its peak around the time of the invasion in early 2003, fully 69 percent of the public felt that an Iraq connection to 9/11 was at least somewhat likely. Thanks to continuing administration domination of the news, solid majorities of Americans continued to believe that Iraq had something to do with the events of 9/11 long after facts to the contrary had come to light.[53]

When Barack Obama took charge of the wars in Iraq and Afghanistan, both governments were so corrupt that their main activities appeared to involve siphoning off US aid money and providing so little security and service to their own people that they may have turned many ordinary citizens into radicalized enemy combatants. Indeed, one observer has credited the United States with inadvertently creating the world's largest organized crime networks in Afghanistan.[54] More recently, a new threat appeared in Iraq and Syria in the form of the Islamic State of Iraq and Syria (ISIS), which suddenly replaced lesser terrorist organizations in the news after it captured large swaths of Iraq on account of the corruption and ineffectiveness of the Iraqi army and government. ISIS captured world attention by beheading captives and burning them alive and posting the grisly videos on YouTube.

When critics look back on such policy failures, they often find that they were poorly deliberated in public and based on incomplete or inaccurate evidence that was papered over by spin. But even when covering such a big event like a war, how is it that journalists get spun? The curious answer is that the press has evolved a set of informal reporting routines that make getting spun the norm rather than the exception.

Getting Spun: Indexing the News to Political Power

Like the reporting on the run-up to the Iraq War, many politically heated stories raise troubling questions about what journalists should do when officials say things that are inconsistent with available evidence. In the case of selling a war, the question is whether one side of a story should be so dominant just because other officials in government are afraid or unwilling to challenge it. There are many variations on this dilemma. What if there are two sides to a story being debated within official circles of power, but one is likely not true? For example, many years after the scientific community had reached consensus that global warming was accelerating because of human causes, many conservative politicians rejected that consensus and got their doubting views into the headlines. During the Bush administration, civil servants in environment-related departments claimed they had been ordered to change scientific reports to bring them in line with the administration position.[55] Even though investigations showed that many of the politicians denying climate change had close political and financial relationships with industries such as oil that contribute to carbon pollution, that was a minor story compared to the long-running political climate debate in which one side simply dismissed the evidence against its position. (This episode is discussed in more detail in the case study in chapter 4.)

Should both sides of a story be covered when one is likely not true? Should a story be allowed to become one-sided when there is evidence to challenge it but powerful officials are simply unwilling to voice that evidence? Either way, American journalism does not have easy answers to these important questions. Finding an answer would require freeing the press from its dependence on government and powerful officials as its reference on reality. According to Thomas Patterson, this sort of "he said, she said" journalism is part of the reason why the news does a poor job of informing the public and clarifying rather than confusing important issues.[56] Despite the seemingly obvious role of the press to sort out facts and evidence, journalists have a surprisingly difficult time when politicians serve up distortions and outright lies, as shown in the case study below.

Why has the American press become caught in this curious dependence on how those in power define reality? I have termed this reporting pattern *indexing*, which refers to the tendency of mainstream news organizations to index or adjust the range of viewpoints in a story to the dominant positions of those whom journalists perceive to have enough power to affect the outcome of a situation.[57] This curious reporting system, as explained further in chapter 5, is a result of the long-standing commitment of the mainstream press to cling to a norm of balance, fairness, or objectivity. If journalists want to appear objective or balanced, they cannot become involved in telling the audience what is really going on. Rather, journalists must channel images of reality through external sources, and the safest sources are those who are elected by the public and who have the power to shape political outcomes. Sometimes those in power also have reasons to confuse or distort the issues—reasons ranging from their own value biases to saying what they must in order to attract the financial support they need to stay in power. Hence the subtitle of this book: *The Politics of Illusion*.

What this reporting system means is that when government is working well, and elected representatives are offering competing alternatives for solving policy problems, the news is filled with competing views that may help engaged citizens think critically about decisions facing the nation. On the other hand, if certain factions in power promote deceptive or untruthful spin in the service of powerful interests, then those ideas also become presented as equally valid alongside more plausible versions of events. Similarly, political parties may decide not to raise doubts about bad ideas because they are hard to explain to inattentive publics, or the parties fear being punished in elections by emotionally aroused publics who buy the spin from the other side. When these things happen, bad ideas become the dominant news frames. If journalists introduced independent evidence to balance such stories, they would be accused of bias or of campaigning for their own agendas. And so spin rules. To return to the example of the Iraq War, the Democratic Party decided not to challenge a then popular President Bush following 9/11 on his claim that Iraq was implicated in the terrorism attacks. The resulting news was dominated by the administration PR campaign to sell the war.

The legacy of the Iraq War raises an uncomfortable truth about the US news system. While many Americans are uninformed because they are inattentive to the news, it may also be the case that paying attention to deceptive news can result in becoming misinformed. In the case of Iraq, some news organizations did a better job than others in helping their audiences critically assess government claims about the war, but many who followed the news from most outlets came away misinformed by the dominant spin. For example, even after claims about weapons of mass destruction and Iraqi links to al-Qaeda had been seriously challenged by sources outside the administration, 80 percent of the viewers of Fox News still shared one or more of these factual inaccuracies about the war, while only 23 percent of Public Broadcasting Service (PBS) and National Public Radio (NPR) audiences were similarly mistaken. Other mainstream news sources misinformed people at rates closer to Fox than NPR, with CBS at 71 percent, ABC at 61 percent, NBC at 55 percent, and CNN at 55 percent—print news sources had an average reader misperception rate of 47 percent.[58]

Even the best news organizations left large numbers of people misinformed simply because they did not check or challenge what those politicians who spoke out were saying. It also appears that the more mainstream or popular news organizations were least likely to challenge government propaganda. The point here is not that journalists were making up facts but that most news organizations simply emphasized what powerful official sources told them, even though other credible sources such as United Nations weapons inspectors were available to challenge those accounts of reality. Such confusions of reality and power may undermine the credibility of news for many citizens. As journalists become spun by officials and join the establishment by sharing often short-lived conventional wisdoms, power becomes the definer of truth. Instead of having a news system that speaks truth to power, the dictates of power produce a news product that comedian Stephen Colbert called "truthiness." Indeed, many citizens seek perspective in political comedy or "fake news" because they cannot find it in the real news, as the case study in this chapter explains.

CASE STUDY
POLITICAL COMEDY REVEALS THE "TRUTHINESS" ABOUT NEWS

NBC News anchor Brian Williams was suspended from his lofty journalism post after telling false stories about his helicopter being hit by enemy fire when he was reporting the invasion of Iraq. Williams's fake war story was challenged by a crewmember of the helicopter that actually got hit on an earlier mission that day. The war veteran's post on the NBC Facebook page about the story said: "Sorry dude, I don't remember you being on my aircraft." The story traveled quickly through social media, the legacy press, and comedy news, raising questions about Williams's trust level, as the journalist's celebrity index score (a marketing measure of brand reputation) tumbled 800 points in a few days.[59]

New York Times columnist Maureen Dowd noted that social media had made the story impossible to ignore and had dealt another blow to an already struggling institution of TV news. Dowd called social media "the genre that helped make the TV evening news irrelevant by showing us that we don't need someone to tell us every night what happened that day." For this and other reasons, Dowd contended that TV news was no longer the authoritative source for information it once was. Pressed by falling ratings and desperate to stay afloat, TV news long ago began chasing audiences with dubious stories, hyperbole, animal videos, and entertainment fare that pushed it into the "infotainment" business. Dowd suggested that the blurred boundaries between entertainment and news might have contributed to Williams's manufactured drama. Williams had long before crossed the line to join the entertainment media with frequent appearances on *Saturday Night Live*, *The Daily Show*, *The Tonight Show* (slow-jamming the news with Jimmy Fallon), and the sitcom *30 Rock*. Dowd noted that as the news becomes more disconnected from reality, "the nightly news anchors are not figures of authority. They're part of the entertainment, branding, and cross-promotion business."[60] Iconic comedy news anchor Jon Stewart (who announced his retirement from *The Daily Show* amid the Williams scandal) commented: "We got us a case here of infotainment confusion syndrome."[61]

Meanwhile, the fake news on Comedy Central and *Saturday Night Live*, among other places, was becoming more credible. Comedy news anchor John Oliver had recently broken a couple of real news stories and was hiring investigative reporters to develop material for his show. Long before Brian Williams's credibility scandal, an online poll conducted by *Time* magazine showed that Jon Stewart was America's most trusted newscaster, beating such journalists as Brian Williams and Katie Couric by a wide margin.[62]

Top comedy news programs often beat serious cable news shows in the ratings. During his run as the king of fake news, Jon Stewart often rivaled Bill O'Reilly on Fox as the top draw on cable news—except Stewart was not delivering real news. The rivalry prompted O'Reilly to dismiss Stewart's audience as "stoned slackers." In fact, comedy news audiences easily beat most TV news audiences in the prime age, education, and consumer demographics sought after by advertisers. What makes fake news so popular at a time when the real news is having such credibility problems?

Many in the fake news audience find that they get perspective on the spin and the staged aspects of TV news. Before moving on to become host of *The Late Show* on CBS, comedian Stephen Colbert hosted *The Colbert Report* on Comedy Central— something of a spoof of *The O'Reilly Factor* on Fox. Among his many contributions to fake news lore, Colbert coined the term "truthiness" to refer to the many political statements that officials introduce into the news that are not entirely consistent with available evidence. As explained by the indexing model of the news, journalists often have trouble introducing evidence independently unless other officials contest the spurious claims. Thus, the news often conveys mainly the trappings of truth: a sincere sense of conviction and all the authoritativeness that earnest officials and journalists can provide. Yet important elements of reality are often missing. This appearance of truth while important evidence is left out is the essence of "truthiness." The missing reality bits make it possible for political comics to point out the political follies that officials offer as serious news. Larry Wilmore, host of *The Nightly Show* on Comedy Central, welcomed Williams to the club "as a fellow purveyor of fake news."[63]

Behind the production of journalistic truthiness is the implicit recognition by powerful figures and their media advisors that what they say in the news generally cannot be challenged effectively by journalists unless they find another Washington source of comparable power or status to do the job. This confusion of power and credibility can lead some politicians to take considerable liberties with the truth in pursuit of strong convictions. Most journalists are not happy about this spin game, and many become cynical about the political situations they cover through the statements of officials, which explains the rise of stories that frame politics as a kind of game. The interplay of press and politicians is often testy and adversarial, with reporters trying to get officials to reconcile their spin with observable realities. Consider a revealing moment during an interview between Ron Suskind, a prominent journalist, and a senior presidential advisor who grew tired of the cat-and-mouse game of journalists trying to get him to admit to inconsistencies in the official script. The official suddenly dismissed the journalist as belonging to the "reality-based community." Suskind recalls the revealing moment in these terms:

> The aide said that guys like me were "in what we call the reality-based community," which he defined as people who "believe that solutions emerge from your judicious study of discernible reality." I nodded and murmured something about enlightenment principles and empiricism. He cut me off. "That's not the way the world really works anymore," he continued. "We're an empire now, and when we act, we create our own reality. And while you're studying that reality—judiciously, as you will—we'll act again, creating other new realities, which you can study too, and that's how things will sort out. We're history's actors . . . and you, all of you, will be left to just study what we do."[64]

While politics still attracts many people of goodwill, even goodwill may become blinded by strong convictions that block out the reality of other views. In these moments, the press often has trouble making independent corrections. Consider an exchange between veteran journalist Ted Koppel and Jon Stewart who described a typical "two-sided" news interview format: "She throws out her figures from the Heritage Foundation and she throws her figures from the Brookings

Institute, and the anchor, who should be the arbiter of the truth says, 'Thank you both very much. That was really interesting.' No, it wasn't! That was Coke and Pepsi talking about beverage truth. And that game is what has, I think, caused people to go, 'I'm not watching this.'"[65]

As communication scholar Dannagal Young points out in her analysis of this interview: "Stewart explicitly rejects the premise that the journalist's role is to present opposing sets of facts from official sources. Instead, he argues that ignoring the underlying truth-value of those 'facts' denies viewers an important critical analysis of political life, and instead the journalist should act as an 'arbiter of the truth.'"[66] As the interview continued, Koppel seemed a bit wistful about the freedom that comedy gives Stewart to point out deception, or BS as Koppel put it, yet he firmly denied that it was the role of journalists to make such corrections:

> Koppel: [You] can use humor to say, "BS." You know, "That's a crock."
> Stewart: But that's always been the case . . . Satire has always. . . .
> Koppel: Okay, but I can't do that.
> Stewart: But you can say that's BS. You don't need humor to do it, because you have what I wish I had—which is credibility, and gravitas . . . I also think that it's important to take a more critical look. Don't you think?
> Koppel: No.[67]

Dannagal Young argues that this greater capacity to get at the truth—or at least point out deception and spin—makes comedy "the new journalism." Indeed, Professor Young has been influential in my thinking about comedy as an important medium for sorting out the truth, as she recounts in an article that mentions how different editions of this book have changed.[68] Her perception is widely shared even by other journalists. When Stewart appeared on the cover of *Newsweek*, the story described him as changing the presentation of news to appeal to a younger audience that has largely tuned out conventional news.[69] It turns out that audiences for programs, such as *The Daily Show* are among the most informed and active members of the public. Despite the worries of many parents and teachers, late-night comedy audiences do not get all their news from the comedians; they bring high levels of news knowledge with them. Otherwise, as Jon Stewart once put it, they wouldn't get the jokes.[70]

Meanwhile, journalists often remain trapped in a symbiotic system dependent on official spin that is largely of their own making. This odd evolution of a mainstream news system that reports mainly what officials say was the subject of one of Stephen Colbert's most controversial comedy routines when he addressed the annual White House Correspondents' Association dinner. This insider affair generally involves a gentle roast of the president and is one of the "A ticket" events in Washington, attended by the elite press corps, powerful politicians, and celebrities. In his appearance, Colbert stepped into his faux Bill O'Reilly character and first took on President Bush and then the press.

> Ladies and gentlemen of the press corps, Madame First Lady, Mr. President, my name is Stephen Colbert, and tonight it is my privilege to celebrate this president, 'cause we're not so different, he and I. We both get it. Guys like us, we're not some brainiacs on the nerd patrol. We're not members of the factinista. We go straight from the gut. Right, sir? . . .
>
> And as excited as I am to be here with the President, I am appalled to be surrounded by the liberal media that is destroying America, with the exception of FOX News. FOX News gives you both sides of every story: the President's side, and the Vice President's side.
>
> But the rest of you, what are you thinking? Reporting on NSA wiretapping or secret prisons in Eastern Europe? Those things are secret for a very important reason: they're super-depressing. . . .
>
> Over the last five years you people were so good, over tax cuts, WMD intelligence, the effect of global warming. We Americans didn't want to know, and you had the courtesy not to try to find out. Those were good times, as far as we knew.
>
> But, listen, let's review the rules. Here's how it works. The President makes decisions. He's the decider. The press secretary announces those decisions, and you people of the press type those decisions down. Make, announce, type. Just put 'em through a spell check and go home. Get to know your family again. Make love to your wife.
>
> Write that novel you got kicking around in your head. You know, the one about the intrepid Washington reporter with the courage to stand up to the administration? You know, fiction![71]

Colbert may have hit the mark too closely, as neither the president nor many reporters in the audience seemed to be laughing as the event was aired on C-SPAN. The *Washington Post* later panned the performance, saying that Colbert "fell flat." *New York Times* coverage did not mention Colbert. On *The Daily Show*, Jon Stewart quipped that Colbert must have been under the false impression "that they'd hired him to do what he does every night on television."[72] Frank Rich, a former media critic and political columnist for the *New York Times*, guessed that Colbert fell flat not because he was rude to the president but because "his real sin was to be rude to the capital press corps, whom he caricatured as stenographers. Though most of the Washington audience failed to find the joke funny, Americans elsewhere, having paid a heavy price for the press's failure to challenge the White House propaganda about Iraq, laughed until it hurt."[73] As Rich noted, even though the national press failed to see its humor, the performance spread virally on the Internet, becoming an overnight sensation on YouTube, blogs, and podcasts. Various clips of the performance posted on YouTube were viewed nearly three million times within a few days and continued to gain viewers for many years thereafter.

Despite Colbert and many other comedians raising such uncomfortable truths about truthiness, the hallowed rules of the reporting game continue to make it difficult for most journalists to act differently. Consider how this journalistic dilemma was handled by the public editor of the *New York Times*, an ombudsman for readers who raise questions about *Times* coverage. Readers challenged a number of cases where *Times* reporters simply passed on claims by politicians that seemed either doubtful or outright wrong. The public editor noted that if reporters corrected lies from politicians, they would be imposing their own judgments in news stories, which, in his view, goes beyond their journalistic mandate to be "objective and fair." He wondered how reporters could be fair in deciding which facts to correct. He also noted that *Times* op-ed columnist Paul Krugman proclaimed that politics had entered a "post-truth" age, adding that columnists like Krugman had the freedom to tell readers when they think politicians are lying. In the end, the ombudsman turned the question back to his concerned readers: "Should news reporters do the same?"[74]

This awkward moment of truth from one of the nation's leading news organizations sparked an outcry from various advocates who propose redefining journalism in order to save it. Critics included Jay Rosen, Clay Shirky, and Glenn Greenwald. Greenwald (who helped report the story of the National Security Agency spying on American citizens) noted that most journalists were offended by Stephen Colbert's charge that they were stenographers taking dictation from politicians, but the *Times* discussion made holding politicians accountable sound like an "exotic or edgy" idea.[75] And so political comedy has become a trusted news source. When Trevor Noah succeeded Jon Stewart as *Daily Show* host, he vowed to maintain the standard Stewart established and continue "the war on bullshit." Meanwhile, many legacy journalists are still convinced they are holding up higher standards and remain puzzled about why they have lost public confidence and why their audiences are shrinking.

What about the People?

The irony of the way the news has evolved is that the often shrill and dramatic efforts to attract audiences drive many citizens away. Many others are only intermittently attentive. Meanwhile, political insiders watch the same news with great interest. Politicians, lobbyists, public relations professionals, and journalists follow the daily spin with the attention of sports fans to see who is winning and who is losing the daily struggle for image control. The symbiosis between journalists and the communication professionals who spin the messages of their political clients keeps the process going, creating what media scholars David Altheide and Robert Snow called a "media logic" that is hard to break out of.[76]

From the standpoint of those on the inside who continue to produce this strange media logic, the shrill voices filling the talk shows and the carefully crafted sound bites in news reports become a substitute for public opinion itself.[77] Not surprisingly, many members of the public express the concern that the news is more for insiders than for them. According to media scholar Robert Entman, this media logic produces a democracy without citizens.[78] Opinion polls and occasional public protests bring citizens into the news frame, but generally in cameo roles rather than starring performances. This noisy media echo chamber of clashing images and slogans ends up driving out more-thoughtful viewpoints, along with space for deliberation and reflection. Woe to the politician who cannot explain health care reform in less than 30 seconds (and woe to the citizen who tries to grasp it in 30 seconds). Foreign policies that address the complexities of international relations become vulnerable to charges of weakness and indecision.

As people become bombarded with spin, and are encouraged to choose sides in a confusing information system in which the press offers little perspective, it is not surprising that there are many different information strategies that people pursue. Many have simply tuned out. Some turn to political comedy. Others choose news with points of view that agree with their own political beliefs and values. And social media recommendations become a convenient filter for many. No matter the personal strategy, the incessant political spin machines are trying to find ways to get through to people.

As social media now reach large numbers of people directly, political information increasingly comes from Facebook, Twitter, YouTube, and dozens of other digital media platforms. As long as it remains relatively open, the Internet lowers the costs of political communication for many citizens who are learning how to communicate with each other in cheap, fast, and effective ways. Communities of environmentalists, pro-choice and pro-life abortion groups, fair labor and fair trade campaigners, human rights workers, and computer privacy groups have mastered communicating with large networked audiences using cheap and available technologies. In the process, many interesting experiments are in progress that may reinvent the news and more generally improve how citizens communicate with each other and with leaders.

While some may object to the quality of citizen-produced information, the degradation of the press system may not seem to offer better options.

Moreover, as the mass media fragment into smaller niche channels, the news is frequently marketed to the lifestyles and political values of different audience segments. When people seek self-confirming information, the news does not so much inform or challenge them as it affirms and reinforces what they already want to believe.[79] All of this complicates answering the simple question: What is news?

A Definition of News

The impact of news on the quality of democracy is always changing. Political communication scholar Bruce Bimber makes a bold assertion about power in American politics: that it is biased toward those with the best command of political information.[80] Bimber follows this claim by tracing the development of American democracy from *The Federalist* to the present day in terms of information regimes. The first great expansion of democratic participation came with the rise of a national mail system that carried many newspapers and publications, perhaps making the US Post Office the most important institution for expanding democracy in the early American republic.[81] A flash-forward to the late twentieth century shows American democracy evolving through the information regime of the mass media, which is now in its late stages. Technologies, such as broadcast television and satellite communication enabled Americans to share common experiences that affected the entire nation. Politicians in the mass media age became experts at "going public" by using the media to deliver messages directly to large audiences.[82] The twenty-first-century information regime is multimedia, with fragmented audiences and channels, often driven by social networks. There are many sources of content: social media, crowdsourced information platforms, and comedy, as well as journalism still doing what defined the news for much of the last century.

As the mass media information regime erodes, many observers worry that multiplying media niches may produce individuals who become informed just about issues and perspectives that suit their personal lifestyles and beliefs. Can a democracy with so many exclusive, personalized media realities have coherent policy discussions, much less share a common purpose?[83] At the very least, we should bring the news down to earth and recognize that it is continually changing, and that these changes are shaped by a chaotic set of factors that may not engineer an information product with the best interests of democracy in mind.

How do the changing interactions among political actors, publics, and the press affect the way we define the news? As a starting point, it makes sense to adopt a simple definition that expands political news beyond just what news organizations produce: *news consists of (a) the reporting of actions and events (b) over a growing variety of publicly accessible media (c) by journalism organizations and an expanding spectrum of other content producers, including ordinary citizens.* As the news process expands beyond the legacy media, standards for selecting, formatting, sourcing, and documenting reports become less shared and more open to challenges about accuracy and relevance. Yet as some properties of news change, others remain the same. Doris Graber suggested that news is not just any information, or even the most important information, about the world; rather, the news tends to contain information that is *timely*, often *sensational* (scandals, violence, and human drama frequently dominate the news), and *familiar* (stories often draw on familiar people or life experiences that give even distant events a close-to-home feeling).[84] In this view, the news is constructed through the constantly changing interactions of journalists, politicians, and citizens often seeking different ends. At the height of the mass media era, journalists were often regarded as "gatekeepers" who screened information (ideally) according to its truth and importance. More recently, as the news habits change and the capacity for direct news production and distribution by citizens grows, gatekeeping by the legacy press is less effective and, in the view of some observers, less important.[85]

Despite all the changes outlined above, the legacy news reported by journalists remains important in the governing process, even as it may undermine the legitimacy of that same process for many citizens who consume it. The core question explored in this book is, *How well does the news, as the core of the national political information system, serve the needs of democracy?* In exploring this question, we examine how various political actors—from presidents and members of Congress to interest organizations and citizen-activists—try to get their messages into the news. Understanding how politics and government work requires understanding who makes the news and who does not. We also want to understand how that news affects elites, public opinion, and the resolution of issues and events.

The Fragile Link between News and Democracy

The diverse forces shaping news and public information raise interesting questions about how to promote the best outcomes for democracy. Many Americans seem to live with the false sense of security that the First Amendment and the Constitution will somehow guarantee a quality press. The chaotic forces outlined in this chapter suggest that there is no overarching plan to keep an ideal democratic information system in order. Even as profit-driven media owners dismantle news organizations and diminish the quality of journalism, they hide behind the First Amendment to defend against attempts by concerned citizen groups to make them behave more responsibly. The irony of this is that the First Amendment with its protections for press freedom was intended to enable an independent press to stand up to government power. While press freedom remains a crucial protection in democracy, it has also become a shield for corporate media to avoid social responsibility. For example, when a citizens' watchdog group challenged the renewal of four Denver television stations' broadcast licenses, it argued that the local stations displayed trends common to local news across the nation, which had become "severely unbalanced, with excessive coverage of violent topics and trivial events," creating "a public health issue" that "goes beyond bad journalism."[86] The Federal Communications Commission that handles broadcast licenses rejected the citizen petition, wrapping its ruling in the hallowed language of free speech: "Journalistic or editorial discretion in the presentation of news and public information is the core concept of the First Amendment's free press guarantee."[87] National broadcaster groups and the Denver stations heralded this formulaic pronouncement as an important victory for free speech—a triumph over censorship and the intrusion of government in the newsroom. Many media and law scholars worry about using the Constitution to defend publicly licensed communication content that is produced with little political or social purpose beyond making money.[88] The citizen group, Media Watch, argued that such high-minded defenses of bad news are part of the reason that we end up with news that "covers schoolyard shootings but not schools, train wrecks but not transportation, bloopers by local politicians but not local elections, and the latest murder but not dropping crime rates."[89]

We may have built a national information fortress with just one wall, protecting the press from formal censorship yet leaving the information system vulnerable to degradation at the hands of poorly controlled business interests. Such interests, as any beginning economics student learns, have no intrinsic reason to embrace social responsibility beyond returning profits to their private investors. Why is something as important as public information left to the current turbulent mix of business profit imperatives, political spin techniques, and consumer tastes? This question would be less compelling if the news was not so important for the quality of democracy. Although it is tempting to assume that the news is somehow geared to the information needs of citizens, this chapter suggests a more disturbing possibility. There is currently little monitoring and few institutional checks to guarantee that the legacy press, as it has evolved, will serve the needs of American democracy. To the contrary, substantial evidence indicates that the news is largely a freewheeling entity shaped by a combination of commercial forces in the news business, technologies of communication perfected by politicians and their media consultants, and the tastes and personal entertainment habits of citizens. More than in any other advanced democracy, political information in the United States is manufactured and sold with few of the quality controls that even far less important household products have.

Yet there is a good deal of complacency about this information system. Perhaps the faith in the free press system in the United States has led Americans to pay far less attention than citizens in other societies to improving the quality of democracy's most important product: political information. How does one of the freest press systems in the world produce news that so often misses the marks of accuracy and relevance? It is hard for most Americans to imagine that freedom and competition do not automatically guarantee the best results. As a consequence of this deep cultural faith in unrestricted political communication, there is stunningly little public discussion about how to design a news and information system that might better suit the needs of democratic politics and citizen involvement.

A goal of this book is to contribute to such a discussion about improving information forms that may emerge from this era of change. A good place to start is by explaining how the current news system has evolved: how legacy news is produced and sold, how it is shaped by political actors, how it is reported by journalists and news organizations, and how it is used by citizens. When this larger news picture is considered, commonly discussed problems, such as the fabled ideological bias of reporters, appear to be the least of the information problems faced by citizens. Moreover, we may begin to see ways in which citizens with direct access to media production via phones and computers can directly shape higher-quality public debate.

2

NEWS STORIES

FOUR INFORMATION BIASES

THAT MATTER

Journalists criticize politicians for spinning their messages and dodging the tough issues. Citizens also find fault with those tactics. Yet journalists and citizens alike punish politicians who speak candidly or play the game badly.

—Thomas Patterson[1]

The 2016 presidential campaign heated up long before the candidates were selected. Many Republicans believed that Hillary Clinton would be the Democratic nominee, and GOP "opposition research" dug up papers from the scandal-plagued Clinton presidency in which Hillary lamented having to "suck up" to the press. Seeking to rise above the news noise in his quest for the Republican nomination, Rand Paul branded Bill Clinton a "sexual predator."[2] Surprise early frontrunner Donald Trump called her use of a private email server when she was secretary of state "criminal." Each election seems more extreme in tone than the last. Many observers called the 2012 election between Mitt Romney and Barack Obama one of the most personally negative on record, with some giving the edge to Obama, who was no stranger to being attacked—he was even accused of being born outside the United States. The Obama campaign went after Romney as a heartless businessman who closed factories, shipped jobs overseas, and cared only about the rich. Surrounding the core attacks were stories about Romney strapping his dog to the roof of the car for a family trip, which added to the impression that the candidate was an "unlikable buffoon."[3]

Personal attacks in American politics are nothing new, but they have become so central to the communication process that they push more useful information aside. Many critics contend that the fragmenting 24/7 media environment and the cutbacks in newsroom staff lead media companies to favor sensationalism as they compete for the attention of weary audiences. This in turn drives communication consultants working for politicians to ramp up the attacks in ads and news events. The result is a loss of control over balance and judgment about what really matters. Press scholar Thomas Patterson likens the news to a "fog of war" that has descended on American politics.[4] Where news exposure once informed the public, Patterson contends that it now often misleads.[5] A blog post by a prominent media critic put it clearly: "Media's myopic obsession with campaign narratives over events of real significance does a disservice to the public."[6] Another observer scolded journalists for their role in keeping outlandish narratives in play, saying that it would be heroic "if commentators with any pretensions left of journalism spent more energy telling us how a crucial piece of legislation might affect American life and public policy than on how the president might most effectively sell it to the skeptical sheeple. At least that's my narrative, and I'm sticking to it."[7]

There is nothing inherently wrong with telling dramatic or personal stories—far from it. Elections may be our most important national storytelling ritual, a time when we remind ourselves, with the help of candidates, what we stand for as a people, what our challenges are, where the next chapter of the national saga is heading, and who may best lead us there. But what happens when journalists and communication consultants, not candidates, do most of the storytelling, or when journalists report the most outlandish things the candidates say and ignore more policy-oriented content? One possibility is that the publics seeking a reasonable discussion tune out while those seeking entertainment and theater tune in.

Who writes the news drama? Politicians lean on consultants to help them tell and sell (spin) their stories, and journalists often weave news plots around the most sensational material. And when politicians and their so-called spin doctors fail to deliver the drama, pundits and journalists charge that they have lost their narrative. This strange preoccupation with who owns the news narrative suggests that the boundary between political spin and independent reporting has become dangerously blurred. As a result, journalists seem to be chasing their own tales, so to speak. Yet politicians who do not like the spin game with its scripted lines written by media consultants find it hard to govern after losing control of the news narrative. This is what *New York Times* reporter Richard Stevenson suggests happened to President Obama from early on in his presidency.[8] Following Mr. Obama's first State of the Union address, the news focused on his slipping narrative rather than his actions as president. A *Washington Post* reporter did an article that was aptly titled "The Obama 'Narrative' Is Overshadowing This Presidency's Real Stories." Many news outlets covered the illusory story about the president losing his story. Even *New York Times* columnist Maureen Dowd wondered how such a gifted storyteller could "lose control of his own narrative."[9]

An intriguing question, of course, is, what is the relationship between an effective narrative and governing effectively? The analysis in this chapter suggests that it is hard to govern effectively without an appealing narrative about things like strength and vision, or hope and change, but those narratives invite opponents' efforts to topple them, and something resembling a political food fight often breaks out in the news. Moreover, having a good narrative does not mean that it has much grounding in reality. As a result, good news narratives may not always produce good governance or smart policies. Journalism mythology has it that it is the job of the press to help sort out the truth of the stories competing for public attention. Yet the forces favoring sensationalism in the press often favor drama over credibility or importance.

Whether the news is about a policy conflict, terrorism, the economy, or an election, mainstream reporting tends to display certain narrative characteristics. This chapter considers the properties of these common journalistic story elements as kinds of information bias in the news. First, it is important to see how the sensationalized story formats that bias the news differ from what critics and the public often talk about when they discuss news bias.

Putting Journalistic Bias in Perspective

Many people blame the problems with our information system on the ideological or partisan biases of journalists themselves. Polls show that growing majorities of people believe that reporters introduce their own political views into the news and generally do not even get the facts straight. According to polls taken by the Pew Research Center for the People and the Press, vast changes occurred in public regard for the press over the last several decades. Even though public confidence in the press had begun its steep decline by the mid-1980s, a majority (55%) still felt that news organizations at least got their facts straight most of the time. This figure dropped to 37 percent in the late 1990s, and continued to decline into the mid-20 percent range in recent years. Meanwhile, the belief that news organizations generally deal fairly with all sides plunged under 20 percent at the time of this writing. Amid this loss of public confidence, there are occasional moments that reveal strengths that the public would like to see more of. For example, coverage of the 9/11 attacks was widely received as fair and informative. And reporting on the more recent revelations about National

Security Agency spying on the public produced an impressive 68 percent agreement that the press can still act as a "watchdog" to keep leaders from doing things they should not do.[10]

The longstanding public concern is that journalists introduce their political biases into reporting. There is the proverbial grain of truth in this stereotype, as survey results show that journalists tend to be more liberal than the general population.[11] Where conventional wisdom breaks down, however, is with the assumption that the personal politics of reporters translate into the political content of their journalism. In an experimental study in which journalists were asked to imagine how they personally would cover hypothetical stories, the ideology of reporters had only a small effect on their professional judgments.[12] And, in reality, journalists do not work in situations in which they have free reign over how to cover a story. The vast majority of individual journalists would have trouble getting consistent ideological slants past editors and owners throughout much of the news industry who are there to enforce norms of balance and fairness. Reporters are small cogs in large business organizations that have a vested interest in producing a marketable, neutral product. As journalism scholar Everette Dennis put it: "Profits are central to the media; the news is more and more driven by market forces and market segmentation. Deliberately or even innocently alienating a portion of the audience through unfair and biased coverage of candidates and causes would be self-destructive. More important, it would be absolutely unacceptable to publishers, broadcast executives, and owners, who, last time I checked, were still running the show."[13] There are notable exceptions, of course, when news organizations intentionally use political perspectives to reach like-minded audiences. For example, Fox News slants conservative, while MSNBC and *Huffington Post* are more liberal.

For the most part, constructing an attention-grabbing story is more important than introducing political slant in the news. Indeed, coverage of recent presidents from Reagan through Obama reveals that most of it has gone against the political bias thesis. Most observers regard news during the Reagan presidency (1981–1988) as generally favorable to Reagan and his "Republican revolution." Even when journalists attempted to take critical stances, they were often diffused by skillful White House press management and by Reagan's media-friendly personal charm—earning Reagan titles such as "The Great Communicator" and "The Teflon President." By contrast, Bill Clinton's presidency (1993–2000) produced some of the most stormy news coverage of the modern era. As discussed in chapter 4, Clinton's press relations contrasted sharply with those of the Reagan administration, both in terms of failing to develop daily communication strategies and by excluding reporters from the back corridors and social life of the White House.

George W. Bush ran the whole gamut of news drama from high praise to deep criticism. Administration news spin from the aftermath of 9/11 through the early years of the Iraq War was reported faithfully by most of the mainstream press. Such successful news management helped Bush reach the highest recorded levels of public approval. That peak followed the Hollywood-style news coverage of his triumphant "top gun" jet landing on the aircraft carrier *Abraham Lincoln* and his declaration of "mission accomplished" pronouncing an end to major combat in Iraq (although the war in Iraq plagues US policymakers to this day). Despite his early triumphs of spin, damaging news coverage soon visited the Bush White House following missteps in handling Hurricane Katrina and amid the growing awareness that Iraq was descending into chaos and corruption.

Attacking Barack Obama became the leading Republican political strategy through both his political terms. Those attacks were reported faithfully by news organizations across the political spectrum (although filtered in different ways by Fox and MSNBC). Perhaps not surprisingly, many more Republicans than Democrats believed the accusations that Mr. Obama was not born in the USA and thus lacked the constitutional qualification to be president. Many of the scandals and dramas of the Obama years were politically manufactured and, in the view of communication scholar Robert Entman, reveal the trouble the press has in adjusting the news drama to fit the underlying reality. This means that scandals often make big news even if there is not much evidence or political consequence to sustain them. It may be difficult to distinguish manufactured scandals from more serious government deceptions such as the NSA spying scandal linked to Obama- and Bush-era policies.[14]

What accounts, then, for the popular perception that members of the press introduce liberal bias into the news? A 2013 survey found that 72 percent of the public believes that the news is ideologically biased, with a 46-to-26 split on whether that bias is liberal or conservative. This suggests that when it comes to politics and its emotional core of values, bias is largely in the eye of the beholder. This generalization is supported by research showing that people in the middle see the press as generally neutral, whereas those on the left complain that the news is too conservative and those on the right think the news has a left-leaning bias.[15] The bias gap between liberals and conservatives may reflect stronger convictions among conservatives that they are right, a belief that has fueled a long-standing conservative campaign against the liberal media.

Even though conservatives are more inclined to publicly attack the news, media criticism groups do exist on both the left and the right, and they continue to muster plenty of evidence for dueling charges of political bias. The reader might be interested in comparing the news criticism of the leading conservative organization, Accuracy in Media (AIM), with that of the leading liberal one, Fairness and Accuracy in Reporting (FAIR). The AIM web address is www.aim.org; the FAIR website is located at www.fair.org.

To be sure, fluctuations in the political content of the news do exist, but they tend to reflect journalistic tracking of the shifts in political power balances between liberal and conservative blocs on the issues in the news. Such political content fluctuations can almost always be explained by factors outside the ideological thinking of individual journalists.[16] Everette Dennis has summed up the endless debate over ideological bias in the press as "pointless and repetitive," concluding that "the media, alas, are centrist, determinedly so."[17] To this, I would add that as the center moved toward the right in recent decades, news coverage reflected the power balances in Washington more than any consistent political bias in the American press. If consistent political bias does not really explain how the press works, how do we account for the all too familiar patterns of distortion, spin, and predictable plot formulas in the news?

A Different Kind of Bias

The general focus of this chapter is on a deeper but less obvious sort of news bias—one that favors *dramatic* and *personalized* aspects of events over more complex underlying political realities. Focusing on individual actors and the dramas and scandals swirling around them makes many political situations seem *fragmented* and confusing. The easiest story plot that connects the actors and their dramas in these fragmentary news episodes is that *politics is a game* in which the actors are trying to win at each other's expense. Portraying politics as a game is among the simplest ways to frame a news story, but it biases the story by not probing for larger issues at stake.

Framing involves choosing an organizing theme that emphasizes some aspects of a situation while downplaying other information in a story. Robert Entman defines framing as creating a thematic connection among selected information in a story to suggest a particular interpretation. For example, those who are concerned about climate change often say that it threatens life on the planet. Opponents claim that imposing environmental policies on businesses will cost jobs. In such cases, a complex situation is reduced to two competing frames offered by leading politicians or parties that are easily depicted as playing a political game to win a policy fight or an election.[18] As Regina Lawrence explains, framing a political situation as a game offers a convenient narrative device for journalists to make the news dramatic and focused on personalities, while giving the fragmented story a self-contained plot that is relatively free of complex policy details or larger historical analysis.[19] As a result, audiences are often left hanging, without much understanding of the pros and cons of various policy options, yet not really caring about who wins and who loses in the game of Washington politics.

A classic example of personalized, dramatized, and fragmented news reporting comes from this opening of a news report of President Bush landing in a jet on an aircraft carrier to declare "mission accomplished" shortly after the invasion of Iraq: "When the *Viking* carrying Bush made its tailhook landing on the aircraft carrier USS *Abraham Lincoln* off California yesterday, the scene brought presidential imagery to a whole new level. Bush emerged from the cockpit in a full olive flight suit and combat boots, his helmet tucked jauntily under his left arm. As he exchanged salutes with the sailors, his ejection harness, hugging him tightly between the legs, gave him the bowlegged swagger of a top gun."[20] This was the ultimate victory frame, full of drama and personal swagger. It appeared that Mr. Bush had personally won the war, and he surely won the media game in the view of most news organizations covering the staged event. Many reports praised the Bush communication team for creating the perfect news event: dramatic, personal, and winning (some even saw it as the image that would help win the next election). The president's personal popularity soared to record heights. The only trouble with the dramatic narrative was that it was fragmented and cut off from the underlying reality of a war that was just starting to heat up and would soon go rather badly.

Consider some of the other choices news organizations had for framing the aircraft carrier landing story. One possible frame might have pointed out the incongruity of attaching a Hollywood "top gun" image to a president with a checkered military service record. Yet the news tendency is to *personalize* stories along the most dramatic and visually immediate plotlines. Thus, the president appeared as the top gun, and for a brief Hollywood moment, the war seemed over. Such framing choices *fragment* connections between surface events (the carrier landing) and underlying realities of situations (the growing violence in Iraq and the spread of terrorism). *What mattered for much of the reporting was that the president was fully in control of his news narrative*: the president was on top of his game and staged the media event of the year—"mission accomplished."

Months dragged into years, and the framing offered by the administration did not sit comfortably alongside continuing disturbing reports of US battle casualties and chaos in Iraq. Yet journalists who tried to shift the framing of the conflict away from White House communication strategies were accused of liberal bias and of being unpatriotic. When reality finally became too much to ignore, the administration simply reframed its story: "Saddam Hussein was a very bad guy, and the world is better off without him," or "Would you rather fight the terrorists here or over there?" For their part, the Democrats failed to offer journalists much of an opportunity to open the news gates to bigger questions, apparently fearing public disapproval if they challenged a popular president (who was popular in part because of the absence of news challenges). As a result, only 34 of 414 stories told by ABC, NBC, and CBS on the buildup and rationale for the Iraq War from September 2002 through February 2003 originated outside the White House.[21]

Communication scholar Shanto Iyengar offers a condensed view of news framing biases by saying that most news is episodic rather than thematic. *Episodic news* parachutes the journalist and the audience into the middle of an already developed situation and puts the focus on the people who are in trouble or in conflict. To put it in our terms, such news is personalized, dramatic, and fragmented; it often tells stories about who is winning or losing a political fight. By contrast, *thematic news* looks beyond the immediate human drama to explore the origins of problems and the larger social, economic, or political contexts in which the immediate news story has developed. Iyengar's research shows that episodic news, which is the most commonly encountered form of reporting, particularly on television, leaves people with shallow understandings of the world around them. For example, viewers of episodic coverage tend to hold the people at the center of news stories responsible for the problems and conflicts that surround them, rather than see more fundamental social, political, or economic causes at work.[22] This is not surprising since the focus of game-framed news is on politicians pointing fingers and blaming each other for the problem of the day.

Not all news reporting displays all these biases, of course, but much of it does. This chapter takes a close look at news content in terms of the information biases that make news hard to use as a guide to citizen action because they obscure the big picture in which daily events take place. While many Americans are caught up in dead-end debates about ideological news biases that are far less evident than commonly assumed, few notice the other information biases that really are worth worrying about. The task for the remainder of this book is to understand the US public information system at a deeper level. Fortunately, most of the pieces to the news puzzle are right in front of us. The roles of government press officers, spin doctors, media organizations, and the public are available for inspection. The openness of the system may be its saving grace when we turn to questions of reform later in the book.

Four Information Biases That Matter: An Overview

Popular expectations about the quality of public information are rather high. Most of us grew up with history books full of journalistic heroism exercised in the name of truth and free speech. We learned that the American Revolution was inspired by the political rhetoric of the underground press and by printers' effective opposition to the British Stamp Act. The lesson from the trial of Peter Zenger has endured through time: *the truth is not libelous.* The goal of the history book journalists was as unswerving as it was noble: to guarantee for the American people the most accurate, critical, coherent, illuminating, and independent reporting of political events. Yet Zenger would probably not recognize, much less feel comfortable working in, a modern news organization.

Like it or not, the news has become a mass-produced consumer product, bearing little resemblance to history book images. Communication technologies, beginning with the wire services and progressing to satellite feeds and social networking, interact with corporate profit motives to create generic, "lowest-common-denominator" information formats that we discuss further in chapter 6. For now, our four common biases make it easy for a large volume of news to be produced in keeping with the budgets of overworked news organizations.

PERSONALIZATION

If there is a single most important flaw in the American news style, it is the overwhelming tendency to downplay the big social, economic, or political picture in favor of the human trials, tragedies, and triumphs that sit at the surface of events. For example, instead of focusing on power and process, the media concentrate on the people engaged in political combat over the issues. The reasons for this are numerous—from editors' and journalists' fears that probing analysis will turn off audiences to the relative ease of telling the human-interest side of a story as opposed to explaining deeper causes and effects. Whether the focus is on sympathetic heroes and victims or hateful scoundrels and culprits, the media preference for personalized human-interest news creates a "can't-see-the-forest-for-the-trees" information bias that makes it difficult to see the big (institutional) picture that lies beyond the many actors crowding center stage who are caught in the eye of the news camera.

The tendency to personalize the news would be less worrisome if human-interest angles were used to hook audiences into more serious analysis of issues and problems. Almost all great literature and theater, from ancient Greece to the modern day, use strong characters to promote audience identifications and reactions in order to draw people into thinking about larger moral and social issues. American news often stops at the character development stage, however, and leaves the larger lessons and social significance, if there are any, to the imagination of the audience. As a result, the main problem with personalized news is that the focus on personal concerns is seldom linked to more in-depth analysis. Even when large portions of the public reject personalized news formulas, as during the chaotic journalistic and political preoccupation with President Clinton's personal sexual behavior, the personalization never stops. This systematic tendency to personalize situations is one of the defining biases of news.

DRAMATIZATION

Compounding the information bias of personalization is a second news property in which the aspects of events that are reported tend to be the ones most easily dramatized in simple "stories." As previously noted, American journalism has settled overwhelmingly on the reporting form of stories or narratives, as contrasted, for example, with analytical essays, political polemics, or more scientific-style problem reports. Stories invite dramatization, particularly with sharply drawn actors at their center.

News dramas emphasize crisis over continuity, the present over the past or future, and the personalities at their center. News dramas downplay complex policy information, the workings of government institutions, and the bases of power behind the central characters. Lost in the news drama (melodrama is often the more appropriate term) are sustained analyses of persistent problems, such as inequality, hunger, resource depletion, population pressures, environmental collapse, toxic waste, and political oppression. Serious though such human problems are, they just are not dramatic enough on a day-to-day level to make the news until they produce crises that appear suddenly and without warning.

Crises are the perfect news material because they fit neatly into the dramatization bias. The "crisis cycle" portrayed in the news is classic dramatic fare, with rising action, falling action, sharply drawn characters, and, of course, plot resolutions. By its very definition, a crisis is something that will reach dramatic closure through cleanup efforts or humanitarian relief operations. Unfortunately, the crisis cycles in the news only reinforce the popular impression that high levels of human difficulty are inevitable and therefore acceptable.[23]

Like personalization, dramatization is not inherently a bad thing. Drama can help us engage with the great forces of history, science, politics, and human relations. When drama is used to bring analysis to mind, it is a good thing. When drama is employed as a cheap emotional device to focus on human conflict and travail, or farce and frailty, the larger significance of events becomes easily lost in waves of immediate emotion. The potential advantages of drama to enlighten and explain are sacrificed to the lesser tendencies of melodrama to excite, anger, and further personalize events.

One thing that makes the news dramatic—indeed, that may even drive news drama—is the use of visuals: photos, graphics, and live-action video. These elements of stories not only make the distant world seem more real, but they also make the news more believable. In many ways, particularly for television, the pictures may help editors and reporters decide which stories to tell and how to tell them. Again, there is nothing inherently wrong with emphasizing visuals in news production. In fact, it might be argued that thinking visually is the best way to engage the senses in communicating about society and politics. There is often, however, a tension between not reporting important stories that are hard to picture and reporting possibly unimportant stories simply because they offer great visual images. The discussion in chapter 7 explains the economics of editorial decisions to start with the pictures and then add the words. The selection of news stories primarily because they offer dramatic images is one of several important reasons the news is often so fragmented or disconnected from larger political or economic contexts that would provide other ways to tell the story.

FRAGMENTATION

As noted, the emphasis on personal and dramatic qualities of events feeds into a third information characteristic of the news: the isolation of stories from each other and from their larger contexts, so that information in the news becomes fragmented and hard to assemble into a big picture. The fragmentation of information begins by emphasizing individual actors over the political contexts in which they operate. Fragmentation is then heightened by the use of dramatic formats that turn events into self-contained, isolated happenings. The fragmentation of information is further exaggerated by the severe space limits nearly all media impose for fear of boring readers and viewers with too much information.

Because of reporting formulas that favor the personal and the sensational over depth and context, the news generally comes to us in sketchy, dramatic capsules. These fragmentary reports make it difficult to see the causes of problems, their historical significance, or the connections across issues. It can even be difficult to follow the development of a particular issue over time as stories rise and fall more in response to the actions and reactions of prominent public figures than to independent reporting based on investigation of events. In addition, because it is difficult to bring historical background into the news, the impression is created of a world of chaotic events and crises that seem to appear and disappear because the news picture offers little explanation of their origins.

POLITICS AS A GAME

The easiest story to tell about many political situations is that they are contests with winners and losers. After all, winning and losing is a core aspect of politics. It is ironic that journalists complain about the scripted and staged events they cover, but they seem unable to find other ways to write stories that might help citizens become more engaged. One of the first discussions of the portrayal of politics as gamelike strategies was Joseph Cappella and Kathleen Hall Jamieson's aptly named book *Spiral of Cynicism*, which argues that portraying politics as an insider's game leaves audiences increasingly cynical and disillusioned with politics and government.[24] Thomas Patterson showed how reporters use the game template for writing stories centered on politicians competing for advantage in policy fights and gaining ground or money in elections.[25] As discussed in more detail below, Regina Lawrence has pointed out how the game frame pushes more useful information out of the news.

Perhaps the most common game frame is the "horse race" narrative of who is ahead, who is behind, and who is gaining in elections. The problem is that this daily update often displaces what the candidates are actually saying.[26] Moreover, since national polls tend to drive the election horse race story, the news narrative is often out of synch with state-level trends that actually determine the results in the arcane US Electoral College system. Despite these distorting effects, studies have shown that as much as 70 percent of TV news about elections is based on variations of the horse race frame, while far smaller percentages (5–15 percent, depending on the news source) focus on candidate ideas and policy positions.[27]

The game frame can be slapped onto a surprising array of stories, from winning or losing the "war on drugs" to defeating terrorism and even combating natural disasters. Consider the news framing of the catastrophic 2010 oil spill in the Gulf of Mexico. The *Deepwater Horizon* drilling rig operated by BP (and several other companies) exploded off the Louisiana coast, and millions of barrels of crude oil gushed for 87 days from the floor of the Gulf of Mexico nearly a mile underwater. Although the spill was not President Obama's fault, he soon became the focus of news attention about whether he was doing enough to control the situation. A photo of the president on a beach talking with workers and officials was captioned "IN CONTROL President Obama went to Port Fourchon, La., on May 28, to look at the oil spill and to look in charge."[28] The game frame received further support from Republicans who spun the story that the president was weak on energy policy when he called for restricting risky drilling. Taking measures to prevent such disasters was suddenly caught up in a larger game over which party would better secure energy independence for America. Focusing the enormous crisis on the president sent his popularity lower, with some polls equating his handling of the crisis with President Bush's lack of command in the aftermath of Hurricane Katrina. We will revisit this episode later in this chapter's case study on how politicians such as President Obama can "lose" their narratives. Before looking at how politicians suffer problems controlling their news narratives, the next sections offer a more detailed look at the four information biases to help bring them into sharper focus.

Four Information Biases in the News: An In-Depth Look

It is important to recognize here that *it is not any inherent flaw with telling stories that creates information problems with the news; it is how stories are told.* If personal or emotionally dramatic elements are used to introduce audiences to more insightful ideas or draw attention to the underlying causes of situations, then narratives and drama can be very useful. The conclusion of this book returns to look at how news stories might be told differently and with more positive effect on citizen engagement. For now, it is important to be able to recognize each of the four types of information bias in action. This section explores more familiar examples of the four biases, with an eye to why news organizations are inclined to pursue stories that fit these information patterns.

PERSONALIZED NEWS REVISITED

Following the discussion above, *personalized news* can be defined as the journalistic bias that gives preference to individual actors and human-interest angles over larger institutional, social, and political contexts. A case in point is the recurring problem of factions in Congress that leverage their issues by inserting them into budget bills that force the president to either take a poison pill on the issue or veto the budget bill and shut down government operations. When the Republican Party gained control of both houses of Congress following the 2014 election, party leaders vowed to end such tactics that raised questions about party responsibility. The new Republican mantra was to show that they could govern more responsibly and perhaps win the White House in the 2016 election. Yet not long after the new Congress was sworn in, Tea Party factions threatened to shut down funding for the entire Department of Homeland Security after President Obama ordered its officers to stop the deportation of some five million people, mainly parents or children from families that would be broken up. The Speaker of the House at the time, John Boehner, tried to separate funding the department from the immigration issue but failed, and produced only a one-week reprieve for a department that is responsible for airport and border security, customs, immigration, and other key functions. A front-page *New York Times* report focused on the *personal defeat* for Boehner and put the whole story into a *game frame*, calling the result a "stunning and humiliating setback for Speaker John A. Boehner and his leadership team."[29] Nowhere in the story was an explanation of who inserted the immigration measures into the budget bill, how his or her local constituencies may differ from national opinion, or why the United States is perhaps the only democracy in the world where such a thing could happen.

Such news is further personalized by creating a brand identity relationship between the consumer and the news product. Television anchors model their delivery styles and even their looks based on the results of market research. News topic selection increasingly keys into the lifestyles and, in the case of some cable outlets, the political views of audiences. For example, Fox News anchor Megyn Kelly aired a number of reports and wrote online columns on the Homeland Security situation blaming the Democrats for not passing the budget while downplaying the role of disruptive Tea Party factions. It the process, Fox promoted Kelly as a celebrity. Her online reports became obscured by pop-up boxes inviting "Megyn Fans" to "like" Megyn on Facebook before returning to the report.[30] Personalized news owes much to communication professionals such as Roger Ailes who moved easily from being a political consultant to heading up media baron Rupert Murdoch's Fox News. Ailes groomed and promoted celebrities such as Kelly and Bill O'Reilly, making Fox the cable news leader with more viewers than all other cable news channels combined.[31] One of the pioneering "news doctors" was Philip McHugh, who summed it up like this: "There has to be an emphasis on human interest and human beings. You have to have an anchorman who can establish rapport with the audience. . . . It takes a very special kind of personality."[32]

The media (led by television, still the major news source for most Americans) has settled on a formula that is profitable, cheap, and easy to produce, but just not terribly helpful to the citizens who consume this news. Powerful personalities enter the news to provide reassurance or sound an alarm about a pending crisis. So important is this private, emotional bias in the news that it is understood as formal policy in most organizations. Here is an excerpt from a 1970s era memo by an executive producer of ABC News to his staff: "The Evening News, as you know, works on elimination. We can't include everything. As criteria for what we do include, I suggest the following for a satisfied viewer: (1) 'Is my world, nation, and city safe?' (2) 'Is my home and family safe?' (3) 'If they are safe, then what has happened in the past 24 hours to help make that world better?' (4) 'What has happened in the past 24 hours to help us cope better?'"[33] One interesting feature of this news maxim is that it has not changed much in the decades since it was written. Consider what Jonathan Wald, producer of NBC's *Today*, said after 9/11: "People want to know when they wake up if their world is safe. They look to us for reassurance that things are OK or not."[34] In today's more sinister news world, the answers to the personalized question of "Is my world safe?" may not be as reassuring, but the personal bias of prominent political actors talking about "my world" remains as dominant as ever.

Examples of personalized news coverage can be found in virtually any newspaper, magazine, or broadcast. Consider, for instance, the personalization of a familiar political issue, welfare reform, followed by the personalization of an important branch of government, the presidency.

Personalizing an Issue: Welfare Reform News coverage of welfare was intensive for more than 20 years, and skirmishes over various food and benefits programs continue to this day. The modern era of welfare politics began with Ronald Reagan's Republican revolution in the early 1980s, a time of fierce political battles over cutting welfare benefits to the poor and chronically unemployed. In the late 1990s, Bill Clinton stole the Republican thunder and welcomed sweeping cutbacks of government benefits. A common feature of the news over the two decades of policy debates was the focus on personal stories, which ranged from demonizing cheaters and charging recipients with being "welfare Cadillac" owners, to featuring the hardships experienced by people whose support was cut, to highlighting the later success stories of people leaving the support rolls to take productive jobs in society.

As Clinton-era reforms of the late 1990s swept through the land, journalists swarmed welfare offices and job-training programs in search of other personal stories to tell. In the process, hundreds if not thousands of poor people got their 15 minutes of media fame. Indeed, the personalization of their stories was so intense that the news often became part of the plot rather than an invisible recorder of personal experiences. When a German film crew asked how a training program in Milwaukee, Wisconsin, had helped a young woman, she did not talk about finding a job or getting her degree. Instead, she announced that "it really helped me with the interview for *Dateline NBC*," adding that her social worker had coached her on press interview techniques. Another newly placed worker had a polished sound bite about welfare from Franklin D. Roosevelt referring to a new beginning of hope. One woman's story cycled from the *New York Times* to ABC, giving her enough news exposure to generate fan mail. In a later *New York Times* interview, she told a reporter that one of her proudest moments in the transition from welfare to work was when her 11-year-old son declared, "Mama, you're going to be on the news."[35]

The personalization of welfare policy continues through more recent times. An opinion piece in the *Washington Post* was headlined "How Obama Has Gutted Welfare Reform."[36] This theme was amplified in charges from Mitt Romney in the 2012 presidential race. The campaign watchdog organization FactCheck.org investigated the claims that the Obama administration had "dropped" the work requirements that were at the center of the 1996 reforms, and found that the story was not supported by the facts.[37] But the facts were beside the point. The personal attack was made for the news.

Personalizing the Presidency As David Paletz and Robert Entman observed, "Prime news generally involves prominent, powerful people in action, or, more desirable from the media's point of view, in conflict."[38] Not surprisingly, a common strategy of opponents is to attack and scandalize sitting presidents with the aim of making them seem personally weak (which is also a nice way to set up the game frame in the press). As a result of various personal scandals, Bill Clinton's public approval ratings hovered under 50 percent during many of his major policy initiatives. As a member of his own administration told a reporter: "Any time you have a 48 percent [approval] president, every major vote is a death struggle. You are dealing with members [of Congress] who don't know whether to embrace him or run from him."[39] For example, a crime bill that Clinton supported was voted down in a procedural maneuver in the House of Representatives. Although a slightly revised version of the bill passed two weeks later, every major news organization played the original vote as a huge personal defeat for Clinton. ABC correspondent and National Public Radio (NPR) analyst Cokie Roberts put it this way in an NPR interview the morning after the defeat: "[For Mr. Clinton, it was] not a good day. I could hear reporters in the [press] gallery hammering out 'Stunning Defeat,' 'Staggering Defeat.' I like your [NPR's] 'Stinging Defeat.'" NPR further personalized its coverage by adding that the president appeared "visibly shaken" as he addressed reporters afterward.[40] These kinds of judgments by reporters become easy to make if the overriding framing of the story is about the political game. Clinton eventually righted his press strategy in time to help him weather the impeachment storm during his second term in office.

The presidency of Barack Obama witnessed a steady stream of personal attacks in the news. Following the rise of the Tea Party movement, the news and the talk show and online echo chambers were filled with claims that he was a socialist or fascist and other attacks because of his support for the bank bailout and health care reforms. Perhaps the most outlandish personal attacks questioned his American birth. Despite the extremism and conspiracy overtones of the so-called "birther" movement, this personal attack on the legitimacy of the president cycled through the news for years, fanned by questions raised by members of Congress in the media. By one count, 17 members of Congress directly or through innuendo questioned the president's citizenship.[41] (Stephen Colbert challenged one of them to prove that he was not the illegitimate grandson of an alligator.) Not only did the president have to produce his birth certificate, but various fact-checking organizations also verified that he was born in Hawaii. Even the Republican governor of Hawaii tried to settle the matter, as reported by CNN: "'. . . I had my health director, who is a physician by background, go personally view the birth certificate in the birth records of the Department of Health.' [Governor] Lingle added, '. . . The president was in fact born at Kapi'olani Hospital in Honolulu, Hawaii. And that's just a fact.'"[42]

When such a controversy cycles through the news, people can choose who and what to believe. A CNN poll following more than a year of official documentation of the president's American citizenship revealed that only 42 percent said that he was "definitely" born in the United States.[43] The dubious birther issue came back before the 2012 election when Donald Trump announced his interest in running for president and amplified his media exposure by challenging the authenticity of the birth certificate.

Obama finally responded with humor at the 2011 White House Correspondents' Association Dinner when he showed a rock video using Hulk Hogan's theme song "I Am a Real American." The birth certificate flashed repeatedly amid photos of American eagles and other patriotic images. Although the birth issue eventually faded, polls taken during the 2016 presidential election campaign showed that 44 percent of all Republican primary voters and 61 percent of Donald Trump supporters believed that Mr. Obama was born outside of the United States, and 54 percent of likely Republican primary voters believed he was a Muslim.[44]

The Political Costs of Personalized News The focus on winners and losers and on personalities and their conflicts gives the news audience a distorted view of power. As Paletz and Entman concluded, "Power seems to be understood in a limited sense by the media. . . . Stories emphasize the surface appearances, the furious sounds and fiery sights of battle, the well-known or colorful personalities involved—whatever is dramatic. Underlying causes and actual impacts are little noted nor long remembered."[45] As a result, the political world becomes a mystical realm populated by actors who either have the political "force" on their side or do not. The surrounding political context of money, interests, political pressures, and institutional constraints often fades into the background.

DRAMATIZED NEWS REVISITED

It is no secret that reporters and editors search for events with dramatic properties and then emphasize those properties in their reporting. Consider the conscious emphasis on news drama in the following policy memo from the executive news producer of a major television network to his editors and reporters: "Every news story should, without any sacrifice of probity or responsibility, display the attributes of fiction, of drama. It should have structure and conflict, problem and denouement, rising action and falling action, a beginning, a middle, and an end. These are not only the essentials of drama; they are the essentials of narrative."[46] The weight of such evidence led Paletz and Entman to conclude that "drama is a defining characteristic of news. An event is particularly newsworthy if it has some elements of a dramatic narrative. . . . American officials held hostage in the far-off but journalistically accessible land of Iran provide a particularly strident example."[47] Indeed, the hostage crisis that dragged down the Carter presidency offered 444 days of sustained news coverage because it contained so many dramatic angles, almost all of which involved personalized themes and plots: What happened in the story today? How are the hostages? Is the president doing anything to bring them home safely? And, of course, there was the overriding dramatic question that kept people tuning in each day: How will it end?

Dramatized news fits neatly with the personalization bias. Drama, after all, is the quintessential medium for representing human conflict. Promising psychological release and resolution, drama satisfies emotional concerns aroused by the development of characters and plots. Although there are occasional walk-on roles for ordinary people, the majority of news plots revolve around a cast of familiar officials who play standard roles in news dramas. There are also the rich, the famous, the powerful, and the glamorous, along with plenty of bad guys threatening the lives of decent people.

Among the most familiar bad guys are terrorists. But who are they? How do they become cast as terrorists in news dramas? There is no universal standard that defines them because our terrorists are almost always someone else's heroes and freedom fighters. A fascinating study by Steven Livingston shows that in nearly all cases, acts of political violence wait for definition in the news until they are labeled as terrorist, accidental, or heroic by government officials who have political reasons for defining who is bad and who is good.[48]

In general, the main principle guiding the casting of newsmakers in their nightly roles has more to do with their potential as dramatic actors than with any natural preeminence they may have in the political scheme of things. For example, in the US government, the three branches share equal power, both under the Constitution and, for the most part, in actual practice. Yet the president is the dramatic news actor par excellence: singular and easy to keep track of, typecast (e.g., as national parental figure, as staunch defender of freedom against terrorists, or as a flawed character), and introduce into almost any political pretext.

By contrast, the justices of the Supreme Court make poor dramatic material, largely because they are reluctant to walk onstage and play for the audience. The small number of articulate, often eccentric, justices would otherwise make wonderful dramatic characters. Also, there is no shortage of available information about court proceedings, but the business of the court, while important, doesn't fit the news bias toward personalized, dramatic coverage. If the media adopted another information format, the court might share the front pages with the president—a place more in keeping with its constitutional and contemporary political roles.

Congress is another political institution with equal standing under the Constitution but with grossly unequal coverage in the media. A handful of glamorous members of the Senate receive the lion's share of coverage, while the House remains largely a jumbled assembly of nameless seat holders. Washington press observer Stephen Hess has noted the following:

> The Senate has the constitutional right to reject a president's treaties and a president's nominees, appealing prospects to a press corps that loves controversy. The Senate is also the incubator of presidential candidates who are then automatically newsworthy. But most important, there are almost four-and-a-half times as many House members as there are senators. As philosopher David Sidorsky notes, the goal of journalists is to transpose "an inherently ambiguous and complex event into a short narrative that can be simply told, have a central plot, and retain the interest of the reader or viewer." It is easier and faster to build a coherent story with a smaller cast of characters. The House of Representatives is too much like *War and Peace*; the Senate is more on the scale of *Crime and Punishment*.[49]

Because of this news bias, members of Congress have learned to play the media game. As Timothy Cook has shown, members of the once-obscure House increasingly rely on news management to bring attention to legislation and put the spotlight on political careers.[50]

How Journalists Write the Script Robert Darnton told of his early problems as a journalist before he had learned to parse the dramatic highlights from the dull details of most stories. On one of his early assignments on the city desk of a paper in Newark, New Jersey, he wrote a story of a bicycle stolen from a paperboy. The story was rejected by his editor. A colleague suggested a much more dramatic version involving the boy's love for the bike, his trauma following the theft, and his Horatio Alger–like scheme to pay for a new one. Upon checking this more dramatic new plot against the facts, Darnton decided that reality was close enough to the dramatized version to write the story—a story that was published in his paper.[51]

Lewis Lapham, a former editor of *Harper's*, tells of similar experiences in his early days as a reporter. He notes how he marveled at the ease with which the senior reporter in the city room "wrote the accounts of routine catastrophe." Finally, the old reporter's secret came out:

> In the drawer, with a bottle of bourbon and the manuscript of the epic poem he had been writing for twenty years, he kept a looseleaf notebook filled with stock versions of maybe fifty or sixty common newspaper texts. These were arranged in alphabetical order (fires, homicides, ship collisions, etc.) and then further divided into subcategories (fires—one-, two-, and three-alarm; warehouse; apartment building; etc.). The reporter had left blank spaces for the relevant names, deaths, numbers, and street addresses. As follows: "A _____

alarm fire swept through _____ at _____ St. yesterday afternoon, killing _____ people and causing _____ in property damage."[52]

Dramatized news is more melodrama than serious theater, more soap opera than Shakespeare. One does not leave the theater after watching *Hamlet* with the feeling that poor Hamlet was a real loser. If journalists pursued more serious dramatic techniques, the results might be less objectionable. It would not require the talents of a Shakespeare to make big changes in the way the news selects and represents reality. In legitimate drama, including many movies and popular novels, one is made aware of the role played by history, institutions, power, conflict, hidden interests, and accidents in human affairs. These factors are usually missing in news melodrama.

The Political Costs of Dramatized News The most obvious effect of dramatization is to trivialize news content with manufactured drama. Even when the drama may reflect an actual feature of the situation, as in the case of a congressional vote, the preoccupation with drama often distracts attention from any broader political significance the event may have. The action imperative feeds on events with some rapidly developing action to report. One result, as Gaye Tuchman has observed so cogently, is that chronic social problems and long-standing political issues often go unreported because they develop too slowly.[53] In these respects, dramatization compounds the effects of personalization. Fiction writer Don DeLillo has captured these aspects of foreign affairs coverage:

> I think it's only in a crisis that Americans see other people. It has to be an American crisis, of course. If two countries fight that do not supply the Americans with some precious commodity, then the education of the public does not take place. But when the dictator falls, when the oil is threatened, then you turn on the television and they tell you where the country is, what the language is, how to pronounce the names of the leaders, what the religion is all about, and maybe you can cut out recipes in the newspaper of Persian dishes. I will tell you. The whole world takes an interest in this curious way Americans educate themselves. TV. Look, this is Iran, this is Iraq. Let us pronounce the word correctly. E-ron. E-ronians. This is a Sunni, this is a Shi-ite. Very good. Next year we do the Philippine Islands, okay?[54]

Dramatized news also creates another information dilemma: the temptation for news organizations to look for the most extreme cases rather than the most representative examples of a subject. The preoccupation with drama makes it hard to draw the line between journalists as reporters of fact and as creators of fiction. After noting that drama is a requirement for a major news story, Paletz and Entman observed that some stories deficient in their own "high drama" may "have drama grafted on": "Journalists have been known to highlight if not concoct conflict and to find characters to symbolize its different sides. One reason: to attract an audience that is thought to have little patience for the abstract, the technical, the ambiguous, the uncontroversial."[55]

In a world where political events are already far removed from the immediate experience of the average person, news dramas may push political consciousness permanently into the realm of fiction. For example, studies of crime waves in the news have shown that they have often occurred during periods of declining crime. Local TV news devotes twice as much time to crime and accidents as to local political affairs, which makes crime a built-in feature of the local newscast. Not surprisingly, people who regularly watch local news tend to think the world is a more dangerous place and list crime as a top political issue. It is an issue that politicians have used to collect a lot of votes and spend a lot of tax money on law enforcement and prisons, making the United States the world leader in prison population.[56]

Dramatized news can reinforce political dysfunction in several ways: (a) by distracting attention from more important causes of problems, (b) by creating a false sense of understanding rooted in personalized explanations, and (c) by promoting dramatically satisfying but practically unworkable solutions. As Murray Edelman has argued, many of the chronic problems that diminish the quality of life both nationally and on the world stage are surely worsened by the way they are represented in the news. The news has become a means of turning problems into political spectacles that drown out serious debate, while creating an appetite for quick, dramatic resolutions on the part of audiences.[57]

FRAGMENTED NEWS REVISITED

News fragments are self-contained dramatic capsules, isolated from each other in time and space. The impression given by the news is of a jigsaw puzzle that is out of focus and missing many pieces. When focus is provided, it is on the individual pieces, and less often on how they fit into the overall picture. When information is delivered in such fragments, people are invited to project their own interpretations onto the world. In these ways, the news defies the old adage that the whole is greater than the sum of its parts. In news reality, the whole is decidedly less than the sum of its parts. Columnist Russell Baker once parodied the typical newscast in the following terms:

Meanwhile, in Washington, the . . . Administration was reported today as fire-
men still sifted through the ruins of a six-alarm blaze in Brooklyn that left two
Congressmen, who were said to have accepted cash contributions from Korean
agents, despite their fifth defeat in a row at the hands of the Boston Celtics. . . .
Seventeen were dead and scores injured by the testimony that two Senators, whom he declined to name, rioted in the streets of Cairo following her
son's expulsion from school for shooting a teacher who had referred to him in
the easy-going style of the . . . White House, as exemplified by the dispute over
the B-1 bomber.[58]

Long-term trends and historical patterns are seldom made part of the
news because it is hard to tell them as simple stories. Events spring full-
blown, from out of nowhere, into the headlines. In place of seeing a coherent world anchored in clear historical, economic, and political tendencies,
the public is exposed to a world made chaotic by seemingly arbitrary and
mysterious forces. Fragmented news has a life and a reality of its own. A
shred of credibility is added by documenting what is reported. Never mind
that much more of what actually happened went unreported. And some of
what happened was staged to make the news.

The Political Costs of Fragmentation There are, of course, numerous
"good reasons" for such reporting. Journalism's hallowed prohibitions
against commentary and interpretation seem to justify the representation
of events as isolated, no matter how interrelated they may be. Moreover,
press releases from official news sources seldom take pains to point out
inconsistencies, complex relations, or other big-picture aspects of events.
These strategies of propagandists are rewarded by the journalistic preoccupation with daily news, which means that the news slate is often wiped
clean each day. Update sections are relegated to the backs of newspapers,
and analysis pieces are saved for slow news days in radio and television
broadcasts.

Consider how personalization and dramatization reinforced fragmented
coverage of the great health care debates of the Clinton and Obama administrations. At stake was finding some way to help some 40 million Americans
who lacked medical insurance for illness or accident. Instead of putting the
focus on how everyone could be accommodated under some new health
plan, news reporting often reflected the spin of opponents who wanted
to scare people who already had health insurance. Would their insurance
change or would costs go up? The main casualty of these fearful stories was
public understanding of the actual proposed plans. A study by the Times
Mirror (now Pew) Center for the People and the Press found that fewer

Americans understood key aspects of the Clinton administration health care plan after three months of intense news coverage than at the time the plan was first announced.[59] The Clinton plan was defeated, which fed into the game-frame coverage described in the next section.

Now flash forward to the Obama-era debates surrounding the Affordable Care Act, which finally passed by a narrow margin. Again, despite years of news coverage and alarming election advertising, popular grasp of key elements of the law remained dim. A study by a team of Stanford University opinion researchers found that many people did not know what the key elements of the law were, and that many others wrongly believed things that were not in the law. The Stanford team concluded that if people properly understood the law, approval would have jumped from just over 30 percent to more than 70 percent.[60]

It is no wonder that public opinion studies show that most people have trouble thinking in abstract, logically integrated ways about political issues. An inventory of findings from public opinion research sounds like a list of the effects of news fragmentation: the average person has trouble stating clear positions on issues, most people tend to remember few facts about important issues, the majority of people see few connections between issues, and many people change their opinions easily about issues. And John Zaller has shown that when people are relatively more informed, it is because they have adopted the viewpoints of partisan officials or parties with whom they already identified.[61]

THE GAME FRAME REVISITED

Both the Clinton and Obama efforts to pass health care reform were framed as political games that snarled the national government with playing politics. In the Clinton episode, the president was described as losing his biggest policy battle to date, and doubts were raised about the ability of government to accomplish major national goals. In the Obama case, the reform passed narrowly, and it was equated with saving his presidency. In the process, the news formats often cut off connections to surrounding political contexts, such as how other countries handle health care for poor people or why so many health industry companies and associations lined up against the proposed reforms. Nor were there many stories about the trails of campaign contributions from the industry to members of Congress who suddenly emerged as opponents to reform. These issues were raised but never became dominant frames for the story. Once again, news biases conveniently capsulized events at the expense of broader understandings.

Johanna Dunaway and Regina Lawrence have identified a number of conditions that help explain when we are likely to see more or less reporting on politics as a game.[62] One interesting pattern is that game frames show up more often in reporting by large media chains owned by conglomerates trying to extract profits from their holdings. The reason seems to be that formula reporting like the horse race in elections or the "winners and losers" in policy contests is much cheaper to turn out than more investigative pieces. Another factor involves the ways in which different types of stories invite or discourage the political game narrative. Again, elections give news organizations relative freedom in how to write about them while requiring frequent updates from the often tedious and repetitive campaign trail. These conditions make horse race and money chase stories popular ways to fill in the daily supply of news.

In an earlier study, Lawrence showed that for big, long-running issues such as welfare reform, game framing often ran ahead of substantive discussions when policies were being debated among politicians, and that substantive policy frames tended to become more dominant only after decisions were made.[63] Breaking up coverage between national and state politics showed the game frame far more prominent in stories about Washington, while reports on welfare reform at the state level were focused far more on the substance of the issues. Moreover, the game frame rose dramatically when the issue entered an election. Even though the same players and positions may move from the policy arena into the election contest, as happened during the Clinton presidency, coverage during the election was more than 70 percent driven by game analyses of how Clinton's positions would win or lose votes.

The Political Costs of Game Framing the News Regina Lawrence cautions that it is precisely at the times when public opinion is forming on issues or candidates that the news offers the least useful substantive information because of game framing. Lawrence concludes: "The game frame marginalizes the substance of political conflicts, undercuts the ability of politicians to communicate their policy positions to the public, and encourages the public to view all politics as self-interested calculation and political manipulation."[64]

There is, of course, the possibility that in many issue conflicts the political sides really are gaming each other, which raises a bit of a chicken-or-egg problem of whether the press is overreporting convenient story formulas. Either way, the ultimate cost is that citizens are discouraged about politics, which is not a good result. In areas such as elections, the press clearly has more leeway to find other ways to tell the story, yet the horse race persists largely because it is the easiest way to keep the election drama going over the unusual length of the American campaign. Journalists have vowed to cut down on this kind of coverage to little avail. Moreover, the increasing levels of journalists as voices and sources in the news make it even harder to avoid narrative formulas that convey insider status, which further alienates many citizens.[65]

As reporters become insiders, they become fascinated with the game often to the detriment of helping people understand why it matters. One of the signs that this trend may be getting worse rather than better is the growing fascination of reporters with whether politicians are winning or losing their struggles over controlling the news narrative itself. One might think that journalists are the ones who actually write news stories, and therefore they should not judge politicians on how good they are at spinning the press. However, when reporters become so taken by strategy and games, they often reward politicians who are good at spinning, and punish those who are not. In many ways, the ultimate game of politics is controlling the news narrative. The biggest political losers are those who do not understand this, or who do not like it, or who are simply not very good at it. The case study in this chapter examines how the press referees this ultimate game of controlling the news narrative.

CASE STUDY
WHO CONTROLS THE NEWS NARRATIVE?

Newly elected New York City mayor Bill de Blasio knew that reporters continuing to ask about his daughter's rumored drug problems could become a distraction from governing. The mayor's communication team interviewed Chiara de Blasio about her struggles with depression and substance abuse and put together a video that looked more like reality TV or YouTube fare than a slick TV ad. The video was uploaded to YouTube, where it received more than one million views and triggered an outpouring of support on social media. By preempting possible critics and bypassing the press, Chiara's story put the issue to rest. The news reported the story largely as packaged by the de Blasio team and told in Chiara's own words. The new mayor had seized control of a narrative about a potentially troublesome problem. In his analysis of this episode in *USA Today*, Michael Wolff noted that storytelling and controlling the narrative have swept America from individuals concerned about their images to corporate and political branding: "Among the most prevalent and up to date phrases in business, politics, and savvy American life is 'controlling the narrative.' That is, telling it your way before someone else gets to it—and possibly tell it better—their way. And getting the public to relate to you on a more intimate level."[66]

When he ran for president, Barack Obama had a simple and effective narrative: the (relative) outsider who promised hope and change in hard times. The nation was entering a serious economic crisis and faced two wars and loss of prestige abroad. Obama's main opponents (Hillary Clinton in the primaries and John McCain in the general election) were Washington veterans who had supported the increasingly unpopular wars and were more easily associated with the failures to regulate the banking industry. Thus he entered office with a strong and emotionally uplifting story—at least for the majority of voters who supported him. As a *Washington Post* article put it: "Journalists and politicians know that voters, like everyone else, are hard-wired to understand the world through stories. Elections are contests between competing story lines, something Obama, himself an elegant writer, and his team of political image editors were keenly aware of as they crafted the protagonist as a transformative Washington outsider, whose unerringly serious, postpartisan belief in competence, bridge-building and doing the right thing would improve the nation. That sympathetic character won 53 percent of general-election voters. . . . But now his narrative has taken on a life of its own."[67]

Indeed, the transition from campaigning to governing proved rough on the Obama story, as personal attacks and dramatic distortions of his legislative initiatives left him seemingly unable to explain and sell his agenda. His tone of civility and reasoned discussion seemed no match for sharp attacks from Tea Party protesters who disrupted health care town halls with signs accusing Obama of being a socialist and a fascist all in the same breath. Images of his iconic "Hope" campaign poster appeared in news and online sites with Hitler mustaches added on. Other images pictured the president as a creepy Joker from the Batman movie. As noted earlier, even his birth in America was challenged. Yet he continued to reach out to offer discussion and compromise. Even his supporters wondered why the Obama team was reluctant or unable to spin the press. In the case of health care, the White House failed to give the plan a brand name and tell its story. Opponents quickly branded it "Obamacare" and spun many misleading stories about it in the press. The persistent negative attacks eroded Mr. Obama's popular support. He entered office with an approval rating at a high of 70 percent, but that dipped quickly to barely 50 percent by the time the health care town halls became disrupted with protesters, and slipped to 45 percent after the oil spill in the Gulf.[68]

Jason Horowitz wrote a *Washington Post* story about how the Obama narrative was overshadowing the real stories of the time: "In this particularly meta moment, the overarching Obama story line hovers a level above events, distracting from the disaster in the gulf, glossing over the question of whether the government's concrete actions are sufficient, removing readers and viewers and listeners from reality. The narrative has been constantly updated—Obama's a hero one day, a goat the next—as ravenous news cycles and impatient audiences demand conclusions, and attention-starved media outlets can no longer subsist on the modest first drafts of history."[69]

As his media fortunes bumped along, Mr. Obama played the narrative game better in the 2012 election and branded his opponent Mitt Romney as an out-of-touch rich guy who didn't care about ordinary folks or the workers whose jobs his investment company sent overseas. Although Romney protested the inaccuracy of that story, he did not effectively counter it with a better narrative. And so the winner of the "brand your opponent before he brands you" contest in 2012 was Obama.

The newly reelected president again stumbled in the storytelling department as the Obamacare sign-up websites turned out to be badly programmed and in many cases simply did not work. A genuine policy failure, magnified by howls from his opponents, sent his popularity to a new low, in the 40 percent range. He attempted to regroup ahead of the 2014 elections by promoting a narrative about how the current minimum wage left millions of hard-working Americans living in poverty. He tried to craft a story about inequality in America that did not produce an outcry of class warfare from wealthy Americans. The president soon found out that stories about inequality are complex and hard to translate into mainstream news. Here is a bit of his story about the shrinking middle class that Mr. Obama told a reporter: "You have an economy that is ruthlessly squeezing workers and imposing efficiencies that make our flat-screen TVs really cheap but also puts enormous downward pressure on wages and salaries. That's making it more and more difficult not only for African Americans or Latinos to get a foothold into the middle class, but for everybody—for large majorities of people—to get a foothold in the middle class or to feel secure there." At one point, he even turned to a gathering of historians at the White House to ask for help finding a narrative that wouldn't immediately trigger the counternarrative of class warfare.[70] In the end, the president was kept off the campaign trail in 2014 by many congressional candidates in his own party who did not want to be seen with him as his narrative and popularity continued to spiral.

Perhaps it is too much to expect a coherent narrative from a leader faced with two distant wars, a long-running economic recession, opposition to nearly everything on his political agenda, and a string of problems from an oil spill to broken health care websites. On the other hand, even if Mr. Obama had crafted a winning narrative that somehow created the illusion of control on all these disparate issues, what would it really help us understand? It is ironic that the logic of the press-politics system in the United States demands so much staged image making and oversimplified storytelling in situations that would benefit from more perspective and thematic reporting. As a result, these news biases become reinforced on all sides: through political spin, newsroom decisions, and a public that has little time for complexity.

Bias and the US Political Information System

The tendencies toward personalization, dramatization, fragmentation, and game-framed news formulas have been developing for some time. They have become more exaggerated with the economic pressures of the news business explained in the last chapter and with the loss of civility in government. Not surprisingly, many good politicians say they have left government because of the relentlessly negative media scrutiny, while others have surrounded themselves with legions of media consultants and handlers, all of which adds to the problem. Many journalists are concerned about their own part in this spiral of staged news, but they confess being helpless to change things under the current system of profit- and ratings-driven business values. And communication scholars such as Joseph Cappella, Kathleen Hall Jamieson, Thomas Patterson, and Regina Lawrence (all discussed above) show that many who continue to consume news become discouraged by the cynicism and negativity of politics and public life.

And so each element of the politician-press-public news triangle affects the others in a dysfunctional manner until nearly everyone is dissatisfied. Rather than a rational process, this information system is more like a dysfunctional system in which different players are operating under different logics:

- Politicians play for public support and favorable insider buzz by using news management and PR techniques intended to put their political bias (or spin) on news content.
- News organizations compete for audiences and profits. The cost-effective formula favors reporting scripted political performances and reactions to attacks from opponents. Ironically, this makes stories look much the same, from one news outlet to another.
- Publics search the news for information that helps them decide what to do politically. They may find useful information if they search for it when motivated by interest in a particular issue. More often, the run of general stories leaves people confused or discouraged, rather like spectators to a game they don't care much about.

Reform Anyone?

Political scientist Murray Edelman described the daily news as political spectacle, attracting attention for its entertainment value even as it often fails to provide much information that is useful to citizens.[71] If we are going to meet the information needs of democracy, citizens need to understand how this information system works and think about how to fix what is wrong with it (and how to fix the underlying political process that generates most of the news). Yet many people have simply withdrawn from politics and joined the chorus of those who hurl easy criticisms at politicians and press alike. Public disapproval alone has not produced the improved quality of information on which a healthy democracy depends. Although criticisms of the news are rampant, relatively few critics offer much in the way of solid proposals for change. Press reform is addressed in the final chapter in this book, but a brief look ahead seems useful now.

There have been various calls for press reform in recent decades, but they have failed because of lack of uptake from various players involved in the current dysfunctional system. One notable reform attempt was the movement for *public* or *civic* journalism that arose in the 1990s. This approach to journalism generally involved local news organizations inviting citizen participation in shaping news coverage that "encourages civic engagement—especially in elections—and supports communities in solving problems."[72] However, the civic journalism trend drew harsh criticism from many prominent journalists and news organizations. For example, editors at the *New York Times* and the *Washington Post* condemned the loss of journalistic independence that comes from letting citizens help decide what is important to cover. Some journalists felt that keeping the focus on popular issues rather than what politicians were doing risked crossing the line from objective reporting to issue advocacy.

Flash forward two decades, and the situation has grown dire. Many news organizations, particularly in the print press, are facing extinction. Online sites churn the spin from government and introduce rumors and dubious stories of their own. More citizens receive their news directly from Facebook, YouTube, or Twitter, without thinking much about how it was produced. Such chaotic developments fail to address how society and government might try to create more useful public information. The closing chapter of the book examines ways in which more recent grassroots media reform movements such as Free Press are trying to promote various changes such as limiting corporate influence on journalism, finding ways for government to support quality journalism, and keeping the Internet open and accessible to all.[73] In addition, as discussed at the beginning of chapter 1, various new journalism start-ups feature investigation and high-quality information and may point a way forward. Meanwhile, the continuing popularity of political comedy offers citizens some relief from the spin. However, the fact remains that the issues and realities of the day for most people are still defined by the mainstream news. This core of our information system continues to shape public opinion in American politics, as discussed in the next chapter.

3

CITIZENS AND THE NEWS
PUBLIC OPINION AND
INFORMATION PROCESSING

Public deliberation is essential to democracy, in order to ensure that the public's policy preferences—upon which democratic decisions are based—are informed, enlightened, and authentic. In modern societies, however, public deliberation is (and probably must be) largely mediated, with professional communicators rather than ordinary citizens talking to each other.

—Benjamin I. Page[1]

Rather than attending carefully to polls, most leaders find their interpretations of public opinion by consulting other leaders and news coverage.

—Robert M. Entman[2]

What information consumes is rather obvious: It consumes the attention of its recipients. Hence a wealth of information creates a poverty of attention.

—Herbert A. Simon[3]

Public opinion is often regarded as the engine of democracy. Public engagement through polls, protests, social media crowds, and other expressions of opinion can define issues, shape policy debates, and affect the outcomes of elections. Politicians, campaigns, and interest groups often try to shape opinion to their advantage. Indeed, many public relations professionals have long argued that managing the attention of publics is essential for taming the noisy communications and passions of the crowd that can disrupt democratic stability.[4]

Sometimes opinion is anchored at least partly in direct personal experiences with such things as the economy, health care, abortion, and taxes. However, many other issues are distant from direct experience and become meaningful primarily through images in advertising and the news, both of which often reflect the "spin" of politicians and interest groups. At the dawn of the modern media era in the 1920s, journalist Walter Lippmann lamented that the only experience most people have of many political realities, from domestic policy conflicts to wars, are those that come through the news.[5] This means that in many areas opinion may be based on news images of distant events, people, and problems. It is therefore important to understand the ways in which such news images are constructed and how they affect our thoughts, feelings, and actions. Consider just three of the many ways in which news content helps people imagine a world they share with others:

- *Focusing attention on selected issues.* News coverage typically focuses a large volume of attention on a few dramatic issues, and scant attention on many others. This emphasis affects the importance that people assign to issues and whether they know enough to even form meaningful opinions about them. Scholars refer to this process as *cueing* issues by associating them with established political leaders, parties, or beliefs.[6] When issues make the news repeatedly, people tend to rank them higher on the agenda of important concerns, which is known as the *agenda-setting function* of media.[7]
- *Forming publics.* News that is repeatedly cued to familiar political figures, parties, or beliefs can shape opinion and divide publics into opposing camps of varying sizes and opinion strengths. These opinion patterns can be reinforced through new episodes of ongoing news stories that are often recycled through talk shows, blogs, and late-night comedy.
- *Shaping political behavior.* The news is often spun by communication campaigns based on marketing research. The core messages in these campaigns may motivate some groups to act, while discouraging others. Even if only small percentages of voters or "issue publics" change their opinions (registering a "bump" in the polls or shifting votes in elections), those changes can affect the outcome of an election or an issue campaign.

The questions of how much and in what ways people rely on media cues still divide many scholars. When citizens are bombarded with messages on multiple channels from TV news to Facebook, they may shift their perceptions about a problem, issue, or candidate. However, many citizens are hard to reach because they avoid the news. Others are hard to persuade to change their views because they seek information that confirms what they already believe. Further complicating the opinion process, the frag-

menting media system makes it hard for communication campaign managers to reach large audiences of the sort that existed in the mass media
era. Despite these developments, politicians, parties, businesses, and other
interests continue to spend record amounts of money on media messaging.
With few restrictions on the flow of money into politics, estimates of total
spending in the 2016 election ran to upwards of $10 billion, with half of that
in the presidential race alone.[8] The soaring costs of elections and spending
on public relations campaigns reflect the persistent belief among political
strategists that even a few points' "bump" in issue polls or voter leanings
can make the difference in winning close contests and policy fights.

News and the Battle for Public Opinion

Opinion can be volatile and hard to manage, particularly in a fragmenting media environment that makes people hard to reach. Thus, the
process of polling and refining messages for different media audiences
is a key element of election campaigns and interest-group politics. Consumer marketing research has been adapted to politics to assess the dispo-
sitions of various segments of the public. Based on this research, messages
are shaped and tested through focus groups and other techniques. Then
those messages are sent through many channels, including direct mailings,
political advertising, local visits, news events, and social media networks.
This communication work is variously called public relations (PR), strategic communication, and spin. We live in an environment saturated with PR
and persuasive images, and likely tune most of them out. However, people
also tend to select information that agrees with their interests and beliefs,
making it challenging to persuade people to take new positions. However,
when new events or crises develop and leaders mount high-visibility communication campaigns, public opinion often follows the cues. But it is hard
to keep people in line when persuasive messages are blatantly contradicted
by policy failures and evidence to the contrary. For example, a sophisticated public relations campaign led by the Bush administration produced
majority support for the Iraq War in 2003, but the inability of either the Bush
or Obama administrations to settle the conflict or produce a viable democracy in Iraq soon eroded that support, so that at the time of this writing, a
majority felt that the intervention in Iraq was a failure.[9]

It is also important to understand the interplay of personalized digital
media and conventional or "legacy" media in shaping opinion. Every time
we go online, we are being tracked by media companies that compile databases on who we are, what we buy, what news and information we consume, what websites we visit, how long we spend on them, what we share

via our social networks and email, and more. Thus, we become often un-witting helpers for political and consumer marketing agents by giving up private information that helps them persuade us to buy, vote for, believe, or value whatever they pitch. Much persuasive communication now takes place through personal digital media channels, but the legacy media continue to play an important role. In particular, communication strategists try to get their messages into the news to create the impression of broader credibility and to invite individuals to join with others in sharing their views through social media, polls, and other means of opinion expression. This "echo chamber" effect of the interaction between personal digital media and selective attention to legacy media helps people feel that their views are well founded and supported by others even when they are extreme or have little evidence to support them.[10]

This selective reinforcement process makes it hard for citizens to have productive conversations—whether personal or national—across areas of polar disagreement. Indeed, the tendency in private life is to avoid talking politics with people who may disagree with us, while the media tone in public life has become shrill and unpleasant, straining norms of civility. Despite the growing dysfunction of the media echo chamber, the news remains an important part of the opinion process. Even though news audiences are losing younger citizens, the legacy mass media remain the most common sources of political information, even as people increasingly tune into the topics and viewpoints they prefer to hear.

The news logic discussed in chapter 2 involves, in part, dramatizing issues to make them more personally accessible. This is not lost on communication professionals who construct public events to fit with this and the other journalistic biases discussed in the last chapter. Issues and events that are packaged in personalized and dramatic terms are the ones that dominate the news. Issues such as abortion, taxes, health care, jobs, terrorism, war, and security are relatively easy to dramatize, and conflicts among competing interests often make them big news stories.

Chasing Its Own Tale: How News Formulas Shape Opinion

When issues stay in the news for extended periods, news organizations conduct polls to measure public reactions. Although they are presented as scientific, these news polls often become part of the spin cycle. This is because the polling firms working with news organizations often phrase poll questions in language similar to the issue frames promoted by politicians, even when those frames may distort or polarize issues. This means that for many issues, the polls tend to follow the language of political spin, and not other, more neutral or realistic terms that might invite more reflective responses. For example, when polls asked people how they felt about invading Iraq in 2002–2003, levels of support for going to war were higher when the questions mentioned weapons of mass destruction or al-Qaeda connections than when these fearful (and largely incorrect) cues were not included. However, polls using Bush administration claims often fit better with news stories on administration justifications for war, and so levels of public support reported by the media were higher than if polling questions had not been tied to political spin.

Because publics are the most important symbol in the grand story of democracy, it is tempting to endow their opinions with greater interest and clarity than actually exists. Thus, news organizations tend to pressure the polling organizations that do their surveys to push respondents to have an opinion even when they do not. As a result, few news polls report high levels of "don't knows," even though many people really do not know much about the issues on which they are pushed by pollsters to express an opinion. Even more disturbing is that news polls seldom probe a deeper aspect of opinion: whether people really care if their favored policies happen or if their pre-ferred candidates win. A series of studies by David Moore (conducted while working as an editor at Gallup) showed that if you asked people whether they would be upset if their stated preference did not occur, the largest seg-ment of responses on almost every issue indicated they would not.[11] Yet news reports seldom include such heavily qualified assessments of opinion. News stories tend to ignore the "don't knows" and "don't cares" in favor of reporting stronger divisions of opinion that suggest a more involved public than usually exists.

David Moore and his colleague Jeffrey Jones asked the "How upset would you be?" question while polling national samples about a variety of issues, including drilling for oil in an Alaskan nature preserve, election campaign finance reform, gay civil unions, missile defense, and human cloning. These were among the most politically contested issues among elites at the time the polls were taken. The surface-level results (typically reported in the news) indicated vigorous public engagement and clear majority opinions on most issues: campaign finance reform (58% favor, 26% oppose), oil drill-ing (56% oppose), human cloning ban (53% favor), building missile defense system (64% favor), and gay civil unions (45% favor, 46% oppose). Yet prob-ing beneath the surface produced majorities or large pluralities that would not have been upset if their preferences did not happen: campaign finance (58% would not be upset no matter how it turned out), oil drilling (44%), gay unions (49%), and missile defense (47%). Of all these issues on which majorities were pushed to have clear opinions (including going to war in Iraq), only human cloning had a majority of supporters and opponents (73%) who actually cared if their preferences did not happen (most opposed human cloning and would be upset if it happened).[12]

These findings raise important questions about the typical characterizations of public opinion in the press. If opinion on many issues is as soft as these findings indicate, then it is a stretch to say that publics strongly support or oppose particular government initiatives. Yet such claims are often made in order to spice up news dramas. *It would be more accurate to say that when elites are deeply divided, the news is written around those divisions, and polls reported in the news are often constructed to push publics into those same divisions.* Political scientist Morris Fiorina has argued that the notion of a polarized America is true only for warring political factions, and not for the public at large.[13]

Exaggerating levels of public engagement and conflict makes for more dramatic news. However this dramatization can also spill back into the political situation itself, in which one side in a policy conflict or election campaign can similarly inflate claims that it is winning. For example, voters may decide to back the frontrunner and sacrifice support for a candidate who is reported behind in the polls—even though support for the frontrunner is really not as solid as the polls make out. In other cases, citizens may quietly accept policy outcomes or decisions (such as going to war) that actually have far less support than dramatically sharpened news polls suggest. Murray Edelman called this symbolically induced state of public mind *quiescence.*[14]

The perpetual conflicts over "hot-button" issues such as race and immigration illustrate how polls can shape reality even as they claim merely to reflect it. A study by Robert Entman and Andrew Rojecki showed that news stories consistently dramatized racial conflict themes and reported poll results that fit the news framing. Thus, the cover of a prominent news magazine blared the headline "Race and Rage." A more reasonable story could well have been written around points of racial harmony and agreement, depending on how the poll questions were worded.[15] Other observers have noted that the polarizing framing of polls enabled the public to become symbolically drawn into so-called culture wars waged by small numbers of elites at the most extreme (in this case, conservative) end of the political spectrum.[16] Those elites found news organizations eager to dramatize their polarizing efforts rather than report more moderate and representative accounts. As Entman and Rojecki observed: "Journalists, it seems, built their frame on claims by elite sources with an interest in promoting the impression of White arousal, a goal that meshed nicely with reporters' constant search for conflict and drama. In fact, journalists appeared to confuse *elite rhetoric* with *average citizens' preferences and priorities*."[17]

Shaping public issues to fit news stories through polling has consequences. One likely result is that this polarizing (or better put, poll-arizing) news may inhibit moderate and progressive politicians from publicly supporting affirmative action or finding new remedies for people experiencing discrimination in education, employment, or voting, as Entman and Rojecki concluded: "It is clear that some of the most important political leaders who set the media agenda—especially presidential hopefuls—turned more actively hostile to affirmative action. . . . It is far from clear that their views reflected the sentiments of ordinary White Americans."[18] The same can probably be said for the immigration debates swirling in the news in more recent times. Even Barack Obama increased the deportation of undocumented people while framing much of his immigration policy around an economic discourse of matching immigrants with jobs.

Immigration politics have introduced hot racial issues into elections and policymaking at all levels of government. In 2010, the state of Arizona passed a law that directed local law enforcement to police the immigration documents of state residents. This was controversial on a number of levels, from pushing local law enforcement into what had traditionally been a federal jurisdiction, to raising the specter of racial profiling, with Latino residents feeling they were more likely to be stopped and screened by police than other racial groups. Extensive polling was conducted by news organizations and other independent survey organizations, with news polling often echoing the dramatized news that filled the 24/7 media. For example, in two national polls taken just a month after the Arizona law was passed, a CNN survey showed that only 6 percent were unsure what to think of the Arizona action, while a Quinnipiac University poll showed fully 18 percent were unsure what to think. The CNN poll evidently created the impression of a much more engaged and clearly opinionated public by pushing as many undecided respondents as possible into the two polar (favor and opposed) camps.[19]

The Arizona immigration conflict illustrates the powerful effects of question wording on polling results. The highly regarded Pew Research organization asked how respondents felt about the decision of the US Justice Department to challenge the Arizona law. The question it asked was carefully worded to describe the basic facts of the situation: "As you may know, this week the U.S. Justice Department filed a legal challenge to the state of Arizona's recent immigration law. From what you know, do you approve or disapprove of the Justice Department's decision to challenge the Arizona law?" In its version, the Quinnipiac University Poll included the more emotionally loaded terms "Obama" and "strike down": "The Obama administration has filed a lawsuit to strike down Arizona's immigration law. Do you think this lawsuit is a good idea or a bad idea?" Loading up the question with "Obama" and "strike down" pushed the numbers who disapproved of the action from 45 percent in the Pew poll to a strong majority of 60 percent in the Quinnipiac survey, while the number of undecided respondents dropped from 19 to 12 percent.[20]

In thinking about the polls in news reports, it is good to remember how poorly formed such opinions can be. Although the Supreme Court eventually struck down some provisions of the Arizona law, the controversial centerpiece involving local police screening was allowed to stand. As other states passed their own versions of such laws, the issue became a huge election focus. Democrats used the issue to try to win Latino votes. Moderate Republicans feared their party was losing those important voters. And Tea Party Republicans sought even harsher policies. Lost in the political drama was a clear sense of how ordinary citizens actually engaged with the issue.

The Public in the News Drama

The moral of the story is that political spin is hard to keep out of the polls, and the polls, in turn, often promote more spin. For most people most of the time, the news is full of emotional images of distant events. As Walter Lippmann noted in his classic work, *Public Opinion*, the news images that people receive often bear little resemblance to the complexity and historical significance of the actual events, leaving much to be desired in terms of deeply informing publics about their choices.[21] From the standpoint of leaders who have high stakes in power struggles and policy contests, the main goal is to win public acceptance or discourage public protest. Thus, public opinion is largely constructed out of competing political visions of reality that often make citizens spectators in the drama of democracy. As noted above, political scientist Murray Edelman referred to the psychological state of these spectator publics as *political quiescence*—going along with the flow of distant events in the news even if they do not fully agree or understand the issues.[22] Edelman described *politics as a spectacle*, full of emotional exchanges among distant actors, sometimes stirring up popular feelings and sometimes leaving people feeling discouraged and manipulated. Either way, the political conflicts dramatized in the news have very real consequences.[23]

Even if publics are not fully engaged in many news dramas, politicians and their communication staff are tuned in. Political communications staffers spin reporters. Then they follow up after stories appear to control any political damage that they failed to spin away. They monitor news to see how their claims about public support are playing in the press and whether news polls echo their framing of questions and interpretations of opinion. In this way, news becomes a barometer for public support and opposition while often leaving citizens on the sidelines. Robert Entman described this process as a "democracy without citizens."[24] In many ways, the news becomes a stand-in for public opinion itself inside the Beltway and in state capitals.[25]

Of course many citizens express their opinions by taking to the streets, writing letters, signing petitions, or even meeting with politicians. Since the advent of the digital age, large crowds such as Occupy Wall Street can rise up more or less spontaneously and be heard—a point to which we will return at the end of the chapter. However, in the day-to-day policy and election battles of government, many more citizens follow the news to see how the battles are going with the issues they care about. As noted above, some issues are beyond the grasp of most citizens. Is Iran building nuclear weapons? What is the best way to address this problem? Some politicians advocate bombing the facilities. Others say this will further destabilize a region already in chaos, and advocate economic sanctions and diplomatic solutions. Public relations that simplify and dramatize these messages can shape what people think and how the sides are drawn. Sometimes events do not have powerful advocates lined up on different sides, and one dominant point of view saturates the news—often with unfortunate results. This scenario happened when the Bush administration sold the idea of going to war in Iraq—a sales effort that succeeded for going to war but failed as sound policy, leaving many citizens disillusioned and confused. When the news reports spin and later the realities that contradict the PR promises, public confidence in both politicians and the news declines. This pattern of declining confidence in both news and politics has been evident since the late 1980s, which many scholars mark as the turning point toward partisan polarization and winner-take-all politics in contemporary America.[26]

Selling the Iraq War

With these considerations in mind, let's think about how political communication experts were able to get images into the news that created the impression of public support for a large-scale invasion of a country halfway around the world. As mentioned briefly in chapter 1, the Iraq War was sold to the American public based on the repeated and carefully crafted insinuations of a connection between 9/11 and Saddam Hussein, with the added consideration that Saddam was building weapons of mass destruction thrown in for good measure. Saddam was a very oppressive leader who triggered strong negative considerations among most Americans. He had even been likened to Hitler by communications managers drumming up support for the first Gulf War in 1991, a war waged to rescue the kingdom of Kuwait following Saddam's invasion of it. But hostility toward Saddam alone did not shift opinion in support of another war with Iraq following 9/11. Drumming up support for that war required adding other considerations to the communication equation, such as associations with Osama bin Laden and weapons of mass destruction, along with menacing references to mushroom clouds by high-level officials. This practice of highlighting particular issues or features in a complex situation to emphasize the considerations around which opinion forms is called *priming*.[27]

The campaign to sell the second Iraq War began in the fall of 2002. Like most persuasion campaigns, it was timed for a period (in this case, after the summer holidays) when sustained public attention could be secured in the news. As former White House chief of staff Andrew Card put it in an interview that the *New York Times* ran in September 2002, "From a marketing point of view, you don't introduce new products in August."[28]

How were news messages designed so that fearful images could be repeated over and over in the echo chamber of the media and appeal to existing considerations that might shift opinion in favor of going to war? It was clear that hostility toward Saddam Hussein alone was not great enough to push support beyond the existing levels that favored the continued monitoring and sanctioning of Iraq. The Bush administration introduced a link between Saddam and 9/11, even though there was no evidence that Saddam had been involved in planning the 9/11 attacks. To get around this nagging detail, White House communication strategists set out to suggest a "relationship" between Iraq and al-Qaeda. Every high official of the administration delivered the same message to journalists. Condoleezza Rice, national security advisor, claimed that al-Qaeda "clearly has had links to the Iraqis, not to mention Iraqi links to all kinds of other terrorists." Secretary of Defense Rumsfeld said, "There is no question but that there have been interactions between the Iraqi government, Iraqi officials and al-Qaeda operatives." Vice President Cheney noted that while there was no evidence that Saddam helped plan 9/11, "there is a pattern of relationship going back many years." And President Bush claimed, "We know that Iraq and al-Qaeda have had high level contacts that go back a decade."[29] Even though outside experts tried to point out that there was little or no hard evidence to support these claims, and that there was a good deal of evidence that Saddam's was one of the secular Arab regimes that Osama bin Laden opposed, the high volume of repeated administration messages primed the news for months leading up to the war. This raises the question of whether the press should report dubious claims from officials just because journalistic formulas give official pronouncements the lion's share of space in the news—a question we will consider in chapter 6.

What were the results of this news campaign? More than 50 percent of Americans soon formed the impression that Saddam had been personally involved in the 9/11 attacks, an opinion formation that peaked around the time of the war. Even if news polls and news drama made these opinions appear more solid than they really were, they became part of an accepted reality for many people, including politicians who pointed to public opinion as a basis for going to war. Such news realities become self-fulfilling, as a majority of Americans believed that they had received generally accurate information from the administration about the al-Qaeda connection and alleged weapons of mass destruction. These perceptions and opinions did not begin to correct themselves until more than a year after the war began when the chaos was too big to spin away, and it became clear that many things were not as they initially seemed.

This example indicates that even though it is not easy to influence opinion, it is possible to do so by dominating the news with simple messages that are personal, dramatic, and fragmented enough to appeal to large numbers of people, particularly when those messages arouse considerations about personal security. This means that the kinds of messages that succeed in shaping opinion are also those that best fit the information biases of news. Television coverage tends to exaggerate these biases, meaning that individuals who get most of their news from TV are less likely to think beyond very personalized considerations when forming opinions. By contrast, those who get most of their news from newspapers tend to reach more complex understandings of problems.[30] Because most people still get their news from television, the incentive is for public relations strategists to create the simplest, most personal, and dramatic made-for-TV events.

The success of its news campaign enabled the Bush administration to claim strong initial public support for the war. Yet the construction of public support in the news may be misleading; recall the earlier point about how news polls tend to complete the political spin process. David Moore's study of opinion strength also asked people who were pushed to have an opinion on going to war if they cared whether their preferences came to pass. Suddenly, the alleged popular support began to look rather thin. Only 29 percent of those favoring the war said they would be upset if it did not occur, while 30 percent of those who opposed the war said they would be upset if it did happen.[31] This simple question puts a different spin on the strength of public support and opposition for going to war in Iraq. Yet news reports seldom include such analysis on grounds that it is too technical and might confuse people.

The moral of this story is that the public relations campaign to sell the Iraq War was built on dubious facts and weak constructions of public support that appeared stronger in the news. This suggests the importance of evaluating the quality of public relations campaigns that shape so much of our news reality. Not all PR is the same. Indeed, some campaigns provide useful information, while others may ignore or hide important facts. Some campaigns build on fear or ignorance, while others encourage more reasoned discussions. Throughout the years, PR has been valuable in national discussions of health issues such as smoking, obesity, and diabetes. In other cases, PR has clouded debates about affordable health care policies. In evaluating the qualities of a PR campaign it is helpful to ask several questions:

- Does it distort/hide important aspects of a situation?
- Does it enable/invite informed public debate and discussion?
- Does it promote good policy choices?

Reaching Inattentive Publics

Part of the difficulty facing communicators who seek to mobilize publics is that the attention of audiences is increasingly hard to gain. This is because both media and society are changing, making audiences hard to reach. In society, people are living ever-more-personalized lives, thus sharing fewer group memberships and other experiences in common that help shape and solidify opinions.[32] The changing media landscape both reflects and reinforces this social fragmentation, with more and more personalized channels of information available to people.[33] These changes make it harder, and often more expensive, to reach individuals. For example, many younger demographics are more likely to be found in gaming environments than watching television, which makes it hard to get conventional messages to them. In 2008, the Obama election campaign purchased ads inside of 18 popular video games, and in 2012 gaming companies offered targeted ads. Xbox even opened an election hub that allowed gamers to interact with the presidential debates and follow the opinion trends of other gamers. In an interesting twist, CNN launched an expanded version of its Political Prophecy game for the 2016 elections. The game aimed to supplement polling by attracting large numbers of players and using a probability algorithm to adjust for various biases. Top players were invited to attend CNN-sponsored candidate debates. The aim was to change how people engage with media while improving the accuracy of crowd technologies in predicting political outcomes. One CNN executive gushed: "It's the gamification of politics—a way for the user to have a daily, addictive habit."[34]

Despite new ways of engaging citizens with media environments, it is difficult to shape public opinion and even harder to control it. Those engaged in political communication put enormous energy and money into these challenges. For example, the staggering costs of winning the support of relatively small numbers of so-called swing voters in elections suggest that the battle for opinion is difficult, expensive, and seldom a sure thing. Despite, or perhaps because of, the saturation of daily life with political spin, citizens live in a noisy media environment in which politics is generally far down the priority list, behind entertainment, fashion, sports, weather, and shopping. Just getting the attention of distracted and often disinterested citizens requires strong measures—usually involving highly dramatic and personal messages that are repeated time and again. The case study in this chapter explores this national attention deficit disorder.

CASE STUDY
NATIONAL ATTENTION DEFICIT DISORDER?

Attention spans are getting shorter. How short depends on the conditions under which we are trying to pay attention. We watch movies in dark quiet places to enhance the chances of following them. However, in much of life, we are multitasking and managing many inputs at once. According to one report, the average attention span—the time people can focus on a task without getting distracted—has shrunk to eight seconds, slightly below that of the average goldfish (nine seconds).[35] Even if such shocking statistics are overblown, most observers agree that people are increasingly distracted by the speed and volume of information in the digital age. If individuals are distracted, what happens when we add those individuals up into publics?

The public attention problem is complicated by the fact that sources of information are expanding rapidly, so that fewer people engage with the same events, and when they do, they may experience them in very different ways. At the height of the mass media era in the 1980s, most Americans sat down and watched the nightly news on one of the three television networks, forming what political scientist Markus Prior called a "captive audience."[36] As media outlets have multiplied and become available on many different platforms on demand, that captive audience has fragmented into thousands of smaller audiences paying attention to different content in vastly different ways.

It is not surprising that this scattered news audience is not terribly well informed about daily political affairs. For example, *New York Times* columnist Charles Blow noted that President Obama's wonky political style left people with little understanding his political agenda because that style did not make for good news coverage. An inattentive public needs sharp and repeated messages to rally them to pay attention even to important issues such as health care. The lack of a focused media campaign to brand the Affordable Care Act only played into the Republican strategy of just saying no. Far from being hurt by their unyielding opposition to health care and many other administration policies, members of the "party of No," as Obama dubbed the Republicans, suffered little relative to Democrats in public opinion for their efforts to obstruct Democratic initiatives. Polls showed approval for the job Congress is doing hovering around 13 percent in 2014, with Republicans receiving only slightly less support than Democrats. Blow cited public inattentiveness as a key reason why the Republican refusal to cooperate or compromise did not seem to hurt them more. He pointed to a Pew survey showing that "only 1 person in 4 knew that 60 votes are needed in the Senate to break a filibuster and only 1 in 3 knew that no Senate Republicans voted for the health care bill." Inattentiveness is even more severe among young citizens, as only 16 percent of 18- to 29-year-olds knew how the Republicans voted on health care. Blow's conclusion about such distressing lack of engagement with a historic issue was to modify H. L Mencken's famous characterization of the American public: "H. L. Mencken once famously opined, 'No one in this world has ever lost money by underestimating the intelligence of the great masses of the plain people. Nor has anyone ever lost public office thereby.' I take exception to that. But if you change 'intelligence' to 'attention span,' I agree wholeheartedly."[37]

Washington Post columnist George Will summarized relevant communication and political science scholarship to conclude that most voters are not interested enough in politics to become informed enough to make good political decisions. Equally problematic is that those who are interested tend to have a "confirmation bias" that leads them to seek information they already agree with. The result is that more-informed citizens fuel the political polarization that turns off the rest, leaving democracy in a bad way. He concurs with a statement often attributed to legendary British politician Winston Churchill: "The best argument against democracy is a five minute conversation with the average voter."[38] Will makes a case for easing the democratic burden on voters by giving them less to decide on. Even if there are good reasons to doubt the interest, attention, and knowledge of the average voter, the public is sovereign in our form of government, and many would surely take exception to being sidelined.

Recognizing the burdens placed on publics that seem ill equipped to handle them, many scholars focus on making news more interesting, engaging, and informative. Despite the appeal of these ideas, the trends do not seem to be heading in the right direction. If anything, the news has lost its once-comforting tone of "what you need to know" in favor of a marketing-driven logic of "what you want to know," aimed at grabbing enough attention from distracted audiences to sell them to advertisers. In his analysis of the economics of the news, James Hamilton suggests that the conventional "who, what, where, when, and why" of journalism is actually determined by another, more important, set of "five W's": "Who cares about information? What are they willing to pay, or others willing to pay to reach them? Where can media outlets and advertisers reach them? When is this profitable? Why is this profitable?"[39] What he concludes from this is that economic markets do not create conditions favorable to the open exchange of democratic ideas. Markets aim to deliver consumers to sponsors by nearly any means that work. What gets the attention of consumers may not be what matters to citizens. What media organizations do with audience attention once they have it may have little to do with informing and encouraging political involvement. It is hard to decide what comes first: the marketing of soft features and shocking stories that deprive audiences of more serious information, or an overriding general withdrawal from civic life that leaves news producers searching for anything to grab audience attention. Either way, the result is a national spiral of inattentiveness to many of the most monumental issues facing the nation.

As marketing shapes information to grab audience attention, what we mean by news is changing in the bargain. For example, a Google search for the NBC news magazine *Dateline* returned the result: "NBC Dateline: News stories about crime, celebrity, and health." Available for streaming from the site were stories about unsolved murders, panicked 9-1-1 calls from residents threatened by a brush fire, and tales of missing children. As the news tilts toward the bizarre and sensational, political news is likely to reflect the information biases discussed in chapter 2. As a result, politicians are reminded by their media advisors to avoid trying to inform or educate publics about issues. Media strategies thus favor emotional, repetitive, and shallow communication aimed at short-term opinion mobilization to get candidates elected and/or keep approval levels up to help elected officials govern.

Even when the attention of some portion of a targeted public is gained, the message still needs to make sense by creating connections to thoughts, feelings, and, then, possible actions such as voting. John Zaller has pointed out that people bring many often conflicting considerations into play when they process even the simplest information.[40] A great deal of polling and focus-group research (probing reactions to messages in small-group discussions) is done to monitor the words and symbols that activate considerations that in turn produce desired opinions.

The resulting battles for public opinion tend to be won by those who are able to create (a) the simplest messages (b) that strike the strongest emotional chord (c) in the right target audiences and (d) then continue echoing through a fragmented media system as long as a public reaction is needed. What works in shaping opinion, then, is aligning different media channels (news, advertising, talk radio, direct mail, email, and social media) to echo simple and attention-getting messages.[41] As noted, information biases such as personalization and dramatization turn out to be important both for political communication consultants in their battle for public attention and for news organizations deciding what makes the news. The news biases introduced in the last chapter arise from, and are reinforced by, this interplay between stories that are easy and economical for news organizations to tell and the political messages that public relations consultants build into those news events. In this interplay between journalism and newsmakers, journalists tend to prefer simple, bounded stories more than complex ones, and communication consultants tell newsmakers to keep their messages simple and free of complication. When these information packages reach large numbers of people who share similar considerations (feelings and beliefs), public opinion can be influenced, often without deeper understanding getting in the way. This of course presents a dilemma for well-informed citizens who are surrounded by less attentive majorities. All of which suggests that there are many different ways in which people process the news.

Processing the News

How can we become adequately informed when many political communication strategies are not aimed at broad inclusion and when that information is further filtered by commercial news formulas that add their own narrowing of the communication flow? One thing that seems certain is that the idea of easy mass persuasion through an all-reaching media is far-fetched, if for no other reason than this is not how communication strategists or media markets work. Nonetheless, some observers may continue to think that mass persuasion is a regular occurrence. For example, political scientists Russell Neuman, Marion Just, and Ann Crigler argue that some scholars continue to believe that mass media messages hold sway with a large passive citizenry: "The traditional view of the way citizens gain information from the media is dominated by imagery of a vegetative audience, passively absorbing media influence."[42] Because they cite me as holding this view, let me set the record straight: There is considerable evidence that individuals actively select, filter, and personalize the meanings that they draw from the news, and as noted above, many people actively avoid much of the news altogether. In short, the fact that communication professionals are trying to spin the news does not mean that people are easily fooled. However, they may be actively avoiding news altogether or seeking information sources they already agree with.

Even if people are not being spun on most news stories, they may not be actively engaged with them either. Nor does the current news system appear to be helping people feel better about society and government, trust others, or act effectively as citizens. Moreover, the failure of news to motivate those who are turned off to the political process means that the escape from public life (particularly among younger citizens) continues to grow. Communication scholars Thomas Patterson and Philip Seib argue that the most important function of the media may not be to directly inform citizens but to first attract their attention and interest. Once people have developed an interest in politics, they are more likely to seek out information that is often available in the media environment.[43]

Without political interest and curiosity, the information environment can seem overwhelming. One of the pioneers in understanding how people "tame the information tide" is political scientist Doris Graber. Her research on how people process the news reveals that many personal factors shape what people pay attention to and what they think it means: personal interests in the issue or problem; the influence of friends who provide news updates and interpretations; and eventually, the personal frames or models of society that people develop to recognize familiar aspects of news stories. One of her later studies explored how to reconnect young citizens with information that engages and motivates them to act politically. She concludes from research on how the brain processes information that more visual, interactive television and web-based formats contain the potential to reconnect young citizens.[44]

Most research shows that people develop personal interpretive strategies that help them actively *construct* meanings from the news they choose to engage with. In some cases, these constructions can be quite surprising and removed from the apparently intentional meanings in the news (or entertainment) content itself. For example, communication scholar John Fiske found that homeless people residing in a shelter often produced "oppositional readings" of popular television shows, cheering for the bad guys and rejecting the good guys—mirroring the way that "proper society" had rejected them in real life.[45]

Sociologist William Gamson shows that people can explore news issues in remarkable depth through everyday conversation, applying various interpretations that were not contained in the news stories they consumed. For example, some people overcome the sense of isolation from events by applying "collective action" frames that address issues of justice, common identities, and the possibilities for social action. Gamson acknowledges that breaking out of the sense of isolation often associated with news frames is easier for people with direct personal experience with an issue. People without direct experience are far more influenced by the framing in news stories.[46] Following along these lines, studies by Neuman, Just, and Crigler show that people are less likely to regard even heavily covered issues as important if they feel powerless to do much about them. People are more likely to wade through dense and complex stories if they contain information about "what you can do about the problem."[47]

It also turns out that the medium matters. Contrary to common stereotypes, people actually learn more from television coverage of most issues than from newspaper coverage (although, as noted above, they may learn claims attached to spin and cues, which may not always represent the best versions of complex realities). Most people find it hard to decode and organize the greater detail of newspaper coverage, unless they already have a personal interest in the issue and unless they have some personal frame of reference to help sort through the dense newspaper format. News magazines are much more accessible than newspapers and nearly as informative as television, perhaps because they offer more of an overview and a thematic perspective in a weekly format than in daily newspaper installments. This research may provide a simple explanation for why the vast majority of people prefer television as their primary news source: they actually learn more from it.[48] However, as noted earlier, when people do have the motivation to dig into print news, they often develop less personal, less episodic, and more complex thematic understandings of issues and events.

WHY PEOPLE PREFER TV: AUDIO AND VISUAL INFORMATION

As just noted, people generally learn more from television than from other news media. Not surprisingly, TV is still the favorite news source across most demographics, while newspapers and radio have dropped dramatically. Cutting across these conventional sources are online news trends that account for half of news consumption. Going online can encompass a broad spectrum of sources, from looking at a CNN or Fox site to getting news feeds from Facebook.[49]

Americans still love TV, along with their Internet-connected devices. A Harris Poll showed that of the things people said they "could not live without," sex ranked below television, mobile phones, computers, and the Internet—although food, cars, and significant others are more important still.[50] Most people watch TV with the explicit expectation of having a pleasurable or emotionally stimulating experience. Perhaps the most interesting commentary on the centrality of television is from an early study of people (680 households, 1,614 individuals) whose TV sets were either stolen (19%) or broken (81%). In 24 percent of these households, people experienced something like a mourning reaction, and 68 percent reported psychological troubles ranging from anxiety symptoms (39%) to moderate discomfort (29%).[51]

Doris Graber notes this and other studies as indicators that TV (and, one presumes, YouTube) stimulates the human brain more fully than other media do. Graber cites research on human brain functions and information processing to conclude that information is not compartmentalized but continually integrated across different kinds of sensory input. Television, unlike most other news media, gives us words, sounds, and sights to work with. This enriches one's sense of understanding and knowing more about televised situations.[52] The important question, of course, is, how do those who produce television news approach their responsibility to carefully select the pictures and sounds that go along with the words?

NEWS AND PERSONAL EXPERIENCE: WHAT GETS THROUGH

To reduce information processing to its simplest terms, we can say that after repeated exposure to a mediated issue or problem, some vague attention and recognition may begin to set in. If there is, in addition, some active personal interest in the issue, people may categorize, or frame, the issue to help keep it in focus, organize future information, and begin thinking more clearly about it. After people have begun to form categories, they can place finer details and bits of information in the categories and start to shade their thoughts and opinions. Following the development of attention, interest, and some basic categorization schemes, people may pick up and evaluate news information in the following ways:

- *Cueing*: looking for cues or labels (left, right; Republican, Democrat; hawk, dove; environmentalist, gun lover, terrorist, etc.)
- *Bolstering*: selecting factoids or bits of information that are offered to support positions attached to political cues and labels
- *Weighing*: using emotions attached to information cues in news reports to direct attention and learning
- *Anchoring*: packaging and narrating this mediated information in terms of personal life experiences

Using these intellectual laborsaving devices, people creatively incorporate the information in various media representations (news, political advertising, editorials, punditry, etc.) into their personal thinking. Each individual develops a strategy for both selecting and tuning out information about politics and, in the process, both draws from and contributes to public opinion. Consider how each of these information-processing strategies operates.

Cueing: Finding Familiar Signals Most of us simplify busy lives by screening political information through familiar and trusted reference groups. We take (or react against) cues from leaders, political parties, interest groups, and other familiar news sources that interpret (frame) news events and offer opinions that may guide thinking about a confusing world. In addition, stereotypes, slogans, and old-fashioned name-calling can provide the basis for simplifying our thinking about otherwise complicated realities. When members of the Tea Party movement denounced the health care reform process of 2009–2010 as fascism, socialism, and Obamacare, among other terms, they invited a larger news audience to identify with them as "Tea Party patriots," who were resisting the evils of government intrusion, while attaching negative sentiments about President Obama to the health legislation. These cues were echoed by Republican leaders in Congress, giving them greater credibility than they might otherwise have had. Then the pundits on conservative talk radio, cable TV, and online blogs and discussion forums magnified the audience impact of these simple cues. The result was a steady erosion of public support for the proposed health care reform.

Research by political scientist John Zaller demonstrates that the more closely people follow an issue in the news, the more their opinions follow the cues offered by leaders of the political parties, recognized ideological groups, and other prominent political viewpoints.[53] This means, in effect, that the more informed people are about issues in the news, the more their opinions conform to those expressed by elites, government officials, interest groups, newsworthy movement leaders, and parties.

Perhaps even more startling, these generalizations apply most strongly to more educated people, who tend to pay more attention to the news—the so-called informed public. Although this is an ironic way to think about being informed, it is not surprising when we recall that most of the information that goes into the news is provided by government officials and other prominent elites.

This does not mean that hearing one news report containing a familiar symbol or information source typically molds understanding of an issue.

On the contrary, as described in the case study above, most people live in a serious state of information overload. They tend not to pay much attention until an issue or event reaches saturation coverage and continues to make the news regularly for an extended period of time with prominent spokespersons taking increasingly clear and simple positions. Once this signal-to-noise ratio (discussed further in chapter 4) becomes very high, people begin to accept the kinds of broad cues discussed earlier to help organize their thinking. Thus, the ability of the Bush administration to dominate the news leading up to the Iraq War and repeatedly link Iraq to weapons of mass destruction and terrorism led majorities of Americans to conclude that Iraq represented an immediate threat.

Bolstering: Selecting Facts That Fit the Cues Even when people are knee-jerk liberals, conservatives, Republicans, Democrats, or Rush Limbaugh "ditto heads," they tend to search for some supporting reasons to accept the cues they get from their favorite political references. This is where *factoids* come in, those bits and pieces of information that fill in emerging understandings of a situation. This is also where news management becomes crucial, with forces on both sides trying to keep a story going and adding elements that reinforce their preferred interpretations while countering those of the other side. For example, in political campaigns where media scrutiny becomes more intense, there is a daily battle in which each side tries to build up its own message while tearing down the images of the other side.

In the political trenches, the lines between news and advertising, information and propaganda, have become increasingly hard to draw. Media consultants often try to insert news and documentary-type images into TV advertisements while setting up news events with advertising values in mind. The synergy between news and advertising can be important in getting public attention and influencing opinions. When themes from advertising hit the news, they gain an important element of "facticity" (seeming objectivity or legitimacy) that can break down resistance.

During an earlier health care reform battle in the Clinton administration, groups in the health care, insurance, and pharmaceutical industries spent millions of dollars on advertising to create doubts about possible negative effects of the president's call for universal health care. A barrage of commercials sent emotional messages about rising costs, government bureaucracy, diminished quality of care, and long waits for treatment to the politically important middle-class audience (most of whom already had health insurance).

Among the most memorable ad campaigns were the "Harry and Louise" spots produced by the health insurance industry, whose member companies stood to lose a great deal from any plan that regulated their profits or required them to extend coverage to people with expensive health problems, such as cancer or AIDS. The millions of dollars they spent on the slick Madison Avenue spots were minor compared with the billions that the big insurance companies had at stake in the reforms. Harry and Louise were depicted as a sympathetic middle-aged, middle-class couple of the sort that appears in TV series and other commercials. They worried about what they would lose under the proposed reforms, and each ad in the series introduced a new element of doubt about the leading plans, particularly the one championed by Hillary and Bill Clinton.

Meanwhile, behind the scenes, the health care industry was spending widely on lobbying and campaign contributions to key members of Congress to pry their support away from the president's plan. Not surprisingly, the authoritative opposition voices from Congress that were heard in the news echoed the same elements of doubt raised in the advertising.[54] A public opinion one-two punch of cueing and bolstering had been set in motion.

These campaigns took their toll on public support. After more than a year of concerted news and advertising information blitzes, a strong majority of 74 percent still favored the idea of universal coverage, a cornerstone of the Clinton plan.[55] However, only 33 percent backed the Clinton plan, reflecting the 76 percent who said they were unwilling to accept less choice in doctors or hospitals, and the 74 percent who believed that universal reform would lead to rationing.[56] As noted in chapter 2, after all the sides had weighed in, the public actually understood less about the Clinton plan than they did at the time it was unveiled.

The health care fight during the Obama administration produced similar results, with the added introduction of unsavory attacks on the president himself, including the claim that he was not born in the United States and thus was not constitutionally qualified to be the president. While this claim was not directly related to health care, it emerged from the same general Tea Party movement that filled the media during the early years of the health care policy debate and clouded the thinking of many people about Mr. Obama. This case illustrates how getting falsehoods into the media offers people convenient information to use in bolstering their beliefs and prejudices.

The moral of this story is that once the big information cues—such as president and Congress, Republicans and Democrats, big government and small government, popular politicians and recognized movements—have structured the information picture, the fine details added daily in the news and advertising can make a big difference. As Robert Teeter, one of the gurus of the information and opinion management business, put it: "People don't decide based on some great revelation. They form their views based on thousands of little bits of information that shake out from television ads and news stories."[57]

Weighing the Positive and Negative Emotions The first two patterns of information processing are seldom enough to account for public reactions to news. In most cases, people would not even attend to stories if there were not some emotional hook or charge in them. It is not surprising in this light that the communication strategies employed by warring political factions can turn downright nasty. This often happens in election campaigns and big national policy battles. The emotions in the long-running national fight over abortion policy come to mind here.

Not only do advocates for a cause challenge factual claims and attack the character of opponents, but they also frequently plant doubts that have little basis in fact. Indeed, when the battle rages for the emotions of the public, the question of what is true or relevant is often the least of considerations. The key concerns of strategic communication become, what gets people's attention? and what creates or resolves doubts in their thinking? Although media managers often have more freedom with advertising, they can obtain the greatest effects when the same messages cross over and become part of news stories.

This is not to suggest that emotions are bad or even less relevant than facts in thinking about politics. On the contrary, research by George Marcus, Russell Neuman, and Michael MacKuen shows that, in many cases, some degree of emotional arousal must occur in order for people to pay attention to other kinds of information in a situation. In some cases, the emotional (or affective) information that people receive may be far more important for their thinking and acting than facts (or cognitions).[58] These important understandings also help explain why TV is more important than other media for most people. Given the emotional satisfactions of social networking sites, and the growing uses by political players to deliver content directly through them, it is easy to see that the future of emotional information processing is online.

Many journalists worry that the loss of quality control through editorial standards may corrupt the communication process and leave it even more vulnerable to manipulation. However, other observers see the current news (and advertising) system as frequently corrupted by spin and political propaganda. The result is that the use of emotion in political communication is often not aimed at enhancing critical thought or judgment, and the reporting tendencies of the press do not always favor the citizen as much as they favor communication strategists bent on winning immediate political battles. For example, given the tendencies of the press to indulge in feeding frenzies (described in chapter 5), allegations and charges from one political camp can often turn into news nightmares for another. The failure to counter even the most scurrilous charge planted in the news can begin to gnaw at people and take root in their opinions, even if they try to ignore the dirt and concentrate on substantial information. All this explains one of the great puzzles of political communication: negativity often works even though a large majority of the public claim that they hate negative communication and that they try to screen it out of their thinking.

A word of caution is in order here: negative communication does not always work. A classic case is the difference between the George H. W. Bush election campaigns of 1988 and 1992. Both were extremely negative campaigns, with conservative estimates of the negative message content running at 50 percent or more of Bush's ads and news statements and increasing to as much as 75 to 80 percent in the closing days.[59] Yet Bush won one of those campaigns quite handily and lost the other one quite convincingly. To simplify the reasons greatly, negative campaigning is less successful if the opponent (or the victim, as it were) understands the importance of information bolstering and counters every bit of negative information with bits of information that deflect it, raise doubts about the other side, or refocus public attention on something else. Where Bush's 1988 opponent Michael Dukakis seemed to lack a strategic response to the negative attacks (thus allowing them to sink in), Bill Clinton in 1992 developed "a wink and a shrug" that suggested that perhaps President Bush's use of negative tactics meant that he was a bit desperate.

In short, when people encounter negative information that goes uncountered, they tend to incorporate the negativity into their thinking even if, consciously, they try to avoid it. In the view of opinion experts Barbara Farah and Ethel Klein, people make the best sense they can of the information they have available to them, even when that information is negative, of questionable reliability, or generally distasteful.[60]

Anchoring New Information in Personal Experiences A popular school of thought about citizen information processing suggests that people are lazy information processors or cognitive misers.[61] Citizens rely mainly on gut feelings, personal experience, and immediate life circumstances to screen information and reach judgments about politics. In this view, much information from the outer world is discounted simply because it does not dent this shell of personal experience. Thus, people take shortcuts in processing information and arrive at judgments about politics that have been described by political scientist Samuel Popkin as "low information rationality."[62] Such experience-based reasoning about politics explains why people cannot remember many facts about particular stories in the news, yet they draw cues, supporting factoids, and feelings from news coverage as the basis for judgments that often turn out to be fairly stable and meaningful.

Charting the terms of public engagement reminds us that beneath the rough indicators and simple judgments recorded in opinion polls are meanings that people construct in the process of arriving at their opinions on issues. For all that individuals may bring to bear in interpreting the news, there is considerable evidence that well-targeted news content can greatly affect the thinking of the average person. This is particularly true when messages have been shaped to appeal to selected or targeted audiences. The work of Shanto Iyengar and Donald Kinder (see chapter 2) showed that just being in the news makes issues seem more important, confirming the hypothesis that the news can tell people what to think about.[63] A follow-up series of experiments by Iyengar found that the personalized or "episodic" *framing* of stories directed audiences to think in short-term, emotional, and personalized ways about issues such as economics and social policy. What is missing in most news coverage, according to Iyengar, are more "thematic" approaches to framing social problems that might encourage people to learn and think about the social, political, and economic forces that affect them.[64] In the process of making judgments that feed into public opinion, people are often shocked, awed, and just plain entertained by the news. Indeed, without these elements of human interest, much of the higher political content would be lost on average citizens and of interest only to news junkies.

ENTERTAINMENT AND OTHER REASONS
PEOPLE FOLLOW THE NEWS

Thus far we have viewed news information in its most obvious democratic context: people following the news to gather information that may help them think about politics, form opinions, and take more effective political action. However, as noted earlier and illustrated in the case study, there are clearly other reasons people follow the news. A great deal of research has been conducted on the so-called uses and gratifications of news and entertainment programming, with a focus on highly personalized decoding of media content.[65] Traditional research on the broader, so-called uses and gratifications associated with the news can be summarized under three general categories:

- *Curiosity and surveillance*: scanning for information that may be useful in everyday life (e.g., word of airline fare wars, weather forecasts, inflation reports, home mortgage rates, etc.)
- *Entertainment and escape*: following the interesting dramas that often develop in politics (e.g., simply enjoying the spectacle of politics as the largest reality TV programming)
- *Social and psychological adjustment*: keeping contact with society and one's own place in it (e.g., how is my world? where do I stand in it?)

News organizations also understand that people have such broader uses for the news, and they adjust their content and coverage accordingly. As popular tastes and interests shift, the news generally follows, creating tensions with the democratic ideal of citizen-engagement-oriented news. Critics argue that pandering to public tastes only fuels the spiral of declining news values. Others counter that people will select and convert information to their own uses regardless of the standards that news or entertainment organizations attempt to maintain. For example, studies of popular American television programs in other countries show that viewers often find meanings that American audiences are far less likely to support, including confirmation of some rather nasty beliefs about greed, violence, corruption, and other images of life in the United States.[66]

News and Public Opinion: The Citizen's Dilemma

What does all this spin chasing inattentive citizens add up to? For one thing it employs a lot of PR agents, spin doctors, press officers, and other communication professionals. Even if there is no guarantee of winning the battle for public opinion, failing to have a comprehensive media strategy generally ensures losing it. In the digital age, increasing attention is paid to using social media to reach publics directly and enlist them in selling candidates and policies through their social networks. As is the case with most advertising hype, people tend to judge the product and see how it matches up to the promises made about it. Although most Americans are unsatisfied with politics and politicians these days, the communication process remains much the same: noisy and negative, with gaps between promises made and policies delivered. In addition, as technologies for targeting particular demographic segments of the public become more sophisticated, public communication becomes increasingly exclusionary. Large numbers of people are often not addressed at all because they are deemed too hard to reach, too difficult to persuade, or simply not necessary for winning an election or generating public pressure on Washington. As a result, increasing numbers of people are tuning out the news and other sources of political information because they find them negative, distressing, discouraging, or simply not speaking to them.

Unfortunately, this escape from the news is too often an escape from politics and civic life as well. Communication scholar Roderick Hart argues that the way we communicate may even make people feel "saintly" about abandoning politics.[67] Like the politicians, pundits, and critics they hear in the news, many citizens adopt the identity of outsiders battling a system run amok. For many, cynicism becomes an angry stance against a political communication process that offers little beyond targeted messages aimed at shaping opinion, shifting votes, or raising and lowering the chorus of public discontent. This does not mean that people necessarily buy all or even most of what the politicians are selling. It does mean, however, that when they enter the political arena, the language and choices they find are products of the communication processes outlined in this book.

Perhaps the most distressing exodus from the news and electoral politics has been among young people, as discussed in chapter 1. This is becoming a vicious circle, as those who run professional communication campaigns often feel that spending resources to reach young citizens is a waste—they are hard to reach, unlikely to get involved, and best left in their state of inattentiveness (although efforts by both parties to mobilize young voters in recent elections have met with some positive results). Moreover, younger citizens live in a social world that is less oriented to joining social groups—the clubs and organizations that their parents and grandparents joined and that created important connections to others in society and to public institutions. As a result of these and other shifts in social and political life, younger citizens participate less in core political activities such as voting, and they have less knowledge of the issues that might engage them in those activities. As Robert Putnam put it: "The post–baby boom generation—roughly speaking, men and women who were born after 1964 and thus came of age in the 1980s and 1990s—are substantially less knowledgeable about public affairs, despite the proliferation of sources of information. Even in the midst of national election campaigns in the 1980s and 1990s, for example, these young people were about a third less likely than their elders to know, for instance, which party controlled the House of Representatives."[68]

This is not just a matter of young people being distracted while they start their adult lives and later becoming more involved citizens. Each generation of young Americans entering society in the last several decades has been less informed, less inclined to follow politics in the news, and less likely to participate in political life than the last. This pattern of generational rejection of politics is unlike anything witnessed in modern times. Here is how Putnam describes it:

> Today's generation gap in political knowledge does not reflect some permanent tendency for the young to be less well informed than their elders but is instead a recent development. From the earliest opinion polls in the 1940s to the mid-1970s, younger people were at least as well informed as their elders were, but that is no longer the case. This news and information gap, affecting not just politics, but even things like airline crashes, terrorism, and financial news, first opened up with the boomers in the 1970s and widened considerably with the advent of the X generation. Daily newspaper readership among young people under 35 dropped from two-thirds in 1965 to one-third in 1990, at the same time that TV news viewership in this same age group fell from 52 percent to 41 percent. Today's under-thirties pay less attention to the news and know less about current events than their elders do today or than people their age did two or three decades ago.[69]

Although these trends cannot be traced entirely to communication practices, there are notable failures of both news and politics to engage and motivate people. Even those who continue to try to find meaning in news content are often frustrated with the negativity and sensationalism. As a result, the news and the political communication logic that feeds it frustrate the formation of interested and informed publics. Those who do follow politics most avidly are disproportionately older, white, conservative males.[70]

In considering whether to become involved in public life, people confront a dilemma: If they ignore or discount what they hear from the officials and opinion leaders who make the news, they become isolated from public opinion. Yet joining the mainstream means adjusting one's views to the available media agenda of issues and credible positions. Either way, opinion is seldom based on impressive levels of information. Most Americans score poorly on basic citizen knowledge tests such as the one developed by Michael Delli Carpini and Scott Keeter.[71] Critics of these tests, such as Doris Graber, argue that they more resemble trivia tests and do not measure the kind of practical understandings that might help people navigate through real political situations.[72] Yet the names of elected officials and the number of votes required in the House or Senate to overturn a presidential veto are not the only things that are vague in the minds of most people. Few people pay much attention to most of what they see in the news. A survey by the Pew Research Center tracked public attention to more than 670 news stories over a 10-year span and found that only 5 percent of the stories attracted close attention from those polled.[73] Perhaps some of these patterns will change as a result of the information abundance of digital media.

Publics in the Digital Age

The ways in which people engage with news suggest a complex picture of political communication. With the generational shift from legacy media to digital media and social networks well underway, more information is available to average citizens than ever before. And as legacy press organizations such as the *New York Times* move into social media environments such as Facebook, the chances increase that friends will alert each other to important news. While this may narrow the range of exposure to diverse inputs, it is not clear what would move people to seek out opposing viewpoints following the decline of the large "captive audiences" of the mass media age. A potential advantage of digital formats is that information often comes personally recommended. As William Gamson has shown, when people tap into personal experiences with political issues, they can begin to identify with others who share those experiences and think in terms of political actions that might make a difference.[74]

The scale of such public engagement can be very impressive when driven by social networks. For example, when the global financial crisis threw large numbers of people out of work and government bank bailouts seemed to help the rich more than the poor, millions of people took to their social networks to share their anger. The Occupy Wall Street protests that spread throughout the United States and the world in 2011–2012 began with a few committed activists occupying public spaces and soon spread through a large digital crowd that discussed and shared a remarkable range of information. Conventional news coverage was cycled back through those networks, and protesters made and circulated their own news using smartphones to record video that was streamed over many different platforms. The proliferation of websites, Facebook pages, YouTube channels, and other sites was made coherent by digital networking mechanisms such as Twitter that enabled people to channel information and resources across physical distances and different layers of participants. When the crowd rallied around popular ideas such as "We are the 99 percent," those sentiments traveled into the mainstream media and sparked a long overdue national conversation about rising levels of inequality that threatened both the American Dream and democratic representation. While the general public was mixed in its support for the occupation of public spaces, there was broad concern about the issues of inequality and the distortion of political representation in favor of corporations and the rich. As a result, a digitally equipped crowd became an organized public that stimulated a national conversation about important issues.[75] Digital media hold this promise to balance the top-down flow of political communication with bottom-up opinion. Although politicians continue to favor PR and conventional opinion management techniques, the capability of publics to communicate among themselves is a force to be reckoned with.

HOW POLITICIANS
MAKE THE NEWS

When information which properly belongs to the public is withheld by
those in power, the people soon become ignorant of their own affairs,
distrustful of those who manage them, and, eventually, incapable of
determining their own destinies.

—Richard Nixon[1]

There is literally no such thing as an idea that cannot be expressed well
and articulately to today's voters in 30 seconds.

—Dick Morris[2]

We have turned into a public relations society. Much of the news
Americans get each day was created to serve just that purpose—to be
the news of the day.

—Walter Pincus[3]

Walter Pincus wrote the above words as a call to arms for
journalists to resist the daily spin from politicians. Although he has won
numerous journalism awards, including a Pulitzer Prize during his distinguished career at the *Washington Post*, Pincus decries the way news organizations chase prizes. He laments that prizes do not reflect the overall quality
of daily journalism. Rather, they boost the brand while distracting attention
from the budget cuts and the decline in everyday news quality. The fire sale
at news organizations that opened the twenty-first century goes on, and
there are growing concerns about how to save journalism as a democratic
institution (stay tuned for chapter 8). The key to democratic journalism is
holding those in power accountable for how well they use government to
serve the public interest. The edge in this struggle over accountability currently goes to the politicians and powerful interests who can hire communications professionals to help them make news.

Public relations events and the framing language used to spin journalists emanate from government, the campaign trail, interest groups, and
business. PR content shapes most of the daily news menu. Indeed, with

fewer and less experienced journalists in newsrooms, and corporate media ownership more concerned about saving costs, PR is ever more important for the supply of the daily news. In the contest between PR and an independent watchdog press, the odds favor communication professionals, whose ranks are swelling as the number of journalists declines. Since 1980 the ratio of PR workers to journalists has soared from about 1:1.2 to about 5:1.[4] As Robert McChesney and John Nichols note: "Even as journalism shrinks, the 'news' will still exist. It will increasingly be provided by tens of thousands of well-paid and skilled PR specialists ready and determined to explain the world to the citizenry, in a manner that suits their corporate and government employers."[5]

The growing resource gap between journalism and public relations reflects a larger problem in the relationship between politicians and the press: the growing code of secrecy in government and the unwillingness of politicians to share much in the way of spontaneity or useful insights with journalists. There are many reasons for the growing distance between elected officials and reporters. The deluge of money in American politics has compromised the representative system to a point where many politicians cannot really talk candidly about the pressures that lead them to take particular positions or actions.[6] In addition, the partisan acrimony in Washington guarantees that moments of candor and spontaneity will be seized upon and distorted by opponents. Moreover, the growth of large audiences on social media gives politicians direct outlets for their messages, reducing dependence on conventional news media. These and other factors have changed the relationship between reporters and officials and created an atmosphere of mutual distrust and hostility.

The Obama White House kept reporters at arm's length from the beginning, provoking many angry reactions from the press. A top reporter for the *Washington Post* became so frustrated in trying to cover a nuclear security summit of world leaders that he characterized Mr. Obama as the "occupant of an office once informally known as 'leader of the free world'" and as "putting on a clinic for some of the world's greatest dictators in how to circumvent a free press."[7] The Obama press control operation even restricted access by press photographers and offered news organizations photos from official White House photographers—provoking journalists to question whether they should even use them, as they were more propaganda than journalism.[8] Santiago Lyon, the director of photography at the Associated Press, wrote an opinion piece in the *New York Times* with the title "Obama's Orwellian Image Control" in which he asked, "Why give reporters any access to the White House? It would be easier to just have a daily statement from the president. . . . Repressive governments do this all the time."[9] Susan Milligan writing in the *Columbia Journalism Review* described relations between the Washington press corps and the Obama White House as a growing "gulf" in which "the relationship between the president and the press is more distant than it has been in a half century." Her review of every official exchange between President Obama and the press during the year 2014 "reveals a White House determined to conceal its workings from the press, and, by extension, the public."[10]

Even as it limited the number of open encounters with the press, the Obama communication team found ever-more-novel ways to communicate directly with publics. In place of holding press conferences with journalists, the president answered citizen questions on YouTube and streamed the event live on the White House website.[11] Explaining the White House communication strategy, Communications Director Dan Pfeiffer said: "Not doing press conferences is equated with not taking questions, and that's not true." This comment reflected a belief among the Obama team that bloggers, entertainment shows, and social media were better at driving messages than the conventional press. Pfeiffer went on to say that, in contrast to the past when it may have been essential to communicate with the public "through the reporters sitting in the first three rows of the White House pressroom. . . . there's no question that the *Huffington Post, Talking Points Memo* and their conservative counterparts can drive a story as well as the traditional powers at the *New York Times* and *Washington Post.*"[12]

The Obama communications team relied more on social media to get its messages out than any earlier administration. Social media strategies played major roles in Obama's two election victories and continued to anchor much of the administration's messaging while he was in office. An article in the *Daily Beast* ominously titled "The Death of the White House Press Corps" pointed out the importance of digital media and direct messaging: "Thirty-one-year-old White House aide Macon Phillips, who directs President Obama's new-media operation, said the White House has 1.7 million followers on Twitter, around 500,000 fans on Facebook, and 70,000 email subscribers."[13] Those numbers all grew considerably over the years as the Obama administration continued to ramp up social media to reach publics directly. At the time of this writing, for example, the @WhiteHouse Twitter account had grown to 8.4 million followers who receive tweets that are microstories about new policy initiatives, official state visitors, or how the family dogs pass their time aboard Air Force One. An even larger

@BarackObama account had grown to around 68 million followers in 2016. Those followers received more personal and political messages on topics such as the president's Alaska adventure trip, as well as calls for financial contributions to Organizing for Action, the Obama political operation that runs the account. Followers of Obama social networks often received video messages from the president at the same time they were released to the press, alleviating the need to wait and watch the news. In some cases, journalists even received notices via social media. Faced with this kind of competition for audiences, the traditional press began questioning its role, as noted by veteran television correspondent Bill Plante: "Technology has made it much easier now for the White House. . . . The availability of all this material means that people have to do their own filtering. The so-called mainstream media, which believes it has the experience to do the filtering, isn't there to do it for them, and for a lot of people that's just fine. They resent the hell out of us anyway."[14]

In what has become almost a caricature of contemporary communication, journalists increasingly monitor politicians through social media such as Twitter. And the communication staffers of politicians also monitor the social media accounts of the press to see how their managed communication is doing. Some observers are even beginning to ask the question that headlines the next section.

Are Social Media Replacing the Role of the Press?

Politicians and their media teams can make news directly by issuing clouds of Tweets that reach a broad public directly and engage reporters who follow the social media accounts of key news sources and other journalists. CNN political reporter Peter Hamby asserts that Twitter has become the primary news source for Washington journalists.[15] He also laments that this source has undermined news quality. Repackaging digital morsels of information into news nuggets places the emphasis on speed over depth and analysis. In the race to get the news out, online sites fueled by social media win most of the time. Hamby reports an informal experiment in the 2012 election that pitted an embedded campaign reporter from BuzzFeed against a colleague from CNN to see which could get a story published faster. They wrote similar stories of the same length based on the same sources. The winner? BuzzFeed posted the story in under five minutes, while it took a bit over half an hour for the CNN story to appear online.[16] These differences matter to executives in news organizations who also follow the campaign on Twitter and push reporters to get the next story

out of the Twitter feed and into publishable form faster than the competition. The stakes in this game of speed over depth are simple: speed draws
the news junkie audience that clicks on stories and ads, capturing revenues
for the faster organization.

Given the limited opportunities for serious reporting, it is easy to see
why the campaign press pack has become younger and less experienced
than in the past. During the height of the mass media era from the 1960s
until the 1990s, presidential campaigns were covered by top reporters. Politicians and their staffs interacted more closely with the "boys on the bus"—
Timothy Crouse's classic phrase for the press pack that followed the candidates.[17] Election reporting combined character assessment, reactions from
voters, and other insights gained from personal encounters with candidates
and citizens. Today, top journalists seldom make road trips. According to
Hamby, the typical campaign reporter today is young, inexperienced, and
digitally savvy. Part of the reason for the waning of experienced journalists
in campaign coverage is the budget savings of sending young digerati instead of an entourage surrounding a "bigfoot" reporter. More importantly,
editors see little reason to send veteran reporters to cover politicians who
seldom mingle with journalists and prefer having their staff post nearly
everything on social media and other digital platforms.

Inside the campaign, there is often a tension between the openness and
spontaneity that make social media authentic and the controlling mentality
of the campaign "war room" where communication decisions are made by
top staff. The war room staff often regards the press as an enemy camp to
be engaged on strategic terms. This wariness is reinforced by fears that fast-
moving digital media can turn a wayward candidate remark into a clip that
goes viral on YouTube or a sound bite that caroms through the Twitterverse.
It is thought to be safer to keep politicians away from reporters and let the
journalists follow the social media streams that are carefully managed by
the professional communication staff. Daniel Kreiss interviewed campaign
communication staff and concluded that their capacity to react instantly to
events using Twitter gave them an edge in influencing story framing over
reporters who value speed more than context or depth.[18] In his discussion
of how Twitter has killed "the boys on the bus," Peter Hamby notes that,
as a result of being kept at a distance, the level of snarky commentary by
reporters has risen, adding to the distance between the camps and feeding the shift in journalistic tone toward negativity and cynicism.[19] A study
by Mark Coddington, Logan Molyneaux, and Regina Lawrence found that
even though Twitter offers journalists a real-time fact-checking capacity on

candidate claims, the dominant campaign uses by reporters were either as stenography (echoing sounds bites from candidates) or commenting on candidate statements.[20]

In sum, politicians now have so many ways to reach the audience that going through the national press is just one strategic option among many. As the media are kept at greater distance and fed more packaged material, reporters often end up following live events by monitoring official Twitter feeds. They also follow each other and use their own accounts to offer running color commentary on debates and other performances. Who are the real leaders? Who are the real candidates? Most journalists won't get close enough to find out. The news becomes a media stream of breathless updates—a mix of repackaged official media feeds and journalists reporting on themselves.

In this fast-moving world of social media updates, is there still is a place for old-fashioned public relations and newsmaking strategies? Indeed, it seems premature to discount the importance of the press in shaping the narratives of power in American politics. Recall here the case study in chapter 2 about President Obama losing control over his news narrative. The mainstream media continues to play a key role in shaping public perceptions simply because it still sends out the loudest signal. Thus, even as the media echo chamber becomes ever noisier with bloggers, webzines, talking pundits, and Facebook news releases, the importance of amplifying clear narrative frames through the mainstream media cannot be underestimated. Television broadcasts and wire service feeds still reach more people than other sources, and they prime the daily agendas of the bloggers and the talk show personalities. As a result, losing control of the mainstream press—whether through poor news management or the belief that the press can be ignored—can spell political trouble. Surely the history of Obamacare—the president's signature health care program—points to his failure to brand the program and tell its story effectively in the press. Like commercial products that are sold through long-running campaigns with catchy stories that connect to popular emotions, politicians and their policies also use branding and image techniques to sell themselves and their policies. Making the news is an important part in the political PR process.

The Politics of Old-Fashioned PR

For all the twitter about Twitter, there is still plenty of good old-fashioned PR aimed at shaping the news. Few communication professionals have been more effective at changing the way many Americans think about issues, politicians, and parties than Frank Luntz. The opening of his book, *Words That Work*, offers a simple formula that, according to Luntz, transcends partisanship and works well for "every product and politician imaginable": (a) figure out who your audience is, (b) learn what they already think about your product or problem, and (c) find a language that brings your issue into the acceptance zone of their thoughts and feelings.[21]

This simple strategic communication model has been applied to many issues, from taxes to health care. Even though majorities of Americans want solutions for things like health care, financial reform, and the environment, Luntz counsels his Republican clients to throw the specter of big government into their framing of these issues. The campaign against "big government" is one of the longest and most successful PR efforts in history. His strategy memo to Republicans said, "The American people are not just saying 'no.' They are saying 'hell no' to more government agencies, more bureaucrats, and more legislation crafted by special interests."[22] The irony of course is that government actions—from decisions to deregulate industries, to appointing former industry insiders to government regulatory posts—allowed private interests to run amok and create problems in the areas of health, finance, and the environment. However, reason is not the thing that drives PR. It is attaching existing emotions to things you want people to love or hate. Government bad. Markets good. Republicans win.

One of the most dramatic examples of an effective communication strategy involved managing public concern about the environment after most scientists reached the consensus that global warming has human causes and seriously harmful effects. Not surprisingly, the prospect of reducing fossil fuel dependence caused alarm among many established business interests: car makers, oil and coal companies, pipeline investors, and the emerging fracking industry, among others. Many politicians were beholden to the political money that flowed from such interests. The question was how to stall environmental legislation and clean energy policies at a time when they seemed most timely?

CASE STUDY
HOW GLOBAL WARMING BECAME A PARTISAN NEWS STORY

Frank Luntz had discovered as early as the mid-1990s that public concern about the environment was growing and that Republicans' alignment with carbon energy interests made them particularly vulnerable. In an early strategy memo to President George W. Bush, he warned, "A caricature has taken hold in the public imagination: Republicans seemingly in the pockets of corporate fat cats who run their hands together and chuckle manically as they plot to pollute America for fun and profit. And only Democrats and their good-hearted friends from Washington can save America from these sinister companies drooling at the prospect of strip mining every picturesque mountain range, drilling for oil on every white sand beach, and clear cutting every green forest."[23]

The solution was to create a new story to counteract being the bad guy in the prevailing public narrative. That story needed to appeal to popular American themes, such as love of nature and preservation of clean and open spaces for all. Luntz counseled his political clients: "First, assure your audience that you are committed to 'preserving and protecting' the environment, but that it can be done more wisely and effectively." In discussing the issue further, candidates should make sure to use the right reassuring terms: "The three words Americans are looking for in an environmental policy are 'safer,' 'cleaner,' and 'healthier.'" As he put it, a story that appeals to common experience and emotion opens the audience to listen to messages on specific issues: "A compelling story, even if factually inaccurate, can be more emotionally compelling than a dry recitation of the truth."[24] If voters sensed that Republicans shared their love of nature, then they would be more open to hearing them out on global warming.

The next step was to stop using the alarming phrase "global warming" and talk in more emotionally neutral language about "climate change." When asked about this framing of the issue, Luntz said: "The public reacts differently to 'climate change' than 'global warming.' Global warming is more frightening to the public. Global warming is something that has a long-term consequence to it, whereas climate change, to Americans, is a little bit more benign."[25]

The final step in transforming public discussion on the environment was the most brilliant of all: attack the science on climate change by claiming that it was not reasonable to undertake big and expensive government programs when the science wasn't settled on these questions.[26] Luntz warned that "the scientific debate is closing [against us] but not yet closed. There is still a window of opportunity to challenge the science."[27] Luntz understood that many people do not fully understand or trust science, particularly because scientists themselves typically portray their findings in terms of complex ideas, probabilities, and degrees of uncertainty. The science challenge even outsmarted scientists themselves who typically employ poor public communication skills when they are asked for reactions or clarification. Lacking communication consultants, scientists often issue fuzzy pronouncements laden with jargon, or, worse, dismiss their critics as ignorant or not worthy of comment. A popular movie about the ways in which scientists often play into the hands of political opponents was aptly named *A Flock of Dodos*.[28]

Armed with a PR strategy built on the seemingly benign idea of science being unsettled, leading conservative politicians had a story they could take to the press.

In the curious way that US journalism thinks about "balance," reporters put the Republican side of the story in the news simply because it came from powerful official sources. Mainstream journalism could not give greater weight to climate science because of the way the *indexing norm* (explained in chapter 1) is used by journalists to create balance in the news. Recall that indexing refers to how journalists select and balance viewpoints based on how much power they think different factions have to shape the outcome of the issue. Even when the Republicans lost the presidency in 2008, they still exercised a veto block in the Senate, and thus commanded press coverage on climate politics.

Just how much press coverage did the Luntz PR strategy win? An analysis of the prestige US press found that more than half the articles were "balanced" to give equal weight to challenges to scientific claims. Maxwell and Jules Boykoff examined a random sample of more than 600 articles that appeared between 1988 and 2002 in the *New York Times*, the *Washington Post*, the *Los Angeles Times*, and the *Wall Street Journal*. They found that 53 percent of the articles were "balanced" by including prominent challenges to scientific claims about human causes of global warming. Another 35 percent favored the human cause viewpoint but mentioned the skeptics. Another 6 percent gave exclusive coverage to the science skeptics. And less than 6 percent gave exclusive coverage to sources claiming human causes of global warming. The conclusion from their study is contained in the title of the article: "Balance as Bias."[29]

Over the years, the climate science skepticism story was fed by dozens of think tanks funded by energy giants like Exxon. On the other side were liberal politicians such as Al Gore who narrated a popular film (*An Inconvenient Truth*). The film won an Oscar and Gore received a Nobel Prize for his efforts to stir attention and action. And so the story that played out in the press was a classic battle between liberals and conservatives. Each side had a story and they were sticking to it. The liberals had science and reason. The conservatives had Frank Luntz. How well did the PR work in terms of shaping public opinion? Polls leading up to the 2008 election showed that popular belief in human sources of climate change was split along party lines: only 23 percent of Republicans believed the human cause thesis, while 75 percent of Democrats accepted the scientific evidence.[30] More importantly, given the lack of clear leadership on the issue, most Americans ranked the environment relatively low on their list of priorities.[31]

In light of these public responses to how the issue was framed, it is not surprising that Frank Luntz answered no when asked whether the environment would be a central issue in the 2008 election. His reasoning is revealing about the very communication strategies he developed. For the environment to become a top public priority, he said, "you have to create a sense of immediacy." By contrast, he pointed out why the issue of immigration has moved more to the center of national political debate: "When we see illegal immigrants coming across the border every single day, . . . every American who's watching this right now says, 'Oh my God, there really is a crisis; we've got to do something about it.' . . . That's the issue with global warming. It may be a crisis, but if it is, it's not right now."[32] Of course, what Luntz failed to add is that both issues have been spun to these effects by PR strategists like him.

While the environment was not a hot election issue, it dominated world concern in many nations during this time period. Much of the world watched as the United States failed to sign a carbon reduction agreement at the United Nations climate summit in Copenhagen in 2009, leading many experts to think that the last opportunity for decisive action had been lost. Yet Americans remained cut off from much of the world by a fog of PR. Between 2008 and 2010, the percentage of Americans who even believed in global warming dropped from 71 to 57 percent, and 41 percent said that they had become much more sure that it was not happening at all. Levels of public concern shrank even further around questions of whether global warming had human causes or whether the consequences were likely to be serious enough to do something about.[33] The factors shaping these opinions are far from "natural." They reflect decades of public relations campaigning.

After winning the climate battle, Luntz walked away by removing his fingerprints from the issue, saying that climate science seemed more settled than when he started the campaign. He also suggested that it might be time to do something, adding that "people are much more interested in seeing solutions than watching yet another partisan political argument."[34] But the lasting damage has been done: climate change continues to sit near the bottom of national political priority lists. It was dead last on a list of 15 issues, garnering "a great deal of concern" from just 28 percent of Americans polled by Gallup in 2015.[35]

Press Politics: Feeding the Beast

Beyond the choice of symbols, the staging of news events, and the development of a news management strategy, the daily working relations between reporters and newsmakers play a part in how officials get their messages out. As the case of Obama press relations suggests, officials can develop uneasy working relationships with the journalists who cover them. The Clinton administration also felt that the press was hostile to it and took the extreme measure of locking the door between the pressroom and the White House communications staff. Perhaps it was no accident that members of the Clinton press staff referred to the press corps down the hall and past the locked door as "the beast." Indeed, locking that door only made the beast angry, as did the Obama communication staff decision to bar news photographers from a signing ceremony. When press relations are bumpy, communication strategists often go around the press, using social media or appearances on entertainment television to get their messages out.

Whether press relations are chummy or chilly, the news continues to be filled with strategically constructed versions of events. With the use of sophisticated polling, message development, and marketing technologies, newsmakers aim to translate the political world into personal terms that trigger the existing emotions of audiences. The mark of skill in the political trade is to make the public version of a situation convincing, no matter how much the actual circumstances may be bent or simplified in the process. As former secretary of state Dean Acheson once said, the task of public officers seeking support for their policies is to make their points "clearer than truth."[36]

Much has changed about the news in recent years, but one important pattern holds: most political news still originates from government officials themselves. Pioneering research by Leon Sigal in the early 1970s showed how much of the news in the *New York Times* and the *Washington Post* reflected three simple patterns:[37]

- Government officials (either domestic or foreign) were the sources of nearly three-quarters of all hard news, and only one-sixth of the news could be traced to sources outside the government.
- Less than 1 percent of all news stories were based on the reporter's own analysis, whereas more than *90 percent* were based on the calculated messages of the actors involved in the situation.
- The vast majority of news stories (from 70 to 90 percent, depending on how they are categorized) were drawn from situations over which newsmakers had either complete or substantial control.

Research by various scholars since Sigal's classic study suggests that much the same patterns persist to this day.[38] The major exception to these patterns is that reporters today insert more commentary in stories than in earlier eras, in part because of the growing portrayal of politics as a game (recall the information biases from chapter 2).[39] The increase of scandals and journalistic feeding frenzies also indicates that journalists have found ways to assert their control over news content, even if these stories often annoy audiences more than they inform them. However, this form of journalistic activism is no substitute for investigative reporting which has declined steadily since the 1980s. The irony is that on stories of greater consequence such as going to war or global warming, journalists are reluctant to insert their own voices or outside sources to challenge official versions of events—even if there is evidence to support the challenge—unless other influential politicians step forward first. A notable exception to this rule was Hurricane Katrina, which devastated New Orleans in 2005, leaving the city in crisis with government response lagging far behind. As officials were slow to respond, the nation witnessed journalists asking where the government response was and informing clueless officials about the problems on the ground. With Katrina, news organizations had entered the eye of a no-spin zone, a rare moment when government officials and press minders were off the job and literally on vacation, leaving journalists to look directly at events without the usual layer of official spin to shape their reporting.

Even with the advent of portable technologies enabling more live event coverage from the scene of disasters and conflicts, journalists continue to seek out officials to provide authoritative viewpoints.[40] The level of official domination tends to be even higher on foreign policy issues, where opposition groups and views from other nations are often pushed to the margins. On domestic matters, such as abortion, health care policy, or taxes, the views of organized interests enter the news with greater frequency. However, the press tends to index the range of diverse viewpoints in a story to the presence of powerful government actors in Washington who also share those views.[41]

By any accounting, the conclusion is inescapable: even the best journalism in the land is extremely dependent on the political messages of a small spectrum of official news sources. This was the moral of the above case study on how global warming became politicized. Elite news organizations such as the *New York Times* or the *Wall Street Journal* may include more detailed background information and vary the perspectives on their editorial pages, but the basic messages in their stories still represent official views. Point-of-view outlets such as Fox or MSNBC will spin the official events in partisan directions, but the focus is still on the surface of staged politics driven by competing partisan strategies.

News as Strategic Political Communication

Walter Lippmann observed more than 90 years ago in his classic work on public opinion, "The only feeling that anyone can have about an event he does not experience is the feeling aroused by his mental image of that event."[42] There is little check on the kinds of images created for political situations when the information received by the masses of people on the outside is controlled by a few people on the inside. As Secretary of State Dean Acheson (who importantly shaped the Cold War and the rebuilding of Europe after World War II) noted, the effective public official does not attempt to educate or convey "objective" images; the official's goal is to represent issues and events in ways that gain support, shape action, and influence outcomes.[43]

If the images contained in official political positions were mere entertainment fare floating about in the electronic ether, there might be less cause for concern. As long as the images in the news are treated as real, however, people may be inclined to respond to them. Even, and perhaps especially, those images with the most dubious links to reality can generate actions in the real world, actions that have real effects: the election of leaders, the acceptance of oppressive laws or ideas, the labeling of social groups, support for ill-considered wars such as the Iraq War, or tolerance of chronic social and economic problems. Thus, news images of the political world can be tragically self-fulfilling. Dominant political images can create a world in their own image—even when such a world did not exist to begin with.

The fact that political actors create PR images to suit their political ends does not mean that the news is filled with diverse and highly imaginative political stories. Most political images are, as Murray Edelman noted so perceptively, based on familiar symbols, formulaic plots, standard slogans, and simple rhetoric.[44] The world of political images is built from predictable symbolic formulas: new beginnings, familiar reassurances, promises to shrink big government, pledges to clean up the mess in Washington, and claims about being a political outsider. Even threats and crises come wrapped in stereotypes of enemy aggression, American firmness, peace through strength, productive and serious discussions, and so on. Political language, in Edelman's view, thrives on banal, predictable, formulaic images that undermine critical thinking in public communication.[45] Both the familiar pronouncements and partisan squabbles of authorities become substitutes for detailed analyses and creative leadership.

It is ironic that newsworthiness often lies not in insightfulness or even importance but in past success as a news formula. In this world of media reality, newsworthiness becomes a substitute for validity. Credibility is reduced to a formula of *who* applies *what* images to *which* events under *what* circumstances. Ordinary logic tells us that the more standardized an image is, the less valid is its application to unique, real-world situations. On the other hand, what David Altheide and Robert Snow have termed "media logic" tells us that reality *is* the image constructed for it as long as that image remains dominant across different mainstream communication channels.[46] A corollary of this logic is that when other officials who hold power in a situation challenge the leading official position, the news will dramatize the conflict (generally in personalized terms), leaving the audience to decide (usually based on prior partisan beliefs) what the issues and their merits really are.

These and other aspects of media logic flow from the basic news information biases outlined in chapter 2. Those biases help explain the evolution of the information and press management strategies used by newsmakers to get their views across in the news.[47] Failure to control the news is often equated with political failure. As the campaign manager for a presidential candidate put it, "The media is the campaign."[48] Or, as a key presidential advisor explained, there is no political reality apart from news reality. That assessment came from one of Ronald Reagan's top aides (and later secretary of state in the Bush administration), James Baker, who was asked by an NBC correspondent why the president seemed so unwilling to compromise on a tough budget proposal he submitted to Congress. Baker said that compromise was undesirable because, in the media, "everything is cast in terms of winning or losing."[49] Thus, the president could not back down, no matter how unrealistic his position. To be seen as unrealistic was preferable to being perceived as a loser because being perceived as a loser would make him a loser. There is a fine line between symbols and reality. We need symbols to represent and act on the real world. But when symbols take the place of reality—become the thing itself—we may lose touch with our capacity to process feedback, act effectively, or communicate well together.

The Symbolic Uses of Politics

Symbols are the basic units of most human communication. Words are symbols that stand for objects and ideas. Flags, emblems, and uniforms are symbols of nationalism, group identity, or authority. Specific people can even symbolize general human attributes, such as heroism, patriotism, beauty, or greed. Because of the existence of symbols, it is possible to communicate about something without having the object of communication immediately present. Thus, the word "tree" is a symbol that permits communication about trees whether or not a tree is present. The term "nuclear war" permits communication about something that does not exist anywhere except in the human imagination. Because a major preoccupation of politicians and interest groups is how to represent actual situations in the most favorable strategic terms, it is obvious why symbols are so important. Through the skillful use of symbols, actual political circumstances can be redefined and people can be moved to action.

To understand how symbols are used and what makes them effective or ineffective, it is useful to know something about their psychological effects.

Every symbol affects us in at least two ways, one *cognitive* and the other *affective*. The cognitive effect refers to the thought and logic engaged by a symbolic message. Affect involves the emotions and feelings triggered by the message. The cognitive associations with a message can be narrow or broad. For example, the term "freedom" has multiple associations for nearly everyone. In contrast, the term "congressional delegation" has a narrow, specific meaning. On the affective side, a symbol may elicit little emotional response or may evoke great outpourings of feeling. For example, the term "freedom" can be used in highly emotional ways, whereas "congressional delegation" provokes relatively little emotion from most people under most circumstances. (However, the term "Congress" can provoke considerable emotional reaction these days.) Symbols that convey narrow meaning with little emotion are called *referential symbols*. Symbols that evoke broad categories of meaning accompanied by strong emotions are called *condensational symbols*.[50] We have even invented symbols to help us talk about symbols!

The kind of image created for a political situation depends on how key actors want the public to react to the situation. A faction interested in broadening the scope and intensity of public involvement may picture a situation in condensational symbols, whereas a faction seeking to narrow the scope and intensity of public concern can be expected to use referential symbols. For example, groups who opposed US involvement in Vietnam represented the bombing of North Vietnam in condensational terms, emphasizing savage destruction, government lying, and dangerous expansion of the war. The government, on the other hand, sought to minimize public concern with the details of the war. Public relations officers in the White House and the Pentagon invented an entire vocabulary of referential symbols to blunt the meanings and feelings attached to military actions. Thus, bombing raids on North Vietnam were referred to as "protective reaction strikes," a term so narrow and bloodless that only its creators understood precisely what it implied. In today's high-technology warfare, it is common to hear that enemy positions in Iraq or Afghanistan were "removed" with "surgical precision" by "smart bombs." Such terms make the news soothing to home audiences, but they may be of little consolation to nearby civilians killed as a target was being surgically removed. "Collateral damage" and "friendly fire" are political code terms to minimize public outrage at the mistaken targeting of innocent people.

Today the term "immigration" is often a highly charged symbol. In some contexts, immigration continues to refer to dry legal categories of people applying for particular categories of government visas. However, in other contexts such as election campaigns, references to particular immigrants can stir great controversy, as Donald Trump found out when he spouted a list of derogatory remarks about illegal immigrants from Mexico causing problems in the United States. While his comments evoked support from a hard core of supporters, they also led to cancelations of various Trump products by sponsors and television channels. Same word, different uses in different contexts.

Few symbols have stirred more conflict than the Confederate flag that continues to be displayed in the American South. A flash point over the meaning and status of that flag came in 2015 in Charleston, South Carolina, after a gunman killed nine people at the Emanuel African Methodist Episcopal Church. Dylann Roof, who joined a church prayer meeting and then began shooting, had posted online photos of himself posing with weapons and the Confederate flag. The shooting and accompanying imagery of the flag sparked a heated national debate over the meaning and propriety of displaying the Confederate symbol. Was the flag a symbol of racism and hatred, or Southern heritage and the valor of Confederate soldiers? As a condensational symbol that became even more invested with emotions following the shooting, the flag held all of these and other meanings for different groups. After heated debates in the South Carolina legislature (and echoing speeches in Washington and elsewhere), the representatives decided to remove the flag from its place above the state capital. South Carolina governor Nikki Haley signed the bill ordering removal of the flag and proclaimed, "It is a new day in South Carolina . . . a day that truly brings us together as we continue to heal, as one people and one state."[51] Such is the power of symbols.

Symbolic Politics and Strategic Communication

The goals of image making are fairly straightforward: design a theme or message to spark the imagination, make sure that message dominates communication about the matter at hand, surround the message with a context of credibility, and tell or act out a story that offers the best framing for the message. Simple though they may appear, these goals are not easy to attain. In the view of communication scholar Jarol Manheim, the technologies of image making today are so advanced that the term "strategic communication" better expresses this sophistication than does the more traditional term "public relations."[52] Frank Luntz would seem to agree. What do the political communication experts do? To put it simply, they use symbols in ways calculated to best satisfy the goals of image making.

Effective image making requires a sophisticated understanding and use of communication technologies, such as polling, message development in focus groups, market research to see how the message plays, and news management to get the message into the news with the right framing. There is, of course, a good deal of time, energy, resources, and personnel devoted to image making in politics. Growing ranks of White House staff are dedicated to media relations and communication. As Martha Kumar notes, it is increasingly common for officials to regard policy and political problems as communication problems.[53] The major preoccupation of the average member of the House of Representatives is running for the next election.[54] The Defense Department spends billions of dollars annually from its huge budget on PR, and has done so historically.[55] The US Army even runs a special school to train its corps of PR officers.[56] In view of these efforts, one observer has concluded that "the vast, interlocking federal information machine has one primary purpose: the selling of the government."[57]

THE GOALS OF STRATEGIC COMMUNICATION

It is clear that controlling political images in the news is a primary goal of politics, and as such, it is important to understand what this entails. Most PR experts agree that successful image making involves the following:

- Being clear about your client's political goals—damaging an opponent, improving the client's leadership image, or representing a policy in terms that will gain popular attention and support.
- Understanding the client's vulnerabilities so that opponents cannot turn the strategic communication back on its sponsors. For example, taking a moralistic stand against an opponent's sexual indiscretions may be ill advised if there are similar behaviors in the client's own past.
- Identifying the audience(s) most important for accomplishing those goals. Perhaps the main audience is a small demographic group that voted against the client in the last election, or the audience may be the key members of Congress who need to be convinced that there is public support for voting against health care reform.
- Using polling and market research to develop a message and a delivery strategy that reaches those audiences in ways that promote the goals of the campaign.
- Creating news events (often echoing advertising and other direct communication techniques) that dominate public discussion and lend authority to the message.

The textbook on how to manage the news was written during the Reagan administration. It is open for others to follow. Few politicians may attempt or even want to manage the press as completely as the Reagan communication staff did, but relations between press and politicians will never be the same again. What does the textbook say about media management for politicians? The first step is to adopt the proper frame of mind. As former White House communications director David Gergen put it: "To govern successfully, the government has to set the agenda; it cannot let the press set the agenda for it."[58] How did Mr. Gergen achieve this goal? Here is the methodology, according to an analysis by Mark Hertsgaard:[59]

- Schedule weekly long-term strategy meetings of policy officers and press handlers to plan the future news agenda and assess the results of ongoing media control efforts.
- Hold daily meetings of the White House communication group to decide, as one member put it, "What do we want the press to cover today, and how?"[60] According to Michael Deaver, one of the masterminds of the press operation in the Reagan years: "We would take a theme, which we usually worked on for six weeks—say, the economy. The President would say the same thing, but we had a different visual for every one of [the regularly scheduled media events]."[61]
- Remember, as the previous step indicates, *repetition* is the key. Feed the press the same message with a new (and therefore newsworthy) visual setting to satisfy the media need for changing video footage and new photo opportunities. As Deaver recalled, "It used to drive the President crazy because the repetition was so important. He'd get on that airplane and look at that speech and say, 'Mike, I'm not going to give this same speech on education again, am I?' I said, 'Yeah, trust me, it's going to work.' And it did."[62]
- Put out the line of the day to all the other potential newsmakers in the executive branch to "make sure we're all saying the same thing" to the press.[63] During the Reagan years, the line of the day was sent out over a computer network to all administration offices. All that any official had to do was call it up on his or her screen before meeting with reporters.
- Coordinate the day's news via conference calls to top administration officials to make sure they understand the line of the day and to orchestrate which officials will say something, when they will say

it, and who will keep their mouths shut, as in "Look, the President's got a statement tomorrow, so shut up today, goddammit, just shut up, don't preempt the President, [we'll] cut your nuts off if you leak anything out on this one."[64]

- Work the press and call reporters and their bosses to see if they understood the story correctly. This has become known as "spin control." During the Reagan years, the White House made it a regular practice to call the national TV network executives just prior to their nightly newscasts to check on what they were running and to offer additional clarification on the stories.
- Conduct weekly seminars for the spokespeople of the various federal bureaucracies to educate them on how to present the administration to the press.
- Produce a heavy volume of opinion polling and market research to see what is on the public's mind and how the president can tap into it through the news. The White House even conducted its own market research on the public images of news people to whom they might give interviews and treat more or less deferentially.

There you have it. Follow the eight easy guidelines, set the media stage, introduce a president who as a former actor was comfortable with the TV lights and cameras, and you have the Great Communicator—someone whose message is on point, salient, credible, and effectively framed. The Reagan press management plan was so effective that chief image maker Richard Wirthlin was crowned Advertising Man of the Year in 1989. He did not receive his industry's top award for his creative work for General Foods or Mattel Toys, but for his accomplishments as director of consumer research for Ronald Reagan.[65] In assessing Wirthlin's award-winning performance, one observer concluded that the mapmaker of the public mind "probed just about every aspect of public affairs on a scale unmatched in U.S. history."[66]

Another measure of the success of the Reagan press program is that even when the press attempted to be critical, the efforts seldom produced results that stuck to the so-called Teflon coating that seemed to protect the president from the press. The classic case of news management operating with even a critical press involves CBS News correspondent Lesley Stahl, who put together a long report showing the gaps between Ronald Reagan's carefully styled news images and his actual policies in office. Stahl was nervous about the piece because of its critical tone and the practice of the White House Office of Communications to call reporters and their employers about negative coverage. The phone rang after the report was aired, and it was "a senior White House official." Stahl prepared herself for the worst. In her words, here is what happened:

> And the voice said, "Great piece."
> I said, "What?"
> And he said, "Great piece!"
> I said, "Did you listen to what I said?"
> He said, "Lesley when you're showing four-and-a-half minutes of great pictures of Ronald Reagan, no one listens to what you say. Don't you know that the pictures are overriding your message because they conflict with your message? The public sees those pictures and they block your message. They didn't even hear what you said. So, in our minds, it was a four-and-a-half-minute free ad for the Ronald Reagan campaign for reelection."
> I sat there numb. I began to feel dumb 'cause I'd covered him four years and I hadn't figured it out. Somebody had to explain it to me. Well none of us had figured it out. I called the executive producer of the *Evening News* . . . and he went dead on the phone. And he said, "Oh, my God."⁶⁷

There it was. The textbook news management system worked even with uncooperative reporters. Television is the medium through which most people get their news. When politicians and their handlers are careful to stage their public appearances for the right production values (i.e., to convey the right visual images), reporters are denied the video evidence they need to back up a hard-hitting script. As one of the Reagan news wizards put it bluntly, "What are you going to believe, the facts or your eyes?"⁶⁸

MANAGING THE MESSAGE

The core of this strategic communication process involves developing and communicating a message that promotes the political goals of a campaign by appealing to a targeted audience and holding the symbolic high ground if it comes under attack. The message construction side of the strategic communication process can be broken down into four important parts:

- Composing a simple theme or message for the audience to use in thinking about the matter at hand. Call this *message shaping*.
- Saturating communications channels (that reach your target audience) with this message so that it will become more conspicuous than competing messages. Call this *message salience*.
- Constructing credibility for the message by finding authoritative settings and recognized sources to deliver it, followed by

endorsements from prominent supporters. Call this *message credibility*.

- Delivering the message with the right scripting (i.e., sound bites) and spin to lead journalists to pick story themes that emphasize the message. Call this *message framing*.

Although these four components of political image making work together in actual political communication, it is useful to consider them separately in order to see what each one contributes to the definition of a political situation.

Message Shaping

The content of a political message is usually simple; it is both emotionally and intellectually accessible. One of Frank Luntz's rules for successful communication is "Simplicity: use small words." Another is "Brevity: use short sentences."[69] Political messages generally begin with a key phrase, idea, or theme that creates a convenient way for people to think about a political object, be it an issue, an event, or even a person. For example, Franklin D. Roosevelt appealed to the hopes of the masses by using the simple term "New Deal" to refer to his complex patchwork of untried economic programs. Borrowing these characteristics of simplicity and idealism, John F. Kennedy added the power of familiarity when he presented his programs to the people under the title of "New Frontier." Ronald Reagan used "New Federalism" to label his efforts to dismantle Roosevelt's New Deal, Kennedy's New Frontier, and Johnson's Great Society. When Bill Clinton stole the Republican thunder in his support for welfare reform, he spoke of "New Beginnings." George W. Bush invoked the concept of an "Axis of Evil" to put the American public and the world on notice that the War on Terrorism would continue after Afghanistan. This example illustrates that simplicity alone does not good communication make, as the (lack of) connections between Iran, Iraq, and North Korea—the three evil axis members—were challenged by critics. Barack Obama took office during a severe financial crisis promising "change we can believe in" and rallying the public with chants of "Yes we can!"

Effective political themes and slogans invite people to bring their own meanings to a situation. Thus, an image is an impression anchored partly in symbolic suggestion and partly in the feelings and assumptions that people have in response to that suggestion. Research by communication scholars Doris Graber, Russell Neuman, Marion Just, Ann Crigler, Michael Delli Carpini, and Bruce Williams, among others, shows that people actively construct personal meanings from the evocative symbols and images of media coverage.[70] When people begin to supply the facts and feelings necessary to complete an image, the symbolic message component of political communication seems increasingly real and convincing. This explains why some of the most simplistic and insubstantial ideas produce some of the most heartfelt understandings. For example, when Richard Nixon's campaign strategists assessed his presidential prospects in 1968, they concluded that the biggest problem was the widespread perception that he was a loser. In response, the campaign introduced the symbolic suggestion that there was a "new Nixon," borrowing a classic advertising ploy to revive sagging products. The "new Nixon" became a much-discussed term that created for many people a concrete reference for new political actions that otherwise might have seemed ambiguous or deceitful.[71] This is the reasoning behind another of the communication commandments offered by Frank Luntz: "Novelty: offer something new." He also suggests creating personal involvement by asking a question such as "Got Milk?"

Message Salience

Many catchy messages elude popular imagination because they fail to capture widespread attention. The need for a message to capture attention explains why the second goal of image making is to saturate communication channels with the message and to stay on message in those communications. The goal of message salience explains why advertisers spend billions of dollars to chant their simple jingles and slogans over and over again in the media. This explains why month after month of the Clinton-Lewinsky scandal involved opponents feeding talk show pundits and journalists a steady message of SEX, SEX, SEX, while justifying this dubious political information by amplifying the Republican congressional message of CLINTON LIED, CLINTON LIED, CLINTON LIED.

Because the environment is full of competing messages, communication consultants are careful to remind (and script) their political clients that whenever the message du jour does go out, it must be "on point," which means not complicating the idea, not drifting to other topics, and punching the current political theme until the strategic campaign of the moment has run its course. In the Luntz school of strategic communication, "consistency matters." Be consistent. Stay on message.

In addition to consistency, message salience can also be enhanced with two other Luntz rules: "sound and texture matter" (make your slogans memorable—even set them to music) and "visualize" (invite the audience to take away an image). That is why speeches have lines, such as "Imagine, if you will for a moment, a debt free economy strong enough that every American can share in the American Dream" or "Imagine a nation of clean coastlines and safe drinking water."[72]

In view of these patterns, it is easy to understand why politicians are so concerned with their images. In a sense, they are right in thinking that image is everything. Images feed on each other. To the extent that politicians can create appealing leadership images, salience is more likely to be conferred on their specific political pronouncements. To the extent that issues can be made to seem important by calling them "crises," opposing voices are more likely to be drowned out. To the extent that public favor can be won, future messages will receive less criticism, thereby escalating the spiral of popularity, thereby increasing future message salience, and so on.

Message Credibility

A public bombarded with strategic political messages cannot always be relied on to accept them—even if they hear them often. Salient political messages are more likely to be supported when they are accompanied by some measure of their validity. Most political communication employs an element of logic, evidence, or authoritative endorsement. Following his advice to keep it simple and keep it short, Frank Luntz offers "credibility" as another rule. The core of credibility is to find a clear, simple message and to embody it. If this message is "No new taxes," be prepared to suffer a huge credibility loss if you give in to pressures for raising new revenues (or call them fees, not taxes!).

In addition, politicians often use staged dramatic settings such as the Oval Office or the deck of an aircraft carrier to lend weight to their announcements. Shocking events may be used to push messages, as when killing sprees are followed by renewed appeals for tougher gun control laws. However, it is striking how messages that are repeated over and over again by high officials may be believed by large numbers of people even when opponents and experts challenge them as dubious. For example, the Bush administration's claimed link between al-Qaeda and Iraq continued to be accepted long after critics pointed out the evidence to the contrary. As we will see in chapter 6, the news system gives credence to many dubious claims because they continue to be reported as one side of a story simply because they are issued by officials.

Message Framing

Simply creating, repeating, and supporting a message is not enough to ensure a successful communication strategy. The news is not just an information bulletin board; more important, it is a storytelling process. Stories become pegged to central ideas or categories of meaning that organize, screen, and emphasize information. These meaning organizers, called frames, can distill large amounts of information into very simple capsule summaries—such as sex scandal, government waste, natural disaster, election horse race, terrorism, or weapons of mass destruction, just to name a few.

Framing often involves engaging many mental activities, emotional, visual, and cognitive. Great political moments have echoed through the fog of daily life with frames, such as "I have a dream," that are powerful because they engage emotions that make people aspire to great things while helping them recognize neglected and perhaps tragic problems. In addition to being good visualizations, such statements also embody another Luntz rule: "Speak aspirationally." Aspirational language often has more impact if it is delivered with the help of this Luntz rule: "Provide context and explain relevance." Dreams can evoke our greatest aspirations. Martin Luther King Jr. had a particular and timely dream that white and black children would grow up living in the same society with the same opportunities. It was a dream whose time had come, and he helped many Americans frame their thinking about race in America differently as a result. Thus, great frames help people visualize, aspire, and put messages into the contexts of their personal lives.

Why the Press Is So Easily Spun

Beyond easy explanations such as the growing numbers gap between PR professionals and journalists, it is interesting to ask why the press is so often spun. Reporters intimately understand the above communication techniques, so they are well aware of being spun. Moreover, most journalists are fiercely competitive and independent. So why does the spin work so well? There are several reasons. First, spin is often all that is being served up, and deadlines and workloads permit no time for deeper digging. Second, reporters and editors from different news organizations watch each other to see what the breaking story is and what the angles are. Journalists who deviate from the conventional wisdom of the press pack are often challenged by their editors to explain why they "missed" the story. Finally, the spin mirrors news values, such as personalization, drama, and neatly self-contained story morsels, which makes it easy to drop into small news holes in papers and broadcast formats.

As a result of being in this spin cycle, the press displays an alternating pattern of cooperation and antagonism. On the face of it, daily reporting suggests that news organizations are easily seduced by PR strategies. At the same time, the press pack can suddenly turn petulant and critical, feeding on personal scandals, political failures, and partisan attacks.

This alternation between being spun and being antagonistic creates an inward-looking world of Washington insiders in which politicians and the press appear to be the ultimate insiders. This Beltway ballet is off-putting to the general public and reflects the dilemma of news organizations having only a dim sense of their obligations to the public.[73] In crafting stories, members of the press are more likely to pay attention to each other and to the politicians and political insiders they associate with every day. The public plays a symbolic cameo role; they are written into stories as polling numbers or parts of outbursts such as protests and riots. The news audience may also come to the attention of journalists when the marketing department pressures editors for more stories that increase the click-through rate. For the most part, however, the press and politicians are locked into a symbiotic relationship in which each side needs the other to some degree, and players who get too far out of line tend to be disciplined (reporters are denied access, politicians receive increased doses of criticism).

Within this symbiotic relationship, there are a number of factors that affect which side may have the upper hand, measured by the degree to which politicians control the press or journalists are able to challenge official versions of events. How well the above communication strategies are executed is of course a key variable. Some politicians and their handlers are simply better at managing the news than others. In addition, the ability of politicians to control events can vary greatly depending on historical circumstances such as crises, scandals, and leaks. The public fortunes of some politicians run relatively smoothly through series of neatly planned events that offer great control over what journalists see and how they can report it. At other times, the forces of history produce unpredictable situations, throwing politicians into scramble mode and giving reporters more opportunities to set the agenda. The next section examines different degrees of control that politicians may have over the settings in which they encounter the press.

Controlling the Situation:
From Pseudo-events to Damage Control

Many newsmakers have the resources required to produce professional media events: writers, media directors, costume consultants, access to dramatic settings, and an attentive press corps ready to cover official announcements and events. Careful preparation of events enables control over key elements of the news story: the scene (where); the status of the actor (who); the motives, or ends, the political action is to serve (why); the means through which the action will accomplish its ends (how); and the significance of the political action itself (what). However, some situations are hard to control, and some political actors perform badly in unscripted settings. Thus, political manipulation of the news runs along a continuum from fully controlled news events at one end to uncontrolled events (the political handler's worst nightmare) at the other extreme.

PSEUDO-EVENTS: FULLY CONTROLLED NEWS SITUATIONS

Fully controlled media presentations are often called *pseudo-events*.[74] Pseudo-events disguise actual political circumstances with realistic representations designed to create politically useful images. A pseudo-event uses careful stage setting, scripting, and acting to create convincing images that often have little to do with the underlying reality of the situation. By incorporating fragments of an actual situation into a dramatized presentation, a pseudo-event tempts the viewer to fill in the blanks and build a complete understanding out of fragmentary facts. According to Daniel Boorstin's definition, a pseudo-event has four characteristics:[75]

- It is not spontaneous, as someone has planned, planted, or incited it.
- It is planted primarily for the immediate purpose of being reported.
- Its relation to the underlying reality of the situation is ambiguous.
- It is intended to be self-fulfilling.

George W. Bush's aircraft carrier jet landing in full "top gun" flight suit followed by a speech that declared "mission accomplished" in Iraq in 2003 was a classic pseudo-event: (1) it was anything but spontaneous (it required practice, costuming, and even holding the carrier off the coast); (2) the event was staged purely for newsmaking purposes; (3) the relationships between the ongoing war and the declaration of victory and between the swaggering president and his dubious military record were made ambiguous by the self-contained performance; and (4) the images of a confident leader and a victory in war were self-fulfilling in the sense that evidence to the contrary was excluded from the performance. It took several more years for the majority of the American public to realize how badly the situation in Iraq was going. As long as news coverage focused on the staged event, the audience received only the images and messages in the dramatic production. And in the case of the carefully staged "mission accomplished" performance, the press played it to the hilt, even commending the White House communications team for producing such a stunning news event.[76] The only trouble was that in reality the war in Iraq had just begun.

PARTIALLY CONTROLLED NEWS SITUATIONS

Some political situations are not as easy to control as a presidential landing on an aircraft carrier. Many public settings have an element of spontaneity in them. For example, press conferences can be controlled insofar as choice of time, place, and opening remarks, but they always contain some risk of unexpected or hostile questions from the press. In other cases, an official may be surprised by an issue and asked to comment, even though he or she is unprepared to do so. As Robert Entman has shown, the escalation of scandals instigated by political opponents has introduced more of these situations into politics in the past several decades.[77]

A common means of handling partially controlled situations is to anticipate and prevent possible moments of spontaneity in advance. For example, press conferences are often structured tightly to promote desired messages and prevent spontaneous distractions. In a press conference, opening remarks are intended to set the tone and make the headlines, reporters can be called on or ignored, time limits can be imposed, and stage settings can be manipulated. However, even press conferences can become testy and can offer reporters opportunities to challenge official claims and push politicians off message. As a result, presidents have tended to give fewer of them over time, with Ronald Reagan, George W. Bush, and Barack Obama setting modern-era lows, as their communications staff preferred media events that communicated messages over the heads of the press and limited situations that enabled the press corps to ask hostile questions.[78] As Dan Bartlett, George W. Bush's White House communications director, once put it: "At press conferences, you can't control your message."[79] There are of course different ways to count what constitutes a press conference. Clinton, Bush, and Obama all favored showcasing visiting leaders and dignitaries with joint press conferences that were tightly scripted and left relatively little room for reporters to ask questions.

Many presidents prefer one-on-one interviews with select journalists or with television entertainment personalities such as Jon Stewart or Jimmy Kimmel. They often grant those interviews only if favorable ground rules are accepted. In contrast to his press conference behavior, Barack Obama set a record during his first year in office with 158 interviews, including 90 television appearances.[80] In 2010, he even went on ABC's daytime discussion show *The View* in an effort to soften his image and connect directly with women. Toward the end of his presidency, Mr. Obama remarked to a journalist that his had been the most transparent administration ever. Shortly afterward, he flew to Hollywood to appear on *Jimmy Kimmel Live*, marking his tenth appearance on late-night comedy shows.[81] As media reporter Howard Kurtz put it, while the White House press corps grumbled about not having face time with the president, he was busy pursuing another media agenda: "In recent weeks, the president has talked to ABC's Diane Sawyer, George Stephanopoulos and Charlie Gibson, Steve Kroft of '60 Minutes' and at Sunday's Super Bowl with CBS's Katie Couric. Each has pressed him on various issues; Obama admitted to Sawyer that he had made a 'legitimate mistake' by promising that all health-care negotiations would be televised on C-SPAN. But with strict time limits and a natural effort by the anchors to touch on several subjects, Obama has a built-in advantage."[82]

All of this is a long way from how politicians used the media in the early days of radio and television. Today, press conferences and presidential addresses do not receive the attention they once did from the networks, as they interrupt scheduled profitable programming. In the early days of radio and television, a political broadcast gave prestige to a network and saved it the production costs of live programs. According to an analysis by Joe Foote, "During 1934, the year Congress was writing the Federal Communications Act, the two networks managed to find free time for 350 speeches by Congressmen and Senators, an average of nearly one program a day. . . . These political broadcasts substituted in many ways for news programs that were just then coming into their own and demonstrated the networks' commitment to public service."[83]

In some cases, officials actively avoid being connected to a risky idea or a development and resort to anonymous news leaks to release information. These controlled leaks are useful when there is uncertainty about how the public will react. An anonymous leak gives the official a chance to change course if the opposition is too strong. Sometimes a leak even increases the chance a dull story will be picked up or given bigger play. This tactic was acknowledged humorously when Ronald Reagan opened a press conference by saying that he did not have an opening remark because his planned statement was so important that he had decided to leak it instead. Controlled leaks also give politicians an advantage over a key political variable: timing. The timing of a leak or a press release is crucial. For example, it is common wisdom that bad news is best released on weekends when reporters are off duty and the public is distracted from worldly concerns. Consider the case of a Reagan administration budget leak. The year was 1983. The proposed budget was a political disaster. There were huge deficits where Reagan had promised a balanced budget. There were painful cuts in already weakened social programs. To top it all off, the country was in serious economic trouble. The news management goal was to soften the blow of more bad news. The Reagan media staff evidently decided that the budget was such a potential news disaster that the budget director leaked it on a Friday by "forgetting" his copy in a congressional hearing room following a high-level congressional briefing. In a few hours, the budget had found its way into the hands of news people without the usual embargo. The story that would have dominated the headlines had it been announced on a Monday was, instead, scattered across the less-visible weekend news channels. By Monday, the budget was old news. When asked about the apparent leak, White House communications director David Gergen denied it and explained that the usual "press embargo" stamp had been omitted "accidentally" from the budget books taken to the briefing.[84]

As noted below, many leaks are not of the controlled variety and can be extremely unsettling and hard to control. One prominent example occurred during the Obama administration when Edward Snowden leaked thousands of documents revealing widespread government spying on the private communications of American citizens, people in other countries, and many world leaders. That kind of leak brings us to the volatile case of uncontrolled news situations.

UNCONTROLLED NEWS SITUATIONS

Few things strike fear in the heart of a politician more than a news story that has gotten out of control. Sometimes control of a story is lost because the underlying reality of a situation is simply too big to hide, as was the case with Lyndon Johnson's increasingly empty assurances that the United States was winning the war in Vietnam. This scenario was replayed 40 years later as the spin from the Bush administration about how things were going in Iraq was eventually swamped by the deteriorating military and political situation that continues to spiral out of control to this day. There is no magic formula for turning out-of-control situations into neatly controlled PR successes. Indeed, many such situations spell the end of political careers. However, the struggle between spin and reality is often epic and has led to greatly expanded communication resources. Research by John Anthony Maltese shows that the White House press operation grew phenomenally both in size and sophistication during the half century after Harry Truman took office.[85] However, there are many situations that go beyond what ordinary damage control can contain, particularly when whistleblowers expose official misdeeds and cover-ups.

In many cases, former insiders blow the cover on a previously contained situation by leaking secret information, as when Daniel Ellsberg, a defense analyst working at the Rand Corporation, leaked secret government documents showing the government lied to the public about key aspects of the Vietnam conflict. In such situations, the responses of politicians and government typically go beyond spin to include legal action and other kinds of intimidation against the leakers and the reporters who may publish the stories. In the case of Ellsberg, the attorney general issued an order that the newspapers to which Ellsberg released the documents cease publication. The legal case was taken to the Supreme Court by the *New York Times*, which won a landmark ruling in *New York Times Co. v. United States* upholding its right to publish. As for Ellsberg, he was a victim of personal intimidation as staffers for then president Richard Nixon formed a covert burglary team that broke into Ellsberg's psychiatrist's office to steal medical records that they hoped to use to embarrass the leaker. Although the files they stole were not personally damaging, the so-called White House Plumbers unit went on to commit other crimes, including a break-in at the Democratic National Committee headquarters in the Watergate building in Washington. That escapade turned into the Watergate scandal that brought down the Nixon presidency.

In more recent times, massive leaks of documents by National Security Agency contract employee Edward Snowden revealed unprecedented levels of domestic spying by the government with collusion from phone and Internet companies. Snowden leaked a cache of documents numbering between one and two million to journalists Glen Greenwald and Laura Poitras beginning in 2013. He met with them after he fled the United States and went into hiding in Hong Kong, where Poitras shot much of the footage for her 2015 Academy Award–winning documentary *Citizen Four* (Snowden's code term for himself in his communications with Poitras). An agreement was reached to publish the key documents in a broad network of world papers and magazines, including the *Guardian* in the UK (for which Greenwald was working at the time), *Le Monde* (France), *O Globo* (Brazil), *Der Spiegel* (Germany), and the *Washington Post* and *New York Times* (US), among others. New documents and stories from this trove of secret information were still appearing at the time of this writing. The press stories caused a global uproar as ordinary citizens discovered their personal communications were being monitored by the US intelligence agency. World leaders, including allies such as German chancellor Angela Merkel and Brazilian president Dilma Roussef, expressed outrage that their private phone calls and email were being intercepted. Snowden had known about the secret program for years, but said he hoped Barack Obama would end the program after becoming president. Instead, Snowden watched in dismay as James Clapper, Obama's director of national intelligence lied to Congress, denying that such practices existed. Soon thereafter, Snowden chose to make a huge personal sacrifice by going on the run and working out arrangements to have his leaks published worldwide.

At the time of this writing, Snowden was living in Russia where he was granted temporary asylum. Snowden's applications for asylum were turned down in more than 20 other countries under pressure from the United States, which sought his return to face criminal charges of treason under the Espionage Act. If convicted of those charges, Snowden could face the death penalty. Needless to say, the stakes become high when such sensitive material is leaked. Snowden is a hero to some and a traitor to others, but the information he leaked created massive domestic and foreign policy problems for the US government.[86]

Playing Hardball:
The Intimidation of Whistleblowers and Reporters

Before becoming president, Barack Obama signaled his discomfort with the national security state that developed after 9/11. However, as president, he aggressively pursued leaks that disclosed the extent of the surveillance and espionage apparatus. By most measures, Obama administration efforts to intimidate leakers and journalists were unparalleled by any other administration since the dark days of the Nixon White House. The Nixon approach to leaks and critical journalists included legal intimidation through the Justice Department and also went to the dark side, making enemies lists, conducting wiretaps, using the IRS to investigate journalists, and even creating the Plumbers unit to commit crimes.

Although the Obama administration has chosen legal methods to try to control leakers and the journalists who publicize their information, its aggressive approach has alarmed many advocates of open government. In 2013 alone the government brought 1,400 cases against whistleblowers.[87] Most of these cases involved reports of corruption and other abuses in government agencies such as the Veterans Administration. However, the most celebrated cases involved leaks of high-security information pertaining to government intelligence, surveillance, military, and foreign policy operations. The aggression against the press has produced cries of intimidation and breach of First Amendment rights. Dozens of journalists and news organizations have reported high levels of fear and intimidation and have abandoned use of personal phones and email accounts in contacting sources. The Obama Justice Department has seized phone records from the Associated Press, the *New York Times*, and Fox News, among others.[88] Investigations have resulted in indictments against six government employees and two contractors. Although most of them, including Edward Snowden, could be labeled whistleblowers rather than spies, they have been charged under the Espionage Act, which pertains to the high crime of treason. The Obama administration has used the Espionage Act more than all previous administrations combined.[89] In most of these cases, various kinds of intimidation have also been used against news organizations, from WikiLeaks to the *New York Times*, for publishing material from the leakers.

Among the most publicized cases is that of Chelsea Manning, an army intelligence analyst who leaked a trove of 700,000 classified State Department cables and other materials on the Iraq War to WikiLeaks. Included in this leak was previously undisclosed information about civilian deaths caused by US soldiers in Iraq. The most highly publicized piece of information was a video taken from an Apache helicopter showing the killing of two Reuters journalists and a number of children and other bystanders. Although Manning admitted to the leak, she denied that her actions fell under the Espionage Act. Yet she was convicted and sentenced to 35 years in prison. As for WikiLeaks, it was branded a terrorist organization by the vice president and some members of Congress, and was placed under criminal investigation by the Justice Department and FBI. The site was also hacked by unknown agents who shut it down for a time, and the payment site PayPal was pressured to stop accepting financial contributions that enabled the site to function. WikiLeaks founder Julian Assange later came under pressure from Sweden to face a sexual assault charge that he said would result in his extradition to the United States on espionage charges. At the time of this writing, Assange was living in the Ecuadorian embassy in London, where he had been granted asylum by the government of Ecuador in 2012. He has been unable to leave the confines of the embassy for fear of being extradited.

A case that spanned the Bush and Obama administrations is that of Jeffrey Sterling, who worked for the CIA. Sterling was charged and later convicted of providing classified information to James Risen, a *New York Times* reporter. The alleged information leak involved a secret spy operation in which a Russian scientist working as a US agent delivered intentionally flawed plans to Iran for building nuclear centrifuges. Risen's account (allegedly based on Sterling's leak) is that the operation was mismanaged, the scientist's cover was blown, and Iran discovered the flaw in the design, making for an all-around harebrained spy caper. The *New York Times* was about to publish the story, but Risen and his editor were called to meet with the CIA director who argued that the operation did not fail and that publishing the story would jeopardize it. The *Times* was next called on the carpet at the White House where Bush national security advisor Condoleezza Rice urged it not to publish the story in the interests of national security. The *Times* relented, as it has on numerous other similar occasions, and withdrew the story.[90] Risen, however, trusted his source and published it in his book, *State of War*, documenting a long list of dubious exploits of the CIA during the Bush years.[91] The Obama administration pursued the case against Sterling and Risen, issuing a subpoena to Risen to reveal his source. Risen fought the legal pressure for years, taking the case to the Supreme Court, where he lost. But he still refused to reveal his source. Without Risen's testimony, the government case was circumstantial, based only on sketchy phone and email records showing that there had been contact between the two, but not indicating its nature. The government nonetheless convicted Sterling based on the argument that he was disgruntled about his career and was the only person who could have leaked the information. The judge who sentenced Sterling gave him a relatively light sentence of 42 months in prison, perhaps because of the circumstantial nature of the case, or perhaps because of the suspended sentence given around the same time to former CIA director David Petraeus, who shared classified intelligence information on the war in Afghanistan with his biographer and paramour.

The Obama war on leaks strikes many observers as odd, given Obama's repeated claims to preside over the most open and transparent administration ever. However, the long-standing friction between his administration and the press may have resulted in an escalating antagonism. More generally, there is little doubt that the scope of the US security and intelligence operations has grown at alarming rates since 9/11, leaving the government vulnerable to charges of conducting undemocratic operations at home and abroad. The prosecution of leakers and the intimidation of journalists becomes an inevitable result when leaders decide to continue upholding the veil of secrecy. This has become an area in which the struggle over democratic values and press freedoms is acutely on display.

Government and the Politics of Newsmaking

As explained in the first chapter, the news remains, for all its failings, crucial to governing. At the same time, the relationships among the key players in the American information system—the people, politicians, and the press—have entered a vicious political cycle:

- As the space for serious news shrinks because of the economic crisis facing journalism, political actors must rely even more on communication professionals to capture that precious space for their messages.
- This means that our public communication is increasingly shaped by the use of the technologies of market research and persuasion to stage, script, and spin news for its most dramatic media effect.
- As a result, with the exception of leaks, the news is made increasingly by and for political insiders, leaving citizens out of the democratic picture.
- All of which feeds the spiral of public disillusionment with both politics and the news.

To make matters worse, the advent of the 24-hour news cycle means that the news never sleeps. There must be developments even when there are none to report. As journalists become more active in keeping stories going, they need reactions and dramatic material from political actors. Failure to "feed the beast" with new installments can result in being on the losing end of a story fed by opponents. Those who market ideas for a living learn quickly that dramatized events, spin, rumor, and reaction are helpful to journalists trying to operate within the low-budget, high-hype constraints of the 24-hour news cycle. Reporters are well aware that most of what they cover is heavily managed, but they generally try to maintain the impression that they are on the outside of events looking in.

This news system does not make many of its players look good. Polls typically show press and politicians competing for last place in public approval. Meanwhile, politicians quietly bemoan the low levels of public understanding of most issues and the selfish attitudes of citizens that hamper solutions for many public problems. This syndrome was summed up by former West Virginia senator Jay Rockefeller, who told a group of reporters: "Voters . . . are angry with politicians like me. And they're angry with you in the media. Well, let me tell you something. The voters are no bargains, either."[92]

In this age of mediated politics, power is, to an important extent, a communication process that must be monitored and maintained by political actors. As a result of the technologies of strategic communications (polling, market research, news, and image management), the news is not just a record of events; it is an event in and of itself—an integral part of the political process linking politicians and people in the competition for government power.

A long-term effect of officially managed news may be to limit the range of problems, solutions, values, and ideas presented to the American people. The political world becomes a predictable terrain of stereotypes, political postures, and superficial images. As Murray Edelman observed, familiar solutions are recycled in melodramatic efforts to solve chronic problems.[93] People come to accept the existence of problems like poverty, crime, delinquency, war, or climate change as facts of life rather than as the tragic results of the concentration of political power, the exploitative nature of economic relations, and the cynical uses of political communication.

The participation of the news media in promoting the official cover stories about these problems—until those stories are attacked or challenged by opponents—further undermines the chances for the kind of public understanding required for effective political action and real political change. As suggested in chapter 3, audiences can be quite independent in interpreting the news, but people cannot interpret what they don't see. What they don't see or hear in the news is often linked to effective press management.

5

HOW JOURNALISTS
REPORT THE NEWS

Dear Glenn: We come at journalism from different traditions. . . .
Journalists in [the impartial] tradition have plenty of opinions, but by
setting them aside to follow the facts—as a judge in court is supposed
to set aside prejudice to follow the law and evidence—they can often
produce results that are more substantial and more credible.

—Bill Keller[1]

Dear Bill: There is no question that journalists at establishment media
venues . . . have produced some superb reporting. . . . But this model
has also produced lots of atrocious journalism. . . . A journalist who is
petrified of appearing to express any opinions will often steer clear of
declarative sentences about what is true, opting instead for a cowardly
and unhelpful "here's-what-both-sides-say-and-I-won't-resolve-the-
conflicts" formulation. That rewards dishonesty on the part of political
and corporate officials who know they can rely on "objective" reporters
to amplify their falsehoods without challenge.

—Glenn Greenwald[2]

Bill Keller is one of the most distinguished journalists in
America, having spent most of his career at the *New York Times* as a Pulitzer
Prize–winning reporter, the Moscow bureau chief, and executive editor. His
side of this exchange with Glenn Greenwald staked out the ideal case for
neutral, impartial or objective journalism. Those standards continue to
motivate journalists in leading news organizations despite the erosion of
the economic model and audience base that once supported them. Greenwald is a leading representative of a resurgent public interest journalism
that operates largely online, with leaner organizations, a narrower topic
focus, and funding from private individuals and foundations. The Keller-
Greenwald discussion of the nature of good journalism appeared in the
New York Times under the title "Is Glenn Greenwald the Future of News?" At
the time of this exchange, Greenwald, along with filmmaker Laura Poitras,
had just broken the bombshell revelations about the US government's elec-

tronic spying on its own citizens and on people and leaders around the world. This National Security Agency surveillance program was revealed in a massive leak of top-secret information from Edward Snowden, who worked as a government contractor for the NSA. At the time, Greenwald worked for the UK newspaper the *Guardian*, and he later went on to join *The Intercept*, an online investigative operation funded by eBay billionaire Pierre Omidyar. This exchange between the old guard and the new reveals a deep divide in contemporary journalism. On one side are legacy news organizations that largely report official accounts of events by "indexing" their coverage to the balance of views among powerful sources. On the other side are growing ranks of more critical journalists who attempt to sift evidence and draw conclusions independently of official claims. Swirling around these two poles are many hybrid sites that blend blogging, citizen reporting, content aggregation, social media distribution, and new syndication models. We explore some of these information hybrids such as *Vice* and *Vox* in chapter 7 but keep the focus in this chapter on the tensions between legacy journalism and the rise of new online investigative organizations.

One of the interesting features of the new online investigative journalism is that it has a political agenda, much like the muckraking journalists of a century ago who sought to expose political and corporate corruption, abuses of workers and consumers, and problems with democracy. Even when such reporting is supported by evidence, it is often labeled as partisan because it is at odds with the views of prominent political officials and powerful interests. Journalists like Greenwald respond that they are trying to hold officials accountable to democratic values by exposing deception and corruption. These different standards of journalism represent a kind of political warp in which legacy journalism that follows the official line is labeled objective, and journalism that attempts to hold officials accountable to evidence and democratic values is often accused of being biased. Viewed from the perspective of journalists such as Greenwald, the legacy press often seems little more than a communication branch of government.

Beyond the debate about whether the press should report neutrally on the government or hold it accountable, there are other aspects of the contemporary press system that also shape our public discourse. For example, an interesting aspect of the legacy press involves occasions when it gets caught up in *news frenzies* that result in intensive bursts of reporting on things like shootings, natural disasters, scandals, crime waves, tragedies, and political blunders. Some of these episodes are event driven, as when a political figure is assassinated or a terrorist attack occurs. In other cases, as Robert Entman has shown in his work on scandals, intensive news coverage is orchestrated by political factions who stage government actions such as congressional hearings and investigations aimed at damaging political opponents.³ Other frenzies are introduced through more stealthy PR techniques such as stories planted with friendly bloggers that act as tempting bait for journalists. Some of these frenzies can end up as "feeding frenzies" (discussed later in this chapter) when journalists begin dissecting the political target and pronouncing him or her wounded or politically dead.

Even when they are of dubious importance, sensational stories generate public attention and political buzz, taking on lives of their own as they travel through online and conventional media. In these cases, social media, blogs, video platforms, and the legacy press become integrated into a densely networked echo chamber that keeps a story going. An earlier example of this involved the rumors about President Obama being born outside the United States, thus disqualifying him to be president. This persistent story rode the waves of social media, and surfaced in the mainstream news for a number of years, fed by statements from conservative politicians and other public figures. Just when the story seemed to die down, none other than Donald Trump brought it back as a key theme in his short-lived bid for the presidency in 2012. Trump displayed an uncanny grasp of media logic, becoming a one-man brand by living large in the media through well-publicized romantic escapades, staged publicity events for his business ventures, starring in his own reality show, and being a presidential candidate. In 2012, Trump secured his moment of media fame when he launched his campaign by joining the "birther" conspiracy and challenging President Obama's American birth. Although there was no evidence for the attack on Obama, the mainstream media could not ignore the charge because it came from a "newsmaker." This circular news logic is what enables newsmakers to continue to get into the headlines, often with baseless claims.

In 2016, Trump topped his earlier performance with a series of inflammatory statements that rallied the Far Right and activated social media spheres, making him a dominant news story in the conventional press as well. Trump launched his 2016 campaign with a scathing speech about Mexican immigrants crossing the border, saying: "When Mexico sends its people, they're not sending the best. . . . They're sending people who have a lot of problems. . . . They're bringing drugs, they're bringing crime. They're rapists, and some, I assume, are good people."⁴ That line immediately put Trump in the lead in media coverage of a large Republican field. After several US and Mexican television networks and sponsors canceled their relationships with him and some of his products, many pundits assumed that his campaign would burn out or that the Republican Party might discipline or disown him. However, the party feared that he could run as an independent, costing them the election. And so his harsh talk gave him a bump in the opinion polls over the rest of the candidate pack. Buoyed by public support and media coverage, Trump next launched a salvo against Republican senator and past presidential candidate John McCain, who was shot down, captured, and tortured as a navy pilot during the Vietnam War. After McCain criticized Trump's remarks about Mexican immigrants as "firing up the crazies," Trump appeared at an Iowa forum and dismissed McCain by saying, "He's not a war hero. He was a war hero because he was captured. I like people who weren't captured."[5] Despite predictions that these unedited remarks would end his campaign, Trump continued to rise in the polls and receive the lion's share of attention on social and conventional media, reaching nearly 2 million mentions across all media in the week after the McCain blast, compared with the next closest candidate, Democrat Hillary Clinton who received around 500,000 mentions.[6] And so, in the early months of the campaign, Trump became his own publicity machine, dominating the news and sending his public approval ratings soaring over a crowded field of comparatively dull Republican primary candidates.

In many ways, this is the best of times and the worst of times for journalism. On the plus side, the rise of new investigative online organizations has revived a long-hibernating strain of American public interest journalism. With so much information now stored in electronic formats, hackers and leakers are able to release it to independent journalists for broader distribution through hybrid networks of conventional news organizations and online platforms. At the same time, the high volume of PR spin keeps legacy journalism producing official versions of events that often fly in the face of the evidence produced by the public interest press. And cutting through this information system are the news frenzies that burst into the headlines and continue as long as they are fed by a combination of spin and social media buzz. The overall effect is a kind of babel of information that leaves many citizens discouraged or confused.

As discussed in chapter 3, people have various strategies for dealing with the information overload: selecting sources they tend to agree with, deciding how to balance facts and values in their information diet, seeking perspective in political comedy, throwing up their hands in dismay, or simply disconnecting from politics altogether. Yet despite all the signs of disruption and discontent, the core of the US news system remains the legacy press with its dependence on official sources, and its tendency to avoid taking sides, even when evidence points to which version of a story is closer to the truth. In this system, the frenzies and scandals provide fig leaves for independence. Why does the legacy press prevail despite the many signs that it is in trouble? One reason the legacy press remains dominant is because it remains an important outlet for those with power. Even though most people who follow the news think that both politics and the press need fixing, they still want to know what those in power are doing. And the legacy press continues to provide free content for the growing numbers of blogs, aggregation platforms, and social media networks outside the mainstream. And so, despite its flaws, the curious dependency of the press on official spin continues to make the news go round.

How Spin Works

It may be obvious why politicians attempt to control the news, but the journalistic response to news control is more complicated. As already explained, the ideal of impartial or objective journalism results in reporting what dominant power players are saying without issuing rulings on their inaccuracy or deception for fear of being accused of taking sides. When news management operations by officials are competent and journalists are heavily spun, the mainstream press often has trouble reporting independently on stories, with the result that the news sounds much the same no matter which mainstream outlet one consults. True, the *New York Times* may have more stories on more subjects and contain more detail than *USA Today*, but neither strays far beyond official messages and spin. Even Fox News and MSNBC, with their distinctive political angles, simply focus more on one side of the official spectrum than the other.

The spin fills the news more easily as shrinking news budgets restrict investigative reporting and squeeze the space for hard news. In addition, the quest for "balance" and fear of being charged with bias result in reporting spin to balance a story even when there is little evidence to support it. As noted in the case study in chapter 4, this results in an information system in which publics can simply choose the "facts" they like best, creating confusion and political paralysis on pressing problems such as global warming and other environmental issues. The quest for balance can be so ritualized that news organizations may impose it even when investigative reporters reveal situations that seem to have the evidence clearly stacked on one side. For example, Ken Silverstein, an investigative reporter for the *Los Angeles Times*, told of his experience doing a solid piece of investigative reporting on Republican efforts to use influence in St. Louis to disqualify African American voters in the 2004 presidential election. He found that the Republican abuses in Missouri might have been significant enough to affect the outcome of the election, while alleged transgressions by the Democrats were comparatively minor. Despite this finding, his editors chose to run a more "balanced" story about the parties charging each other with dirty practices. In such cases, the game frame is the default plot option for writing stories. In Silverstein's view, creating artificial balance out of political spin rather than reporting the actual independent findings was anything but balanced. He went public with his frustrations, saying: "I am completely exasperated by this approach to the news. The idea seems to be that we go out to report but when it comes time to write we turn our brains off and repeat the spin from both sides. God forbid we should . . . attempt to fairly assess what we see with our own eyes. 'Balanced' is not fair, it's just an easy way to avoid real reporting and shirking our responsibility to readers."[7]

The greatest irony of this system is that considerable competition exists among journalists for what generally amounts to a pretty homogeneous result—with the notable exception of the marketing of partisan content on Fox and MSNBC. Perhaps the next greatest irony is that so much antagonism between journalists and politicians also exists, even though they frequently end up serving each other's mutual interests. What keeps this system from looking too much like the more managed press systems of authoritarian regimes are the regular frenzies in which journalists turn against politicians at the hint of a slip, a rumor, or an accusation from an opponent. Thus, politicians may suddenly find reporters biting the hand that feeds them (recall "feeding the beast" from the last chapter) if they slip or indulge in a spontaneous moment that can be interpreted as a problem. As a result, the press is often kept at a distance from the officials it covers. The result is that journalists seldom have much to distinguish their stories from one another. Former White House correspondent for CNN Charles Bierbauer has described the intense scramble for some nugget or nuance that makes a report different, something that leads someone else's editor to call and say, "Bierbauer's got the story. Where's yours?"[8]

This strange American news pattern alternates between publicizing patent political spin and trying to trap politicians in slips and scandals. Far from enhancing public respect, the press politics game conveys an air of smug insiders often struggling over little of substance while ignoring gaping realities. Indeed, this conformist reporting that often misses the larger story gives political comedy programming its daily material. When the press pack attacks, the adversarial behavior appears largely ritualistic. This "gotcha" journalism often comes across to audiences as posturing—as a game that journalists play to make themselves appear independent and adversarial. Again, providing a steady supply of comedy material.

This chapter explores why so much journalism falls into the two broad categories of (a) reporting the official lines of the day and (b) playing personal "gotcha" games, often with the same officials and newsmakers. Both of these tendencies of the legacy press present serious problems for citizens and their relation to government. The tendency of the press to open the gates to officials and their carefully managed messages is hard to reconcile with the common assumption, as advocated by Glenn Greenwald above, that the media should be more independent, and even adversarial, in their relations with news sources. The problem of a free press relying so heavily on what officials and their handlers feed it is so perplexing that the reasons have been explored by a number of researchers in the fields of communication (e.g., Jay Blumler, Michael Gurevitch),[9] sociology (e.g., Herbert Gans, Gaye Tuchman),[10] and political science (e.g., Bernard Cohen, Timothy Cook).[11]

The countertendency of the press to bite the hand that feeds it is in many ways equally puzzling because the resulting adversarialism is more often personal than substantive. As Thomas Patterson has pointed out, the resulting news content is an odd mix: a narrow range of political ideas, interspersed with cranky criticisms by journalists of politicians and the games they play. Patterson describes the rising levels of journalistic negativity as follows: "Negative coverage of politics has risen dramatically in recent decades. Negative coverage of presidential candidates, for example, now exceeds their positive coverage. . . . By 1990, negative coverage of Congress and its members was over 80%. Each president since 1976—Carter, Reagan, Bush, and Clinton—has received more negative coverage than his predecessor. Federal agencies have fared no better; in the 1990–1995 period, for example, not a single cabinet-level agency received more positive than negative coverage. As portrayed by the press, America's public leadership is universally inept and self-serving."[12]

Thus, the game framing of politics is more about winners and losers, and their inside strategies, and not enough about the issues or the reasons why the options often seem to narrow. Although different researchers propose different specific reasons for why the news comes out in this odd way, all seem to agree that the general answer is a combination of three factors: (a) the economics of the news business, (b) the dependence of journalists on sources who control the information that journalists need, and (c) the routine news-gathering practices of reporters and their news organizations (along with the professional norms and codes of conduct that grow up around those organizational routines). Since two of these factors (the political economy of the news and the information management strategies of news sources) are discussed extensively in other chapters, this chapter and the next look inside journalism itself. We begin with the organizational news-gathering routines that keep reporters and officials locked into their strange dance.

Journalistic Routines and Professional Norms

Organizational routines are the basic rules and practices that journalism schools and news organizations train reporters and editors to follow. These routines help in deciding what to cover and how to cover it. Journalistic routines give the news its reassuring familiarity and create a steady supply of news product about particular topics. *Professional norms* are those moral standards, codes of ethics, and guidelines about inserting voices and viewpoint into stories. Both work routines and professional norms are shaped strongly by the industry business practices and pressures explained in chapter 7. The recent wave of economic change sweeping the news industry not only introduced changes into reporting practices, but also created serious strains in important journalistic norms, such as objectivity, as discussed in chapter 6.

These everyday work routines inside news organizations bias the news without necessarily intending to do so, resulting in the information biases described in chapter 2. In addition to explaining how reporting practices bias the news, it is important to understand why these habits persist and why neither the press nor the general public seems to grasp their true political significance. For example, many members of the press continue to defend their reporting habits as being largely consistent with the professional journalism norms of *independence* and *objectivity*. These standards may go by different names, such as "accurate," "fair," "unbiased," or "nonpartisan," but the point is that a surprising number of American journalists continue to espouse some notion of objectivity. The peculiar nature of objectivity is so important to understand that the next chapter is devoted primarily to its origins and its defining consequences for American news.

A word of clarification is in order here about the intent of this critical discussion. In many instances, the practices and professional standards of American journalism have been commendable. In a few celebrated cases, reporters and editors have waged legal battles and even risked going to jail to protect the confidentiality of sources or to defend the principle of free speech. Moreover, when it comes to the many moral divisions that trouble the nation—our struggles over abortion, guns, or race—journalism has done a good job of presenting the issues and the reasons for impasses. However, on matters of economic, environmental, or foreign policy, political reporting becomes an insider game subject to the limitations of a deferential press. In such key areas, American journalism may have become trapped within an unworkable set of professional standards, with the result that the more objective or fair reporters try to be, the more official bias they introduce into the news.[13] A five-nation study of political journalists by Thomas Patterson and a group of international colleagues produced a startling finding: although the American press is arguably the most free or politically independent in the world, US journalists display the least diversity in their decisions about whom to interview for different hypothetical stories and in what visuals they chose for those stories. Patterson concluded that the strong norm of political neutrality or independence among American journalists actually homogenizes the political content of their reporting. By contrast, reporters in countries such as Italy, Britain, Sweden, and Germany (the other nations studied) are more likely to regard political perspectives as desirable in covering events. As a result, journalists in other nations tend to cover the same events differently—that is, by interviewing a broader range of political sources and using different visual illustrations.[14]

HOW ROUTINE REPORTING PRACTICES
CONTRIBUTE TO NEWS BIAS

Much like any job, reporting the news consists largely of a set of routine, standardized activities. Despite some obvious differences involving the nature of assignments and personal writing styles, American reporters (as noted earlier) tend to cover news events in remarkably similar ways. A fascinating example of how these work routines affect news content was discovered by Timothy Cook in a study of international crisis coverage in the United States and France during the first Iraq War in 1990–1991. In the months after the Iraqi invasion of Kuwait, crucial international diplomatic efforts attempted to prevent the looming war. When news of these efforts broke, television networks in both countries assigned their reporters to get reactions from key sources. American newscasts flipped through the "golden triangle" of Washington news beats: the White House, State Department, and Pentagon. Even though there was no official US reaction to be had, the reporters were pressured to say something, and they effectively invented the kinds of vague pronouncements that one might expect from officials in sensitive political posts at the early stage of a world crisis. By contrast, French reporters (who do not operate with a US-style beat system) interviewed various political party leaders and generated a comparatively broad range of political views about the meanings and implications of the diplomatic talks.[15]

The existence of standardized reporting behaviors and story formulas is not surprising when one considers the strong patterns that operate in the news environment. For example, the events staged by political actors tend to reflect the predictable political communication goals outlined in chapter 4. In parallel, news organizations tend to impose constraints on reporters in terms of acceptable deadlines and story angles. Those organizations watch each other, further standardizing coverage and making the official spin the common denominator. In short, reporters confront three separate sources of incentives to standardize their reporting habits:

- Cooperation with, and pressures from, news sources
- Standard work routines and pressures within news organizations
- Daily information sharing and working relations with fellow reporters

Each of these forces contributes to the development of standardized reporting formulas that favor the incorporation of official political messages in the news, interspersed with the feeding frenzies that may undermine those same officials when they make mistakes or become targets of scandals organized by their opponents. These reporting patterns also lead reporters to write personalized, dramatized, and fragmented news stories. The spice of those stories typically comes in the form of insider analysis of the political games their official sources are playing. We will now explore each source of everyday pressure on journalists.

REPORTERS AND OFFICIALS: COOPERATION AND CONTROL

Most political events are so predictably scripted that reporters can condense them easily into formulaic plot outlines: who (which official) did what (official action), where (in what official setting), for what (officially stated) purpose, and with what (officially proclaimed) result. For example:

President _____ met at the White House today with Prime Minister _____ from _____ to discuss mutual concerns about _____. Both leaders called the talks productive and said that important matters were resolved.

It does not take a careful reading to see that such a formula is virtually devoid of substance. The pseudo-events that provide the scripts for such news stories are generally designed to create useful political images, not to transmit substantive information about real political issues. Because such events are routine political occurrences, reporters quickly develop formulas for converting them into news whenever they occur. Compounding the temptation to report official versions of political events is the fact that reporters live in a world where the "divide and conquer" mentality is ever present. Careers are advanced by receiving scoops and leaks and are damaged by being left out in the cold, excluded from official contact. Like it or not, reporters must depend on the sources they cover.

In view of the patterned nature of political events combined with the spin tactics of politicians, it is not surprising that the news seems to emerge from formulas that virtually write themselves.[16] Of course, there are occasional departures from these scripts. However, in a workday world filled with short deadlines, demanding editors, and persuasive news sources, the formulas become the course of least resistance. In the illusory world of political news, the seal of official approval becomes a substitute for truth and authenticity, which in turn makes the formulas seem legitimate.[17] Robert Scholes developed these ideas a bit further when he said: "Perhaps the credulous believe that a reporter reports facts and that newspapers print all of them that are fit to print. But actually, newspapers print all of the 'facts' that fit, period— that fit the journalistic conventions of what 'a story' is (those tired formulas) and that fit the editorial policy of the paper."[18]

The formulas used to select and arrange facts in the news are produced through mutual cooperation between reporters and newsmakers. These partners may not share exactly the same goals or objectives, but together they create information that satisfies each other's needs. It is all in a day's work. Perhaps that famous slogan of the *New York Times* (All the News That's Fit to Print) should be changed to "All the News That Fits, We Print."

THE INSIDER SYNDROME

In addition to developing work habits that favor official views, reporters are also human beings. It can be heady to feel like an insider in the game of politics. When officials court favor and understanding from reporters, they are often paid back with sympathetic coverage that sticks close to the officials' political lines.[19] Journalists who cooperate with powerful officials often receive recognition and flattery and are taken into the confidence of those officials. In the intensely political environments in which most of our news occurs, nothing is valued as much as power. If one cannot possess power (and there always seems to be a shortage), then the next best thing is to be on the inside with the powerful—to be seen with them, to be consulted by them, to socialize with them, and perhaps even to have them as friends. As Tom Bethell puts it, "To be on close terms with elite news sources is to be an 'insider,' which is what almost everyone in Washington wants to be. It is interesting to note how often this word appears on the dust jackets of memoirs by Washington journalists."[20] Even in the current era in which journalists tend to be kept at a distance from officials, they can create the aura of being insiders by pontificating on the game of politics, talking about the players and their moves as though they were privy to the view from the inside.

Whether being friends with the powerful they cover, or just being in the know about them, there are dangers to the insider syndrome. Ellen Hume, a journalist and scholar of the press, says that she has come to feel that journalists can be "more powerful than any elected official" and that something "urgently" needs to be done to "dynamite" the insiders out of their privileged positions.[21] Steve Goldstein, Washington correspondent for the *Philadelphia Inquirer*, suggested term limits for Washington journalists. If news organizations would agree to rotate their stars out of Washington, the power of the "unelected media elite" might be diminished. Even more important, says Goldstein, media term limits "might counteract the potential for disconnection, whereby the correspondent suffers a loss of understanding of issues that Americans really care about. Federal policy-making and the impact on the folks at home is supplanted by the view from Washington. There is a difference between Here and There. In Sodom-on-the-Potomac the political culture is secular, while most of America is religious. Here the character issue is often framed as: Did he/she sleep with her/him/it? Out there, the issue is often one of fairness, justice, integrity. All the sleaze we print doesn't fit."[22]

NEWS ORGANIZATION PRESSURES TO STANDARDIZE

If the daily spin from officials breathes new life into news formulas, the norms inside news organizations reinforce the use of those formulas. Novice journalists experience constant pressures (subtle and otherwise) from editors about how to cover stories.[23] Those pressures are effective because editors hold sway over what becomes news and which reporters advance in the organization. Over time, reporters tend to adjust their styles to fit harmoniously with the expectations of their organizations.

In many cases, these organizational expectations are defended by journalists as simply preserving the "house style" of the news organization—the tone, editorial voice, and format that makes one news outlet distinguishable from another. This level of formula reporting is inevitable in any kind of organization that has standard operating procedures. However, at a deeper level, there are industry-wide norms about story values that define what news is and that, in turn, open the news to the kinds of biases outlined in chapter 2. For example, one young reporter serving an apprenticeship with a major big-city newspaper talked about the somewhat mysterious process of having some stories accepted and others rejected without really knowing the basis for many of the decisions. Equally mysterious were the conversations with assignment editors in which the editor seemed to know what the story was before it had been covered. Over time, the socialization process works its effects, and young reporters learn to quickly sense what the story is and how to write it.

Beyond the style of this or that news organization, the whole media system begins to emulate particular formats, themes, and news values. Bending news genres to fit commercial values and socializing reporters to recognize how potential stories fit the familiar formulas are the roots of the news biases discussed in chapter 2. In all their variations, however, organizational pressures result in news that typically fits a formula.

WHY FORMULAS WORK

Standardized news is safe. Managers in news organizations must constantly compare their product with that of their competition and defend risky departures from the reporting norm. As Edward Epstein observed in his classic study of television network news, even TV news assignment editors look to the conservative wire services for leads on stories and angles for reporting them.[24] The wires cover the highest portion of planned official events and stick closest to official political scripts. Following the daily lead of the wires becomes the most efficient way to fill the daily need for news, particularly in economically strained organizations that find syndicated content more affordable than hiring their own reporters.

Other organizational arrangements also strongly influence standardized reporting. Among the most powerful standardizing forces are daily news production routines. Newspapers and news programs require a minimum supply of news every day, whether or not anything significant happens in the world. Perhaps you have seen a television news program on a slow news day. In place of international crises, press conferences, congressional hearings, and proclamations by the mayor, the news may consist of a trip to the zoo to visit a new "baby," a canned report on acupuncture in China, a follow-up story on the survivor of an air crash, or a visit to the opening of baseball spring training in Florida. Slow news days occur during weekends or vacation periods when governments are closed down. News organizations run fluff on slow days because their daily routines report official happenings from the news centers of government. Whether the news day is slow or fast, the same amount of news must be produced to fill the "news hole."

FILLING THE NEWS HOLE

For a news organization to function, it must fill a minimum "news hole" every day. Producing a large amount of cheap, predictable news normally means assigning reporters to events and beats that are sure to produce enough acceptable stories to fill the news hole by the day's deadline. During normal business periods, the public relations (PR) machinery of government and business fills these organizational needs by producing events that are cheap, easy to report, numerous, and predictable.

With the advent of 24-hour news channels and websites that are linked to papers and broadcast organizations, or that stand alone (such as the *Huffington Post*, *Vox*, or the *Daily Beast*), the news hole has become a canyon. Pressures increase to update stories many times a day, in contrast to once or twice a day in the old era of morning and evening news. The journalistic credo of "advancing" a story has become an obsession for many organizations. Reporters learn to ask leading or challenging questions, often based on little more than trying to elicit a reaction from a newsmaker in an effort to generate new material to report. "The president denied rumors today . . ." becomes a familiar lead in a news age with an ever-larger news hole to fill.

BEATS

Filling the daily news hole on time means that news organizations must figure out how to make the spontaneous predictable. The obvious solution to this problem is to anticipate when and where the required amount of news will happen every day. Because this task is made difficult by the size of the world and the smallness of reporting staffs, the solution is to implicitly adjust the definition of news so that things that are known to happen on a regular basis become news. Reporters can be assigned to cover those things and be assured (by definition) of gathering news every day. As a result, the backbone of the news organization is the network of beats, ranging from the police station and the city council at the local level to Congress, the Supreme Court, and the presidency at the national level. Beats produce each day's familiar run of murders, accidents, public hearings, press conferences, and presidents entering helicopters and leaving planes.

BUREAUS

In addition to beats, large news organizations also have geographically assigned crews. For example, television networks have news crews stationed in large cities and locations around the world where news is expected to happen. The assumption is that enough news will be generated from these areas to warrant assigning personnel to them, and these crews will get the news faster and with more local knowledge than would teams dispatched from the home office. The locations chosen for these bureaus naturally become more covered. As Epstein discovered in his study of television network news, almost all non-Washington news originates from the handful of places where the networks station their crews.[25]

To an important extent, the reliance on bureaus has decreased in recent years because of budget cuts that eliminated many of these branch offices. As the profit imperative has been felt at both print and broadcast organizations, expensive bureaus are often the first things to be cut. Among American television news operations, only CNN has retained a substantial network of worldwide information-gathering outposts—in large part because CNN also runs an international channel that demands serious world coverage. However, all major news organizations have dropped bureaus and reporting staff. The result is that ABC, CBS, and NBC have increasingly settled for buying their raw product secondhand from a variety of world TV wholesale news suppliers. In the newspaper business, pressures to cut luxuries such as remote bureaus have been equally intense. Many big-city papers have been purchased by large conglomerates, which feed all the papers in the chain the same material from centralized bureaus. The few remaining independent big-city papers increasingly rely on secondhand suppliers, such as the Associated Press, the *New York Times*, and the *Washington Post*, which continue to maintain extensive bureaus and sell their stories to smaller organizations. The overall trend is an increasing consolidation of the information channels on which media organizations rely for their daily supply of news. All of this produces more limited news coverage in the legacy press.

Reporters as a Pack: Pressures to Agree

As a result of the routine nature of news gathering, reporters tend to move in packs. They are assigned together to the same events and the same beats. More than most workers, they share close social experiences on the job. Together they eat, sleep, travel, drink, and wait, and wait, and wait. They also share that indescribable adrenaline rush of "crashing" a story— hurtling through those precious minutes between the release of key information and the deadline for filing the story. As a result of such intimate social contact, reporters tend to develop a sense of solidarity. They learn to cope with shared pressures from news organizations and news sources. They come to accept news formulas as inevitable, even though they may cynically complain about them in between mad scrambles to meet deadlines. They respect one another as independent professionals but engage in the social courtesies of comparing notes and corroborating story angles.

As discussed in the last chapter, Timothy Crouse called the reporter's social world—particularly on the campaign trail—"pack journalism."[26] He concluded that reporters come into such close contact while under such sympathetic conditions while covering such controlled events that they do not have to collaborate formally in order to end up reporting things in much the same way. Once a reporter has been assigned to a routine event for which news formulas are well known, there is a strong temptation to produce a formula story. Added to this are a tight deadline and an editor who will question significant departures from the formula used by other reporters; as a result, the temptation to standardize becomes even stronger. Finally, put the reporter in a group of sympathetic human beings faced with the same temptations, and the use of formulas becomes easily rationalized and accepted with the social support of the group.

So strong are the pressures of the pack that they were felt by a trained sociologist posing as a reporter to study journalism from an insider's perspective. While working as a reporter for a small daily paper, Mark Fishman was assigned to the city council beat. He quickly fit into the routine of writing formula stories that mirrored the council's careful efforts to create an image of democracy in action—complete with elaborate hearings, citizen input, serious deliberations, and formal votes. In a rare case when an issue before the council got out of control and turned into a hot political argument, the reporters at the press table reacted strangely: they ignored the disruption because it did not fit the mold of what counts as news. And they had to work together to classify the event as not being newsworthy. As Fishman described it: "The four members of the press [including Fishman] were showing increasing signs of impatience with the controversy. At first the reporters stopped taking notes; then they began showing their disapproval to each other; finally, they were making jokes about the foolishness of the debate. No evidence could be found in their comments that they considered the controversy anything other than a stupid debate over a trivial matter unworthy of the time and energy the council put into it."[27]

Fishman noted the strength of group pressure operating against independent news judgment: "Even though at the time of the incident I was sitting at the press table [as a reporter] making derisive comments about the foolishness of the council along with other journalists, it occurred to me later how this controversy could be seen as an important event in city hall."[28] Just as Fishman succumbed to the pressures of the pack while still recognizing them at a conscious level, most reporters are aware of group

pressure but seem unable to escape it. In a study of the Washington journalism corps, the nation's reporting elite, Stephen Hess found that reporters
regarded pack journalism as their most serious problem.[29] As Hess noted,
however, pack journalism will persist as long as news organizations establish their routines around the predictable actions of officials. Although the
pack generally feeds on the handouts offered by spin doctors and political
handlers, it can also turn on the unprepared or vulnerable politician, resulting in a *feeding frenzy*.

FEEDING FRENZY: WHEN THE PACK ATTACKS

Although the political content of the mainstream press may be remarkably uniform, it does not always follow the scripts of politicians. What is
often mistaken for a critical, independent press is a phenomenon popularly
known as the "feeding frenzy."[30] When politicians become caught up in personal crises, scandals, or power struggles, the news media may descend like
a pack of hungry dogs or sharks to devour the political prey. Add the hint of
a sex scandal or produce the proverbial smoking gun of political corruption,
and the frenzy can bring down the high and mighty.

Cases of the pack devouring its political prey are legendary: Lyndon Johnson fell to a feeding frenzy over the Vietnam War; Richard Nixon lost control
of the press during the Watergate crisis; Jimmy Carter was himself held hostage in the Oval Office by the press for 444 days during the Iranian hostage
crisis of 1979–1980; the first George Bush plummeted from his standing as
the most popular president in the history of modern polling as the press
pack followed the Democrats in attacking him for an economic recession;
and Bill Clinton saw the customary presidential honeymoon period cur-
tailed prematurely by feeding frenzies over a series of minor "scandals" in
White House operations. The growing chaos and criticism surrounding the
Iraq crisis provided openings for the press pack to turn on George W. Bush,
but those openings were balanced against the somber fact that the country
was at war. And, as discussed in chapter 2, the press pack reached consensus early in the Obama administration that the president had lost control
of his "narrative."

Few politicians have felt the sting of the feeding frenzy as repeatedly as
Bill Clinton. The news was spiced during the 1992 election by charges of
Clinton's extramarital affairs, pot smoking, draft dodging, and other personal issues. Clinton's character became a major preoccupation of the press
during the campaign.[31] The resulting challenge for the Clinton communication team was to reassure voters about the character defects raised in
the news and reinforced by opponents during the primaries and the gen-

eral election. The fact that Clinton survived the nearly nonstop negative news and then won the election struck one Republican media consultant as something close to a miracle. He likened Clinton to the crash test dummy of American politics: "I've never seen anybody come back from being attacked in that fashion. It's like going through a car crash with no seat belts and then going through the window and hitting a wall and walking away. It's absolutely astounding."[32]

After the election, Clinton and his staff remained bitter about their treatment by the press during the campaign. When they came to Washington, it seemed as if they felt that they could govern much as they had won the election—by going over the heads of the press through electronic town halls, controlled news events, and heavy polling and image construction. The daily world of Washington politics proved different than the campaign trail, where paid advertising and controlled events stand a better chance of countering press attacks. The now-famous decision to close the corridor between the pressroom and the White House Office of Communications amounted to a declaration of war on journalism's elite corps. The icy relations left the press pack surly and ready to pounce at the hint of a scandal or personal failing. Clinton's run of personal incidents continued after the inauguration, and the press pounced on such items as Clinton's expensive haircut aboard an idling Air Force One on a Los Angeles International Airport taxiway and a scandal in the management of the White House travel office that was quickly dubbed "Travelgate" in the media.

One analysis of this nonstop feeding frenzy opened with the observation that "twelve days after President Clinton took office—with *only* 1,448 days left in his term—Sam Donaldson of ABC *News* was on a weekend talk show saying 'This week we can all talk about, Is the presidency over?'"[33] Another reflective piece was titled "The White House Beast" after the derisive nickname given the press corps by George Stephanopoulos, who was Clinton's early (and disastrous) communications director, and who now serves as a pundit and anchor for ABC News. As *Washington Post* correspondent Ruth Marcus put it in that article, "The White House press corps is like this large, dysfunctional family. It's weird. It's not normal. Half the time I'm at the White House, my attitude is: No one would believe this."[34] Influential *New York Times* correspondent (now an influential columnist) Maureen Dowd listed numerous instances of poor press handling during a European trip commemorating the 50-year anniversary of D-Day. She recounted a reflective moment at a British pub after a missed deadline: "Sipping champagne ordered by the *Paris Match* reporter, I fantasized about replacing the corner dartboard with the head of one of Clinton's prepubescent press-minders."[35]

Several lessons can be drawn from the series of feeding frenzies that plagued the Clinton presidency. As these factors often contribute to other feeding frenzies, they are stated here in more general terms:

- Cooperative relations between the president's communication staff and the press had broken down. (See the discussions of press-politician cooperation earlier in this chapter and in chapter 4.)
- The communication staff seemed to think it unnecessary (or beneath the dignity of the office) to follow the basic rules of news management in response to the initial outbreaks of negative coverage, as outlined in chapter 4. They had no apparent game plan to spin the incidents that kept the feeding frenzies going.
- Opponents in Congress converted the incidents into hearings and investigations that resulted in numerous uncontrolled news situations.

The lessons from the Clinton years apply equally to the Obama presidency. Even though Barack Obama took office facing large challenges at home and abroad, he was unable to spin his circumstances to his political advantage, and spent most of his presidency fending off attacks from Republicans and rumors bubbling from deep social media networks. Even his signature health care program became a frenzied press problem as he displayed little ability to sell it to the public, and poorly defended attacks from critics who sought to kill it. And so, as discussed in chapters 1 and 2, President Obama lost his narrative, and opposing Republicans were ever ready to supply theirs to the press. The Republican opposition managed to capture a substantial portion of the news by threatening to filibuster Obama initiatives in the Senate while echoing various birther and other slurs on his character from Tea Party activists in the streets. Meanwhile, the administration seemed unable to generate or stay on messages of its own, preferring to continue to communicate directly with supporters through social media networks, which worked far better to mobilize public support during the election campaign than in the governing process. The Obama years were an odd mix of orchestrated opposition spin interspersed with frenzies stirred by online attacks and the Tea Party movement.

Ever a popular target for scandalmongering from the Right, Hillary Clinton launched her 2016 presidential campaign amid waves of scandal promoted by Republicans in Congress. Using hearings and investigations to attract ongoing media coverage, political opponents continued to raise questions about Clinton's use of a private email server as secretary of state, and her handling of security at the US diplomatic compound in Benghazi,

Libya, where an attack resulted in the death of the American ambassador. In between bouts of damage control on these scandals, Clinton was trying to get press coverage for her positions on the economy and the environment. With opponents spinning the press, and the pack poised for attack, maintaining control of the news narrative was tricky.

During a week in which Clinton issued major policy announcements on the economy and a sweeping solar energy proposal, her statements were swamped by a *New York Times* front-page story that the Justice Department had launched a criminal investigation into her use of a private email server during her time as secretary of state. That set off another media frenzy as the story ran through other news outlets and echoed back again as political opponents such as Donald Trump piled on and made news of their own. Trump fueled the news frenzy by claiming that storing official email on a private server was clearly criminal activity that should disqualify her from running for president.[36] The only trouble is that the story was not true. There was not a criminal investigation, and Clinton was not specifically named as the target in what turned out to be a less-focused bureaucratic investigation to determine whether classified information had been handled properly. This detail was lost in the press frenzy as Twitter erupted and other news outlets ran the *Times* story and politicians commented on it.

When officials in positions to know about a criminal investigation were asked for confirmation on the record, they stated that no such investigation had been called for. It is impossible to know, of course, whether the officials who denied the story on the record were the same ones who planted it off the record. Even more embarrassing for the *Times* was that since no such investigation had been called for and there was no clear legal charge to be found, the original news report awkwardly avoided any clear discussion of what the specific legal problem might be. After several days of changing the headline and attempting to correct, or "skin back," the story in back-page correction boxes, the *Times* eventually had to retract it. What now exists in the paper's digital record is a much more benign story with two vague corrections at the bottom stating that revisions were made in other versions.[37] Kurt Eichenwald, a former *New York Times* writer, published an analysis in *Newsweek* dissecting the *Times* story based on documents released under Freedom of Information Act requests covering the same events that were framed as a criminal investigation in the *Times* story. He concluded that those events were low-level bureaucratic examinations of State Department handling of classified material. Accusing the *Times* of reckless distortion, Eichenwald concluded: "This is no Clinton scandal. It is no scandal at all. It is about current bureaucratic processes, probably the biggest snooze-fest in all of journalism."[38] However, the lasting impression in the minds of many citizens who follow the news casually was that Clinton engaged in some kind of criminal activity. The political impact of the months of scandals and recurring feeding frenzies was that Clinton suffered eroding trust levels among voters polled in key states.

Many big stories in recent years, including the Bush administration rationale for the Iraq War, have been based on rushing to publish scoops handed out by anonymous sources that may either have poor information or political motives for spinning the press. This kind of journalism is commonly criticized, as in Glenn Greenwald's remarks at the start of this chapter, yet continues to be widely practiced. Among the many critics in the Clinton case was the *Times'* own public editor (ombudsman) who wrote a column noting that the paper's editors had defended the problematic story based on the information given them by trusted sources. The public editor noted that accepting information from anonymous sources should always raise caution flags, and that rushing to publish before other organizations got the story only compounded the chances for error. In her words, the postmortem editorial discussion inside the paper should have been less defensive and more focused on "the rampant use of anonymous sources, and the need to slow down and employ what might seem like an excess of caution before publishing a political blockbuster based on shadowy sources. I'll summarize my prescription in four words: Less speed, more transparency."[39]

The Paradox of Organizational Routines

Whether being spun, joining the pack in feeding frenzies, or some combination of the two, the press ends up reporting much the same news across different mainstream outlets. The paradox is that because there are so many different papers, radio programs, and television broadcasts from which audiences can receive the daily news, it is hard for competing organizations to establish a competitive edge in the news market. As a result, routine reporting may be efficient, but it limits the share of the market that any media source can capture. Thus, efficiency may impose an unintended ceiling on audience share, which limits the growth of profits in the news organization—and news is, after all, a business. The ways around this dilemma involve marketing strategies, budget cutting, and the various other business moves described in chapter 7—none of which improve the quality of news.

Breaking out of the news routine toward more independent, less sensational news has not been attractive to legacy news organizations because it is not clear what the alternative would look like even if it were profitable enough to worry about. For example, television executives may point to the *NewsHour* on the Public Broadcasting Service (PBS) as an example of how more in-depth reporting only drives audiences away. Some critics argue, however, that PBS news, while more detailed and more likely to broadcast hard news over soft, is otherwise very similar in content to that available on the commercial networks. Why should audiences seek a bigger dose of the same product? Indeed, the ratings suggest that far more people prefer the news on ABC, NBC, CBS, and Fox.

Because news is largely the result of convenient conventions between politicians and reporters, it is not clear where to look for guidance in reforming the product. Any new format would surely draw criticism from politicians and other news organizations, and it might startle the public, risking the possible loss of audience share. As a result, the media do not like to think too much about tampering with the standard news-gathering routines. Instead, the competition in most news markets tends to be waged in terms of marketing strategies, brand images, and other matters of style over substance.

Should marketing and delivering key demographics to advertisers rule the news? Such questions are dodged by news doctors and media executives, who reply simplistically that they are only interested in making the news more relevant to people. It is doubtful that marketing surveys really measure popular demand at all.[40] For example, most media surveys are designed with the assumption that formula news is a given. Audiences are not asked whether they would prefer alternatives to news formulas; they are simply asked which news formulas they like best. Thus, the standard excuse that the news reflects what the people want might be stated more properly as "the news reflects what people prefer among those choices that are profitable and convenient to offer them." This is not the same thing as saying that the news is responsive to popular demand.

One thing that seems clear is that the emphasis on marketing to generate revenues has opened the content of news organizations to more economical fare such as recycled exploits of reality TV celebrities; fluffy features on fashion, health, and food; and dramatic scandals and political clashes that resemble food fights. In addition, the Internet keeps bubbling up with tempting rumors and wild claims that newsmakers can use to get publicity. All of this points to an erosion of the legacy press as the arbiter of what is most important in society and as the most reliable judge of authoritative sources and information. These hallmarks of *journalistic gatekeeping* are eroding in a changing media system.

The End of Gatekeeping and the Challenges of Change

During the heyday of the legacy press, the reigning assumption was that the leading news organizations set the tone for what was important for the country to think about. Legendary CBS anchor Walter Cronkite ended his nightly newscast with the authoritative tag line "And that's the way it is." Even though the press during the mass media age also relied mainly on official definitions of events, there was a much clearer capacity to mind the national information gates to keep out much of the hype, frenzy, fake scandals, and game framing that fills the news today. *Gatekeeping* is a term often used to refer to *whose voices and what messages get into the news*.

Journalists and their news organizations make choices about what to cover and how to report it. In an ideal world, journalists might find the sources representing the most credible, insightful, and diverse points of view. These ideal news sources would try to engage their opponents in convincing debate aimed at helping the public decide the best course of action. And the ideal public would want to take the time to learn about different approaches to important social issues. In the real world, many factors work against these ideals of a democratic press, from business pressures in news organizations to lazy citizens and deceptive politicians. The growing importance of spin, and the rise of tempting rumors on the Internet have undermined the capacity of news organizations to mind the gates with uniform or high-minded standards. Stories easily spill back and forth between news and entertainment programming in ways that seem to further diminish the capacity of the press to authoritatively develop perspectives on what is important and why it matters.

Communication scholars Bruce Williams and Michael Delli Carpini suggest that for many stories, the news has become a secondary information source behind talk shows and late-night comedy monologues. They argue that the mass media news regime once dominated by the nightly news on the three broadcast networks is ending. Along with its demise, the once-hallowed gatekeeping function of journalism is dissolving. Politics now spills outside the bounds of news and throughout other media formats from political comedy to YouTube mash-ups that are better suited to telling dramatic and entertaining stories.[41] Williams and Delli Carpini describe the emergence of a much more chaotic public information order. In their view, the new order gives rise to questions such as: Is there a difference between comedian Tina Fey and news anchor Katie Couric?[42]

Journalists and the academics who study them are acutely aware of these signs of change. Yet it is very hard for established press institutions to change in creative and adaptive ways. More often, change is a slow corrosive process resulting in replacement of archaic institutions with new and disruptive ones. Indeed, even when staring at their own demise, many journalists cannot abandon the values of their profession that establish their identity. The exchange between Bill Keller and Glenn Greenwald at the opening of this chapter is a good illustration of this point. Keller is bent on upholding the ideals of a profession and pointing to some iconic moments such as Watergate when brilliant reporting brought those ideals to life. And so those ideals persist even as the iconic moments become few and far between.

Indeed, the leading organizations of the legacy press have become easy prey to comedians and to the new breed of critical journalists who lampoon the legacy media's often slavish reporting of official spin and practice of safeguarding the identity of the officials who did the spinning. For example, Glenn Greenwald dissected a prominent *New York Times* article in which high-level officials granted anonymity claimed that the NSA leaks revealed by Edward Snowden had directly helped ISIS and other terrorist groups figure out how to evade US efforts to monitor them.[43] Greenwald then showed that there is no evidence for these claims, either in the *Times* article or in subsequent media rehashes of that report. Moreover, he showed evidence suggesting that the claims were false. However, since the official government sources were anonymous, there was no way for other journalists to question them. Perhaps most damning, since the claims appeared in the prestigious *New York Times* (which got the scoop by promising anonymity to the sources), other media outlets reported the story as the gospel truth. And so the spin cycle of the legacy media goes on, aided by journalists clinging to ideals that blind them to the realities of their daily practices. Greenwald noted that similar deference to official spin, compounded by granting the sources anonymity, aided and abetted the deceptions and falsehoods in the Bush administration PR campaign to sell the Iraq War through the mainstream press. Despite promises by prestige news organizations to be more critical in the future, the same practices continue to this day, as illustrated in the NSA story discussed here and the Clinton email scandal discussed earlier. Established press organizations that are locked into dependency relations with those in power simply cannot change even when their ideals are compromised. This syndrome of dependence on officials is made worse by the failing business model of the commercial press. And so there are now many challengers to the dominance and gatekeeping authority of the legacy press. Among the most interesting of these challengers is the rise of a critical, investigative press dedicated to holding government officials accountable to the public.

The Rise of the New Investigative Journalism

The economic crisis in journalism, combined with the loss of popular confidence in mainstream news, is producing waves of innovation and experimentation. The array of mostly online news organizations, blogs, and hybrid organizations is impressively large and growing. An investigation by Pew Research identified 172 nonprofit digital outlets launched between 1987 and 2012, with most of them still in operation today. These range from prominent national investigative organizations such as ProPublica, discussed in the case study below, to Portland Afoot, a site aimed to report on how to beat the car culture in Portlandia.[44] Depending on how one defines a news outlet—which is becoming more challenging in this era of hybrid media—the list of for-profit operations is likely even larger, including the *Daily Beast, Huffington Post, Vox, Vice,* and many others. Like their nonprofit cousins, these relatively recent additions to the news world vary in terms of the range of topics covered, the degree to which they feature original reporting or reprocess news from other sources, the balance between evidence and opinion, whether they are staffed by paid professionals or amateur content creators, and the sizes of the audiences they pull in. A number of these organizations claim to be dedicated to investigative journalism that holds officials accountable to public standards of integrity, transparency, and other democratic values. Many of these operations contrast themselves to legacy news organizations that they regard as too dependent on the officials they cover. This emerging class of investigative news organizations merits attention as potential challengers to the legacy press. Indeed, many of the stories they have produced are among the major news events of our time, rocking governments and drawing large audiences.

CASE STUDY
HACKTIVIST JOURNALISM: THE NEW
INVESTIGATIVE REPORTING IN THE DIGITAL AGE

The exchange between Bill Keller and Glenn Greenwald opening this chapter suggests a changing paradigm that is emerging to challenge the troubled legacy press. Many reporters who represent conventional news organizations—as embodied by Keller in this exchange—continue to practice the modern-era code of impartial or objective journalism that leads to close reliance on official sources. For many journalists, this professional paradigm serves as a defense against charges of bias, even though such charges continue to be made anyway as a means of keeping the press on notice that it is being constantly policed from all sides. Critics such as Greenwald argue that maintaining this thin veil of objectivity comes with the high price of being spun and failing to hold officials accountable to the public when their spin crosses the line into deception and lying. In this disruptive period for legacy journalism, many news organizations have folded, and numbers of good journalists have left legacy news organizations as they cut staff—often joining new digital start-ups. In addition, many young reporters are skeptical about working in low-paying and insecure jobs for organizations that seem unable to find a news format that meets with much public enthusiasm. As a result, a new era of more critical investigative journalism has developed.

The rise of these organizations is aided by the ease of public access to online sites and the low cost of producing them compared to that of conventional news organizations. One of the first sites was ProPublica, which began publishing in 2008 and defined itself this way: "ProPublica is an independent, nonprofit newsroom that produces investigative journalism in the public interest. Our work focuses exclusively on truly important stories, stories with a 'moral force.' We do this by producing journalism that shines a light on exploitation of the weak by the strong, and on the failures of those with power to vindicate the trust placed in them."[45] Its reporting has won a number of major journalism prizes, several of which were the first time they were given to an online journalism organization. With funding from foundations and philanthropic donors, ProPublica's innovative model involves sharing stories freely under Creative Commons licenses with other news organizations. This free syndication model has resulted in over 120 "publishing partners" since its founding.

Another recent investigative organization is *The Intercept*, which launched in 2014 with funding from eBay billionaire Pierre Omidyar. With a founding editorial team of Glenn Greenwald, Laura Poitras, and Jeremy Scahill, the online site declared its mission as "producing fearless, adversarial journalism. We believe journalism should bring transparency and accountability to powerful governmental and corporate institutions, and our journalists have the editorial freedom and legal support to pursue this mission."[46] *The Intercept* site has a page inviting readers to "become a source," along with a link "How to Leak to The Intercept." Indeed, the availability of large troves of electronic data about any manner of subjects makes many ordinary people potential news sources simply by downloading files at the office or hacking into systems remotely and leaking the information to journalists. This is of course a high-stakes game, but the playing field that once greatly advantaged public officials and secrecy against public accountability is being leveled somewhat by such organizations. Many of the top stories in *The Intercept* during its early era came from the NSA archives leaked by Edward Snowden.

This emerging trend is interesting in many ways, and could signal a second muckraking era of the sort that became popular after the turn of the twentieth century before the birth of the professional, objective press in the 1920s. Political communication scholar Adrienne Russell has called this new trend the rise of "hactivist" journalism, in which conventional news formats are "hacked" or repurposed for the ends of activists who gather and share information they feel publics should receive without being clouded by official spin and contrived journalistic neutrality.[47] Some of these hactivist reporters are also activists for various causes such as the environment, economic justice, and personal privacy, among others. At the same time, they actively seek solid information that they publish using various digital technologies that they may develop or hack together to aid their reporting. Another sense in which these journalists display a hactivist spirit is that they may hack into databases or receive information as leaks from others who do. The overriding rationale is that information about what governments are doing should be free and available to the public.

As a result of these more aggressive forms of gathering and publicizing information, the tensions run high between government officials who guard their secrecy and the whistleblowers and hackers who would expose their behind-the-scenes activities. In many ways this journalism has become a hallmark of larger struggles to keep the Internet free as a public space by tilting the balance toward citizen interests and away from surveillance and data mining. As discussed in the last chapter, many hackers and leakers have been prosecuted, and journalists have faced increasing government pressure in recent years. Figures like Chelsea Manning, Jeffrey Sterling, and Edward Snowden discussed in chapter 4 are heroes to some and traitors to others. They have raised questions about the balance between government secrecy and surveillance versus protecting fundamental human rights and democratic principles.[48]

In addition to operating outside conventional news organizations, these new journalists often have very different methods of gaining and publicizing information. Indeed, some have been successful as solo citizen journalists without belonging to a larger organization at all. Adrienne Russell compares the personal profiles of four prominent examples.[49] Activist Tim Pool was involved in the Occupy Wall Street protests and wanted the public to witness the action from the inside rather than from the distant remove and official spin applied by the mainstream press. He developed technology to live-stream many Occupy activities, from marches to police raids, using personal equipment and the streaming platform Ustream. His audience soon numbered in the millions, and his reports were picked up by a number of conventional news agencies whose reporters could not get as close to the action with the same degree of authenticity. Pool was subsequently hired by other organizations such as VICE News to cover protests in a number of other countries. Another activist journalist is environmentalist Bill McKibben, who published a number of influential books on the environmental crisis. He decided that the impact of information alone was not enough without providing his audience with opportunities to act on it. He created an activist organization (350.org) to help his reading public take action on the information he provided them. Glenn Greenwald, already introduced in this chapter, has become a critic of conventional journalism, initially as an influential blogger, and subsequently as a risk-taking reporter who helped publicize the Edward Snowden NSA leaks. Juliana Rotich is one of the founders of Ushahidi, a crowdsourcing platform that has enabled direct citizen reporting and aggregation of human rights violations, elections, natural disasters, and other events that conventional journalists either cannot reach or often get wrong because they may not understand them (or because they think that their home audiences will not grasp foreign situations that are not translated into more familiar story lines).

As these examples indicate, there is no single form that this new investigative reporting takes. In fact, operating outside legacy news organization and using technologies to help organize their activities frees these journalists to create formats best suited to different stories and events. The result is a fluid information system that contains many different hybrid news organizations. Instead of being bound by routines, and competing for scoops and tidbits of information from offi cials, the new investigative reporting has generated some of the biggest stories of our time and reached large audiences by hacking improvised networks together. As Andrew Chadwick and Simon Collister observe, these divergent models were inspired by the initial WikiLeaks release in 2010 of US government cables and other artifacts pertaining to the Iraq War.[50] In a novel twist, WikiLeaks formed an international partnership with leading news organizations in different countries. Editors and reporters in those organizations sifted through the documents, performed the editorial and writing work, and published the stories to their large international audiences. After years of disruption by financial blockades and prosecutions from a host of world governments, WikiLeaks relaunched in 2015, offering new security protections to its informants and publishing dozens of stories about ways in which governments around the world are spying on their own citizens, other nations, and business corporations.[51] All of this occurred while publisher Julian Assange was holed up in the Ecuadorian embassy in London facing sexual assault charges in Sweden and espionage charges in the United States.

The global publishing partnership model pioneered by WikiLeaks was also adopted after Edward Snowden released his trove of documents to Laura Poitras and Glenn Greenwald. They coordinated the selection and release of stories across different news organizations in the United States (*Washington Post*), the UK (*Guardian*), Germany (*Der Spiegal*), France (*Le Monde*), Brazil (*O Globo*), and a number of other countries.

All these changes suggest an interesting set of trends that may redefine journalism as we have known it:

- High-quality information produced and distributed by citizens and activists
- Hybrid and flexible networks created with a mix of digital platforms and conventional news organizations
- Global distribution of news about issues such as climate, economics, wars, human rights
- News environments in which citizens can both contribute and consume information, and take action

This journalism promises to challenge official authority and deception as conventional journalism only rarely does. Governments and officials do not appreciate these efforts and often attempt to suppress them by punishing the individuals involved. However, the hacktivist culture that has adopted the slogan "Information wants to be free" may well prevail, ushering in a new era of public interest reporting.

Democracy with or without Citizens?

Recall from chapter 1 that political communication scholar Robert Entman has argued that the mass-mediated democracy of the legacy press is in danger of becoming a *democracy without citizens.* This is in part because most news coverage uses formats that place the audience more as passive consumers than active citizens.[52] For both politicians and journalists, the public has become more of a market to be tested, persuaded, and sold than an equal partner in communication and government. The reality of much opinion and participation is anchored in electronic images that move people psychologically in private worlds that may be detached from society and face-to-face politics.[53]

The irony in this is that the technology exists to communicate more information—farther, faster, from more sources, and to more people than ever before. At the same time, the political and business pressures operating behind the legacy press create just the opposite results. Perhaps the electronic age would not be so worrisome if politicians and the press used the potential of today's electronic technology to communicate critical ideas to people and help them take action. The question is how to move politicians and journalism away from the paths of least political and economic resistance in their communication strategies. The promise of the new investigative journalism is to bring citizens directly into the news by making government more transparent and often providing ways in which people can act and react to the information they receive.

The informal partnerships that have emerged between investigative organizations and conventional media may signal a path for change in the legacy press. In addition, the appearance of high-quality news sites covering topics such as climate change or prison reform may signal another direction for a press that better informs and engages citizens. As journalists are laid off from news corporations and conventional jobs dry up, idealistic journalist-activists may find niches in the digital realm and join the hacker culture, exploring how digital technologies may attract more active audience involvement. Recent years have seen the rise of blogs, discussion forums, instant polls, YouTube channels, social networking sites, and invitations for citizens to report stories they have documented on cell phones and digital cameras. What do you think? What kind of news best fits the needs of a *democracy with citizens*?

6

INSIDE THE PROFESSION
THE OBJECTIVITY CRISIS

Journalistic objectivity is an effort to discern a practical truth, not an abstract perfect truth. Reporters seeking genuine objectivity search out the best truth possible from the evidence that the reporter, in good faith, can find. To discredit objectivity because it is impossible to arrive at perfect truth is akin to dismissing trial by jury because it isn't perfect in its judgments.

—Alex S. Jones[1]

"Objectivity" placed overwhelming emphasis on established, official voices and tended to leave unreported large areas of genuine relevance that authorities chose not to talk about. . . . .It widened the chasm that is a constant threat to democracy—the difference between the realities of private power and the illusions of public imagery.

—Ben Bagdikian[2]

So much for Objective journalism. Don't bother to look for it here— not under any byline of mine; or anyone else I can think of. With the possible exception of things like box scores, race results, and stock market tabulations, there is no such thing as Objective journalism. The phrase itself is a pompous contradiction in terms.

—Hunter S. Thomson[3]

The exchange between Bill Keller and Glenn Greenwald that opened chapter 5 indicates an emerging divide in how journalists understand their professionalism. Many mainstream journalists continue to think of themselves as objective observers who are able to put aside personal political biases in order to get to the bottom of a story. Critics argue that this impartial or objective stance actually produces a serious bias by relying on official sources, thus bringing spin into the center of the news. The growing ranks of critical "accountability journalists" discussed in the last chapter prefer to challenge official versions of events when there is available evidence to cast doubt on the spin. These critics argue that journalists in a democracy should act like public "watchdogs" to hold officials accountable. Mainstream reporters respond that when they present contrasting viewpoints that challenge each other, they are offering a form of accountability that enables the public, rather than journalists, to decide the most credible version of a story. Both sides in this debate believe that they are pursuing the truth by different methods.

Despite growing criticism that objectivity has become conflated with spin, the commitment to the norm of neutral, impartial, or objective reporting runs deep in the legacy press. Where did this norm come from? How did it somehow get caught up in the "he said, she said" journalism that gives officials their say with minimum challenges from reporters? Can reporters be objective? Should they be? These questions fuel much public debate and offer instant topics for pundits on 24/7 cable channels. At the time of this writing, a Google search on "journalism bias" produced a healthy 29,000,000 hits. Despite the extensive discussions of what it is and how to detect it, we are not likely to resolve the problem of bias for reasons outlined in chapter 2. In particular, if you ask them what's wrong with the press, most people view the world through their own political biases and think that perspectives deviating from their views are unbalanced. Because there are so many different views operating in the public on almost any issue, the quest for news coverage that strikes a majority as fair, balanced, or objective appears to be an impossible dream. It is commonly assumed that news bias involves journalists abandoning objectivity to insert their personal prejudices into their reporting. In this chapter, we will consider the disturbing possibility that the most serious biases in the news actually occur when journalists cling most closely to the ideal of objectivity.

The indexing model introduced earlier in the book reveals several patterns of news coverage. When officials are split on an issue, with two or more sides faithfully representing broad viewpoints among knowledgeable experts or the public, the news tends to offer a broad spectrum of credible views. However, when one faction in power dominates a political situation and there is no substantial opposition, then the news tends toward one-sided coverage, even if that side is out of touch with important evidence or popular viewpoints. In still other cases, there may be two sides in conflict, but one or both represent narrow interests or misleading positions, resulting in "balanced" news that contains serious information biases. Because authorities often filter what they say and do through political calculations, this makes the news more a window on power and political strategy inside government than a platform that examines politics critically in some broader factual or democratic context.

Thus, the methods used by mainstream journalists to achieve balance, fairness, or objectivity can produce results that seem anything but balanced, fair, or objective. In an acerbic look at how so many competing news organizations manage to converge on such an unhelpful information format, Joan Didion describes the code of Washington reporting: "The genuflection toward 'fairness' is a familiar newsroom piety. In practice the excuse for a good deal of autopilot reporting and lazy thinking but in theory a benign ideal. In Washington, however, a community in which the management of the news has become the single overriding preoccupation of the core industry, what 'fairness' has often come to mean is a scrupulous passivity, an agreement to cover the story not as it is occurring but as it is presented, which is to say, as it is manufactured."[4]

Criticisms of objectivity as practiced by the mainstream press have been around for some time. The epigram above by Hunter Thompson was written in the 1970s and reflected an earlier counterjournalism movement, popularized by Thompson, Didion, Tom Wolfe, and others, that combined long-form reporting with stylistic elements of fiction. Today's critics are more inclined toward evidence-based, watchdog journalism that holds officials accountable for false statements, empty spin, and breaches of public trust. This chapter explores the origins of objective journalism, with an eye toward explaining the paradox of how the news is biased not in spite of, but precisely because of, the professional journalism standards intended to prevent bias. The central idea is that the professional practices embodying journalism norms of independence and objectivity also create conditions that systematically favor the reporting of official perspectives. At the same time, the postures of independence and objectivity created by these professional norms give the impression that the resulting news is the best available representation of reality. In short, professional journalism standards introduce a distorted political perspective into the news yet legitimize that perspective as broad and realistic. This professional stance is increasingly challenged, but it is still the hallmark of the legacy press. The following discussion explores how this odd perspective emerged and why it persists.

The Professional Vocabulary of Objectivity, Fairness, Balance, and Truth

Journalists sometimes substitute terms, such as "accuracy," "fairness," "balance," or "truth" in place of "objectivity" to describe the prime goal that guides their reporting. Objectivity is a tough standard to achieve, particularly with so many critics and citizens charging that journalists today do not even come close to achieving it. "Accuracy," "balance," and "fairness" are softer terms. They seem to be more reasonable reporting goals in light of all the obstacles to objectivity:

- The values inherent in political events
- The deceptions of newsmakers
- The difficulty of achieving a wholly neutral point of view
- The impossibility of covering all the sides and gathering all the facts
- The rush to meet unreasonably short deadlines
- The pressures of breaking information online and the 24/7 news cycle

Because of these difficulties, the press is sure to come under fire no matter how hard it tries to present the facts. To many embattled journalists, accuracy, balance, and fairness sound like the best defenses against criticism from all sides. In a sign of the times, the Society of Professional Journalists dropped the word "objectivity" from its code of ethics after many years of featuring it as the core principle. However, journalism historian David Mindich notes that "objectivity" was replaced in the code with terms such as "truth," "accuracy," and "comprehensiveness." In his view, the decision to replace "objectivity" with these synonyms signals that many journalists are tired of defending an embattled word yet remain committed to its meaning and guiding spirit.[5] There is strong evidence that no matter which name it is called, the vast majority of journalists subscribe to an ideal of objectivity. For example, in a national survey conducted by the Pew Research Center for the People and the Press, three-quarters of journalists polled agreed that their ideal standard is to report the "true, accurate, and widely agreed upon account of an event."[6]

These reporting standards are so familiar and commonsense that they seem to have been put there to serve obvious and laudable purposes. Yet the following discussion suggests that the evolution of norms such as objectivity, fairness, and balance had more to do with the somewhat haphazard course of the developing news business than with the rational or determined pursuit of truth. In short, practices were dictated more by historical, technological, or business circumstances than by rational human design. The resulting reporting practices later became rationalized as good and even noble things.

The Curious Origins of Objective Journalism

It is tempting to think that modern journalism values such as objectivity derive from an enlightened evolutionary process. Yet the historical story involves a radical shift from a nineteenth-century press supported largely by political parties to an early twentieth-century model based on the sale of advertising. Journalism historian Gerald Baldasty describes this transformation in these terms: "In the early nineteenth century, editors defined news as a political instrument intended to promote party interests. By century's end, editors defined news within a business context to ensure or increase revenues. News had become commercialized."[7]

In the early days of the American republic, the news was anything but objective. Most newspapers were either funded by or otherwise sympathetic to particular political parties, interests, or ideologies. Reporting involved the political interpretation of events. People bought a newspaper knowing what its political perspective was and knowing that political events would be filtered through that perspective. In many respects, this is a sensible way to approach the news about politics. If one knows the biases of a reporter, it is possible to control for them in interpreting the account of events. Moreover, if reporting is explicitly politically oriented, different reporters can look at the same event from different points of view. The idea was that people would encounter different points of view and bring them into face-to-face debates about what the best course of action might be—an idea that came directly from some of the nation's founders, such as Thomas Jefferson.

The commitment to political analysis in news reporting began to fade as the nature of politics itself changed after the age of Andrew Jackson from the late 1830s on. As Baldasty notes, politicians became less dependent on party papers to communicate with voters as, among other things, strict norms against candidates campaigning directly in public began to change.[8] With these changes, party financial support for papers began to dry up. The early partisan papers were modest operations with small, local readerships. These small and increasingly impoverished newspapers could not compete for large audiences as the nation and its communication system grew.

As the country grew, the economics of the news business changed. For example, the population began to move to the cities, creating mass audiences for the news. Also, the expansion of the American territory during the nineteenth century created a need for the rapid and large-scale distribution of national news. Breakthroughs in printing and communication technologies made possible the production of cheap mass media news that could be gathered in the morning on the East Coast and distributed by evening on the West Coast.

These and other patterns in the development of the nation produced dramatic changes in the news. By 1848, a group of newspapers made the first great step toward standardized news by forming the Associated Press

(AP).[9] Pooling reporters and distributing the same story to member news organizations (today numbering 1,400) turned the news into a profitable mass-market commodity. The broad marketability of the news meant that it had to be stripped of its overt political messages so that it would be appealing to news organizations of all political persuasions. An early prototype of objective reporting was born. Moreover, the need to send short messages through an overloaded mail system was followed by the transmission of national news over telegraph wires that also dictated a simplified, standardized reporting format. The *who, what, where, when*, and *why* of an event could be transmitted economically and reconstructed and embellished easily on the other end. The "inverted pyramid" style that places the most important facts early in a story and lesser details toward the end may have originated with Secretary of War Edwin Stanton, who wrote a series of important communiqués about the Civil War.[10]

As the market for news grew, the demand for reporters grew along with it. Whereas writing persuasive political essays required skill in argumentation and political analysis, it was far easier to compose stories, which are the basic media for communicating about everyday events. The use of stories also guaranteed that the news would be intelligible to the growing mass-news audience that could easily digest and share simple narratives.

As this account suggests, the elements of objective reporting arose in piecemeal fashion, at very different points in time, and often under odd circumstances. The overlapping effects of communication technology, economic development, and social change gave rise to large-scale news-gathering and news-marketing organizations. Along with these organizations came a standardized set of reporting practices. As noted above, news services like the AP ushered in the *documentary report*. The use of wire transmission, along with untrained reporters, promoted the shift to the *story form*. The discovery that drama sold newspapers promoted the first *adversarial reporting*. Early reporters were rather like provocateurs stirring up controversy and conflict in order to generate dramatic material for their stories. Thus, the collection of practices that eventually came to define objective reporting appeared, one at a time, by the end of the 1800s.[11] However, the idea that they might be called "objective journalism" did not occur until after the turn of the century. This retrospective labeling of objectivity was, in part, an ennobling claim by a journalism trade looking to become a profession. It was also a rhetorical appeal to an increasingly educated middle-class news audience who responded favorably to those claims about professionalism.

There was initially stiff competition between this highbrow press and the tabloids or "scandal sheets" (also known as the yellow press) at the turn of the twentieth century. The tabloids ran highly sensationalized versions of news, marketed to a less-educated, working-class population seeking escape as much as information from the media. By the 1920s, urban life and local politics were increasingly dominated by an affluent middle class of business and professional people with formal education. Representing the news as objective, nonpartisan, and tasteful was an effective marketing ploy geared to the lifestyle of this group. Consider, for example, the early slogans of the *New York Times*, "All the News That's Fit to Print" and "It Will Not Soil the Breakfast Cloth."[12] High-minded standards of good taste guaranteed that a news product would be inoffensive to the mass market. This professional image of mainstream journalism became a convenient means to discredit the muckrakers on the journalistic left and the sensationalistic scandal sheets on the political right.[13]

This new professionalism was fed by growing concerns among intellectuals following World War I that democracy faced many challenges that could be addressed by a professional press dedicated to the mission of providing objective information to the public.[14] This noble purpose helped define a movement for a professional press and a code of objective journalism. Led by persuasive intellectuals like Walter Lippmann, journalists began to regard objective reporting as both a description of their existing work practices and as a high moral imperative.[15]

In these ways, journalism, like many professions, developed a set of business practices first and then endowed those practices with an impressive professional rationale. The logic of objective reporting began with a solid business rationale: political neutrality attracted a wider audience than partisan reporting.[16] As bureaucratic organizations grew in response to economic success, professional editorial review practices became expedient means of processing the huge flow of news. Successive generations of reporters began to regard their work as a skilled occupation that should demand higher status and better wages. The move toward a professional status both enhanced the social image of reporting and paved the way for higher wages by restricting the entry of newcomers off the street into the journalism ranks. Professionalism meant that formal training and screening could be required for skills that had been acquired formerly on the job.[17] As a result, journalism programs emerged at universities and began to formalize and refine the received practices as professional standards. Perhaps the best capsule summary of this curious transition of journalism from a business into a profession is Lou Cannon's observation that what began "as a technique became a value."[18]

Putting Professional Norms into Practice

After conducting a review of journalism texts, David Mindich found a common set of orientations that reporters learn as the defining elements of objectivity: *detachment, nonpartisanship, reliance on "facts," balance*, and the use of the *inverted pyramid* writing style (which puts the most important facts in the lead paragraph).[19] These core attitudes are translated into a set of standard working habits and methods. Based on the work of Mindich and others, the standards and practices that embody objective journalism include the following:[20]

1. The professional journalist assumes *the role of a politically neutral adversary*, critically examining both sides of an issue and thereby ensuring impartial coverage. Journalists see adversarialism as an important counterpoint to becoming too close to their sources, ensuring detachment and balance in their reporting. As discussed in the last chapter, the adversarial role has been corrupted by "gotcha" journalism in recent years, but many journalists and scholars continue to think of this as adversarialism.

2. The journalist resists the temptation to discuss the seamy, sensationalistic side of the news by *observing prevailing social standards of decency and good taste*. Standards of taste establish boundaries as a story makes its way toward becoming "objectified." Like adversarialism, this norm has also become strained with the increase of sex scandals and tabloid coverage in the mainstream press. Many critics wonder whether news organizations are losing their commitment to sticking to important issues and avoiding rumor and sensationalism.

3. The truthfulness and factuality of the news is guaranteed by *the use of documentary reporting practices* that permit reporters to transmit to the public "just the facts" that can be observed or supported with credible sources.

4. News objectivity is also established by *the use of a standardized format for reporting the news: the story*. Stories serve as implicit checks on news content by requiring reporters to gather all the facts (who, what, when, where, how, etc.) needed to construct a consistent and plausible account of an incident. Because stories are also the most common means of everyday communication about events, they enable the public to judge the consistency and plausibility of news accounts. Within the story format, journalists use other conventions, such as writing in an inverted pyramid style,

meaning, as noted earlier, that the most important elements of the story appear in the lead paragraph.

5. Because these methods apply to different beats and topics, news organizations often favor the idea that reporters should be generalists, not specialists. The use of standardized reporting formats enables any reporter to cover any kind of story, further separating reporters from personal bias vis-à-vis the subject matter of the news. The *practice of training reporters as generalists*, as opposed to specialists, also helps minimize undesirable interpretive tendencies in news reporting.[21] In recent years, specialization has appeared in areas such as the environment, health, science, and technology, but many key areas such as business and politics still favor generalists.

6. Practices 1 through 5 are regulated and enforced by the important practice of *editorial review*, which is a check against violations of the practices and norms of the profession.

The following discussion shows how each element of objective journalism actively constructs the standardized information formatting of mainstream news. This standardization gives thousands of news organizations a standing within the institution of the (legacy) press. Scholars such as Timothy Cook, Bartholomew Sparrow, and Rodney Benson have argued that the remarkable uniformity of the practices that define the American press make it a governing institution without which politics and politicians could not function.[22]

THE ADVERSARIAL ROLE OF THE PRESS

If reporters were always adversarial in their dealings with politicians, they would face a serious dilemma: the news could end up discrediting the institutions and values on which it depends for credibility. In some ways, the drift toward a more cynical, game-framing tone in recent years has pushed the press toward just that outcome, as public confidence in both the press and institutions such as Congress has plummeted. To a still important degree, however, maintaining the illusion of news objectivity depends on the general reliance on official views to certify reports as credible and valid. As sociologist Gaye Tuchman put it:

Challenging the legitimacy of offices holding centralized information dismantles the news net. If all of officialdom is corrupt, all its facts and occurrences must be viewed as alleged facts and alleged occurrences. Accordingly, to fill the news columns and air time of the news product, news organizations would have to find an alternative and economical method of locating occurrences and constituent facts acceptable as news. For example, if the institutions of everyday life are delegitimated, the facts tendered by the Bureau of Marriage Licenses would be suspect. One could no longer call the bureau to learn whether Robert Jones and Fay Smith had married. In sum, amassing mutually self-validating facts simultaneously accomplishes the doing of newswork and reconstitutes the everyday world of offices and factories, of politics and bureaucrats, of bus schedules and class rosters as historically given.[23]

It is equally true, of course, that the news would also lose its image of objectivity if reporters catered too openly to the propaganda interests of public officials and government institutions. If neither extreme adversarialism nor its polar opposite support the illusion of news objectivity, then there is an obvious implication: much adversarial behavior on the part of the press is ritualistic, something that is selectively applied in keeping within the cooperative interests of reporters and officials. A ritualistic posture of antagonism between press and government creates the appearance of mutual independence while still keeping most news content in line with the political perspectives certified by authorities. Such ritualistic posturing dramatizes the myths of a free press and an open government that have long defined American democracy. It is the nature of rituals to evoke such myths and beliefs without challenging them.[24]

If the adversarial relationship is a ritual that both mystifies and legitimizes the reporting of narrow political messages, then the following characteristics should be observed: (a) the incidence of criticism and confrontation will occur in regular patterns, as a matter of everyday reporting orientation, as opposed to just when there is a serious political issue at stake; (b) challenges and charges will aim to provoke personal mistakes or political confrontations between politicians rather than deeper investigations of issues; (c) charges against officials will be restricted to them personally and generally separated from their institutions and offices; and finally, (d) these characteristics will pertain equally to routine news coverage (e.g., reporters' beats) and nonroutine coverage (e.g., crises and scandals).

As illustration of these points, consider C. Jack Orr's study of earlier presidential press conferences.[25] Analyzing data from a sample of Kennedy, Johnson, and Nixon press conferences, Orr found that the proportion of hostile or critical questions was virtually constant across presidents, conferences, issue categories, and political contexts.[26] Not only did the incidence of confrontational questions fall into a routine pattern, but nearly all hostile questions were personal in nature. Yet many of those personal questions also signaled clear deference to office and institution. Moreover, questions that could have held the line on an issue contained open invitations to the president to redefine the issue or dismiss the entire question. Based on these patterns, Orr concluded that the adversarial postures of press and president create a dramatic image of journalistic aggressiveness while communicating a subtle message of institutional deference.

Broad ritualistic elements have also been observed in the reporting of less routine events such as scandals and crises, although some observers have argued that crises and scandals have become routine news events, complete with standard reporting formulas.[27] For example, David Altheide and Robert Snow showed how a scandal involving an aide to Jimmy Carter was cast quickly into a standard reporting formula that emphasized political damage to the president while offering little measure of the importance of the issue itself.[28] Similar patterns ran through the Whitewater scandal involving Bill and Hillary Clinton, as they were subjected to guilt by association with a number of shady real estate dealings. Despite saturation coverage implying the possibility of serious wrongdoing, few members of the public ever understood what the scandal was about. Such scandals and rumors leave residues of image damage and doubt, as illustrated by Barack Obama's continuous engagement with questions about his birth certificate and religious beliefs.

For their part, politicians contribute to the enduring antagonism ritual by routinely attacking the press as liberal, biased, or hostile. Such attacks frequently appear in elite publications and occupy the agendas of business, government, and journalism symposia.[29] Occasionally, such charges are dramatized through formal political attacks, such as the ones during the McCarthy era and the Nixon administration. One analyst found the Nixon-Agnew attacks on the press so ritualized that he interpreted them in terms of ethological concepts of animal aggression and territorial defense.[30]

None of this means that politicians or the press take their often antagonistic relations lightly. Indeed, the mark of a good ritual is that those involved are deeply moved by it. For example, Bill Clinton raged in a *Rolling Stone* interview with William Greider that he was the most poorly treated and misrepresented of presidents.[31] Clinton was hardly alone. The list of presidents claiming this distinction is a long one, dating from George Washington and Thomas Jefferson to Lyndon Johnson and Richard Nixon. Few have taken their press treatment as personally as Nixon, who kept a personal enemies list, which included a good number of journalists who were singled out for wiretaps, IRS audits, and other special punishments.[32] Although the press ritual can be quite animated and engrossing, both for those who play it and for the audiences who watch it, this should not distract us from understanding what this ritual accomplishes: narrowing the focus of human attention to convincingly exclude large categories of more important issues from public discourse.

The press-politics adversarial rituals work as long as neither side undermines its credibility by questioning the system that legitimizes their roles. Even Watergate, long regarded as the model of modern investigative reporting, stopped short of challenging the authority of government or pushing too far into institutional failings. Most of the focus was on the misdeeds of Nixon and his associates, and little attention was paid to flaws in the secrecy and espionage systems that may have contributed to presidential abuses of power. For the most part, the press pack settled for the limits established by congressional investigations. Despite the rich possibilities for a story that might go well beyond the personal failings of one flawed president, the press avoided them all in favor of reporting the steady stream of leaks from a fabled inside source nicknamed Deep Throat (later revealed to be the second in command at the FBI), along with the activities of various congressional investigations at work on the case. This brand of investigative reporting ignored questions about institutional problems or abnormalities in favor of dramatizing the personal culpability of the most publicly visible actors involved.[33] Whereas all the institutional paths for the story led to questions of change and reform (questions the press chose largely to avoid), the personal drama held out the promise of returning the political system to normal as soon as the individuals were accused, charged, and removed from office. When Nixon resigned from office under threat of impeachment, NBC correspondent Roger Mudd led the nation in the cheer "The system worked!" Even at the level of personal melodrama, "The system worked" seems an ironic ending. After all, the system pardoned the worst offender, gave light sentences to most of the others, and turned criminals like G. Gordon Liddy into media celebrities in the process.

Perhaps the most important outcome of Watergate was the myth of a crusading press that uncovered the crimes. The Watergate news story reported by *Washington Post* reporters Bob Woodward and Carl Bernstein was fed by leaks from the FBI, the Justice Department, and congressional investigators. Stories based on the leaks built public support for continued investigations that finally led to the resignation of the president. The movie *All the President's Men* (based on the Woodward and Bernstein best-selling book) became a popular classic, and the myth of the crusading American press was launched.

Standards of decency and taste aim to keep the focus of news on important issues and away from the seamy, sensationalistic aspects of political life. These standards have clearly changed in recent years, as the lines between news and entertainment have become blurred and moral standards in society have relaxed somewhat. Among the signs that moral sensitivities have softened from earlier times is the volume of sex scandals in the news. For example, the sex-drenched coverage of the Clinton-Lewinsky affair suggests a tabloid trend in the press. During that scandal, audiences learned of oral sex in the Oval Office, presidential semen stains on a blue dress, and graphic sexual accounts published in the report of special prosecutor Kenneth Starr. Such a media spectacle would be hard to imagine even ten years earlier. While an earlier era of media morality would have avoided such things, current moral standards seem to involve publicizing them with expressions of shock and disapproval. Even as they drag up seamy details, journalists are also quick to pronounce moralistic judgments. It would have been useful during the Lewinsky affair to do a count of the number of raised eyebrows on the Sunday morning news shows or the numbers of shocked and disdainful expressions uttered by the cast of journalists-turned-shouting-pundits. Whereas an earlier generation of journalistic morality police may not have published such material in the first place, a later generation driven to sensationalism will publish first and then decry its sorry content.

Although the media seem to have become obsessed with the private lives of politicians and other public figures, there are other areas that continue to be avoided, although some with growing difficulty. For example, graphic images of gruesome death, profane language, erotic art, or depictions of the human anatomy seldom appear in the news. Even as standards of news taste evolve, there remains a curious strain of middle-American morality that the mainstream press long ago adopted as part of its professional code. Even coverage of scandals generally carries the moral message of family values and the enduring obligation of politicians to uphold them. As for the collection of things regarded as too tasteless, offensive, or obscene to include in the news, excluding them may often be at odds with the actual events that reporters witness. For example, it took more than two years during the 1980s for the mainstream media to explain that one way in which the dreaded disease AIDS (acquired immune deficiency syndrome) is spread, among other means, is through anal intercourse. The threat posed by a large-scale, life-threatening AIDS epidemic would seem to call for rapid delivery of as much explicit information as possible to the public. Yet in the early, panicky years of the disease, the decency code governed information content about AIDS. Early stories suggested that the disease was transmitted "not through casual contact" but through the "exchange of bodily fluids." As one editor put it, "We would make the reader guess what was going on rather than use the term 'anal intercourse.' . . . We wouldn't spell it out."[34] It took years for consensus to emerge in the media that informing the public about health risks was more important than censoring offensive language from the news.

What is the obligation of the press to communicate information that people may not want to hear, read, or see? Imagine, for a moment, that you were an editor for a news organization covering the first Gulf War in 1991. The United States just routed the Iraqi army from Kuwait City, and the fleeing army has been attacked by American airpower, creating a scene that was widely described as "the highway of death." The carnage was so distressing that some of the American pilots involved asked the commanders to stop it. Behind the scenes, a high-level debate was raging about whether to go on with the war, knowing that it would produce a massacre of the enemy's disorganized army, or whether to stop it and leave the enemy with a substantial portion of its fighting force intact for the future. A photojournalist visited the highway of death and took a terrifying picture of the remains of an Iraqi soldier burned alive with a hideous expression on his face, his arms raised in the macabre position in which he died while trying to climb out of his flaming vehicle. It was an image right out of a horror movie.

Would you run the picture? Why not run a picture in the news that is no worse than an image that millions of people might pay money to see in a horror movie? More to the point, why not run a photo that appeared in leading English and French newspapers on the grounds that it brought home the fact that at least 100,000 Iraqis died in the war, and people should be forced to consider the human consequences of decisions to go to war? However, the newspaper and magazine editors of America never even had the chance to struggle with these issues because the leading photo wire service that had the option to buy and distribute the picture censored it at the source. The picture never even went out over the wires. The AP editor explained that he did not buy and distribute the photo because he already knew what the reaction of newspaper editors would be: "Newspapers will tell us, 'We can't present pictures like that for people to look at over breakfast.'"[35] The picture editor at *Time* magazine later said this about the picture: "It's dramatic. It's horrific. It says it all about war." However, he admitted that even if he had seen it in time, *Time* probably would not have printed it because, "whenever we run a picture like that, we're heavily criticized. We get a lot of reader mail."[36]

Should such images be part of the news? Are they worse than images commonly shown in movies? How should the news limit its representations of reality? The case of the photo of the Iraqi soldier and many similar episodes from recent wars raise the troublesome question of whether people in a country at war should see comforting images of war as they prefer to think about it, or whether they should be stimulated, even shocked, into thinking about the consequences of political decisions to go to war.

Many such decisions on what to show and how to describe important events are difficult ones. When the ISIS army began to take territory in the Middle East, it also launched a propaganda war that included videos of executions and beheadings. One incident involved a video uploaded to YouTube showing the beheading of American journalist James Foley in 2014. The mixed reactions of news organizations ranged from showing the images, to refusing to show them to avoid shocking children and other sensitive viewers, to deciding not to give publicity to ISIS propaganda. These ethical considerations reveal the spectrum of difficulty in applying moral standards.[37]

The morality code in the news is among the most rapidly changing aspects of legacy journalism. In part, this is due to changing morals in society. In addition, recent court rulings have rolled back federal regulations against profanity on the air. The rise of cable programming has further relaxed standards on language, nudity, and graphic images. And the availability of original images on YouTube and other digital sites makes cleansing them from the news an empty gesture for those who want to find them (although YouTube has taken down a number of beheading videos). While news organizations continue to have discussions on how to apply standards of decency, the lines are increasingly difficult to draw.

DOCUMENTARY REPORTING PRACTICES

Objective reporting assumes that journalists do not embellish their stories, advocate particular interpretations of ambiguous events, or otherwise make up the news. These principles define the practice of documentary reporting. Reporters trained in the documentary method report only the information that they have witnessed and only the facts that credible sources have confirmed. Although the goals of documentary reporting are hard to fault, in practice the method creates a trap for journalists confronted with staged political performances. Only in rare cases, when performances are flawed or when behind-the-scenes staging is revealed, can reporters document what they otherwise already knew to be the case: the news event in question was staged for propaganda purposes. The problem, as Daniel

Boorstin pointed out, is that manufactured news events, or pseudo-events, contain their own self-supporting and self-fulfilling documentation. Thus the documentary method highlights the very aspects of events that are designed to be reported, blurring the underlying reality of the situation.[38] The paradox of the documentary method is clear: the more perfectly an event is staged, the more documentable and hence reportable it becomes.

A more common practice reflecting the "new cynicism" that seems to characterize the press in recent times is to frame political situations as games between manipulative actors. This tendency is described by various scholars noted in chapter 1, including Kathleen Hall Jamieson, Regina Lawrence, and Thomas Patterson, and discussed as one of the information biases in the news in chapter 2. Reporting the political game based on spin and leaks from rivals may continue to look like objective reporting to journalists, but it may undermine the sense of news authority on the part of audiences.

THE USE OF STORIES AS STANDARDIZED NEWS FORMATS

Although adopting the story as the basic news unit also had economic roots, stories quickly became justified under the norm of objective journalism. Stories can be defended as standardized and mechanical means of communicating information. This representation gives journalists a claim to a universal methodology of objective reporting. The problem with this definition is that it is a very selective rendition of what storytelling is all about. Telling a story requires choices about what information to include, what words to assign to the included information, and how to tie together all the chosen symbols into a coherent whole. These choices in turn depend on assessing the audience, deciding what point to make to that audience, and choosing what plot techniques (flashbacks, sequencing, character development, climax, etc.) will best make that point. In short, stories are not mirrors of events.[39]

A well-constructed story may be plausible, but plausibility and truth in the world of storytelling have little necessary connection.[40] An obvious implication of these features of storytelling is that they give reporters room to emphasize dramatic and narrative aspects of events.[41] Edward Epstein suggests that the use of artistic (i.e., literary and dramatic) forms in news construction is encouraged by editors, one of whom even issued a memo containing formal instructions about how to incorporate dramatic structure into stories.[42] Herbert Gans notes the frequency with which reporters "restage" aspects of stories to heighten their dramatic qualities.[43]

The dramatic license in storytelling creates a tension: the wholesale invention of news plots would place enormous strains on the norm of objective reporting. This tension between the value of dramatic news and the commitment to documentary reporting helps explain the receptivity of news organizations to events that are staged dramatically by news sources. Staged events are designed to be documented, and their dramatic features are built in. So important is the dramatic element in political performances that they are often judged for newsworthiness on this criterion. Gans observed that "an exciting story boosts morale; and when there is a long drought of exciting stories, they [reporters] become restless. . . . Some magazine writers, left 'crabby' by a drought of dramatic domestic news, joked about their readiness to be more critical of the President and other public officials for their failure to supply news that would 'make adrenaline flow.'"[44]

The use of stories further constrains news content by promoting the use of standardized plots in news reporting. Any communication network based on stories will become biased toward particular themes. For example, criminal trials are dominated by such familiar plots as mistaken identity, victim of circumstances, and others relevant to the legal judgment of cases.[45]

In politics, consensus and legitimacy can be promoted through the frequent use of dominant values, beliefs, and myths of the political culture.[46] Gans has noted that the news is dominated by a remarkably small number of recurring themes. These plot devices include ethnocentrism (America first, America-the-generous, America-the-embattled, etc.), altruistic democracy, responsible capitalism, and individualism, among others.[47]

Political performances scripted around routine themes legitimize the status quo at the price of severely limiting the range of political discourse.[48] The formula-story syndrome enables reporters to use plots to screen and organize facts so that few details are left dangling, and the resulting story can be viewed as an exhaustive representation of reality. This naive approach to objectivity gives news writing a mystical quality described by Robert Darnton: "Big stories develop in special patterns and have an archaic flavor, as if they were metamorphoses or *Ur*-stories that have been lost in the depths of time. . . . News writing is heavily influenced by stereotypes and by preconceptions of what 'the story' should be. Without preestablished categories of what constitutes 'news,' it is impossible to sort out experience."[49]

Just as stories lock in the narrow political messages of routine news events, they can introduce distortions into investigative reporting. Stories, by definition, encapsulate events, making them seem self-contained and independent of external forces. Yet the tips provided by inside sources to investigative reporters are often motivated by the source's own political considerations. These motives are seldom included in the stories fashioned by reporters. Recall, for example, the earlier discussion that the Watergate story based on the investigative reporting of Woodward and Bernstein may have been only part of a much larger political scandal (see chapter 2). The source of the inside information necessary to keep the story unfolding seemed to provide only information that would turn the story toward the Oval Office. Epstein noted that there might have been other political actors who could have been caught up in the Watergate scandal had the reporters not encapsulated the issues in a story centered on the president and his men.[50]

It took 30 years to find out who provided the initial leaked information that trapped Nixon within the damaging Watergate story. The obvious need to protect the confidentiality of sources is not the only or even the most important reason the political contexts of news stories are seldom disclosed. The elevation of the story form to a professional practice places an even more subtle prohibition on revealing the politics behind political news. It would be devastating to the simple view of news reality to show that behind many big stories are other stories that come closer to revealing the true politics of the situation. As Epstein explained, the story-behind-the-story approach to news reporting would blow the cover off the normative claim that objective reality can be encapsulated somehow in stories.

REPORTERS AS GENERALISTS

Stories play another role in journalism as a universal reporting methodology employed by all reporters, whether of politics, sports, or business. Most reporters are trained as generalists who are able to write stories on any subject. Although a small percentage end up reporting in a specialized area such as science or fashion, the majority change beats periodically and pride themselves on their ability to cover any news story.[51] The emphasis in the profession on training reporters as generalists has obvious origins and payoffs. As Gans noted, "The news is still gathered mostly by generalists. One reason is economic, for general reporters earn less and are more productive. Beat reporters can rarely produce more than one story per television program or magazine issue, while general reporters can be asked, when necessary, to complete two or more assignments within the same period."[52]

Despite these obvious economic advantages, generalism is justified almost exclusively in normative terms. A key element of the journalism code is informing the average citizen. The use of generalists who tell simple stories is justified as the best means of presenting comprehensible information to the average person. If a reporter has special knowledge or expertise on a topic, he or she may run the risk of complicating a story or violating the story form altogether by lapsing into technical analysis. Editors and news producers seem to widely believe that the general public cannot follow news produced by specialized reporters. For example, Epstein reported this response by an NBC News executive to a Justice Department suggestion that the TV networks use correspondents with special knowledge of ghetto problems to cover urban riots: "Any good journalist should be able to cover a riot in an unfamiliar setting. . . . A veneer of knowledgeability in a situation like this could be less than useless."[53] In another case, Gans reported a comment by an executive producer to his economics reporter following a good story on a complicated subject. "You scare me with your information; I think we'll put you on another beat."[54] Gans also noted that many specialists shared a general anxiety that they were becoming too knowledgeable for the tastes of their audiences or their superiors.

Although generalism is justified normatively as a necessary concession to a mass audience, the audience may pay a high political price in exchange for the alleged gains in news comprehension. Generalist reporters are often at the mercy of the news source. In technical areas, they are seldom qualified to ask critical questions.[55] As a result, reporters may have to ask news sources for guidelines about appropriate questions. Even when generalists are assigned to fairly straightforward political stories, they may have to fashion their stories almost entirely from official pronouncements and the story angles pursued by other reporters.[56] Because generalists are more dependent on their sources than are specialists, the odds are even greater that they will report fabricated events. Moreover, generalists may be less likely than specialists to spot flaws in performances that would make it possible to expose the contrived nature of an event. For example, Gans noted of generalists: "Not knowing their sources well enough to discount self-serving information, they may report an opinion or a hopeful guess—for example, the size of an organization's membership—as a statistical fact. In this way, enterprising politicians sometimes get inflated estimates of their support into the news. . . . Occasionally, general reporters may cover only one side of a story without ever knowing that there are other sides."[57]

This generalization about generalists applies even to areas in which we might expect more perspective and sophistication. For example, most business reporting seriously neglects the political or social impacts (or the inner politics) of corporations in modern life. Instead, business news tends to be a mix of shallow reports of mergers and profit analyses, alongside personality profiles of corporate celebrities such as Donald Trump or Bill Gates. As noted by Diana Henriques of the *New York Times*, one of the relatively few investigative business reporters in the mainstream news business, even business editors at prestigious news organizations often have little sense of big business as a social or political force. Indeed, because these editors often parachute into the business desks as generalists with little understanding of economics or the inner workings of corporations, their news assignments and decisions about what to run reinforce the tendency to report a shallow mix of profit and loss and profiles of companies and executives. Lacking much depth or perspective, such business news implicitly promotes the myths of business virtue, the superior rationality of free markets, and the prowess of chief executives.[58]

Of course, executives that seem brilliant this year may be the subjects of scandal and malfeasance the next. When the giant Enron Corporation went bankrupt in 2001 and the unbelievable story of its shady pyramid schemes and corrupt accounting practices came to light, there was little in the business press to prepare the public for the spectacle. Enron CEO Kenneth Lay was regularly profiled as a business genius, friend of the president, and noted philanthropist. Even the *Wall Street Journal* investigation of Enron the year before stopped short of blowing the whistle on the company because the journalist assigned to the story could not understand how the company actually worked. Similarly, the political story of Enron's involvement in shaping Bush administration energy policy was not even hinted at until after the collapse of the company in a cloud of deception and corruption.

Perhaps the biggest missed business story of the century was the global financial crisis that began in 2008 and swept the planet, throwing the world economy into the worst downturn since the Great Depression of the 1930s. At its core, the problem involved selling home mortgages to unqualified buyers and then distributing the mortgages to millions of investors through dubious financial products that banks were ultimately unable to justify, or even reassemble to establish ownership of many properties. The result was a housing bubble that burst, leading to the collapse of a number of big banks, and resulting in an epidemic of home foreclosures, bank failures, and government bailouts. While some members of the legacy press claimed that stories were published on the dubious lending practices, many critics argued that the prominence of those reports was dwarfed by business channel euphoria about soaring home values and bank profits. More importantly, the lack of investigative reporting made it impossible to put the story together until it was too late.

It is hard to imagine that the practice of editors reviewing, checking, and approving reporters' preliminary accounts of events could be criticized. The review policies of most news organizations are represented as ensuring that the professional practices discussed above will be used in reporting the news. In a sense, editorial review does serve this function, thereby also ensuring the news distortion produced by these journalistic practices. Editorial review exerts its own influence on the political content of the news as well. Editors are not just the overseers of news production; they are accountable to management for the competitive position of their news product in the marketplace. As a result, editors and owners (or managers) typically develop guidelines that their reporters must follow in order to be successful and professionally respectable in their eyes. Studies of the internal workings of news organizations make it clear that these editorial pressures are major influences on reporters and on the political content of news.[59]

Editorial filtering might not be so worrisome if it were idiosyncratic, giving each news organization its own perspective and encouraging reporters to be different. However, the safest editorial course is often to cover the same stories in the same ways as other organizations while packaging them differently, using brand-name anchors, catchy theme music, or bold headlines to attract the audience. It is no secret that most editors take their leads from the wire services and the prestige papers, such as the *New York Times*, the *Washington Post*, or the *Wall Street Journal*. The reliance on the wire services and the prestige papers as implicit standardizing mechanisms applies to both print and broadcast media.[60] In addition, editors tend to standardize their product further by comparing it with the competition. It is easier for them to justify similarities in the coverage of stories than to account for differences between organizations. To put it simply, the transparency of the objectivity or fairness claim becomes most evident when the coverage of one organization differs from the others and, as a result, journalists must defend it against queries by publishers, politicians, and the public. The best defense of objectivity is contained in the implicit standardization of editorial review practices.

The obvious political consequence of standardized editorial policies was captured nicely by Edwin Diamond, who noted that editorial practices reinforce the worst tendency in the news business to stereotype stories. News stereotypes conform to the major plot outlines of fabricated news performances and give the news its obvious status quo bias. As Diamond notes, none of this bias can be attributed directly to political motives on the part of reporters. On the contrary, the professional standards of journalists cleanse the news of such motives; yet, somehow, the resulting product does seem to display a particular slant:

> The press isn't "racist," though as the skins of the participants become darker, the lengths of the stories shrink. The press isn't "pro-Israeli," though it is very sensitive to Jewish-American feelings. The press isn't afraid of the "vested interests," though it makes sure Mobil's or Senator Scott's denials appear right along with the charges. The paranoids are wrong: there is no news conspiracy. Instead there are a lot of editors and executives making decisions about what is "the news" while constrained by lack of time, space, money, talent, and understanding, from doing the difficult and/or hidden stories.[61]

In short, the editorial review standards pointed to as the fail-safe mechanism for preventing news distortion are, paradoxically, the very things that guarantee it.

Each of these defining practices that make up objective journalism makes a direct contribution to news bias by creating or reinforcing conditions favorable to the reporting of news filtered by Washington officialdom. This collection of practices that later became institutionalized as professional journalism were developed to sell mainstream social and political values to a mass audience. By the height of the mass media era in the last half of the twentieth century, the political perspectives that dominated mainstream news had narrowed to the viewpoints of key power blocs in Washington (and the social groups they recognized), while alternative media left and right had small audiences and were easily discredited as not objective. This circular logic equated the official views that dominated the mainstream press with being somehow objective. Buying this logic was aided by a simple fact that as one reality comes to dominate all others, the dominant reality begins to seem objective. It no doubt helped that in these earlier times, the political parties were less polarized, the tone of the press was less cynical, and public confidence in the press and government was much higher.

These conditions supporting broad acceptance of the professional practices of the legacy press have all begun to change. As they suffer erosion of public confidence, journalists also face growing criticism from both political comedians and critical investigative journalists. When such high-profile challenges to professional standards are raised, legacy journalists often seem unable to engage with them convincingly. Among the most difficult of these challenges is what is commonly called the problem of "false balance" in the news, as explained in the case study in this chapter.

CASE STUDY
FALSE BALANCE IN THE NEWS

Among the mainstream reporting practices facing the greatest criticism these days is forcing balance into stories just to achieve the appearance of objectivity and impartiality. Balance seems a very reasonable reporting guideline in cases where evidence is in dispute or political conflicts are playing out over contested values in society. However, the overriding pressure to insert balance whenever possible often leads to reporters being spun by political interests that are promoting dubious or even patently false ideas. Recall, for example, the case study in chapter 4 showing how in order to achieve the appearance of balance, reporters inserted skeptics as roughly half of the sources in climate change stories. Such balance undermined the overwhelming consensus among scientists that human activity is causing dangerous levels of global warming. As is often the case, political comedy offered the best insight into the problem of false balance. John Oliver asked a prominent climate skeptic to debate Bill Nye (the science guy) on his HBO show *Last Week Tonight*. However, in order to make the discussion truly representative, Oliver also invited 96 other scientists onto the stage to voice their consensus on the human causes of global warming.[62]

The problem of false balance is compounded when dubious positions are introduced into the news through "indexing" the views of powerful politicians who take positions to stir up supporters or promote the corporate interests that finance their political careers. Such spin will continue to get into the news as long as journalistic training instills the idea that stories need to be balanced whenever possible by including two sides. As a result, the incidence of false balance has become a chronic problem for the credibility of legacy journalism.

Encouraging signs of awareness of false balance are appearing in a few news organizations. For example, the British paper the *Guardian* that publishes a US edition criticized how American papers covered a political fight in Washington that threatened a government shutdown over the budget. In October 2013, a *Guardian* headline proclaimed: "False Equivalence: How 'Balance' Makes the Media Dangerously Dumb." In the article, media reporter Bob Garfield criticized the US press for reporting the budget dispute and shutdown threat as equally the fault of both political parties when a more accurate account would point to the internal gridlock in the Republican Party between more centrist elements and Tea Party radicals. However, pointing the blame at the Republicans would appear biased (and bring on the wrath of Republican spin), so the mainstream press story blamed the Democrats and Republicans equally. It is interesting that polls showed that many citizens were able to decode the news and figure out that the forces pushing government to the brink of shutdown and debt default were in fact coming from within the Republican Party.[63]

Not only are comedians and more critical journalists exposing the strained nature of these efforts to be impartial, but audiences are pushing back against the practice as well. For example, John Oliver's efforts to introduce real balance into the climate change discussion received over five million views on YouTube. And there is now a *Wikipedia* page on false balance in the news.[64] In the end, if false balance in the news is likely to be changed, the credit may go to news audiences, who have increasing voice in responding to stories through social media and comment sections of news sites. *New York Times* public editor Margaret Sullivan wrote a column titled "Another Outbreak of 'False Balance'?" in which she said that the problem is among the top three concerns of readers, right after fairness and accuracy. She discussed the topics heading the list of reader complaints: "In the past, this discussion has arisen on the subjects of teaching evolution, the reality of climate change and whether voting fraud is widespread enough to demand 'reform' that would inhibit voting rights. (Stating the facts briefly: evolution happened; climate change is happening; and there's virtually no evidence of voter fraud.)"[65] To this list she added the national controversy over parents who resist having their children vaccinated against infectious diseases, leading to a resurgence of childhood maladies that were once controlled. The question is whether those who argue that vaccines are dangerous and may cause problems such as autism have been given too visible a public platform, when there is little or no evidence to support their position. She notes that beyond elevating the prominence of sources that are not credible, the resulting news coverage may contribute to the problem (e.g., encouraging more parents to refuse having their children vaccinated). Indeed, this concern gets at the core of false balance: in striking a ritualistic pose of objectivity to satisfy professional norms, the news actually introduces bias into public discussions that affect the outcomes of the real-world situations. Sullivan questioned the *Times*' standards editor about the problem. He said he was aware of it but had not formulated rules or guidelines. However, he felt that the newsroom was becoming more sensitive to the issue as a result of reader comments and occasional Twitter bursts about stories that try too hard to achieve balance.

Other news organizations are ahead of the *Times* in addressing the problem. The BBC, for example, has long held an internal discussion about misleading balance in its reporting. As early as 2011, the venerable British news organization issued a report that discussed "over rigid application of guidelines on impartiality," citing several areas in which there was cause for concern, including vaccines, genetically modified organisms, and climate change. That report found the problem of false balance to be compounded by generalist reporters who did not "fully understand the nature of scientific discourse." As a result, those journalists were guilty of "false impartiality" in the form of "presenting the views of tiny and unqualified minorities as if they have the same weight as the scientific consensus." The report concluded that this practice has become so widespread as to "distort public perception."[66] The controversy was fueled more recently by members of Parliament who formally called on the BBC to examine practices in which scientists were pitted against political lobbyists on news programs. A parliamentary committee on science and technology issued a report that charged: "Some editors appear to be particularly poor at determining the level of scientific expertise of contributors in debates, putting up lobbyists against top scientists as though their arguments on the science carry equal weight . . . Lobbying groups and other interested parties should be heard on the issue, [but] the BBC should be clear on the role of its interviewees and should not treat lobby groups as disinterested experts."[67]

In response to its own internal discussion and to this parliamentary report, the BBC introduced a new editorial guideline called "due weight" in which editors and reporters are trained to assess the weight of evidence in selecting and balancing sources. Bringing this discussion back home, Katrina vanden Heuval wrote an opinion column in the *Washington Post* denouncing the outdated commitment to "he said, she said" journalism, and blaming it for the confusion and lack of concern among the American public about issues such as climate change. Citing the BBC's shift in editorial policy, she called for similar introspection in the US press, describing false balance as an ethical issue: "Ultimately, forcing balance where there is none is not journalistically ethical. It is not part of the proud and essential tradition of truth telling and evaluation, either. At best, it's lazy. At worst, it's an abdication of the media's responsibility."[68]

Objectivity Reconsidered

A number of observers (including many journalists, when they are not being pressured by critical academics) have argued persuasively that whatever the news is, it is not an objective mirror of the world. Nevertheless, it would be a mistake to leap from this to the conclusion that both the ideal of objectivity and professional reporting practices do not matter. Professional standards still work in several ways that are worth noting. For example, high-minded norms such as objectivity, even if they are not always clear, hide the connection between the news and its economic, organizational, and political contexts. Above all, the objectivity norm gives the press the look of an independent social institution. Even when reporting practices distort the political content of the news, they can be rationalized and defended conveniently under the objectivity code, thereby obscuring their political effects. In this fashion, journalistic norms and reporting practices operate together to create the aforementioned information biases in the news—biases that are hidden behind the facade of independent journalism. Indeed, the cluster of practices with objectivity or fairness at their center may have the ironic result of often replacing the pursuit of truth with the best available political spin.

When viewed at a distance, claims about "objective" (or even fair and balanced) reporting rest on shaky foundations. For every source included, another is excluded. With each tightening of the plotline, meaningful connections to other issues and events become weakened. Above all, when officials are allowed to script the news, journalists give up their most important democratic function: to assess and critically examine public officials and business elites on behalf of the public interest. Yet the unstated assumption underlying the commitment to objectivity, neutrality, or balance is the reliance on official sources. Because journalists do not have a scientific method to filter political values, the implicit understanding is that the essential facts of most stories can be conveyed through the statements offered by authoritative sources.[69] The irony is that this notion of objectivity is not easy to defend: officials are known to have biases, facts are easily disputed, and the news can never include all the viewpoints that may be important to understanding events.

Although these and other factors make it impossible for the news to be objective, it is important that it seem objective or, in the terms of the trade, "believable." Perhaps most important of all, the practices and perspectives that go into creating the appearance of objectivity or believability depend heavily on striking the right balance between adversarialism and deference toward official sources. It is this balance that seems most in danger of tipping in ways that damage the credibility of news. Not only do reporters and officials seem to vacillate between cooperation and antagonistic posturing, but these displays clearly leave most of the public cold toward both sides of the news process.

Journalism and the Crisis of Credibility

As explained in chapter 2, the cynicism and game framing that dominate today's news have produced a crisis of credibility for legacy journalism. The mean-spirited tone of government and partisan politics no doubt feeds into this. A more acceptable stance might be for journalists to gain greater distance from the political spectacle rather than channel it directly to the public. Yet commercial news pressures for sensationalism, emotion, and drama feed a steady stream of cynical, game-framed politics into the 24/7 news cycle. This results in a vicious cycle as politicians use negative rhetoric and public attacks on opponents to trigger formula news.

Both news producers and politicians seem to have bought into the formula of "shock them and they will watch." The trouble is that after watching for a moment, people often change the channel.

Alternating with the channeling of spin are the feeding frenzies when the press pack attacks and exposes moments of political deceit and weakness. Recall the argument by sociologist Gaye Tuchman from earlier in this chapter: The illusion of news objectivity depends on journalists treating the world of officialdom as authoritative.[70] If this is true, then "gotcha" journalism may also have the effect of undermining public confidence in news objectivity. And so both of the press tendencies in covering politicians, being spun and playing gotcha, end up not playing well to the public. As it has evolved in recent years, the ideal of objectivity appears to be flawed, no matter how journalists try to pursue it.

Despite exposing mainstream journalism to loss of public confidence and charges of bias from all sides, the commitment to objectivity or neutrality continues to provide a defense mechanism in a difficult job: if everyone is mad at us, we must have gotten it right. Tuchman called objectivity a "strategic ritual" that offers a defense against career-threatening moments in which a risky report might receive the brunt of official or other public condemnation.[71]

When journalists and their audiences grow far apart in their perceptions of whether a defining concept such as objectivity is really being practiced properly, we know that serious tensions exist in the news system. The curious result of pursuing objectivity as defined in this chapter is that the US legacy press is perhaps the most standardized reporting system in the free world—a system that blurs the lines between objectivity and political authority, and between fact and political spin. Those who produce news and those who consume it appear to have different understandings of what they are doing. In the process, they may have lost an important measure of respect and understanding for each other. Is objectivity possible, or even desirable? That is a question for the reader now to decide. One thing, however, is sure: we live in a time where there is little consensus on just what good reporting might be. Such moments in history tend to open the way for change. As the coming chapters show, there are many new forms of journalism and new types of news organizations competing to take center stage.

7

THE POLITICAL ECONOMY
OF NEWS

Journalism is in crisis. This claim no longer invites controversy, but the nature of the crisis and possible solutions still elude broad agreement.

—Victor Pickard[1]

If we are serious about democracy, we will need to reform the media system structurally.

—Robert W. McChesney[2]

Most of the buzz about the journalism crisis is focused on the painful situation of newspapers. There are many reasons for the concern about the health of papers, not the least of which is that print news organizations produce much of the journalism content that cycles through the rest of the media system. Continued production of quality news cannot occur with the business in freefall. Newsroom staffs dropped 30 percent between 2001 and 2012, and then took another nosedive between 2012 and 2015, totaling a roughly 40 percent loss since the century began.[3] During this period, hundreds of "native digital" organizations have appeared, including *Huffington Post, Vice, Politico,* BuzzFeed, *Gawker, Vox,* and *Business Insider,* among others. They are called native digital because they have only existed online, and they use different marketing, distribution, and business models than the legacy media. One survey of these digital-only organizations counted some 468 outlets with roughly 5,000 jobs created. Much of what these organizations produce resembles news in some ways—particularly since a great deal of content is reposted or reformatted from legacy media—but much of it is different. The emerging content trends include blurring the boundaries between reporting and opinion, partnering with advertisers and other sponsors to develop content, mixing serious news with cat videos to keep traffic flowing, letting readers decide what matters, making it easy for readers to share what they like with their social networks to drive traffic to the sites, and getting free content from people who want the exposure or paying content producers according to how much traffic they attract. Despite pressures to innovate, legacy media have been held back by concerns about maintaining journalism standards and by the need to keep online formats similar to what appears in print or on the air. These concerns place severe limits on both content formats and the uses of technology in legacy media—limits that do not apply to native digital operations.

In addition to the proliferation of native digital sites that are driven by audience tastes, there is a smaller group of native digital organizations that are reinventing watchdog journalism and putting the heat to legacy media for their cozy relationships to officialdom. As discussed in the last chapter, these more serious journalism organizations include ProPublica, *The Intercept, GlobalPost,* and, on good days, *Huffington Post* and *Vox*. These sites are drawing upon earlier traditions of watchdog and investigative reporting and using custom technologies to receive, process, report, and distribute original information, often from leakers. Most of the digital watchdog sites are supported by some combination of gifts, grants, or wealthy owners. By contrast, most of the audience-driven digital operations began as start-ups infused with venture capital betting on big profits down the line.

The native digital world is engaged in a frenzy of experimentation to see what works. For example, BuzzFeed has pioneered a successful model of sponsored content that resembles its regular articles. One article was headlined "18 Hacks You Didn't Realize You Could Do with Google."[4] The text was similar to a tech column, but the content was provided by Google, and the graphics promoted ways to use the company's products. BuzzFeed has developed a profitable model and more than doubled its staff (700) and user base (75 million a month) in a single year, while aiming for 200 million users in the near future thanks to infusions of venture capital. Following such growth potential, the smart money is going away from the legacy media and toward native digital start-ups. The valuations of many native digital media far exceed most legacy operations. For example, Amazon founder Jeff Bezos paid a paltry $250 million for the *Washington Post,* and the *Boston Globe* was sold for $70 million some 20 years after the *New York Times* paid over $1 billion for it. By contrast, BuzzFeed has been valued at close to $1 billion, as has Flipboard (a slick magazine format media aggregator). The *Huffington Post* was rumored to have received a bid for $1 billion at the time that its owner AOL was being sold to Viacom for $4.4 billion, a deal that included the *Post*. Meanwhile, in just the decade or so since the first native digital sites appeared in the early years of the century, legacy media have lost huge sums of stock market value. The *New York Times* has lost 70 percent of share value, Gannett (90 daily papers, nearly 1,000 other publications) has lost 60 percent of value, and McClatchy, with over 100 papers and online holdings, has lost 93 percent of market value.[5]

It is clear that the business model of the legacy press has collapsed. The loss of reporting and editorial jobs is just the tip of the iceberg. If one examines newspaper revenues since the start of this century, papers were far more profitable than online-only enterprises, based on total ad revenues topping $50 billion per year from 2003 to 2006. Then the bottom fell out, and ad revenues declined steadily, to around $20 billion by 2014.[6] Meanwhile, Google's ad revenue alone was the mirror opposite of newspapers, soaring through the $60 billion mark by 2014, and hitting more than $17 billion in the first quarter of 2015 alone.[7] By contrast, the entire newspaper industry's revenues from all sources (circulation, advertising, paywalls, etc.) fell short of $40 billion. Google's stock market value has soared 1,000 percent during this time. The trouble is that while newspapers produce news content, Google aggregates and curates content that it does not produce. At no point in the last century has the business model behind the news been so poorly aligned.

Newspapers are not the only legacy media under siege from native digital companies. As people access content differently than in the past—increasingly going mobile and wireless—even television is being threatened. Both Google (which owns YouTube) and Facebook rival television for audience reach.[8] Within the next decade, roughly half of younger demographics under 30 (prime advertising targets) will be so-called "cord cutters" and "cord nevers" who bypass cable subscriptions and television programming for their content, shifting to content providers such as Netflix, Amazon, Hulu, Apple, Google, and YouTube. Much of this content will be streamed on mobile devices. Needless to say, this creates challenges for both cable companies and television networks. The advertising dollars have yet to fully catch up with these changing audience habits because ad technologies have lagged in delivery to mobile devices and monitoring the reach and impact of digital ads. Thus the movement of ad revenues from legacy to native digital media is likely to continue.

How all of this affects news is the important question here. What will news look like as these native digital operations settle on profitable content formats that are not likely to resemble legacy journalism? Will the new advocacy journalism rise in prominence? Will the legacy press find a niche somewhere in the new digital ecology? Surveys indicate that people receive news from many different sources but that contact with conventional journalism remains important. More than 80 percent of people still get some news directly from news organizations. Roughly half also rely on news aggregators, half use search engines to find news, and 40 percent also use social media.[9] If the news aggregators, search engines, and social media sites are making money from the content produced by less profitable news organizations, something has to give. The case study looks inside the dizzying world of the news business in a time of rapid change, as conventional news organizations attempt to remain viable, while new information delivery enterprises seek to overtake them.

CASE STUDY

ADAPT OR DIE: THE FUTURE OF NEWS IN NATIVE DIGITAL MEDIA

The profit pressures on legacy media are enormous. Behind this economic crisis is a generational shift in how people consume, process, and share information. Even if legacy media figure out a formula that keeps them afloat, they need to reconcile changing information habits that may redefine what people think of as news and how they want it formatted and delivered. However, the innovation going on in legacy media is often underwhelming. A combination of unwillingness to rethink journalism standards and the desperate financial picture led many legacy media companies to retreat behind paywalls as a means of guarding—and getting paid for—their content. Some publications continued to offer limited access to articles through search and news aggregator referrals, giving away a limited number of free articles to tempt subscribers. However, the paywall experiment has had mixed results. Some specialty publications such as the *Wall Street Journal* have had success selling their specialized content. However, general news organizations such as the *New York Times* showed little net gain. Paywall subscribers are roughly balanced by lost readers who go elsewhere for free content. Thus, paywalls typically do little to boost ad revenues. While subscribers were gained, many others went elsewhere in search of much the same content for free—thus, not boosting the audience levels that ad revenues depend on.[10]

And so the quest for the next business model goes on, with many experiments under way. One of the most intriguing new possibilities is the move by the *New York Times* and a number of other legacy media companies to launch content inside of Facebook. The hope is that news feeds and social network distribution may yield new ad revenues shared between the content-producing companies and Facebook. The initial experiment was launched with nine media companies, including one native digital (BuzzFeed) and eight legacy organizations (*New York Times*, *National Geographic*, *Atlantic*, NBC News, *Guardian*, BBC News, *Bild*, and *Spiegel Online*, the latter two being prominent German companies). Such experiments may change the nature of news based on a complex set of factors that are not always coherently related to each other. For example, the *New York Times* stories inside Facebook are delivered on news feeds by algorithms that tend to filter stories according to what kind of content people have liked in the past and shared with friends. Such delivery logic signals the acceleration of audience fragmentation and the creation of multiple news worlds down to the fine-grained news reality of each individual. Since Facebook is always changing its feed algorithms to enhance its own business model, it is unclear how legacy companies will adapt within its proprietary environment. However, there appear to be reasons on both sides to make these partnerships work. Facebook is seeking to elevate its brand to include being a place where people become informed. The media companies already get a good deal of traffic from Facebook, and they want to be inside the environment where they can begin pushing content into potentially vast social networks and receive some of the ad revenue flowing over those networks. At the time of their moves inside Facebook, the *Times* was getting around 15 percent of its online traffic from the social networking site, and *National Geographic* was getting about 25 percent of its traffic from Facebook, where it already had 35 million fans. The potential for all parties to prosper seems great. At the time that this experiment was launched, roughly half of all Internet users were getting news from Facebook each week, rivaling the impact of local TV news.[11]

Some native digital organizations have figured out how to expand their reach with an economy of resources. For example, *Huffington Post* has become a large organization employing some 850 people and producing 13 editions around the globe for audiences as diverse as India, Germany, Italy, Japan, and Brazil. This operation produces nearly 2,000 content posts per day—contrasted with 350 at the *New York Times* and 60 at *Slate*.[12] While *HuffPo* has won a Pulitzer Prize for a series of stories about wounded veterans written by a respected senior journalist on its staff, most of its content is produced far more cheaply. Many stories are reposted and reformatted from other news organizations, and many more are posts from unpaid bloggers who are happy to receive large audiences for their ideas.

Recall from the last chapter that many of the norms that define professional journalism actually grew out of a collection of business and technology-driven practices that had little coherent rationale beyond delivering information in a timely fashion to people who paid for it. As the news world turns toward new digital platforms, another chaotic combination of social and technological forces is reshaping the kinds and forms of information that people receive. Some of the native digital enterprises of recent times have been spearheaded or given greater visibility by people who tried to launch digital features from inside legacy organizations but found the constraints too frustrating. One example is Ezra Klein who pioneered the successful *Wonkblog* inside the *Washington Post*, offering rapid analytical looks at breaking news. He sought to expand the operation into a model digital newsroom within the paper, but the idea of investing large sums in something that was not quite like journalism was rejected. Klein soon left the *Post* and joined *Vox*, saying, "We were badly held back not just by the technology, but by the culture of journalism."[13]

What Klein meant by the constraints of the culture of journalism is that his stories were rich in context, commentary, and political analysis, which put them at odds with regular news because of the biases discussed in chapter 2. In addition, the *Vox* technology platform (developed by Vox Media, the parent company of a number of sites) enables a richer multimedia and interactive format that includes embedded videos, continuous updating of content, extended interview segments with experts, and background features such as the "card stack" that invites people to drill down on more information if they seek it. Just as earlier technology helped shape the journalism of the twentieth century, the integrated digital platforms of the twenty-first century may redefine the news as an interactive, socially mediated, and potentially richer interpretive experience. The dilemma, of course, is whether people want such serious engagement with political information at a time when politics is viewed negatively and people use social media for other purposes. There are no guarantees that the tastes of the crowd, and the content that makes money, will naturally end up being high-minded.

Let's look at the *Vox* business model and how it affects content on the site. The *Vox* technology platform is called Chorus. It is a content management system (CMS) used on a variety of Vox Media properties such as SB Nation, The Verge, Polygon, Curbed, The Eater, Racked, Re/code, and hundreds of affiliated sites. Chorus continues to evolve as a partnership between developers and content producers, with a sharp eye on user habits and reactions. The result is an emerging model of a digital culture based on these defining elements:[14]

> *Community and identity*: Each Vox Media site invites users to join a
> community in which they may contribute content and rise through
> the ranks if their posts are popular and deemed effective by site
> administrators.
> *Automated editorial workflow*: Both Vox Media sites and the CMS (Chorus) are
> user-friendly interfaces that help community members learn how to rise in
> the system by creating the right kind of content and developing strategies
> to get the attention of other community members.
> *Multimedia publishing platform*: This enables content producers to gather
> materials from around the web and drag and drop them into storyboards,
> with automated tagging and editing of emerging content. The copyright
> status of images is also automated, and the platform offers easy photo-

editing tools. At the end of the process, the author decides how to promote the article through social media. All of this is done with interfaces simple enough for people to move through the whole process.

User experience: The look of the site is attractive and flexible for users, whether they want to drill deep or surf the site. Content is easily shared with social networks. Users can also create content, starting with comments and ending up with articles that rise in the community.

Statistics: The platform feeds data back to content creators and site editors about how a story is doing, what Google search trends look like on the topic, how similar stories have fared in the past, and how they differed in terms of timing and social media strategies. Such stats help users position and launch stories and figure out social media strategies in real time.

Revenue: While Vox Media properties are still tied to ad revenue, the idea of a community of users makes their interests far more focused than most audiences for legacy media. As a result, content can be surrounded by ads that directly appeal to common community interests. The effectiveness of ads can be tracked at a fine-grained level and adjusted for better performance. Vox Media reports high revenue growth and an unlimited range of topic areas for which its platform can be cloned.

The example of *Vox* illustrates all the reasons why legacy organizations are having trouble competing with native digital start-ups. Journalist and tech blogger Frédéric Filloux identifies 10 dimensions on which legacy media are limited: *funding* (there is little investor interest), *resource allocation* (there are seldom enough resources to scale new products—e.g., the *Washington Post*'s decision not to grow Ezra Klein's *Wonkblog* operation), *timing* (they operate under a desperate short-term profit orientation), *scalability* (new ideas either challenge existing conceptions of journalism or lack the resources to grow), *customer relations* (the old model of delivering a product on a take-it-or-leave-it basis makes it hard to create community), *agility* (old bureaucracies are conservative and hold on to the past), *hierarchy* (a vertical organization limits new ideas unlike the more horizontal organization of native digital organizations—witness Google's decision to free up its growing chain of businesses in a looser company called Alphabet), *attitudes toward risk* (legacy organizations are risk averse whereas native digital operations accept experimentation, risk, and failure), *competition* (legacy organizations have a sense of the inherent superiority of the journalism product whereas a highly competitive and innovative ethos prevails in the native digital world), *production constraints* (legacy media have expensive facilities and older, higher-paid workers, and native digital organizations use online production and a younger, more mobile workforce).[15]

The conditions facing legacy and native digital media could not be more different. This means that the factors shaping the information regime of the future will likely result in different ways of thinking about news, resulting in fewer boundaries between serious and nonserious information, more input from the audience in creating content, distribution over social networks rather than mass distribution to individuals, and, most likely, a greater degree of direct communication between officials and publics. Somewhere in this changing media landscape the legacy media will likely find a niche for those who seek a daily record of events. Even as bloggers and crowdsourced content become more important, the legacy press still offers a sense of authority and editorial skill that helps important information reach large audiences and hold officials accountable, creating a link between publics and their political institutions. For example, economist and *New York Times* columnist Paul Krugman has recognized the importance of economic bloggers who have generated informed public discussions about economic policy in a time of crisis. However, as one observer has suggested, "It takes someone like Krugman writing regularly about such matters in the *Times* for that discussion to reach a broader audience, enter the political discourse, and make a difference. When it comes to impact, traditional news organizations retain an overwhelming edge. . . . Even the revelations of Wikileaks and Snowden, while involving leaks of digital information, were delivered to the public via print-based outlets."[16] And so legacy media are beginning to nest inside native digital platforms. We will see how this experiment goes.

The Legacy Media Try to Hold On

As serious reporting falls away, the news is increasingly based on catchy hooks that are easily updated to keep audiences coming back and buzzing. When Lady Gaga told her Little Monsters on Facebook to press for gay rights in the military, the story became packaged as news with a comment from a politician thrown in for authenticity, and then it spread through the blogosphere with hyperlinks flowing far and wide. When Donald Trump ran for president in 2016, his Twitter stream @realDonaldTrump was a continuous source of amusing material: lashing out at opponents, slamming journalists who asked him tough questions, and bloviating on his own greatness. Such news is aimed at grabbing people when they check in briefly at work or on the commute home. Pablo Boczkowski has found this cycle of more numerous and less substantial content proliferation to be something of a global media trend, occurring in Argentina as well as the United States.[17]

The trend is driven in part by doing more with less, and in part by the assumption that keeping the online version of a news organization refreshed and full of short, attention-getting features is the future of the business. This new information content model is rapidly replacing what was formerly known as journalism across the industry. Even organizations that are still profitable see this buzz-driven, continuous-update process as a means of becoming even more profitable. For example, Dean Starkman studied the *Wall Street Journal* (*WSJ*), which is generally regarded as one of the two best papers in America. The *WSJ* is interesting on several counts: it is still profitable because it feeds information to a special interest audience of high-income investors and firms, it was purchased by media baron Rupert Murdoch's giant News Corp and put through a profit-ratcheting reorganization, and so it stands out as a profitable exception that nonetheless reflects industry trends toward shallower and less analytical stories. Between 2000 and 2008, the number of *WSJ* stories increased from 22,000 to 38,000 per year as the staff shrank at least 13 percent.[18] Starkman's analysis of what he calls the "Hamster Wheel" indicates that distant corporate owners of failing businesses believe that more and shorter content bits are what busy people want. News on the go is like fast food—momentarily satisfying but ultimately unhealthy.

Many other former high-quality news organizations, from the *LA Times* to the *Washington Post*, have been pushed to go even faster on the hamster wheel of legacy newsrooms. The irony of all this, according to Starkman, is that there is no evidence that this trend is even leading to a successful stabilization of the business. He notes, for example, that the measures for web ratings and site traffic are woefully unreliable, and, in any event, few online news operations are turning a profit. Moreover, as we will discuss in chapter 8, there are now so many competing information models for people to choose from that the current effort to do more with less in the news business may well be bypassed by publics who discover more satisfying media formats beyond the news that offer deeper information about the topics they care about. This is what Starkman means by the real-time undoing of the mainstream media. Later in this chapter, we will see that what media executives think people want is generally severely limited by what they decide their organizations can afford to feed them at lowest cost.

Meanwhile, what is being lost is serious reporting. At the height of the mass media era, news organizations were more independent and less likely to be driven by sheer goals of maximizing profits. Journalism was once thought to be valuable in itself because it was an important good or resource for the public in a democracy. The government once helped media organizations maintain commitments to these values by holding them to some public service standards as a requirement for license renewal. Newspapers were often run by people committed to journalism and who made a commitment to balance their profits with the value of political reporting as a public good. The rest of this chapter tells the story of what happened to these values and sets up the discussion in chapter 8 about the future of news.

The bottom line in the present system is that the economic collapse has produced a double blow to the public interest. First, the amount of serious political information is shrinking in favor of rumor, scandal, and increasing focus on entertainment and lifestyle news. Second, much of the political news that remains comes through public relations events and spin. Thus, the mainstream news media are ever more tied to officialdom, even as they cling to the norms of objectivity discussed in chapter 6. The result, according to Starkman's hamster wheel analysis, is this: "The Paradox of the Wheel is that, for all the activity it generates, the Wheel renders news organizations deeply passive. The greater the need for copy, the more dependent reporters are on sources for scoops and pitiful scraps of news."[19] How did all this happen?

Ownership Deregulation and the End of Social Responsibility Standards

The corporate concentration of media ownership that undermined commitment to the news as a public service was well underway by the mid-1980s when the government all but abandoned the mandate for the Federal Communications Commission to monitor and enforce the "fairness doctrine." That key regulatory standard required broadcasters to present issues of public importance in a balanced fashion. For decades, this had been regarded as a reasonable protection of the public interest in exchange for granting commercial corporations the use of public airwaves for commercial gain. Increasing pressure from corporations during the Reagan era of deregulation driven by antigovernment PR led a Republican-dominated FCC to abolish the doctrine in 1987. Many stations quickly abandoned news and public affairs programming in favor of cheaper formula programming that could be pumped through multiple stations.

Yet the pressures continued from media companies for further reductions of government limits on ownership of multiple types of media (e.g., newspapers, television, and radio) in particular markets. These limits were intended to keep small independent media companies alive in local areas and to promote competition among local media, with the hope of stimulating content diversity and local voices. However, media companies had invested widely in the campaign funds of both parties, and by the 1990s, both

Republicans and Democrats had for the most part become advocates of free-trade deregulation and the powerful idea of synergy in the media. Bill Clinton (who had powerful Hollywood backers) explained how enabling media concentration was a good thing because it would build capital for new investment and make the US entertainment industry even more dominant in global markets. As for competition and diversity, those questions were waved off with vague ideas about how huge conglomerates would have to encourage diversity and competition so their subsidiaries would not duplicate each other.

All of this culminated with the Telecommunications Act of 1996, which the *Wall Street Journal* heralded as "the first major overhaul of telecommunications law since Marconi was alive and the crystal set was the state of the art."[20] The most highly publicized aspects of the law promised increasing competition and lower rates for consumers in phone and cable services. However, the meat of the legislation was a maze of reduced barriers to ownership of a number of media outlets (e.g., stations, papers, cable channels), ownership of outlets in different media sectors (e.g., radio, TV, newspapers, cable), and the number of outlets that can be owned by the same company within the same city or media market. Along with these reduced regulations came what was termed a necessary relaxation in community service requirements for distant owners who can now operate multiple outlets in the same local markets. For example, if the entire program feed for a rock station in Boston comes from an automated control room across the country, there is little room for news or even local tastes in music to be reflected—only the cheapest program content that continues to deliver enough listeners to sell commercials at a profit.

Why don't listeners simply flee to other channels? With the sweeping deregulation written into the Telecommunications Act of 1996, most of the stations in most cities have become owned by a few corporate giants who gradually put the local competition out of business and replaced high-quality and often diverse programming with the cheapest, most standardized fare that still keeps listeners tuned in for commercials. An activist from Prometheus Radio Project, which supports community radio stations, described a typical situation: when one company owns "eight radio stations in one town plus all the billboards and all the concert venues, and all the promotion machinery, suddenly they have a level of power that their competitors have no way to compete with. Once their competitor[s] are out of business they have free reign to do just about anything that they please, that is the same just as any other monopoly."[21] Is that assessment too harsh or radical? On the contrary, it is precisely the goal of many corporate owners, which is why corporate media spent so much money lobbying for the 1996 legislation (and spent so little time reporting it to their audiences as news).

A few owners, such as Lowry Mays, who founded Clear Channel radio, were even happy to tell you exactly what their business model is. As he put it to a *Fortune* magazine reporter: "We're not in the business of providing news and information. We're not in the business of providing well-researched music. We're simply in the business of selling our customers products."[22] This philosophy was literally licensed and unleashed on the nation by the Telecommunications Act of 1996. Clear Channel quickly grew to take over more than 850 radio stations in 50 states, reaching 110 million Americans. Within a few years after the Telecommunications Act passed, the company's website claimed to reach 45 percent of all people between the ages of 18 and 49 every day. However, like many other big companies, Clear Channel became an attractive target for a buyout. Bain Capital (of Mitt Romney fame) led a successful effort to buy the company, renaming it iHeartMedia, firing thousands of workers, and automating its programming even further, so that many stations now operate with no local on-air staff and with announcers piping their recorded programs from a central base to the rest of the network.

A noted above, ownership restrictions and community service standards were once regarded as firewalls for information diversity and competition in the American democracy. The old public responsibility thinking went like this: (a) local owners might be more responsive to community values, (b) different ownership of different sectors (types of media) was good for program diversity, and (c) limits on a single company's control of a particular sector would prevent strangleholds on advertising revenues that might put smaller local companies out of business. The business-driven thinking that was used in lobbying both Democrats and Republicans to support the deregulation went like this: (a) markets inherently create diversity through competition; (b) competition within each company's holdings will be created by the drive for audiences and profits; (c) therefore, even companies that own many media outlets in a community will be driven to diversify and reflect community values. As for public service, if communities want some sort of service from their media outlets, they will support broadcasters who provide it.

This easy reasoning ignores the fact that conglomerates like iHeartMedia enter communities with the intent of closing down local programming and piping the same music or talk formulas from central production facilities to hundreds of niche markets around the country. During the critical days after 9/11, many local people found that they could not get any information about what was happening in their communities because distant radio corporations had no provision for monitoring the local scenes in which they broadcast. Indeed, some had no news production at all and had to patch into CNN in order to provide communities with any news about the crisis. These realities of community service were glossed over by hasty and shallow debates on media regulation and deregulation.

Therefore, without much public discussion, Congress and President Clinton ended the old regime and announced the new. In what has been termed "The Full Employment Act for Telecommunications Lawyers," a consolidation frenzy was unleashed. This came on the heels of a decade in which few thought that merger mania could get any more intense. For example, before the new law, corporate giants bought out the TV networks (GE swallowed NBC, Westinghouse gobbled CBS, and Disney added Cap Cities / ABC to its portfolio of assets). The world's book publishers were also merged, stripped, and consolidated in breathtaking leaps. But the Telecommunications Act set the media world spinning even faster. The year following the new law was called the "Year of the Deal" by many in the industry, as indicated by just a few of the deals that the new legislation enabled. Murdoch's News Corporation (which earlier had swallowed Fox, HarperCollins Publishers, and *TV Guide*) bought New World Communications, making News Corp for a short time the nation's largest TV station owner. Westinghouse/CBS bought Infinity Broadcasting, giving it a chain of 77 radio stations to go with its string of other stations, creating multiple outlets in the top 10 markets in the country. Viacom bought CBS and all its media holdings, making it (until the later CBS spin-off) the largest TV and radio station owner. Time Warner and Turner Broadcasting merged into the world's largest media company, and, not long after, America Online bought Time Warner, making it the largest media company for a few years. Gannett bought Multimedia Entertainment and expanded its newspaper holdings to become the national leader in circulation. Gannett then bought Belo Corporation, which owned a string of TV stations, and later split off those holdings to become Tegna, one of the nation's largest TV chains. The frenzy of mergers, breakups, and industry shakeups continues at a dizzying pace. For example, after a very short marriage, AOL and Time Warner split up, and AOL was then bought by Viacom, the world's sixth-largest media company, owning 160 cable networks that reach 600 million people globally. By the time this edition of *News* gets into print, some of these mergers will have fallen apart and new ones will be announced as blockbuster deals.

Indeed, the media merger circus is about just that: deals that make money for the players involved. Little attention is given to the quality of the content or the potential costs to the public interest. These stories unfolded largely as business and financial news, with the focus on corporate profits and growth prospects. The press (whose parent corporations lobbied furiously for the new legislation) seldom raised the question of whether the proliferation of choices would really provide the "diversity of voices and viewpoints" promised by Bill Clinton when he signed the bill into law.[23]

The Media Monopoly: Four Decades of Change

As noted above, sweeping deregulation has aided concentration of media ownership and created considerable turbulence in media companies. When journalist-turned-media-scholar Ben Bagdikian published the first edition of his classic book *The Media Monopoly* in 1983, he showed that 50 large media corporations controlled roughly half the content consumed by Americans, in terms of movies, radio, television, magazines, newspapers, and books. By the time the second edition was published in 1987, the number was 29; by the third edition in 1990, it was 23; by the fifth edition in 1997, the number was 10; by the sixth edition in 2000, the number was 6, where it has stayed since then, although the names of those 6 have changed many times as the mergers and breakups continue. In recent times, the rise of the Internet and mobile content delivery have created new challenges and new players.

The conventional wisdom among the chieftains of giant media corporations since the heyday of the 1990s has been *bigger is better*, as expressed in the mantra of *synergy*. The common goals were (a) to become large enough to own the production, marketing, and distribution of media content; (b) to have enough channels and publications to dominate advertising markets; (c) to use free internal advertising to draw audiences from one channel or publication to others in the media empire; and (d) to recycle both new content and old programming within the system to reduce the costs of filling the schedules of multiplying cable and broadcast outlets. However, the model did not anticipate various changes in the media environment that affected the profitability of both print and broadcast news. Although the merger mania continues to this day, it is driven more by making money for those involved than by proven advantages to creating megacorporations. Today the companies that own the lion's share of media we consume are Comcast, Viacom, CBS, Time Warner, News Corp (and its spin-off 21st Century Fox), and Disney. However, as audiences increasingly move to mobile content delivery and escape the bonds of cables and cords, these patterns may change dramatically.

Wait a minute, isn't Comcast a cable service provider that also owns content channels? Named the world's largest media company by Forbes in 2015, Comcast delivers cable and Internet to roughly 113 million Americans. Comcast also owns a long list of content channels, including a string of NBC companies (e.g., NBC, CNBC, MSNBC), a number of local network affiliates in top markets, The Weather Channel, SyFy, Telemundo, and Universal Studios, among many other properties. The classic definition of a monopoly is to use control of a dominant market position to create unfair competition—as when you can give your own properties a sweet deal and make it more expensive for competitors to use your delivery system. For example, Comcast can fill its cable packages with its own content more cheaply than with competitor channels. And despite huge profits on Internet service delivery, Comcast has repeatedly threatened to slow down the delivery of rival content, along with other content that is not profitable. For example, Comcast and Netflix, along with Internet service provider Verizon, were locked in a fight over Comcast and Verizon letting their service degrade so that Netflix content was not viewable for many subscribers. Comcast refused to upgrade service despite its huge profits based on high customer rates supported by monopoly licenses in many local markets. Instead, Comcast cut a deal with Netflix that resembled blackmail by asking payment from Netflix to assure speedier service to customers. Nextlix complied, rather than losing customers, but then filed a government complaint against both Comcast and Verizon.

At the time of the Neflix squabble, Comcast was trying to take over Time Warner Cable. Time Warner had spun off its cable operation into an independent company that was the target of the takeover bid by Comcast in 2014. The merger would have created the largest cable operator in the country with a dominant position in control of as much as 80 percent of the cable market in California, for example. The volume of public protest against this merger (along with the Netflix complaint) led federal regulators to turn down the deal. However, Time Warner Cable was not on the market long before being bought by smaller Charter Communications in a $55 billion deal.

All this merger mania produces huge fortunes for law firms, the banking and finance industry, and media executives. Those wealthy interests contribute to political campaigns and lobby intensely for freedom from regulation, and so the government has been reluctant to intrude very often. However, episodes such as the Netflix slowdown and the proposed Comcast–Time Warner Cable merger have fueled advocates for a policy knows as "net neutrality" (calling for all content to be treated the same). Indeed, a citizens' media reform movement discussed later in the chapter has done some impressive campaigning and lobbying against giving cable and wireless operators greater powers over the content they carry.

Questions about whether most of these mergers are in the public interest, or even make good business sense, seem lost in the financial fog. Many of these mergers make little sense when examined in terms of real synergies achieved. Distracted by windfall profits, executives in the boardrooms often fail to see how rapid changes in technology and society can turn the winners in today's media monopoly into tomorrow's lesson in business failure. The story of AOL (formerly known as America Online) is illustrative: the company went from being the giant among dial-up service providers in the 1990s to becoming the dominant merger partner with Time Warner in 2000, creating a $350 billion deal, just at the time that cable began stealing AOL's Internet business. Within three years, AOL was dropped from the company name, in what the business press continues to discuss as one of the great business disasters of our time. AOL was cut adrift as an independent company, and in 2015 was bought for a paltry $4.4 billion by monopoly giant Verizon that valued its ad delivery technology, along with a few prize properties such as the *Huffington Post*. It may be just a matter of time before behemoths like Time Warner and Verizon will be replaced by native digital companies as people are leaving cable in favor of wireless and mobile content delivery. Few customers or competitors are likely to shed a tear when Comcast and Verizon leave the list.

Big Business versus the Public Interest

The experience of many journalists today is one of losing the battle for maintaining public interest standards against corporate managers who think of news as just another product. Quality news in the television industry is in many ways just as endangered as in print journalism. One case in point is the resignation in 2010 of David Westin as president of ABC News. Westin reportedly gave up fighting with Disney executives over what profit level the news division should be expected to deliver. A very good investigative report in the *New York Times* noted:

> The ABC News staff member informed of the decision said that Disney and ABC managers had pressed Mr. Westin for years to make the division more profitable, but had been unhappy with his efforts to accomplish that goal. ABC announced in February that it would reduce its staff by up to 400 employees, about 25 percent of its work force.

. . . Another senior ABC News executive said the division had been consistently profitable, but ABC had sought to increase its profit margin to 15 percent, from 5 percent.[24]

Since government deregulation of the media industries began, as described above, journalists have been under increasing pressure from corporate executives promoting cheap news to generate higher profits. The loss of advertising to native digital sites in the first decade of the twenty-first century was magnified by the Great Recession at the end of the decade, which led to the wholesale collapse of any remaining balance between profits and the public interest value of the news product.

Rank-and-file reporters in newsrooms across the land have long been forced to accept the "lite" news and features that turned newspapers and television stations into highly profitable businesses by the 1990s.[25] The story here is not that audiences really demanded lite news. On the contrary, in most markets, TV news audiences and newspaper readership began shrinking, particularly in the audience demographics that advertisers pay more to reach: people under 35. So the cheapening of the product came at the expense of the long-term viability and public appeal of the industry.

If audiences were running away, why did the downgrading of news content continue? The simple reason is that most media calculate their business model in terms of delivering prime demographics to advertisers and using as cheap a product as possible to attract those demographics. Thus, the loss of absolute audience numbers was initially not as serious a blow to some organizations, as long as they were able to produce a product that still appealed to target audiences of high value to sponsors. For example, newspapers turned out to be highly profitable in the early days of profit-driven media consolidation. Many of them actually saved money on production and distribution as they lost noncritical readers, and they added lifestyle (e.g., fashion, food, and travel) features that continued to draw key demographics (e.g., 30–50 age brackets with disposable income) that drove the heyday of consumer spending in the prosperous 1990s. Later in the first decade of the twenty-first century, newspapers suffered the double blows of Internet advertising and the Great Recession. Television network news declined steadily from a peak of more than 50 million viewers until it leveled off at slightly more than 20 million following the Great Recession. The Pew report *State of the News Media 2015* showed slight upticks in local and national network TV audiences, balanced by sharp declines in cable news, and modest declines in newspapers. The revenue picture tells more of the story, as only local TV showed impressive revenue growth in recent years

(7 percent in 2014–2015). By contrast, native digital revenues were up 18 percent in 2015.[26] In order to stay afloat, serious news operations must cut resources. How do business decisions translate to the editorial side of news organizations?

HOW CORPORATE INFLUENCE SHAPES NEWS CONTENT

Executives at Disney, Comcast, or Gannett do not need to issue many direct orders to distant journalists to cut back on serious coverage of politics and government, or to run more sex and crime. The demise of serious news is a mere casualty of sensible-sounding business decisions. As a managing editor of the *New York Times* explained it,

> News coverage is being shaped by corporate executives at headquarters far from the local scene. It is seldom done by corporate directive or fiat. It rarely involves killing or slanting stories. Usually it is by the appointment of a pliable editor here, a corporate graphics conference there, that results in a more uniform look and cookie-cutter approach among a chain's newspapers, or it's by the corporate research director's interpretation of reader surveys that seek simple common-denominator solutions to complex coverage problems. Often the corporate view is hostile to governmental coverage. It has been fashionable for some years, during meetings of editors and publishers, to deplore "incremental" news coverage. Supposedly it is boring, a turnoff to readers, and—what's worse—it requires news hole. The problem with all of this is that government news develops incrementally. And if you don't cover it incrementally, you don't really cover it at all. Incremental is what it is all about.[27]

Journalist and communication scholar Doug Underwood examined changes in business values of news organizations at the newsroom level, and he found increasing limits on the content of news that stem from the manufacture and sale of news as a commercial product. Real press freedoms are limited each news day simply because, in his words, "MBAs rule the newsroom."[28] Assignments are made increasingly with costs, efficiency, and viewer or reader reactions in mind. Newspapers, in particular, struggle to survive in the video age; they are run with fewer and fewer concerns about informing the public. As Underwood describes it: "Today's market-savvy newspapers are planned and packaged to 'give readers what they want'; newspaper content is geared to the results of readership surveys; and newsroom organization has been reshaped by newspaper managers whose commitment to the marketing ethic is hardly distinguishable from their vision of what journalism is."[29] The paper that set this trend was *USA Today*, which was dubbed "McPaper" and "the newspaper for people who are too busy to watch TV." However, in this era of newsroom cutbacks, *USA Today* does not look so bad.

CHEAPENING THE PRODUCT

The bottom line throughout the industry during the corporate buyout era at the turn of the twenty-first century was to cheapen the news product itself. Serious political news costs more to report because it often requires the time and initiative of experienced journalists who know whom to call, what to ask, and where to follow the leads. Cheaply produced news often requires no reporters at all, save perhaps sending a camera crew to shoot fires, floods, accidents, and other disasters that can be scripted back at the studio. Much of the other content circulates through generic news feeds and wires, requiring only repackaging for putting on the front page or for the anchor to report on the air. As a former chairman of General Electric (GE), the company that bought NBC (and later sold it to Comcast) put it so bluntly: "Network news isn't the strategic center of what happens here. . . . News is not the core of the asset."[30] News simply became a tiny piece of the corporate profit and synergy picture. When the networks like NBC and CBS were independent companies, profits were not as important for the news division, which was regarded more as an asset that added prestige to the brand image. Legend has it that CBS founding owner William S. Palcy once told his news division to concentrate on the best reporting possible, and he would make profits from sports and entertainment. That idea of using news quality as something of a corporate loss leader to build the brand was encouraged by far stronger government requirements. Before the deregulation waves in the late 1980s, broadcasters had to produce some public responsibility programming in exchange for getting free licenses to use the public airwaves for profit. Most of those responsibility requirements have been dropped or diminished as advocates of deregulation point to profits as the number-one public value that government should encourage.

CBS News (the home of Edward R. Murrow and Walter Cronkite) was merged in 2000 with cable giant Viacom (a former CBS subsidiary), and then it was split in 2005 into two companies called CBS and Viacom, all out of judgments about growth and investment potential. During this profit-driven era for CBS, news content and delivery formats were continuously adjusted to fit the lifestyle interests of the audiences already tuning in to entertainment programs. When CBS decided to lower the median age of its audience with programs like *Survivor*, the move set in motion a reformatting of other network programming, including news. The trouble is that with news in general being less interesting for young people, the network news programs have entered a steady and seemingly irreversible decline with aging audiences tuning in to programming supported by commercials for medicines and health products. The tough challenge facing news executives is to create content that shifts the demographic and changes the product mix in the advertising surrounding the news: "Network executives yearn to lower the median age for the news, which is about 57 or 58 depending on the network, and replace Immodium and Zoloft ads with ones for the iPod and Mountain Dew. If they cannot attract youth to the current brand of news, they think they can tailor news to be more attractive to youth."[31]

Saving the costs of reporters, remote news bureaus, and other aspects of quality journalism produced such a boost in the profits that the corporate consolidation reached unprecedented levels, as more and more news organizations were bought up solely for their investment potential. The average profit margin was a healthy 14.8 percent for companies in the newspaper industry. The prospects of even greater profits stimulated an even larger wave of mergers and buyouts in the 1990s.The mega media companies squeezed a whopping 21.5 percent average profit from their expanding newspaper holdings by the end of the decade.[32] During this time, the government gave the green light to media concentration by passing the Telecommunications Act that gave virtually no consideration to its impact on the quality of public information.

The purchase of these cash machines by larger media companies and investment conglomerates made the demand for high profits a requirement. This set up a collision course with Internet sites that siphoned advertising revenues online, along with news and entertainment fare, which drove more of the audience away as well. What were news organizations to do to keep the profits high? The answer, of course: cut reporting staff even more and shore up the content with more "news lite." While local TV was an early adopter of the lite-news formula, many cities still had quality newspapers for those who wanted to stay in touch with politics and community affairs. Yet, fueled by government deregulation that enabled more concentrated ownership of media outlets (as discussed in the case study in this chapter), high-quality papers were bought and stripped by big corporations beholden to distant investors rather than to the public. The story is the same in Chicago, Los Angeles, Philadelphia, Atlanta, San Jose, Dallas, and many other cities: Papers and television and radio stations that once reported serious news became milked by investors concerned about short-term gains rather than long-term stability or community responsibilities. Indeed, some venerable institutions, such as the *Philadelphia Inquirer*, were simply cast adrift by new owners seeking steep profits and were left to struggle under unstable ownership or simply fade away.

Consider the case of the *Dallas Morning News*. At the turn of the twenty-first century, the *Dallas Morning News* was rated in a national survey of newspaper editors as the nation's fifth-best daily paper.[33] However, the large company that owned it, Belo, had made a number of bad investments and decided to raise profits where it could. Rather than seeing the Dallas paper as a gem of good journalism and an asset to the brand, Belo viewed it as a place to make cuts and reap short-term gains. When the *Morning News* was named one of the nation's top papers by the *Columbia Journalism Review* in 1999, it had a newsroom staff of 600 employees. Between 2004 and 2006, under Belo profit squeezing, 200 newsroom staff members were laid off, and 100 more were to follow in the next few years. The paper soon led the country in declining circulation (with a whopping 14.3 percent decline in one six-month period in 2007), and reader satisfaction plummeted from 79 to 60 percent.[34] Gone were bureaus in Europe, Asia, the Middle East, Cuba, South America, Houston, and Oklahoma City. The Washington bureau was cut from a staff of 11 to 2 reporters and 1 columnist.[35] More of the news was simply ripped from wire feeds. Even though Belo profit margins continued to slide because of various problems, the CEO was given a 50 percent raise. Journalism scholar Phillip Meyer surveyed the damage: "It seems to me that papers that do what Dallas did have decided to liquidate the business and get as much money out of it as they can. That's not crazy. That's a rational strategy if you only care about what happens on your watch as a manager because it takes a long time for a newspaper to die, and while it's in its death throes, it can still be a pretty good cash cow. But it's really bad for the community and for the business in the long run."[36] In the end, concerns about community are pushed aside by business decisions. Belo was later bought by Gannett, which, in turn, split the television stations off into a separate company named Tegna. Left behind in the deal was a tiny remnant, the A. H. Belo Corporation, named for Alfred Horatio Belo who founded the *Morning News* in 1885. That small remaining company is down to operating the *Morning News* and one other paper.

Throughout this chaotic era, profits have been squeezed out with a three-step industry formula: (a) cheapen the content, (b) market content directly to the audiences that are most attractive to advertisers, and (c) allow the less profitable audiences to wither away, producing a net savings of printing and distribution costs. Indeed, within the shortsighted economic logic of the time, dwindling audiences did not set off as many alarm bells as one might think, since cheap content could be thrown at them to keep the balance sheets in line. Moving away from quality information made everything seem economically viable for a time. Putting the political news focus on personalities at the center of dramatic conflicts may have accentuated the fragmentation bias discussed in chapter 2, but it made stories easier to report in terms of generic plots. Echoing some of our themes about news biases from chapter 2, here is how Matthew Baum describes the trend:

> The net effect is that traditional news programming has been supplemented, and in some respects supplanted, by a variety of new types of entertainment-oriented informational programs, which I have collectively termed soft news media. Relative to traditional news programs, soft news outlets place a greater emphasis on episodic human-interest-oriented stories with highly accessible themes—themes that are particularly suitable for cheap framing. Conversely, the soft news media are far less likely than their traditional news counterparts to employ *thematic* frames, which provide broader context for understanding the causes and consequences of a given issue or event, but which also tend to be more complex, and, hence, less accessible for politically uninterested individuals.[37]

Baum also notes, however, that many disconnected citizens might never hear of important world issues at all unless they appear in news magazines or on entertainment programs such as those on E! and MTV. The good news seems to be that infotainment gets information about a select few big issues to people who are otherwise walled off from politics. The bad news is that the information may be so fragmented and personality driven that it offers little useful understanding. As political comedy becomes increasingly popular, the line between hard and soft news is difficult to draw. Indeed, the context and insight provided by political comedy may make so-called soft news more informative. However, the argument that comedy may be superior to news, or that it is a necessary complement, hardly speaks well of the state of corporate journalism today. Indeed, the trends discussed above have alarmed many citizens who have joined in a national movement for media reform.

The Citizen Movement for Media Reform

The level of media concentration soon became so worrisome that a grassroots citizen movement emerged (see, e.g., www.freepress.net) when the Federal Communications Commission (FCC) moved to relax ownership restrictions even further in 2003. Two of the five FCC commissioners voted against provisions that would have enabled a single corporation to own a newspaper, three TV stations, eight radio stations, and the cable system in a single market. Hearings were held around the country, and owners of remaining independent media outlets protested that the latest rules would surely mean the death of local media. A citizen lobbying campaign targeted Congress with hundreds of thousands of emails, faxes, and phone messages, and in an impressive display of bipartisanship, the US Senate voted to block the changes. The Bush administration regrouped around possible executive measures to restore good relations with its corporate donors, and FCC chairman Michael Powell went public to express his shock that the Senate would block a pro-business deregulation move. Robert McChesney described Powell's charge that

> the rule-making process had been upset by "a concerted grassroots effort to attack the commission from the outside in." Seemingly unaware that a public agency like the FCC could, in fact, be addressed by the public, he expressed amazement that as many as 3 million Americans have contacted the FCC and Congress to demand that controls against media monopoly be kept in place. Capitol Hill observers say that media ownership has been the second most discussed issue by constituents in 2003, trailing only the war on Iraq. Following Brecht's famous dictum, Michael Powell wanted to fire the people.[38]

The citizen movement to restore social responsibility in the media continues to gain momentum. However, even with the restoration of a Democratic administration in 2008, the FCC was scrambling to get a grip on the changing media landscape. More of the action in media was happening online, including news and other political information sources. Yet the Bush FCC had thrown a wrench into the agency's capacity to regulate the Internet by unilaterally declaring that service providers were not "common carriers" of information like phone companies that are obligated to provide service to all who want it within their licensed monopoly jurisdictions. This meant that giant service providers, such as Viacom and Comcast, were essentially free to decide who could download what and at what charges.

Members of Free Press and other concerned citizen movements reasoned that if all content and users were not treated alike, then a company could promote its own products over competing content, as discussed above with the Netflix episode. Moreover, civic groups and public interest organizations that use the Internet to communicate with large numbers of members and list subscribers might be restricted, slowed down, or charged higher rates. The result is that content could be controlled to suit the business plans and even the politics of the service providers. Those companies are already highly profitable and have in many cases been given monopolies in lucrative markets. Like the television and newspaper conglomerates that came before them in the days after the Telecommunications Act, the big cable and Internet companies just want more. The eternal belief in synergy prevails in the boardroom, even though it drove the old media to the brink of profit-driven collapse. Nevertheless, the titans of the new media industries are also jockeying for dominance and control, and the Internet service providers turn out to be in critical positions to shape the game.

The early efforts by the Obama FCC to regain some regulatory authority in this rapidly changing mediascape were rebuffed by a court ruling that made the path back to public interest regulation unclear. Perhaps Congress needed to pass new laws made for the Internet. In the meantime, events and mergers were rapidly unfolding. Faced with a challenge to its own authority, the FCC invited giants Verizon and Google to meet and propose a plan for balancing profits with an open Internet. Not surprisingly, they were happy to propose how to regulate themselves, and they made reference to what citizen activists have called "net neutrality" or open and equal access to the Internet. Yet the solution of letting corporations help set their own standards sounds eerily similar to what happened with the telecom regulations of the last era.

Should the Internet be turned into a collection of giant shopping malls policed against political content that might reduce bandwidth and distract the shoppers? Should media companies regulate download privileges, file sharing, and enforce copyright policing in favor of their own products? These are important questions that affect the future of the Internet and its potential for a viable public information space where experiments may enable citizens to discover the next form of public information to replace the currently crumbling news system.

The battle for a noncommercial Internet goes on. As recently as 2014 the chairman of the FCC proposed rules in favor of companies creating "pay-to-play" fast lanes, which resulted in millions of protesters voicing their concerns. As a result, he reversed himself and proposed a much more public friendly ruling in favor of net neutrality (all traffic flowing equally) that was accepted by the commission in 2015.[39] However, this battle will go on because the stakes are so large for the industry. Politicians receiving corporate financing in Congress and running for president may well shift the balance back toward the big Internet companies when the opportunity arises. All of which suggests the rationale for continuing public mobilization on these and other media reform issues.

Most cities now have media justice and media reform groups, and many of these citizen networks are currently pressing for *net neutrality*, along with other policies such as regulating corporate ownership in favor of preserving local media. No matter what one's main political issue or concern may be, media democracy is rapidly becoming a companion concern as citizens begin to understand the shrinking public communication space devoted to their main issues.

Technology, Economics, and Democracy

Much of this book focuses on three core elements of political communication: (a) journalism and the news business, (b) the communication strategies of political actors, and (c) the information habits of citizens. However, we cannot ignore how other factors, such as technology and economics, shape each of the others in important ways. Some of the greatest changes in news content were created by developments in communication technologies. As discussed in chapter 6, the nineteenth century witnessed the formation of modern news as an overburdened horse-drawn national mail system was followed by the telegraph, forcing news dispatches to adopt a "just the facts," or "telegraphic," information structure, launching the "who, what, where, when, why" format for the news.[40] In the twentieth century, first photography, then film, and, finally, television put the news emphasis on visual information, creating vivid images that communicate without words.

People talk of the twenty-first century as an age of technological convergence in which word, image, and sound will be translatable, storable, editable, and programmable on devices that will blur the distinctions among television, computers, and telephony. The electronics of a house, from TV to Internet devices, down to the art images on the walls, and even the kitchen toaster, may be fully integrated, interactive, and run from a single remote control the size of a cell phone. In the next chapter, we explore how these and the many other coming technological developments may change the news.

The potential for reinventing public information online depends on many factors, such as restricting large corporations from owning the Internet. Jochai Benkler has argued persuasively that if left to be relatively open, the Internet has fostered a very different and competing economic model based on sharing (e.g., open-source platforms, operating systems, and software; a Creative Commons copyright system for public distribution of creative property under the control of those who created it rather than corporations that own it).[41] This economic model and the future of public information that may be based on it depend a great deal on how the Internet is regulated and whether big media corporations, such as Google, Comcast, Verizon, and Apple, get to decide how that goes.

As noted in chapter 1, there is no guarantee of optimal information in any political system, including one that displays the First Amendment as a sort of broad guarantee of information quality. As a challenge to conventional wisdom, consider the argument of communication scholar Robert McChesney, whose historical analysis indicates that commercial press systems contain little inherent basis for public service or responsibility. McChesney suggests that if we lift the veil of press freedom, we encounter corporate interests that invoke the First Amendment less often to protect their freedom to publicize politically risky or challenging information than to defend their pursuit of profits against obligations to serve the public interest.[42] Today's catchphrase is *freedom of the market*, which means profits over social responsibility. As we have seen, the raw pursuit of profits does not mean that giant corporations will necessarily prosper, however much they cheapen the product.

In the end, something like news as we currently know it will likely persist inside of social media platforms, but it will not be as easily controlled by journalism institutions. Moreover, the range of information formats and quality will continue to expand, making some citizens extremely well informed and leaving many others operating in grey areas of rumor and fantasy. At the same time, the release of important information via hacking and leaking will continue to expose official deceit and breach of public trust. Moreover, there is a natural link between such digital information releases and the uses of social media to help people organize and take action to make their voices heard, as illustrated in the waves of protests around the world in recent years. Readers of this book will be part of this new information order as it emerges.

8

THE FUTURE OF NEWS
IN A TIME OF CHANGE

News from the Past
Where the press is free, and every man able to read, all is safe.
—Thomas Jefferson[1]

News from the Present
The new market-oriented communications and information system . . .
addresses people predominantly through their identities as consumers.
. . . In the process, the system marginalizes or displaces other identities,
in particular the identity of citizen.
—Graham Murdock and Peter Golding[2]

News in the Future
More than one-half of all teens have created media content, and
roughly one-third of teens who use the Internet have shared content
they produced. In many cases, these teens are actively involved in what
we are calling participatory cultures. A participatory culture is a culture
with relatively low barriers to artistic expression and civic engagement.
—Henry Jenkins[3]

Thomas Jefferson could probably not have imagined the
state of the contemporary American press. One suspects that he might prefer searching for information on the Internet, and participating in its creation, over the passive communication style promoted by corporate media outlets. As veteran reporter Walter Pincus has observed: "Today, the mainstream print and electronic media want to be neutral, presenting both or all sides as if they were refereeing a game in which only the players—the government and its opponents—can participate. They have increasingly become common carriers, transmitters of other people's ideas and thoughts, irrespective of import, relevance, and at times, even accuracy."[4]

Indeed, being a perceptive observer, Jefferson would likely notice that there are at least two important public information models in play in the United States. The old press model is fading—both because of the collapse of its business model and, related to this, because its product is no longer trusted or relevant for many citizens. The other model involves ever-expanding applications of interactive and social technologies that create networked audiences who participate in sharing and often producing content.[5] We are beginning to see the importance of this second model in the native digital sites discussed in chapters 6 and 7. The participatory media culture described by Jenkins and others has also entered election campaigns, protest movements, and the viral flow of partisan information across desktops, phones, and tablets. These two political information models have parallels in many information sectors, from politics and business, to reference sources such as *Encyclopedia Britannica* (the legacy model, but now published only online) and *Wikipedia* (the native digital model). The case study in this chapter shows how both the legacy press and native digital sites are trying to harness audiences that were much more "captive" in the mass media era. The dilemma is that the native digital sites are freer to use the full capabilities of social and participatory media, while the legacy press imposes greater limits about how much the audience should participate in creating and driving content. This becomes a source of friction in a system where much of what we continue to regard as serious news is produced by legacy journalism organizations that remain out of step with the emerging communication logic of the future.

To frame the problem in sharp terms: the logic of legacy journalism comes into conflict with the logic of the participatory media culture, raising questions about what the news of the future will look like as this conflict plays out. The current period is one of creative, but chaotic ferment—creative destruction in the parlance of the digital age. As legacy media die off, or move inside native digital sites, more and more experimental hybrids emerge, as discussed in chapter 7. Many different business models power those sites, including ad revenues, foundation funding, and wealthy donors. As long as legacy journalism is stuck on traditional ideas about reporting, and cannot take full advantage of the participatory technologies that power native digital sites, the likely outcome is a chaotic reinvention of journalism in a profusion of new formats.

One story that illustrates the current era of experimentation involves a venture capitalist who reports sitting through a particularly "stultifying" meeting where representatives of a dying newspaper proposed running "more photos of pets and cute couples." The investor's growing concern was that journalism was never mentioned. He realized that in the golden era of papers, their large profits had subsidized some degree of quality political reporting. This rare case of businesses using profits to subsidize a public good began to disappear as the corporate takeover of news organizations squeezed the profits out to the last drop. Suddenly the venture capitalist had a revelation: "That's when the light went on for me that maybe public-service journalism . . . is a public good just like national defense, clean air, clean water . . . [and something that] market forces, left to their own devices, won't produce enough of."[6] After that revelation, the venture capitalist went on to help start the *Texas Tribune*, a lean online investigative reporting operation (www.texastribune.org). The *Tribune* describes its mission as "a nonprofit, nonpartisan, public media organization. Our mission is to promote civic engagement on public policy, politics, government, and other matters of statewide concern."[7] In addition to being nonprofit, the aim of citizen engagement is another departure from the long-standing dominant press model in America. The legacy press aims to keep citizens informed, but whether and how those citizens engage with politics is their personal concern.

One scenario for the news of the future is for citizens to become reporters by asking personally relevant questions, finding answers through information and database interfaces, and sharing what they find across various media platforms. Perhaps social media such as Facebook or Twitter will enable people to share and act on such information, rivaling the scale of old mass media audiences, while coordinating collective action over social media. On the other hand, individuals have the option of consuming just the media realities they prefer, and thus isolating themselves from the information realities of others in society. The result may be the fragmentation of public voices into more isolated communities of interest that have trouble being heard. How can digital native citizens bridge their different information realities and develop intelligent public engagement with issues and ideas?

Information Technology and Citizenship: Isolation or Deliberation?

The personalized potential of the digital information age has clearly captured the popular imagination. What is changing most about the conventional news, as many media consultants see it, is that our daily information handouts are becoming more personalized and tailored to individual consumer tastes. It may be tempting to think that the more personalized the information delivery system, the better. But is this necessarily true for democracy? Imagine that a presidential election campaign hits full swing and you get information on your smartwatch sent by an infobot operated by a political candidate. The bot draws from a large database of personal information: what kind of car you drive, the books you read, the websites you visit, the vacations you take, the restaurants where you eat, the products you order online, your past voting patterns, how much time you spend reading about various topics online, and more. These patterns are matched with other voter profiles to assess your receptivity to various kinds of messages. Perhaps your smartwatch senses that you are stressed for some reason. Processing all this information triggers distressing news from the bot about illegal immigrants receiving public benefits from your tax dollars. Or, if you are of a different political persuasion, the message is about another issue that you find worrisome. Then a soothing message arrives telling you how the candidate whose campaign runs the bot will fix this problem if elected. Meanwhile, your next-door neighbor is getting a very different message from the same candidate's infobot geared to that neighbor's personal profile.

Such trends in personalized information might be desirable if democracy were something that thrived inside the heads of individual citizens, instead of in some more widely shared public life. Critics like political scientist and communication scholar James Fishkin argue that communication systems are counterproductive for democracy when they simply feed unchallenged beliefs and prejudices back to individuals—creating isolated audience fragments. Fishkin argues that a better idea would be to assemble interactive citizen bodies that would be exposed to information and expert debate on key issues. These citizen panels would be allowed to question the experts, hold group deliberations, and then announce their conclusions to broader publics.[8] Based on such deliberative models, communication scholar John Gastil recommended that states assemble citizen panels to deliberate on ballot propositions. Their recommendations and their ratings of the partisan positions on the various ballot issues could be delivered to voters along with their ballots.[9] He has developed such a model in Oregon. Both Gastil and Fishkin aim to create a more meaningful voice of the people.[10]

Despite many experiments indicating that these deliberative polls can work in different settings (including online), the political and media trends seem to be moving in the opposite direction: toward less face-to-face deliberation and more personalized information delivery. According to Fishkin, what is missing in many schemes for citizen input, such as instant polls or comment boards on news sites, are mechanisms to facilitate learning and critical exchanges about issues. Indeed, the expanding online universe may not be as easily adapted to focused interactive public experiences as many optimists initially thought. Many observers of online communities note that they seldom produce ideal results: "Chat rooms, bulletin boards, news groups, listserves, blogs and wikis afford users considerable opportunity for talk, but that online talk tends to be undisciplined, intolerant and superficial, rather than deliberative."[11] The tendency to seek reinforcement for prior attitudes is also evident in face-to-face interpersonal relations. For example, Diana Mutz shows that most people avoid engaging in discussions with others who may disagree with them.[12]

Can democracy in America survive more fragmentation and personalization of the political experience? Have we become a democracy of one? For perhaps the first time in human history, large numbers of people have substantial choice about who they are and how they want to be identified socially.[13] As noted by many social theorists, a major reason for this is that the identities once attached to institutional memberships in class, church, business, social clubs, or community associations are weakening. As these elements of personal identity weaken, they are increasingly replaced by choices in lifestyles driven by consumer images. Our communication media deliver information packaged with ads tailored to very personalized data about us. This chapter explores the future of citizen information, looking at both legacy news and emerging digital media with an eye to how citizens may become active participants in the public information process.

Whither the Public Sphere?

The idea of democracy implies a public life in which, ideally, people think critically about solutions to common problems. The quality of public input into democratic decisions depends on whether people share public communication forums in which they express concerns, try out new ideas, and see how they stand up in everyday debate. The collection of these public spaces, from cafés and taverns, to town meetings and book clubs, to online sites and forums, constitutes what the pioneering communication theorist Jürgen Habermas termed the *public sphere*.[14] Many contemporary observers sense that the public sphere is shrinking or at least splintering perilously in contemporary society. Ironically, the expansion of sophisticated personal communication technologies seems responsible for much of the shrinkage. For example, sociologist Todd Gitlin argues that in place of any coherent public sphere, it makes more sense to think about the proliferation of tiny and shifting "sphericules."[15] These sphericules of interest can be extremely engaging, and they often offer a comforting escape from the pains of society at large. However, if people increasingly use communication technologies to construct and live in their own private worlds, where can people meet and share the concerns and the information required for coherent political discussion, much less for consensus to emerge?

To put it simply, the nature of our political communication process has something to do with how we act together politically—how we define our goals and chart our actions as a nation. At one extreme of national politics are the political crusaders who zealously fill the airwaves with moral ultimatums for everyone to follow. Their "flaming" on talk shows provides a low-budget media spectacle for the fragmented audiences who tune in, but it also sets bad examples for the greater numbers who tune out. As noted earlier, many Americans today are more inclined to avoid politics, or at least to seek it close to home, than to welcome open-minded debate in everyday situations about common national concerns.[16]

Today's citizens, in the view of communication scholar Michael Schudson, differ from the citizens of past eras in their acute awareness of a protective armor of personal rights and the way they casually monitor the larger environment for threats to those rights and other personal concerns.[17] Prickliness about rights and related identity issues may have the ironic result of further driving wedges between personal lives and the public sphere. Some celebrate the liberation of individuals from oppressive public norms and obligations, while others decry the decline of coherent societies and nations.[18]

These changes in personal relationships to society and public life may explain some of the declining confidence in both national leaders and the press discussed in earlier chapters. Add to this the surrounding fragmentation of many social institutions, from schools and political parties to churches and families, and it is easy to see why many observers conclude that the authoritative basis of public information itself seems to be in decline. People simply have fewer common institutional bases for sharing and respecting the same information. These personal information trends are not helped by the politicians and news organizations using communication technologies to tailor information more to personal emotions and consumer tastes than to more challenging views of the public interest. When viewed from different perspectives on the information system—whether from the standpoint of the press, political actors, the people, or emerging technologies—the information environments in which we live are changing in important ways.

Three American Myths about Freedom of the Press

Understanding how to improve the information system in the United States is made more challenging by the layers of belief and mythology that have built up to defend the very things that may be weakening that system. As discussed throughout the book, common sense is not always the best guide to discovering how things work. We learned, for example, that the popular belief in liberal press bias is not only off the mark, but it may also actually keep people from recognizing more serious biases. The biases outlined in chapter 2 run far deeper than ideology; they actively discourage many citizens of different political persuasions from engaging critically with the political world around them. We also examined the myth that sensational news is what the public wants. This belies the fact that sensationalism and infotainment are mainly the products of corporate profit pressures because they are cheap to produce.

When a system is not working well, it is often because popular beliefs and misperceptions keep the dysfunction going. Conventional wisdoms are often taken on faith without much evidence to support them. Because they are resistant to rational argument or evidence, such beliefs help support larger myths, such as the legend that the US press system is free and independent. And when that system is not working to our satisfaction, it is easy to rationalize that the problems are due to superficial failings such as the liberal bias of journalists or the venality of politicians. Among the broadly shared conventional wisdoms that help support the myth of the free press (and discourage deeper thinking about the news and democracy) are these:

- Support for private corporate ownership of the news media
- Resistance to government support for public broadcasting
- Belief that news should be objective or politically neutral

What if these conventional wisdoms that importantly define our communication system actually contribute to the failings of news? Consider how each of these core elements of the American legacy press system may actually limit its capacity to produce quality news.

THE NEWS ABOUT CORPORATE OWNERSHIP
IN THE MEDIA SYSTEM

Americans too easily regard private ownership of public information as a good thing. Economic competition is often imagined to produce informational diversity and quality. Yet markets that have been deregulated to the extent they have in the United States present opportunities for concentration of ownership and control, resulting in oligopoly or monopoly. This is why democratic governments nearly everywhere else regulate key markets more strictly—particularly media markets—in order to protect the people from the many unhappy effects of unchecked economic power. Many other government regulations are taken for granted: most Americans trust that they can safely drink the water from the tap or that the new toaster they bought will probably not burn down the house. Government regulations concerning health or product safety have become invisible guarantees of decent lives that few would argue with (beyond skirmishes over putting fluoride in drinking water or vaccinating children). Yet there is surprisingly little public concern about protecting the quality of ideas that ultimately define the quality of democracy.

As discussed in chapter 7, the corporate ownership of most of the news business in the United States does not advance the quality or citizen-friendliness of information. When John Stuart Mill long ago discussed the importance of a *marketplace of ideas* for democracy, he thought about how to design election and press systems that would bring the most diverse ideas into public debate and link them to governing.[19] Many other democracies still think seriously about how to best represent and stimulate the thinking of the diverse publics that make up complex societies. Unfortunately, the American faith in the rule of markets means that there is not much serious policy-level thinking about just what kind of press system citizens should have.

Even when scholars and journalists engage with this important question, there is little interest from government or most citizens in imposing public responsibility guidelines (beyond some guidelines of public taste) on private media corporations. Public information standards in this age of free enterprise would be denounced by media corporations and by the politicians they support as dangerous violations of free speech and free enterprise. Many citizens would echo these concerns and many more would reject the idea of strengthening public service broadcasting.

THE NEWS ABOUT PUBLIC BROADCASTING

The government regulates the quality of air, food, and water much more actively than it regulates the quality of political information. There is probably more truth in product advertising than in political advertising. People fear government intervention in the area of political information and cannot imagine government regulations that might actually expand the range of ideas in circulation. This hands-off approach to the press has been criticized by communication scholar Robert McChesney as actually limiting the range of ideas in American political debate. Compared with most other advanced democracies, the United States provides little airspace or financial support for public service broadcasting. Repeated government decisions to limit public broadcasting have served up the public airwaves to commercial corporations with little accompanying obligation to serve the public interest.[20] The journalism crisis of recent years provoked McChesney and John

Nichols to think about how to restore public support for the most precious public good: information. They note that in the early days of the republic, the main government expenditure after national defense was the large federal subsidy for the exchange of information through the US Postal Service.[21] If the founders felt that the government should find ways to support the flow of ideas, why is our public communication system so weak today?

Despite its bare-bones operation, public broadcasting in this country faces continual attack from conservative members of Congress and media critics. In many ways, public broadcasting in the United States is not as independent as it could be because it is forced by limited government support to take money from commercial sponsors and audience members. As an alternative to this fragile public system, why not shift a tiny portion of the money spent on corporate subsidies or other tax breaks for business, to support an independent media system chartered to expand the range of ideas and experiment with news formats beyond those found in commercial media?

The repeated conservative attacks on public broadcasting alternately charge that it reflects a liberal bias and that it is dangerous to have such a system at all because it may be prone to government pressures on content. As if to realize those fears, the Bush administration stacked the board and management of the Corporation for Public Broadcasting (CPB) with Republican appointees. Those operatives inserted more conservative content into programming, even though their own polling showed broad public satisfaction with the programming on both public television (the Public Broadcasting Service, or PBS) and radio (National Public Radio, or NPR). One of the first moves was to push out Bill Moyers, longtime journalist and host of the PBS program *NOW*, under charges that his program was liberally biased. Moyers's program was eventually restored after an investigation found that the management overstepped its bounds. Even if the charge of liberal bias were true, the idea that there should be no program reflecting a critical or liberal viewpoint on the air seems an extreme way to impose impartiality. In any event, packing the management of public broadcasting with conservatives was an ironic move given the history of conservative warnings about government meddling in public broadcast content.[22]

Most other advanced democratic nations have far more developed public service news and entertainment media systems than the United States. Sweden even subsidizes local newspapers in areas where there would otherwise be no community voice. The most respected news sources in many countries are the public radio and television news services. Yet Americans generally have trouble imagining how government-funded journalism could avoid being a mouthpiece for the government itself. In thinking about this issue, it may help to remember that the current US press system has not achieved such impressive levels of independence from officials, or set high standards for critical reporting, either. There are many ways to insulate journalists from direct government pressure in public service media systems. A common model is to appoint oversight commissions balanced with representatives from different parties and political groups, along with members of major religious, educational, business, and labor institutions. These commissions monitor news content and negotiate norms and standards for journalism.

THE NEWS ABOUT OBJECTIVE JOURNALISM

When combined with a highly commercial and minimally regulated press system, the cultural ideal of neutral or objective journalism may be the greatest limit on the communication of political ideas. No matter how independent they may be, journalists who avoid introducing political perspective in their coverage all end up reporting much the same news based on official spin. Worse, as shown in chapter 6, objectivity may force reporting of one side of a story that is not true just to guarantee balance. Yet the powerful ideal of a free-but-unbiased press leaves most journalists and citizens unable to imagine another way. It seems that politicians, like the voters who elect them, believe that it is possible to separate the news from politics and arrive at something resembling objective information. Thus, Americans grudgingly receive a similar replay of the same events and ideas from virtually every mainstream news channel. Political communication scholar Thomas Patterson describes this as the "irony of the free press" in America: "American journalists have concluded that the marketplace of ideas is enhanced when they are 'free' or 'independent,' in the sense that they are not connected organizationally, editorially, or legally to any political institution or mandate. In this view . . . news decisions should be the free choices of unregulated journalists. . . . [Yet] when journalists are detached from political moorings . . . they tend to generate a form of news that, first, underplays political ideas and, second, is consensual as opposed to competitive in its content."[23]

Patterson's comparative study of journalists in five nations found that American journalists may be the freest in the world—at least they cited fewer limits on their reporting than their counterparts in other democracies. American reporters, however, also made the narrowest range of choices about how they would cover various hypothetical news situations.[24] Such findings, along with a large literature on how the press is dependent on official spin, suggest that we are operating in the realm of a myth about the free press that is out of touch with underlying realities of power in American politics.

News and Power in America: Myth versus Reality

In the ideal civics-book version of American democracy, power rests with the people, who are, in effect, the voice of the political system. Leaders are supposed to take cues from the people and express their voice politically. The journalist in this scheme occupies the role of the independent monitor who reports to the people on how well leaders handle the public trust. In simple picture form, this ideal version of power in America looks like figure 8.1.

It is obvious that the reality of power in America does not look much like this ideal picture. As numerous examples in this book have indicated, leaders and organized interests have usurped enormous amounts of political power and reduced popular control over the political system by using the media to generate support, compliance, and just plain confusion among the public. Grassroots opinion drives various battles over rights and morals such as abortion and religious expression, but on matters affecting economic policy and other sensitive areas of state and corporate concern, the battle for public opinion is waged largely by organized interests and political elites who use polling and marketing techniques to deliver images to generally inattentive publics. Which came first, the inattentive public or the blocked communication channels? Either way, the result is not encouraging for public participation.

The conventional commercial media also play a different role in the reality of American politics than the one they play in the ideal version. News organizations are more often political transmission lines to the people than they are monitors or watchdogs of the information they transmit. The news gates are opened most often to voices from below when government officials or other prominent newsmakers are already in conflict about an issue. Citizen groups seldom get into the news unless they first get on the govern-

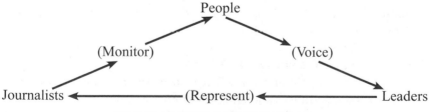

Figure 8.1. Ideal version of power in America

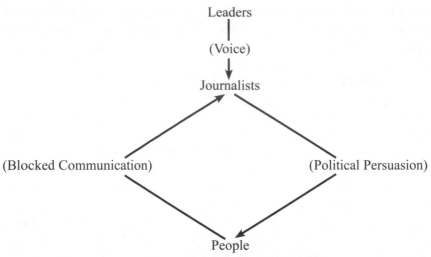

Figure 8.2. Realistic picture of American political power

ment agenda, or they engage in disruptive tactics such as occupying the streets and public spaces. Figure 8.2 provides a more realistic picture of the place of journalism in the American political power system.

As discussed throughout this book, there are a number of obvious reasons the media do not monitor government actions in an adequate way. To begin with, the news as it currently exists is a profit-making enterprise (albeit an endangered one). As long as profits can still be extracted, even by dismantling the basis of quality journalism, the owners of news organizations have little incentive to change what they do. Those elite national journalists who still have jobs derive a large measure of professional success and personal satisfaction from their status and have few incentives to rock the boat. In addition, critical watchdog reporting often brings social and political pressure to bear on reporters and their organizations. Even routine news reporting is constantly criticized by (largely conservative) media-monitoring organizations and by political and economic elites for not being sufficiently objective. Such media criticism has become an important lever in the power system by helping extreme voices gain greater credibility in public discourse. All these developments raise the question of why the myth of a free press in America persists.

Why the Free Press Myth Persists

As they pass through school, citizens learn inspiring things about the free press. These ideals are based on dramatic events in American history. The free press legend is reinforced by inspiring endorsements, such as these thoughts of Thomas Jefferson: "The people are the only censors of their governors [and they must have full] information of their affairs through the channel of the public papers. . . . [Were] it left to me to decide whether we should have a government without newspapers or newspapers without a government, I should not hesitate a moment to prefer the latter."[25]

Ideas like these have been passed down by every generation of journalists, educators, and politicians throughout American history and have come to represent the spirit of a nation and a people. The real meaning of those sentiments in today's society is hard to imagine, yet ideals that are given such powerful reinforcement and that endow people with such noble purpose often take on a life of their own. They are inspirational, hopeful, ennobling—giving substance to a national history that would otherwise become vague in the minds of new generations. Such are the characteristics of myths. Unfortunately, myths like the free press stand in the way of seeing the realities of power.

The myth of a free press and a free people and its guiding principle of objective reporting would seem to provide different but compelling benefits for different groups. However, there is an irony here: the groups at the top of the power structure gain the material advantages of power and control, while the groups at the bottom trade real power (because in reality the myth works to limit their political involvement) for psychological reassurances. Thus, the broader the support is for the idea of fair or objective journalism, the more firmly established the inequalities of power become. A brief overview of the interests of politicians, journalists, and the public illustrates the different (and even contradictory) bases of loyalty to the myth.

POLITICIANS AND THE MYTH

Most political actors promote the free press / free people myth because it is useful politically. Equating deregulation with free markets and a free press makes it easier for them to deregulate media ownership and continue to win favor from the media owners who sponsor them. It is also necessary for politicians to endorse the free press myth to avoid being attacked by other politicians and the press. And since there is little public discussion of how well the media system is working for democracy, many citizens would question politicians who fail to echo the reassuring myths. Even though interest organizations and spin doctors work overtime to influence the news and public opinion, publics demand at least the illusion that their system of government represents their will. It matters little whether politicians are conscious of the contradiction between their public support for the free press myth and their political efforts to control information or aid the concentration of media ownership. The political benefits accrue as much to those who truly believe the contemporary relevance of the story of the free press and the free people as to those who embrace the free press myth cynically.

As discussed in the last chapter, media activists are pressing politicians to support policies that create greater press independence from corporate influence and better public access to media. Given their lack of resources, groups such as Free Press (freepress.net) have had impressive success in areas such as keeping the Internet open. This suggests that public input matters, and that the more people speak out in favor of a press system that promotes public accountability and popular voice, the more politicians may think and act differently in these areas.

JOURNALISTS AND THE MYTH

The benefit of the news myth for the journalist is not power (at least in the conventional sense) but professional credibility. Without public claims to objective or fair reporting, and independence from government influence, mainstream journalists could not project professional status. Even if this status is tarnished in the eyes of the public, it is supported by the values operating within the journalism profession itself. The myth provides the reporter, like the politician, with a ready-made role in the ideal picture of American democracy. Because that role is so easily dramatized with the help of the politician, it would be hard to imagine many reporters not embracing the part. Reporters who become frustrated with what objectivity means in practice may simply leave the major news organizations, perhaps to become freelance writers or reporters outside the mainstream.

Some journalists, like some politicians, may cynically mouth the news myth while harboring a fuller private sense of its emptiness. However, many journalists fail to see the contradictions in their pursuit of news objectivity. At some point, most career journalists accept the fact that reporting what officials say and do is really the highest form of professionalism. When former NBC anchor Tom Brokaw was questioned about whether the press failed to raise enough questions about the Bush administration's case for the Iraq War, he noted that in the end, "Congress voted overwhelmingly to approve the war—and we had to reflect that."[26] The moral here seems to be that when in doubt, the edge goes to the government. From this assumption, it is a small step from embracing the activities of professional, objective journalism to the idea that these activities really are the truth about politics. Telling it like it is in the official circles of Washington politics can become equated, however erroneously, with telling the truth.

This does not mean that journalists do not worry about objectivity and other elements of the news myth. They do. The problem comes in finding a new journalistic stance that provides more critical distance from the power holders they cover. For example, after the invasion of Iraq, the *Columbia Journalism Review* ran a cover story called "Re-thinking Objectivity." The story's lead idea was that "in a world of spin, our awkward embrace of an ideal can make us passive recipients of the news." The lesson emphasized was the failure of the mainstream press to challenge the Bush administration's rationale for the war: "In his March 6 press conference, in which he laid out his reasons for the coming war, President Bush mentioned al-Qaeda or the attacks of September 11 fourteen times in fifty-two minutes. No one challenged him on it, despite the fact that the CIA had questioned the Iraq–al-Qaeda connection, and that there has never been solid evidence marshaled to support the idea that Iraq was involved in the attacks of 9/11."[27] The trouble is that calling for better investigative reporting—or more reporting of credible sources beyond official circles—is unlikely to make it happen. Change requires the rise of new professional norms of the sort that the current era of media disruption may generate.

THE PEOPLE AND THE MYTH

What do citizens gain from embracing the news myth? To answer this perplexing question, we must return to the two pictures of power in America presented earlier in the chapter. In the second picture (fig. 8.2), which better represents the reality of power in America, the people are locked into a weak power position with their choices structured for them. Their efforts to respond politically are filtered through the gatekeeping rules of news formulas. In such situations, people either withdraw from the source of their distress (e.g., from politics and public life) or embrace idealized images that are frustratingly out of touch with realities they experience. The tensions between the ideal and the reality of the news start at an early age, as the free press myth is taught in schools as an academic subject for which there are right and wrong answers. Students who question the myth are likely to do poorly on tests. When we look at other education systems that impose myths uncritically as fact, we brand them as propaganda. What do we make of this civic education system?

The learning process that reinforces the free press myth continues throughout life in the form of stories in the news itself. Idealized versions of democracy in action fill the daily news. Both journalists and politicians continually dramatize the illusory appeal of figure 8.1, the free press / free people myth, for the benefit of the public. They offer news stories as reports to the people about choices or problems that face them. Leaders in the news claim to be speaking for the people, and appeal for popular support and understanding. If people can suspend their disbelief about such claims, they can live in an illusory world in which democracy is operating just fine. For many citizens, however, the dissonance is too great, and they either withdraw or condemn the press and politicians without having access to clarifying public discussions to sort out the root of the problems. As a result, many who become disillusioned tend to think that the failings of the system can be fixed with more honest politicians and more neutral journalists. Such solutions, while popular, fail to address the deeper problems with the national information system such as the distortion of our public debate on account of pressures from special interests and spin. The following discussion explores various changes that citizens, journalists, and politicians can make.

Proposals for Citizens, Journalists, and Politicians

It is naive to think that some magic wand of government, journalism, or citizenship can be waved and all will be changed. Yet even small changes within each sphere can make important differences. Above all, it would help to recognize the roots of our communication problems and talk about them differently in public. As we enter an age of electronic democracy and information abundance, the opportunity exists once again to have a critical national debate about how we should inform ourselves and engage with politics. New information technologies through which citizens can interact with politicians, journalists, and each other may help us think creatively about striking a new balance of media power.

PROPOSALS FOR CITIZENS

Citizens can make a difference by thinking more creatively about how information comes to them. Participating in public life without the illusions of the free press / free people myth is a good start. The next step is to begin thinking freely about alternatives. There is little cost to brainstorming about a more perfect information order. Should we encourage more partisan political reporting? Seek out reporting that contains more analysis? Celebrate political comedy that builds perspective? What about government incentives for news organizations that pioneer new formats for covering issues, elections, and chronic social problems? These and other ideas are worth exploring openly without concern that they would somehow violate our mythical notions of a free or objective press.

In addition to thinking more creatively about designing a better national communication system, people would also do well to learn how to better use the one we currently have. The critical analyses contained in this book can be used in decoding the news. If people learn to read between the lines and see beyond the images, they can reduce their frustration and confusion with the news. In short, becoming informed does not mean simply reading more papers or watching more television. It means decoding the information from these and other sources with a critical eye. In other words, becoming informed entails more than just memorizing the who, what, where, when, and how of the isolated events of the day. Understanding the political causes and social consequences of public affairs is also useful for clarifying feelings and deciding how to respond. Armed with the basic introduction provided in this book, it is possible to recognize and decode the most common information biases in the news. The following guidelines should help in becoming a more critical news consumer.

Recognize Stereotypes and Plot Formulas When new information is translated into standard plot formulas, there is no challenge to replace prejudices with new insights. Yet the easiest stories for politicians to tell and journalists to write are based on familiar images of the world. Unless these warmed-over schemes are detected and discarded, the news remains an unhelpful forum, reinforcing superficial understandings and old ideologies. It is important to detect and discard loaded descriptions and buzzwords. When opponents routinely called President Obama a socialist, the news was sure to set off knee-jerk reactions among conservatives, who wanted to see him in negative terms, while angering progressive supporters. Terms like "leftist," "right-winger," "big government," "freedom," "populist," or "religious fundamentalist" are often planted by spin doctors to undermine their opponents. Yet such terms often stick as though they were objective descriptions. This is not to say that there are no leftists or rightists or other "-ists" in the world. However, accepting those terms as though they are inherently meaningful may shut down any desire to know more about political actors and their motives.

Another common reporting practice is to give anonymity to sources spinning the news yet lend them credibility by calling them "well placed" or "informed." Savvy information processors should beware that these sources are often high officials using their cover of anonymity to plant rumor and innuendo in the news. In general, more weight should be given to sources that are identified. The exception, of course, is when sources fear for their lives or livelihoods by blowing the whistle.

Also beware of tired formulas such as *The War on* _____ (drugs, crime, terrorism, etc.). For example, declaring war on terrorism has in many ways clouded a spectrum of important issues such as who the terrorists are, where they come from, what the best responses are, and what kinds of personal liberties we may be sacrificing in the war against them. In some cases the blanket declaration "War on Terror" may block understanding of disenfranchised groups who have resorted to violence as a last desperate measure to have their problems addressed. For example, the complex situation involving the Kurdish people is muddled in the news. The Kurds have been allies of the United States in Iraq by fighting ISIS, yet the same Kurdish fighters have been attacked by another US ally, Turkey. Because US officials do not speak out about why they have tolerated Turkey attacking one of the few effective forces fighting ISIS, the news remains a puzzle. What seems clear is that one nation's terrorist is another nation's freedom fighter, and the news must wait for officials to pronounce the good guys and the bad guys. This was the conclusion of political communication scholar Steven Livingston, who showed that the news does not assign labels until officials make the call, and that labeling actors as terrorists is a strategic form of spinning the news by those officials.[28]

The emotions stirred up by terrorism can pave the way for sweeping policy agendas, from war to domestic spying. As Douglas McLeod and Dhavan Shah have shown, emotional public responses to terms like "war" and "terrorism" following the attacks of 9/11 enabled a number of policies compromising the civil liberties of the American public.[29] It surely would have been more difficult for the government to claim such powers without having a loaded term such as "terrorist" to use when taking away civil liberties.

Seek Additional Sources of Information This does not mean consulting the *New York Times* to check on *USA Today*. Rather, it means consulting alternative publications that look at a situation from the standpoint of critics, opposition groups, or expert observers. Information in the news can seem true simply because it fits so neatly with a powerful image, a familiar plot, or a deeply held belief. A useful reminder is that reality is seldom neat and clean. Raw data are always messy and ambiguous. The ambiguity of data is their real advantage—they make us think critically and probe for new patterns. When facts and claims fit too neatly, they provide psychological affirmation, not a reality check. Thus, many Americans were prepared to hear that there was some connection between Saddam Hussein and al-Qaeda following 9/11, and few stopped to see whether there was evidence to challenge this administration claim. The result of that deception continues to haunt us these many years later, with chaos and failed states in the region.

The Internet makes it easy to gather diverse information on almost any subject. The major search engines tap into different domains of news and information. It is important to recognize that not all the results of these searches are reliable, but it is possible to detect patterns of information from known sources that challenge the too-convenient spin of official news accounts.

Find Sources of Perspective Such as Political Comedy As discussed earlier in the book, few people use political comedy as a substitute for other information sources, but instead they use it as a way of putting information from other sources into perspective. When news becomes mostly spin, and reality edges dangerously toward the absurd, comedy may be the best way to straighten it out.[30] When citizens share their sense that official dramatizations of events are not credible, governments may be less inclined to think that people will buy anything. Comedy often exposes staged events as resembling bad reality TV. When he left *The Daily Show* in 2015, Jon Stewart challenged his viewers to spot "bullshit," which is everywhere. What matters, according to Stewart, is to call it out. As mentioned in chapter 1, Trevor Noah vowed to continue this mission in his first program after replacing Stewart as *Daily Show* host.

Learn to Become Self-Critical At this point, you may be concerned that these guidelines will turn you into a cynic rather than a critic. Who or what can be trusted? The goal of news criticism is not to reject everything—it is to think confidently and independently about world events in the face of a lot of pressure to think like everybody else. Nor is the point to distrust all authorities—it is to trust your own judgment.

This brings us to what may be the most important guideline: Recognize the importance of prior beliefs (and prejudices) in screening and accepting news information. And, wherever possible, challenge those beliefs with information that is at odds with them. The point of being self-critical is not to get rid of beliefs altogether or to tear them down as fast as we build them up. The goal is to make sure that our beliefs do not stand as a wall against reality. Beliefs are most useful when they help us engage constructively in the ongoing solution of social problems. When beliefs are proclaimed as absolutes to be defended against all evidence to the contrary, they become the causes of social problems. Because the news contains two sides to most stories, people can simply select the version of reality that comes closest to their prior beliefs and never change their thinking about the world. What if neither side represented in the news provides a particularly useful way to think about an issue? What if both sides have some merit? Escaping our current political dilemmas requires the will to challenge existing political beliefs, and there is no better way than by resisting the daily temptation to look to the news for confirmation of what we already hold to be true about the world.

PROPOSALS FOR JOURNALISTS

Reporters and editors often argue that they would like to do more with the news, but time, space, profit pressures, and fickle audiences just do not permit it. In response to these journalistic laments, consider this challenge: it is the responsibility of the press to hold government accountable even when it fails to do so itself. Journalists may also aspire to prepare the citizenry for participation, or at least try to write news with citizens in mind. Here is a discussion of how to implement these goals.

Beware Information Biases of Personalization, Dramatization, Fragmentation, and Game Framing As suggested in chapter 2, news biases such as drama can be used constructively in communicating important information. However, current news formats are more often melodramatic, sacrificing the deeper issues for the trials and tribulations of political actors. Journalists could easily reduce the melodramatic overtones of the news by developing the historical and institutional contexts in which action is played out. This does not mean eliminating the actors involved—it is hard to tell a story without characters—but rather placing them in the larger political context. Thus, many crime stories could be removed from the realm of the bizarre, grotesque, and sinister, and placed in the social world of poverty, loss of community, alienation, group conflict, and psychological disorders. Budget deficits could be removed from frames personalizing them around big-spending politicians, and placed in the context of the trade-offs and political constraints that create them. International violence could be taken out of the personalized world of tough talk, and shown in the context of economic, military, and international relations that sustain many conflicts. And the continual portrayal of politics as a game distracts from the deeper analysis of why politicians often resort to such tactics. If the reasons why political actors try to undermine opponents and resist cooperation were exposed, perhaps the public exposure would discourage those behaviors.

Indeed, the press could shift from channeling political spin to more analysis and accountability. Virtually every news story could be enriched in favor of more useful social, historical, and institutional analyses. This shift corresponds to Shanto Iyengar's recommendations for less episodic and more thematic reporting discussed in chapters 1 and 2.[31] Such journalistic shifts would make it possible for the general news audience to grasp the larger political implications of events without resorting to so much laborious decoding.

Many reporters and editors believe that more attention to social, institutional, and historical factors would only make the news more complicated and confuse people. Most people probably could not be any more confused about the world than they are at present. It is also possible that this confusion is the direct result of personalized, fragmented, melodramatic, and game-framed news formats that fail to provide intelligible contexts for developing events. Given the forces of change at work in the current media environment, there may be opportunities to disrupt the cycle of simpleminded coverage aimed at simpleminded publics.

Introduce More Background Knowledge into Stories To continue the line of reasoning from the previous section, journalists could use more of what they have learned as expert witnesses to the situations they cover. A Pew Research Center survey of journalists revealed that fewer than half of television news workers felt that "providing an interpretation of the news" was a core journalistic principle.[32] Mark Levy and John Robinson suggest that reports must pass the "so what?" test:

> It's used implicitly all the time in the newsroom to decide if something is newsworthy. Why, for example, was it important that a space suit had been recovered from the shuttle wreckage . . . ? The TV journalists who covered that news knew the answers; they had to in order to get their stories on the air. But most reports in our . . . sample never explicitly conveyed that "so what?" element of the news. Sometimes it was there—between the lines. But in our experience, information reported between the lines tends to remain there.[33]

Legacy reporting leans heavily toward letting the actors tell the story. In these source-driven narratives, the reporter's voice sets the tone of a story. As noted earlier, this tone is often cynical or game focused, precisely because journalists cannot find ways to say what they really know or think about the situations they are covering. Moving away from actor-centered narrative toward observer-centered narrative would place control over the development of a news story with the journalist, where it properly belongs, not with political actors, whose interest is in manipulating the story to their own advantage. The place where reporters could add most to stories is in the explanation of how different policy proposals were developed, why others were rejected, and what the competing proposals might accomplish if implemented. In her cogent analysis of news coverage of the 1990s welfare reform, Regina Lawrence noted that during the extended period in which the various proposals were being debated between Congress and the White House, journalists mainly contributed commentary about the games and strategies. However, after the reforms were passed, journalists introduced an impressive review of the substance of the new policies.[34] Such journalistic discussions of political substance could have clarified the issues if they came earlier in the coverage.

Define Political Situations in Terms That Appeal to Ordinary People When reporters clearly define the terms and concepts in a situation, the news audience may begin to see what is going on. New information is hard to assimilate under the best of circumstances. In fragmented, fast-paced news, definition and repetition of new information are essential to comprehension. Pointing out that TV viewers miss the main ideas in two-thirds of all stories, Levy and Robinson urged a revamping of current formats. They concluded that TV news is "produced for people already in the know, it's filled with the jargon of policymakers and riddled with cryptic references to continuing stories. What TV journalists forget is that most viewers need some help in understanding the news, no matter how often the story has been told."[35]

When Congress passed a historic health care act in 2010, the Democratic leadership and the Obama administration did a poor job of explaining what was in the bill and how the new plan would work. Opponents filled the news with shouts of socialism and destruction of freedom of choice. Few news stories went beyond the political battle to sort out the actual details of the new law and make it accessible to people. Whether people would like what they heard cannot be known, since they were not given the information. However, what is clear is that leaving the news to become a spin contest— that the Republicans clearly won—resulted in a majority of Americans opposing the new law while still favoring health care reform.

Involve the Audience in Producing and Sharing Content The social media revolution makes it possible for individual citizens to produce and distribute often high-quality and insightful reporting. For example, the news about democracy protests in Iran, Tunisia, Egypt, and other countries in the Middle East depended on videos and messages sent directly from protesters. Blogs offer other ways for citizens to interact with journalists and stories. As the example of the *Texas Tribune* illustrates, the development of interactive databases may be the answer for many government watchdog stories that are increasingly hard to support in failing news organizations. These and other innovative approaches to public information are illustrated in the case study below on innovative solutions and public information experiments.

PROPOSALS FOR POLITICIANS AND GOVERNMENT

If politicians spent less time spinning the emotions and fears of isolated individuals and actually led publics by educating them on complex issues, they might be more popular. Indeed, many politicians would secretly like to shift their public relations strategies in these directions but fear being attacked by opponents. An unfortunate reality of the contemporary communication system is that politicians who attempt to educate, discuss complex issues, or propose new ways of thinking about problems are routinely attacked as unrealistic, big-spending, big-government politicians who want to rob Americans of their freedoms and create more government programs that do not work. As a result of this tired tone of Washington politics, many of the most talented members of Congress from both parties have left government in recent years, frustrated at the inability to speak or act creatively. The communication system that has evolved in the United States seems designed to drive out careful, open, thoughtful discussion of public problems in favor of stereotypical and stifling appeals to fear and divisive emotions.

Appealing to politicians individually to change how they communicate may get some sympathetic responses, but few are brave enough to fire their spin doctors and pollsters and step in front of the television cameras to talk openly about complex problems. What, then, is the solution for politicians? One approach is to put public pressure on government to referee the national marketplace of ideas just as it referees every other market to protect consumers from fraud, deception, and safety hazards. Why should citizens have less protection against public information "fraud" than against stock market fraud and faulty products? The following are four simple recommendations for government that would greatly improve the quality of political information.

Limit the Flow of Big Money into Politics Getting elected to high public office in America is extremely expensive. And, as Lawrence Lessig has argued, money in politics corrupts the system in several ways: (1) politicians spend enormous amounts of taxpayer time in fund-raising, rather than attending to public business; (2) public trust in government is depressed both because the system looks bad and because people believe that issues favored by big donors get special attention at the expense of more popular policies; and (3) former politicians often get rich when they leave office and go to work for lobbying firms, law firms, and corporations that they once helped when in office, which perpetuates the corruption.[36]

In 2002, Congress passed campaign finance reforms that promised a start on the problem, but in 2010, the Supreme Court issued the 5–4 landmark *Citizens United* ruling that struck down legal provisions limiting corporate spending in elections. Fox News ran the headline: "Founding Fathers Smiling after Supreme Court Campaign Finance Ruling."[37] Hamilton may have approved of this, but it is hard to imagine Madison, Jefferson, Franklin, or many others applauding. Denouncing the partisan ruling by the court Republican majority was a 90-page dissent penned by John Paul Stevens that said, in part: "While American democracy is imperfect, few outside the majority of this court would have thought its flaws included a dearth of corporate money in politics." Furthermore, "the court's ruling threatens to undermine the integrity of elected institutions across the nation."[38]

Subsequent Supreme Court rulings (e.g., *McCutcheon*, 2014) have further removed limits on money in politics. Now there are many channels for unlimited money in politics, including the sinister category of "dark money" in which unlimited amounts flow into tax-sheltered 501(c)(4) organizations claiming to serve social welfare functions that allow them to evade disclosing donors or amounts. The ever-more-creative ways of sheltering money and donors make paper trails increasingly hard to construct.[39] However, it is clear that as a result of the removal of limits and thanks to ever-more-creative financing options, the amounts pouring into elections continue to escalate to breathtaking heights. The 2012 presidential campaign alone ran over $2.5 billion. Estimates for the 2016 presidential contest were around $5 billion at the time of this writing. Today in the United States, less than one percent of campaign donations are under $200, leading Supreme Court Justice Ginsberg to lament that "we have all the democracy that money can buy."[40]

Not surprisingly, most Americans feel that moneyed interests have too much power in American politics. Since the original 2010 ruling, polls consistently show that super majorities (typically over 80 percent) of Americans feel that wealthy individuals, big companies, banks, and lobbyists have too much influence over government and politicians, and that the general public has far too little.[41] A 2012 poll found that 86 percent felt that government corruption was the second-most important problem facing government, just behind job creation.[42] In a 2015 *New York Times*/CBS News Poll, 84 percent felt that money had too much influence in politics, and 85 percent believed that elected politicians sometimes or often helped out those who gave them money.[43] The money problem is magnified by the increasingly uncompetitive system of congressional districting, and by conservative efforts to discourage voting among poor and minority citizens. As a result of these various sources of corruption, government policies in the United States are at odds with majorities of Americans on a number of issues, such as gun control, tax rates on the wealthy, bank and finance regulation, the minimum wage, public subsidies for wealthy individuals and corporations, and Medicare benefits, among others.

In addition to making government unresponsive to the demands of the people, the corrupting influence of money has introduced turbulence into politics. The Tea Party movement that rose up after the financial crisis in 2009 is one result of popular disgust with government. The oddly popular candidacy of Donald Trump in 2015–2016 is another. To the shock of party professionals, Trump turned the Republican primaries into his most popular reality TV show ever, making unscripted and often offensive remarks to the approval of more voters than sided with any of the other, more tightly managed early candidates. In trying to explain the Trump phenomenon, *New York Times* columnist Maureen Dowd said: "It's deeply weird, but the jeering billionaire reality star seems authentic to many Americans. Trump is a manifestation of national disgust—with the money that consumed politics, with the dysfunctional, artificial status quo and with the turgid return to a Bush-Clinton race with a less adept Bush and Clinton."[44]

Meanwhile, other countries have devised many different ways of limiting the corrupting influences of money. For example, Germany provides public financing to parties while imposing strict reporting on large donations, limiting the length of its campaigns, and giving parties free airtime on TV. There is overwhelming popular support to fix the American system, with 85 percent saying that major changes are necessary, yet 58 percent were pessimistic that such changes would be made.[45] Meanwhile, the continuing corruption of American democracy means that the news is often filled with spin as politicians attempt to cover up the distorted policy agenda of government.

Control Media Monopolies As discussed in chapter 7, the concentration of media ownership is detrimental to the diversity and the quality of information reaching the public. The singular concern about profit maximizing has changed the landscape of corporate journalism: fewer documentaries, more mayhem news, less investigative reporting, more dependence on spin, more cheap reality TV programming, news increasingly selected to fit audience demographics, and little programming for economically marginal audiences and ethnic communities. Antimonopoly laws and public responsibility standards once existed, and new ones could be written with the quality of information expressly in mind. Over the past two decades, government has given the green light to most media mergers with little consideration of public values. For their part, the corporate media are notably silent regarding the political and social responsibilities of big business. On the contrary, many corporate opinion leaders promote the idea that the only obligation of business is to make profits for the investors. A positive development in recent years involves the emergence of a citizen media reform movement (see www.freepress.net) that has put pressure on the FCC and Congress to consider the public interest when writing media legislation and conducting regulatory activities.

More Funding (and Creative Freedom) for Public Broadcasting Current government policies on public broadcasting restrict funding. The resulting dependence on listener donations and corporate sponsorship forces struggling local stations to play it safe. More enlightened policies could encourage public broadcasters to be what the commercial media are not—that is, to find ways to promote more diversity, more grassroots input, more minority voices, and more challenging viewpoints. If all of this is too much to accomplish under one roof, split the current public broadcasting corporation into multiple organizations under the directorship of different public sectors: political parties and related interest networks (perhaps channels for Republicans, Independents, and Democrats), public interest organizations (e.g., think tanks, citizen watchdog organizations, and foundations), and social groups (churches, educators, arts and culture organizations). Alternately, government can ensure that the current public broadcasting organizations have boards of directors and political firewalls that broaden programming beyond the comfort zones of the political factions currently battling for the soul of public broadcasting.

Many other nations have designed strong public broadcasting systems to meet the public communication requirements of democracy. Continuing debate and scrutiny accompany those systems as they face government pressures and adapt to stronger private competition. By contrast, the United States has not had a serious debate since the 1930s and 1940s about the ideal balance between public and private media or the possibilities of more useful public information systems.

Strengthen Public Service Requirements for License Holders Many Americans find it difficult to understand that the airwaves that bring them television, radio, and mobile communications, and the local franchises that bring them cable, are sold or granted by the government. Just as we expect companies granted rights to use public lands to undertake some stewardship, so should we require holders of communication licenses to have obligations other than to commercial advertisers and corporate shareholders.

In the view of communication scholar Robert McChesney, one of the great turning points in the American information system came in the 1930s when Congress granted the great proportion of the radio and television bandwidths to private operators with relatively few responsibilities to create public forums or cover social issues in any depth.[46] Over the years, the FCC, with the encouragement of Congress imposed some modest public service requirements on licensees. The lobbying efforts of increasingly powerful communication companies, combined with the growing anti-regulation mood in the nation, have resulted in rollbacks in operator obligations to run public affairs programs, community forums, and even basic news programming.

Yet just as governments decide how broadband cable monopolies and new digital spectra will be allocated, they have leverage over what public service obligations the license holders should have. Local governments can extract subsidies from cable operators for high-quality local arts and politics channels that might promote citizen involvement in local affairs. As discussed in the last chapter, the openness of the Internet, which many people take for granted, is seriously affected by regulatory decisions about whether Internet service should be like the phone and postal services that are mandated to be available equally to all citizens. The battle over the freedom of the Internet is just one of the issues facing the future of public communication. One policy goal to develop the potential of digital democracy would be to create a publicly supported communication commons so that people can find resources, create and share information, and take political action.[47]

Time for a Public Discussion about the Role of the Press

The role for the press that the founders of this country imagined was far removed from the corporate media and the deteriorating condition of legacy journalism today. Thomas Jefferson imagined that communities would have many partisan news sources. The idea was not that any individual would achieve balance by reading them all, but that diverse viewpoints would be in circulation and provide for discussion and debate when people met. In today's society, many native digital sites come closer to the Jeffersonian idea, but society has fragmented so much that people do not meet in communities to discuss public affairs. People are confronted with do-it-yourself networking via social media, which has produced some impressive levels of public engagement, but offers little enduring foundation on which to build new groups, movements, or parties. The changing society and media system of the current era have eclipsed the pleasant fantasy of how a community-based partisan press might spark a vibrant democracy.

By the mid-twentieth century, the press was already coming under fire for becoming too big and too close to business and government interests. In an effort to fend off calls for more regulation and enhanced public media funding, publishing magnate Henry Luce convened a distinguished panel of journalists and academics under the chair of University of Chicago president Robert Hutchins. This Commission on Freedom of the Press (now commonly known as the Hutchins Commission) spent four years debating the responsibilities of the press to democracy and society. An official report was issued in 1947 outlining norms and guidelines that influenced journalism for much of the mass media era, until deregulation became the trend in the 1980s. The report opened with an account of the long-since-faded ideal of the founders: "Nor was it supposed that many citizens would subscribe to all the local journals. It was more likely that each would take the one which would reinforce his prejudices. But in each village and town, with its relatively simple social structure and its wealth of social contacts, various opinions might encounter each other in face-to-face meetings; the truth, it was hoped, would be sorted out by competition in the local marketplace."[48]

As the Hutchins Commission report made clear, we no longer live in such a world. Even in the mid-twentieth century, it was clear that competing partisan news sources were not commonly available and that people did not live in close-knit communities where they would deliberate until reaching higher understandings of situations. For better or worse, the news had become distilled into commercialized and highly uniform reports that presented themselves as neutral. Citizens were expected to draw their own personal conclusions—generally without confronting fellow citizens with whom they disagreed. The Hutchins Commission concluded that the changing conditions of press and society placed important responsibilities on contemporary journalism. In particular, news organizations should attempt to challenge dominant points of view that are dominant simply because they are better publicized by government or political interests. News organizations also had the responsibility to bring into their reporting the perspectives of diverse voices from communities who lacked the resources to hire PR agents to help them make the news. The report also recommended standards of fairness and balance in which competing viewpoints would be presented to help audiences experience a kind of mediated deliberation that was often lacking in society. Most of the standards recommended by the Hutchins Commission have been abandoned over the years, as corporations successfully lobbied against government regulations and downgraded their news operations in pursuit of profits.

As communication scholar Victor Pickard has argued, we are long overdue for another visible public examination of the role of the press in American democracy. We need to address the balance between corporate interests and the needs of democracy. Pickard warns that the future of information on the Internet is similarly threatened by the desires of corporations to turn the Internet into a commercial space, colonized by large corporations, with room only for content that benefits business.[49] Until a high-profile national discussion occurs, we do not know the fate of the profusion of chaotic experiments, new business models, and hybrid information formats that define the current transitional period. Indeed, this chaotic time is reminiscent of the era of changing technology and society that brought about the modern (legacy) press a century ago. The question is, what set of forces will converge to establish the next news system? The case study looks at some of the changes and trends that are underway and that we may look back on as producing the next era of news.

CASE STUDY
INNOVATION AND CHANGE IN NEWS FORMATS

The growing crisis in the news industry has produced an array of interesting experiments that may offer glimpses of how that future will look. There are now dozens of independent investigative news organizations that are not tied to large corporations, and hundreds more digital sites offering information from the neighborhood to the global level. Some of these are long-standing operations, such as the Center for Public Integrity and the Center for Investigative Reporting, that have made the transition from the predigital age to the present. However, the vast majority of these sites are native digital platforms that have appeared within the last decade.

As discussed in the case study from chapter 7, some of these native digital sites are well-known operations such as the *Huffington Post*, which combines some original reporting with stories produced by a mix of other organizations and volunteer bloggers. On a given day, the home page of *HuffPo* may run an original report on the crisis in the Middle East alongside a cat video. Other operations are smaller start-ups such as InvestigateWest (www.invw.org), which does stories of interest to the western region of the country, focusing on topics such as power, environment, budget crises, prison populations, housing markets, homelessness, and jobs. These native digital investigative operations are often begun by top journalists from failing news organizations, such as the *Seattle Post Intelligencer* in the case of InvestigateWest. All these organizations face questions about how to generate revenues to support the production of content and how to distribute that content to substantial audiences.

The key issue for the future of news is how to take full advantage of the social technology and crowdsourced logic of the participatory media culture without abandoning journalism to the unpredictable dictates of content-sharing networks. As noted earlier, more-serious news organizations tend to limit audience participation in content production, while many native digital operations are more willing to bend content to audience tastes. It is instructive to look at how different nonprofit and commercial organizations are adapting participatory media logic to their ends.

One of the most interesting experiments with the future of news is going on at ProPublica, which is dedicated to high-quality investigative reporting. ProPublica has the luxury of not being driven by the bottom line, since it is operated as a nonprofit largely through contributions from foundations. As a result, ProPublica is already doing many of the things recommended for journalists above, albeit to a far smaller audience than many legacy news organizations attract. For example, it has run a series of investigations on money in politics, numbering more than 120 reports at the time of this writing. While its decisions about what to report and how to cover it are relatively free of business pressures, ProPublica faces a parallel issue of how to get its product out to audiences large enough to give its stories exposure and impact. One strategy has been to partner with other news organizations to develop and distribute content. NPR has become a steady partner with ProPublica on a number of stories. Indeed, the partner list is an impressive array of legacy and native digital organizations ranging from ABC, the *New York Times*, and *USA Today*, to *Vice* and Amazon. ProPublica in collaboration with the *New York Times Magazine* won a Pulitzer Prize for a long investigative piece on deaths and decisions in a New Orleans hospital during Hurricane Katrina, raising larger questions of how well hospitals are equipped to handle emergencies. In a very different partnership, Amazon sells a subscription service for ProPublica, along with single copies of long reports, through its Kindle reader. Despite these innovative ideas, the Kindle audience remains relatively small, and the partnership model is uneven in terms of selecting and sustaining stories and creating a clear brand signal that draws audiences directly to the ProPublica site.

Hence, the challenge for ProPublica and many other high-quality native digital sites discussed in chapter 7, such as *The Intercept*, continues to be how to reach an audience large enough to create impact and public accountability for its stories—without giving over control of editorial decisions to the tastes of the crowd. An early effort at ProPublica was a "get involved" program that helped people connect with each other and take action about the stories in the news. This idea had been tried previously by other organizations such as the BBC when it attempted to better harness the participatory logic of digital media. In one example, ProPublica ran a series of investigations on how mistakes are often made in hospitals, such as operations that go wrong and result in death. Following that series, the "get involved" program issued a call for readers to react to the articles based on experiences they have had with friends and loved ones. Soon a Facebook page developed where people could exchange support and ideas about action. Like other experiments with community building around news reports, the scale of audience response was relatively small, and there was not much connection between reporter and audience in the development of the stories. A more integrated model is now under way thanks to a $2.2 million grant from the Knight Foundation aimed at better integrating reporting and audience interactions. The goal is to create a "crowd-powered news network" in which communities form around topics and develop stories with inputs from networks of journalists, bloggers, and engaged citizens.[50] Depending on how ProPublica tunes the crowd input, this may become a model that sustains quality journalism alongside scaled-up distribution through social networks.

Commercial news organizations are also looking at ways to harness crowds and build communities. As noted in the last chapter, the tilt on the for-profit side is more on generating profitable buzz than citizen engagement. *USA Today*, for example, has created a position, director of social and strategic brand marketing, responsible for training journalists on how to understand social media and how to assess likely audience reactions to different stories and ways of telling them. Reporters compose stories using dashboards that assess which angles are of greatest interest to demographics that bring in ad revenues, and what kinds of graphics, data, and social media strategies are likely to engage those readers.[51] In a similar move, *Fortune* created the position of engagement editor, which, like the *USA Today* post, is more business than civics driven.[52]

In a sweeping look at the present and future of these kinds of news experiments, Leonard Downie and Michael Schudson raise cautionary notes about what sort of content they will generate:

> The questions that this transformation raises are simple enough: What is going to take the place of what is being lost, and can the new array of news media report on our nation and our communities as well as—or better than—journalism has until now? . . .
>
> Some answers are already emerging. The Internet and those seizing its potential have made it possible—and often quite easy—to gather and distrib-

ute news more widely in new ways. This is being done not only by surviving newspapers and commercial television, but by startup online news organizations, nonprofit investigative reporting projects, public broadcasting stations, university-run news services, community news sites with citizen participation, and bloggers. Even government agencies and activist groups are playing a role. Together, they are creating not only a greater variety of independent reporting missions but different definitions of news.

Reporting is becoming more participatory and collaborative. The ranks of news gatherers now include not only newsroom staffers, but freelancers, university faculty members, students, and citizens. Financial support for reporting now comes not only from advertisers and subscribers, but also from foundations, individual philanthropists, academic and government budgets, special interests, and voluntary contributions from readers and viewers.[53]

The open question is whether these experiments will alter the nature of news in unforeseen ways. As explained in chapter 6, another set of commercial, societal, and technological factors dating to the late nineteenth and early twentieth centuries shaped the legacy news system that is now in transition. If we are to avoid some of the haphazard forces that shaped that system, we might invite more public discussion of what kind of news best suits democracy today and how to help engineer effective outcomes.

In this spirit, Downie and Schudson offer a number of proposals. First, they suggest that any news organization substantially devoted to public affairs should be able to claim nonprofit tax status. Some organizations, such as National Public Radio, are already in this bracket and can receive tax-deductible contributions from supporters. Broadening and clarifying the terms for inclusion in this category would help other start-ups find a sustainable path. They also suggest that foundations expand subsidized reporting on more issues. A third recommendation is that public broadcasting refocus its priorities to include more local news coverage. The fourth recommendation is for colleges and universities to expand the scope of journalism programs to do more active news production and engage in partnerships with various innovative journalism start-ups. A fifth proposal is to create a small fee for broadcast license holders and cable providers to fund local news under the supervision of the Federal Communications Commission. The FCC already uses tax and fee monies to support various public interest communication initiatives, so this would be consistent with its current regulatory mission. Finally, they propose that news organizations, government agencies, and interest groups create easy-to-use interfaces for databases that enable citizens to get direct answers to many of their political questions.[54]

These ideas resonate with proposals from other observers such as Robert

McChesney and John Nichols, who suggest the government create a *citizen news voucher* system that people would be able to use to support any news organization, broadcast or print, that is substantially nonprofit.[55] Funding for this plan would come from taxes on commercial media operations through broadcast and mobile licenses. With a citizen news voucher system, citizens, not government, would drive the public information marketplace. In defense of such a system, they note that the founders regarded government subsidies for public information as an essential part of a healthy democratic public. It is unfortunate that much of this history has been lost in the fog of propaganda against "big government." As a result, the United States spends far less per citizen per year on public media than any other democracy (around $3), contrasted with Spain and France at $68, and eight nations over $90, led by Norway ($180), Switzerland ($164), and Germany ($124).[56]

The idea of promoting corporate interests over the public interest is to be expected of business, but the fact that so many Americans have bought the sales job that corporate media are somehow serving the public interest separates the United States from most other democracies. Not surprisingly, the news cultures of other countries are more diverse and engaged. In particular, relatively few Americans understand that information is a public good and that government regulation—with proper firewalls against political meddling—is the best way to protect it.

In Closing: How to Fight the Information Overload

The great peril of the digital age is the production of so much information that we are drowning in it. The output of information today is measured in exabytes and zetabytes, where one exabyte equals one million terabytes (one billion gigabytes), and one zetabyte equals one thousand exabytes. Former Google CEO Eric Schmidt once proclaimed that the world produced roughly five exabytes of information between the dawn of civilization and 2003, and that since then an equivalent amount of information is produced every two days. Schmidt, who went on to become executive chairman of the more recently hatched parent company Alphabet Inc., made that statement in 2010, so the volume of daily information is likely far larger today. While it is hard to check those figures for accuracy, it seems safe to say that we have entered a radically different era in which information has become one of the important commodities—if not the most important commodity—being produced, gathered, and managed. Schmidt's point in making that comment was that people are caught unawares by these developments and are not ready for the technology revolution that is inundating them.[57]

Adding to the challenges of sorting, organizing, and processing this flood of information is its addictive nature, fed by the seductions of the many devices over which content flows. It is hard to resist the constant rush of incoming information: texts from friends, Snapchats, news alerts, and incessant reminders from pings, dings, buzzes, and pulses. Information is pushed at us, and we become easily habituated to attend to its flow. Like most addictions, info addiction ends up not being very satisfying: it dulls the senses and proves hard to shut off. In recent years, I have banned Internet-connected devices from my classrooms on grounds that many students cannot resist drifting away from lectures or discussions and entering private worlds of SMS, Facebook, Pinterest, Snapchat, shopping, or sports. There is by now plenty of evidence that students who have devices connected to the Internet in class tend to do less well on assignments, distract others around them who also do less well, and, in the end, find the class experience less satisfying. It turns out that putting pen to paper and taking notes by hand actually improves information retention because that information must be judged for its importance and coherence as it passes through the brain during the more reflective act of writing. When I began this experiment, I expected something of a revolt in the classroom. As it turns out, many students have expressed their thanks. Their grades went up over earlier classes, and the increased focus of attention was palpable. Is there a lesson here about the news?

It turns out that similarly distracting results occur when people stream news chaotically online, checking for shallow updates, with little time for reflection or critical processing. When native digital media began seriously challenging legacy media for public attention, the Associated Press conducted a study of the news habits of young consumers. What it found was that the information most readily available when surfing the net or checking Facebook was often shallow and unsatisfying. The more people continued to check for updates, the more frustrated they became at not really understanding what was happening in important events. The AP report concluded that "participants in this study showed signs of news fatigue; that is, they appeared debilitated by information overload and unsatisfying news experiences. . . . Ultimately news fatigue brought many participants to a learned helplessness response. The more overwhelmed or unsatisfied they were, the less effort they were willing to put in."[58]

The difficulties of sorting the important from the trivial, and being unable to control the flow, have created the national attention deficit disorder described in chapter 3. As the Nobel economist Herbert Simon noted: "What information consumes is rather obvious. It consumes the attention of its recipients. Hence a wealth of information creates a poverty of attention."[59] Tony Schwartz has argued that the way we often engage with information has turned the Internet into a distraction system keeping us from being able to focus on complex tasks and issues.[60] People need to recognize this problem and deal with it. Spending more time without devices connected is a good start. Seeking depth over surface knowledge by reading books is another good idea. It may even be a good idea to reduce the time spent with cat videos and other ephemera. In addition, when we are receiving information, it is important to learn to assess its quality and to experiment with new ways to process and use it. The many innovative forms of news—and the technologies for managing them—offer interesting options for becoming informed and engaging with others. We are shifting from an era of largely passive citizenship tethered to the one-way communication of legacy media toward platforms that enable people to produce, share, and act together on quality information. These technologies for networked information engagement hold the promise to overcome the personally addictive aspects of the information age and help avoid fatigue, disconnection, and withdrawal. If that promise can be realized, we may reinvent citizenship in the process. Perhaps the next generation of citizens will also reinvent government, along with the ways in which news connects people to it.

ACKNOWLEDGMENTS

Each time I revise this book I realize that I have learned new things about publics, politics, democracy, and the importance of communication in the governing process. I owe much of my continuing engagement with these topics to the many colleagues with whom I have discussed these subjects over the years. Not all of those who have commented and reacted to the ideas in this book agree with my views and interpretations, but their lively engagement has stimulated my thinking and helped me reach new insights about a rich and complex subject. It is not possible to acknowledge all the people who have influenced my thinking, but I am particularly indebted to Regina Lawrence, Steve Livingston, Bob Entman, Jay Blumler, and the late and dearly missed Tim Cook. For other insights that continue to inform my thinking, I thank Bruce Bimber, Jerry Manheim, Barbara Pfetsch, Bruce Williams, Ann Crigler, Marion Just, Michael Delli Carpini, Susan Herbst, Bob McChesney, John Zaller, Michael Schudson, Dan Hallin, Kathleen Hall Jamieson, David Altheide, Thomas Patterson, Shanto Iyengar, Stephen Coleman, Rod Hart, Scott Althaus, Victor Pickard, Danna Young, and Doris Graber. I am also grateful for the comments by Sabine Lang, who is my partner in life and ideas. And the enduring influence of the late Murray Edelman lives on in these pages. Murray was an inspiring mentor to me as a young scholar thinking about the first edition of this book so many years ago.

A long publishing relationship with Pearson-Longman has come to a happy close, and I am indebted to them for the return of my publishing rights. The new relationship with Chicago is a welcome change that enables me to breath new life into a beloved book. I am particularly grateful to John Tryneski for signing the book and for his incisive editorial touch. Kelly Finefrock-Creed delivered a superb copyediting job. And thanks to Rodney Powell for doing all of the little things that count.

NOTES

CHAPTER ONE

1. Bruce A. Williams and Michael X. Delli Carpini, *After Broadcast News: Media Regimes, Democracy, and the New Information Environment* (New York: Cambridge University Press, 2011), 19.

2. Mike Isaac, "Amazon's Jeff Bezos Explains Why He Bought The Washington Post," *New York Times*, December 2, 2014, accessed January 26, 2015, http://bits.blogs.nytimes.com/2014/12/02/amazons-bezos-explains-why-he-bought-the-washington-post/?_r=0. Appeared in the print edition December 8, 2014, on page B8.

3. Nicholas Negroponte, *Being Digital* (New York: Vintage Books, 1995).

4. Marc Prensky. "Digital Natives, Digital Immigrants" (2001), http://www.marcprensky.com/writing/Prensky%20-%20Digital%20Natives,%20Digital%20Immigrants%20-%20Part1.pdf.

5. Paul Sparrow, "Let's Start Talking about a Radically Different Future of News," *American Journalism Review*, October 28, 2014, accessed January 28, 2015, http://ajr.org/2014/10/28/radically-different-future-news/.

6. Thomas E. Patterson, "Doing Well and Doing Good: How Soft News and Critical Journalism Are Shrinking the News Audience and Weakening Democracy—and What News Outlets Can Do about It" (Working paper, Joan Shorenstein Center on the Press, Politics and Public Policy, John F. Kennedy School of Government, Harvard University, 2000), http://shorensteincenter.org/wp-content/uploads/2012/03/soft_news_and_critical_journalism_2000.pdf.

7. Andy Kohut, "Pew Surveys of Audience Habits Suggest Perilous Future for News," *Poynter*, October 7, 2013, accessed February 7, 2015, http://www.poynter.org/news/mediawire/225139/pew-surveys-of-audience-habits-suggest-perilous-future-for-news/.

8. Monica Anderson and Andrea Caumont, "How Social Media Is Reshaping News," Pew Research Center, September 24, 2014, accessed February 7, 2015, http://www.pewresearch.org/fact-tank/2014/09/24/how-social-media-is-reshaping-news/.

9. Cass Sunstein, *Republic.com* (Princeton, NJ: Princeton University Press, 2001).

10. Markus Prior, *Post-Broadcast Democracy: How Media Choice Increases Inequality in Political Involvement and Polarizes Elections* (New York: Cambridge University Press, 2007).

11. Jay Rosen, "The People Formerly Known as the Audience," *Huffington Post*, May 25, 2011, accessed January 28, 2015, http://www.huffingtonpost.com/jay-rosen/the-people-formerly-known_1_b_24113.html.

12. Williams and Delli Carpini, *After Broadcast News*, 20.

13. Pew Research Center Project for Excellence in Journalism, "The State of the News Media 2013," accessed February 19, 2014, http://stateofthemedia.org/2013/overview-5/.

14. Elizabeth Mendes, "Americans' Confidence in Newspapers Continues to Erode," Gallup, June 17, 2013, accessed February 19, 2014, http://www.gallup.com/poll/163097/americans-confidence-newspapers-continues-erode.aspx.

15. Pew Research Center Project for Excellence in Journalism, "How News Happens: A Study of the News Ecosystem of One American City," January 11, 2010, accessed July 27, 2010, www.journalism.org/analysis_report/how_news_happens.

16. Paul Starr, "Goodbye to the Age of Newspapers (Hello to a New Era of Corruption)," *New Republic*, March 4, 2009.

17. See the report by Judicial Watch, "New Judicial Watch / Zogby Poll: 81.7% of Americans Say Political Corruption Played a 'Major Role' in Financial Crisis," October 21, 2008, accessed July 27, 2010, www.judicialwatch.org/news/2008/oct/new-judicial-watch-zogby-poll-82-7 -american-say-political-corruption-played-major-role.

18. Transparency International, "Global Corruption Barometer 2013," accessed February 27, 2014, http://www.transparency.org/gcb2013/country/?country=united_states.

19. Attributed to Stewart Brand at the first hacker's conference in 1984. *Wikipedia*, s.v. "Information Wants to Be Free," accessed July 27, 2010, http://en.wikipedia.org/wiki/Information _wants_to_be_free.

20. See Robert W. McChesney and John Nichols, *The Death and Life of American Journalism: The Media Revolution That Will Begin the World Again* (New York: Nation Books, 2010); Leonard Downie Jr. and Michael Schudson, "The Reconstruction of American Journalism," *Columbia Journalism Review*, November/December 2009, 28–51.

21. See W. Lance Bennett, Regina G. Lawrence, and Steven Livingston, *When the Press Fails: Political Power and the News Media from Iraq to Katrina* (Chicago: University of Chicago Press, 2007).

22. Thomas E. Patterson, *Informing the News: The Need for Knowledge-Based Journalism* (New York: Vintage, 2013), 110.

23. Paul Starr, *The Creation of the Media: Political Origins of Modern Communications* (New York: Basic Books, 2004).

24. McChesney and Nichols, *Death and Life of American Journalism.*

25. Joel Simon, "Identity Crisis: Why Journalists Should Drop the Push for Special Protection and Just Defend Freedom of Expression," *Columbia Journalism Review*, September/October 2013, 30.

26. Clay Shirky, talk at the Joan Shorenstein Center, Kennedy School of Government, Harvard University, September 22, 2009, www.hks.harvard.edu/presspol/news_events/archive /2009/shirky_09-22-09.html. For a full transcript, see www.niemanlab.org/2009/09/clay -shirky-let-a-thousand-flowers-bloom-to-replace-newspapers-dont-build-a-paywall-around -a-public-good/ (accessed July 27, 2010).

27. Jane Sassen, Kenny Olmstead, and Amy Mitchell, "Digital: As Mobile Grows Rapidly, the Pressures on News Intensify," in Pew Research Center, "State of the News Media 2013," accessed February 28, 2014, http://stateofthemedia.org/2013/digital-as-mobile-grows-rapidly -the-pressures-on-news-intensify/.

28. Thomas E. Patterson, "Young People and News" (report from the Joan Shorenstein Center on the Press, Politics, and Public Policy, Kennedy School of Government, Harvard University, prepared for the Carnegie-Knight Task Force on the Future of Journalism Education, July 2007).

29. American Press Institute, "Social and Demographic Differences in News Habits and Attitudes," March 17, 2014, accessed February 9, 2015, http://www.americanpressinstitute.org/pub lications/reports/survey-research/social-demographic-differences-news-habits-attitudes/.

30. See Martin P. Wattenberg, *Is Voting for Young People?* (New York: Pearson/Longman, 2008). Also W. Lance Bennett, "The Twilight of Mass Media News: Markets, Citizenship, Technology, and the Future of Journalism," in *Freeing the Presses*, 2nd ed., ed. Timothy Cook and Regina G. Lawrence (Louisiana State University Press, 2013), 117–40.

31. Wattenberg, *Is Voting for Young People?*, 5.

32. Pew Research Center for the People and the Press, "What the Public Knows about the Political Parties," April 11, 2012, accessed February 28, 2014, http://www.people-press.org/2012/04/11/what-the-public-knows-about-the-political-parties/.

33. See Prior, *Post-Broadcast Democracy*.

34. Timothy Cook, *Governing with the News: The News Media as a Political Institution* (Chicago: University of Chicago Press, 1998).

35. William Schneider, remarks delivered at the conference "The Clinton Presidency: Campaigning, Governing and the Psychology of Leadership," held at the Graduate Center, City University of New York, November 18–19, 1993. (A video of Schneider's talk is available from the university's PhD program in political science; attn: Stanley Renshon.)

36. Philip Rucker, "Bill Clinton Begins Campaign for Democrats in 2014 Midterms," *Washington Post*, February 25, 2014, accessed February 28, 2014, http://www.washingtonpost.com/politics/democrats-unveil-their-midterm-secret-weapon—bill-clinton/2014/02/25/2c94dec0-9e4e-11e3-b8d8-94577ff66b28_story.html.

37. Marvin Kalb, "Press-Politics and Improving the Public Dialogue," *Political Communication Report* 3 (June 1992): 1.

38. Timothy Cook, "Afterword: Political Values and Production Values," *Political Communication* 13 (October/December 1996): 469.

39. Shanto Iyengar and Donald R. Kinder, *News That Matters* (Chicago: University of Chicago Press, 1987).

40. Samuel Kernell, *Going Public: New Strategies of Presidential Leadership*, 3rd ed. (Washington, DC: Congressional Quarterly Press, 1997).

41. John Zaller, *Nature and Origins of Mass Opinion* (New York: Cambridge University Press, 1992).

42. Shanto Iyengar, *Is Anyone Responsible?* (Chicago: University of Chicago Press, 1991).

43. See Stephen Coleman, "From Big Brother to Big Brother: Two Faces of Interactive Engagement," in *Young Citizens and New Media: Learning and Democratic Engagement*, ed. Peter Dahlgren (New York: Routledge, 2008).

44. Angie Drobnic Holan, "PolitiFact's Lie of the Year: 'Death Panels,'" PolitiFact, December 18, 2009, accessed January 2, 2016, http://www.politifact.com/truth-o-meter/article/2009/dec/18/politifact-lie-year-death-panels/.

45. One of hundreds: "Don't Kill Grandma - Obamacare Video," uploaded July 25, 2009, accessed August 1, 2010, www.youtube.com/watch?v=wJb-TrmJl80.

46. "Limbaugh Discusses 'the Similarities between the Democrat Party of Today and the Nazi Party in Germany,'" Media Matters, August 6, 2009, accessed August 1, 2010, http://mediamatters.org/mmtv/200908060023.

47. John Hinderaker, "Who's Insane?," *Power Line*, August 9, 2009, accessed January 2, 2016, http://www.powerlineblog.com/archives/2009/08/024235.php.

48. Jordan Fabian, "Death Panels May Be in Final Healthcare Reform Bill," *The Hill*, December 22, 2009, accessed August 1, 2010, http://thehill.com/blogs/blog-briefing-room/news/73371-palin-death-panels-may-be-in-final-health-bill.

49. David Espo, "2014 House Races Are Already Testing Obamacare as an Election Issue," *Huffington Post*, February 22, 2014, accessed February 28, 2014, http://www.huffingtonpost.com/2014/02/22/2014-house-races-obamacare_n_4839219.html.

50. Alan Greenblatt, "An 'Absolute Will to Forget': Iraq Casts Shorter Shadow than Vietnam," National Public Radio, March 19, 2013, accessed February 28, 2014, http://www.npr.org/2013/03/15/174425566/an-absolute-will-to-forget-iraq-casts-shorter-shadow-than-vietnam.

51. Daniel Trotta, "Iraq War Cost US More than $2 Trillion, Could Grow to $6 Trillion Says Watson Institute Study," *Huffington Post / World Post*, March 14, 2013, accessed February 28, 2014, http://www.huffingtonpost.com/2013/03/14/iraq-war-cost-more-than-2-trillion_n_287 5493.html.

52. For a more complete analysis, see Bennett, Lawrence, and Livingston, *When the Press Fails*.

53. Steven Kull, "Misperceptions, the Media, and the Iraq War" (report of the Program on International Policy Attitudes, University of Maryland, October 2, 2003). Statistics based on national polls of 3,334 respondents taken from June to September 2003.

54. Sarah Chayes, *Thieves of State: Why Corruption Threatens Global Security* (New York: Norton, 2014).

55. See Bennett, Lawrence, and Livingston, *When the Press Fails*, ch. 5.

56. See Patterson, *Informing the News*.

57. See W. Lance Bennett, "Toward a Theory of Press-State Relations in the United States," *Journal of Communication* 40 (Spring 1990): 103–27.

58. Kull, "Misperceptions."

59. Kyle Stock, "The Single Number That Could Seal Brian Williams's Fate," *Bloomberg Business*, February 10, 2015, accessed February 11, 2015, http://www.bloomberg.com/news/articles /2015-02-10/the-metrics-behind-brian-williams-s-fall-from-grace.

60. Maureen Dowd, "Anchors Aweigh," *New York Times*, February 8, 2015, SR11.

61. Dave Itzkoff, "Jon Stewart Will Leave 'The Daily Show' on a Career High Note," *New York Times*, February 11, 2015, accessed February 11, 2015, http://www.nytimes.com/2015/02/11/arts /television/jon-stewart-leaving-daily-show.html?ref=business&_r=0.

62. Reported in Nancy Snow, "Jon Stewart: Still the Most Trusted Newscaster in America," *Huffington Post*, July 23, 2009, accessed March 1, 2014, http://www.huffingtonpost.com/nancy -snow/jon-stewart-still-the-mos_b_243646.html.

63. Jon Blistein, "Larry Wilmore Supports 'Fellow Purveyor of Fake News' Brian Williams," *Rolling Stone*, February 10, 2015, accessed February 11, 2015 http://www.rollingstone.com/tv /videos/larry-wilmore-supports-fellow-purveyor-of-fake-news-brian-williams-20150210.

64. Ron Suskind, "Faith, Certainty and the Presidency of George W. Bush," *New York Times*, October 17, 2004, accessed August 1, 2010, www.nytimes.com/2004/10/17/magazine/17BUSH .html?ex=1255665600&en=890a96189e162076&ei=5090&partner=rssuserland.

65. *Nightline*, ABC, July 28, 2004, from Dannagal Young, "The Daily Show as the New Journalism" (paper presented at the Annual Meeting of the National Communication Association, Boston, November 17–20, 2005).

66. Ibid.

67. Ibid.

68. Dannagal G. Young, "Lighten Up: How Satire Will Make American Politics Relevant Again," *Columbia Journalism Review*, July/August 2013, 27–32.

69. Marc Peyser, "Jon Stewart: Seriously Funny," *Newsweek*, January 5, 2004, 70–77.

70. Dannagal G. Young and Russell M. Tisinger, "Dispelling Late Night Myths: News Consumption among Late-Night Comedy Viewers and the Predictors of Exposure to Various Late Night Shows," *Press/Politics* 11 (2006): 113–34.

71. Daniel Kurtzman, "Stephen Colbert at the [2006] White House Correspondents' Dinner: Transcript of Colbert's Presidential Smackdown," updated November 4, 2015, http://political humor.about.com/od/stephencolbert/a/colbertbush.htm.

72. *Wikipedia*, s.v. "Stephen Colbert and the 2006 White House Correspondents' Dinner,"

accessed March 4, 2014, http://en.wikipedia.org/wiki/Stephen_Colbert_at_the_2006_White
_House_Correspondents'_Association_Dinner.

73. Frank Rich, "All the President's Press," *New York Times*, April 29, 2007.

74. Arthur S. Brisbane, "Should the Times Be a Truth Vigilante?," *New York Times*, January 12, 2012, accessed March 3, 2014, http://publiceditor.blogs.nytimes.com/2012/01/12/should-the -times-be-a-truth-vigilante/.

75. Glen Greenwald, "Arthur Brisbane and Selective Stenography," *Salon*, January 13, 2012, accessed March 3, 2014, http://www.salon.com/2012/01/13/arthur_brisbane_and_selective _stenography/.

76. David Altheide and Robert P. Snow, *Media Worlds in the Postjournalism Era* (Hawthorne, NY: Aldine, 1991).

77. Susan Herbst, *Reading Public Opinion* (Chicago: University of Chicago Press, 1998).

78. Robert M. Entman, *Democracy without Citizens: Media and the Decay of American Politics* (New York: Cambridge University Press, 1989).

79. W. Lance Bennett and Shanto Iyengar, "A New Era of Minimal Effects? The Changing Foundations of Political Communication," *Journal of Communication* 58 (2008): 707–31.

80. Bruce Bimber, *Information and American Democracy: Technology in the Evolution of Political Power* (New York: Cambridge University Press, 2003).

81. See also Richard R. John, *Spreading the News: The American Postal System from Franklin to Morse* (Cambridge, MA: Harvard University Press, 1995); and Timothy E. Cook, *Governing with the News: The News Media as a Political Institution* (Chicago: University of Chicago Press, 1998).

82. Kernell, *Going Public*.

83. See various perspectives on this in W. Lance Bennett and Robert M. Entman, eds., *Mediated Politics: Communication in the Future of Democracy* (New York: Cambridge University Press, 2001).

84. Doris A. Graber, *Mass Media and American Politics*, 3rd ed. (Washington, DC: Congressional Quarterly Press, 1989).

85. See Clay Shirky, *Here Comes Everybody: The Power of Organizing without Organizations* (New York: Penguin, 2009).

86. Lawrence K. Grossman, "Does Local TV News Need a Nanny?," *Columbia Journalism Review*, May/June 1998, 33.

87. Quoted in James Brooke, "The F.C.C. Supports TV News as Free Speech," *New York Times*, May 3, 1998, 27.

88. Robert W. McChesney, *Rich Media, Poor Democracy: Communication Politics in Dubious Times* (New York: The New Press, 2015).

89. Grossman, "Does Local TV News Need a Nanny?," 33.

CHAPTER TWO

1. Thomas Patterson, "Phony Balance, Manufactured Conflict: The Media Just Confuses the Truth," *Salon*, October 5, 2013, accessed March 7, 2014, http://www.salon.com/2013/10/05 /phony_balance_manufactured_conflict_the_media_just_confuses_the_truth/.

2. "2016 Political Attacks Get Personal," *NBC Nightly News*, February 10, 2014, accessed March 11, 2014, http://www.nbcnews.com/video/nightly-news/54338378#54338378.

3. John F. Harris and Alexander Burns, "Verdict Is In: Obama Levels More Personal Attacks," *Politico*, September 6, 2012, accessed March 11, 2014, http://www.politico.com/news/stories /0912/80810_Page4.html.

4. Thomas Patterson, "Phony Balance, Manufactured Conflict: The Media Just Confuses the Truth."

5. Thomas E. Patterson, *Informing the News: The Need for Knowledge-Based Journalism* (New York: Vintage, 2013).

6. Eric Alterman, "Blowhards and Windbags," *Guardian* blog, January 11, 2008, http://www.theguardian.com/commentisfree/2008/jan/11/blowhardsandwindbags.

7. Matt Welch, "The Obama 'Narrative' Narrative: Imagine What the President Could Do If Only He Had a Better Bumper Sticker!" *Reason*, March 18, 2010, accessed August 8, 2010, http://reason.com/archives/2010/03/18/the-obama-narrative-narrative.

8. Richard W. Stevenson, "The Muddled Selling of the President," *New York Times*, January 29, 2010, accessed August 8, 2010, www.nytimes.com/2010/01/31/weekinreview/31stevenson.html?scp=7&sq=stevenson&st=nyt.

9. Jason Horowitz, "The Obama 'Narrative' Is Overshadowing This Presidency's Real Stories," *Washington Post*, June 20, 2010, accessed August 8, 2010, www.washingtonpost.com/wp-dyn/content/article/2010/06/18/AR2010061803052.html. The quote from Maureen Dowd is also from this source.

10. Pew Research Center, "Amid Criticism, Support for Media's 'Watchdog' Role Stands Out," August 8, 2013, accessed March 14, 2014, http://www.people-press.org/2013/08/08/amid-criticism-support-for-medias-watchdog-role-stands-out/.

11. This finding is reported, for example, in David Weaver and G. Cleveland Wilhoit, *The American Journalist: U.S. News People at the End of an Era* (Mahwah, NJ: Lawrence Erlbaum, 1996). A 1996 Freedom Forum / Roper survey of 139 Washington news people indicated that those with a left-of-center leaning outnumbered those leaning right-of-center by a margin of 61 percent to 9 percent. See Neil Hickey, "Is Fox News Fair?," *Columbia Journalism Review*, March/April 1998, 31.

12. Thomas Patterson and Wolfgang Donsbach note a slight but significant difference in how liberal and conservative journalists approach hypothetical stories. However, it is not clear whether even such small differences persist when hypothetical stories are replaced by real ones and subjected to editing processes within news organizations. See Thomas E. Patterson and Wolfgang Donsbach, "News Decisions: Journalists as Partisan Actors," *Political Communication* 13 (October/December 1996): 455–68.

13. Everette E. Dennis, "How 'Liberal' Are the Media, Anyway? The Continuing Conflict of Professionalism and Partisanship," *Press/Politics* 2 (Fall 1997): 116.

14. Robert M. Entman, *Scandal and Silence: Media Responses to Presidential Misconduct* (Cambridge: Polity Press, 2012).

15. Gallup–Times Mirror, *The People and the Press* (Los Angeles: Times Mirror, 1986), 28–29. See also Robert P. Vallone, Lee Ross, and Mark R. Lepper, "The Hostile Media Phenomenon: Biased Perceptions and Perceptions of Media Bias in Coverage of the Beirut Massacre," *Journal of Personality and Social Psychology* 49, no. 3 (1985): 577–85.

16. See, for example, W. Lance Bennett, "Toward a Theory of Press-State Relations in the United States," *Journal of Communication* 40 (Spring 1990): 103–27.

17. Dennis, "How 'Liberal' Are the Media, Anyway?," 119.

18. Robert Entman, "Framing: Toward Clarification of a Fractured Paradigm," *Journal of Communication* 43, no. 4 (1993): 51–58.

19. Regina G. Lawrence. "Game-Framing the Issues: Tracking the Frame in Public Policy News," *Political Communication* 17, no. 2 (2000): 93–114.

20. Dana Milbank, "The Military Is the Message: Triumphant President Casts Strong Image for '04 Election," *Washington Post*, May 2, 2003, A24.

21. Brent Cunningham, "Re-thinking Objectivity," *Columbia Journalism Review*, July/August 2003, 24–32.

22. See Shanto Iyengar, *Is Anyone Responsible? How Television Frames Political Issues* (Chicago: University of Chicago Press, 1992).

23. Murray Edelman, *The Symbolic Uses of Politics* (Urbana: University of Illinois Press, 1964).

24. See Joseph Cappella and Kathleen Hall Jamieson, *Spiral of Cynicism: The Press and the Public Good* (New York: Oxford University Press, 1997).

25. Thomas E. Patterson, *Out of Order* (New York: Knopf, 1993; New York: Vintage Books, 1994).

26. Ibid.

27. Johanna Dunaway and Regina G. Lawrence, "What Predicts the Game Frame? Media Ownership, Electoral Context, and Campaign News," *Political Communication* 32, no. 1 (2015): 43–60.

28. Matt Bai, "Obama, the Oil Spill and Chaos Perception," *New York Times*, June 10, 2010, accessed August 9, 2010, www.nytimes.com/2010/06/06/weekinreview/06bai.html.

29. Ashley Parker, "Congress Pushes Shutdown Back Another Week," *New York Times*, February 28, 2015, A1.

30. Megyn Kelly, "What Will Really Happen in the Event of a Homeland Security Department Shutdown?," *Fox News Insider* (blog), *The Kelly File*, February 24, 2015, accessed February 28, 2015, http://megynkelly.us/96848/what-will-really-happen-in-the-event-of-a-homeland-security-department-shutdown/.

31. Jim Rutenberg, "The Megyn Moment," *New York Times Magazine*, January 25, 2015, 28–35.

32. Quoted in Edward W. Barrett, "Folksy TV News," *Columbia Journalism Review*, November/December 1973, 19.

33. Reported in David L. Paletz and Robert M. Entman, *Media Power Politics* (New York: Free Press, 1981), 17.

34. Howard Kurtz, "Since September 11 Attacks, TV Morning Shows Rediscover World News," *Seattle Times*, November 25, 2001, A2.

35. Jason DeParle, "From the Welfare Rolls to the Starring Roles: TV Offers Recipients Brushes with Fame," *New York Times*, June 25, 1999, A10.

36. Robert Rector, "How Obama Has Gutted Welfare Reform," *Washington Post*, September 6, 2012, accessed March 14, 2014, http://www.washingtonpost.com/opinions/how-obama-has-gutted-welfare-reform/2012/09/06/885b0092-f835-11e1-8b93-c4f4ab1c8d13_story.html.

37. Eugene Kiely, "Does Obama's Plan 'Gut Welfare Reform'?," FactCheck.org, August 9, 2012, accessed March 14, 2014, http://www.factcheck.org/2012/08/does-obamas-plan-gut-welfare-reform/.

38. Paletz and Entman, *Media Power Politics*, 16–17.

39. Quoted in Ann Devroy and Don Balz, "The White House Wins Again, but Was the Victory Pyrrhic?," *Washington Post National Weekly Edition*, November 22–28, 1993, 12.

40. National Public Radio, *Morning Edition*, August 12, 1994.

41. Gabriel Winant, "The Birthers in Congress," *Salon*, July 28, 2009, accessed August 9, 2010, www.salon.com/news/feature/2009/07/28/birther_enablers.

42. Quoted in Eric Zimmermann, "Poll: 27 Percent of Americans Doubt Obama's Birthplace," *The Hill*, August 4, 2010, accessed August 9, 2010, http://thehill.com/blogs/blog-briefing-room/news/112619-poll-27-of-americans-doubt-obamas-birthplace. Zimmermann's ellipses; my brackets.

43. "CNN/Opinion Research Poll—Obama Birth," August 4, 2010, accessed August 9, 2010, http://politicalticker.blogs.cnn.com/2010/08/04/cnnopinion-research-poll-obama-birth/.

44. Celeste Katz, "Many of Donald Trump's Supporters Also Think Obama Is a Muslim Born Outside of the United States, Poll Finds," *New York Daily News*, September 15, 2015, accessed January 16, 2016, http://www.nydailynews.com/news/politics/donald-trump-supporters-obama-muslim-poll-article-1.2344533.

45. Paletz and Entman, *Media Power Politics*, 17.

46. Reported in Edward Jay Epstein, *News from Nowhere* (New York: Random House, 1973), 4–5. Such a conscious statement of a defining characteristic of news is all the more remarkable considering that most journalists have difficulty clearly defining their professional product.

47. Paletz and Entman, *Media Power Politics*, 17.

48. See Steven Livingston, *The Terrorism Spectacle* (Boulder, CO: Westview Press, 1994).

49. Stephen Hess, "Covering the Senate: Where Power Gets the Play," *Washington Journalism Review* 9, no. 3 (June 1986): 41–42.

50. Timothy E. Cook, *Making News and Making Laws: Media Strategies in the U.S. House of Representatives* (Washington, DC: Brookings Institution, 1989).

51. Robert Darnton, "Writing News and Telling Stories," *Daedalus* 104 (Spring 1975): 190.

52. Lewis H. Lapham, "Gilding the News," *Harper's*, July 1981, 34.

53. Gaye Tuchman, *Making News: A Study in the Construction of Reality* (New York: Free Press, 1978).

54. Don DeLillo, *The Names* (New York: Vintage, 1982), 58.

55. Paletz and Entman, *Media Power Politics*, 16.

56. A summary of evidence for these points can be found in Patterson, *Informing the News*, 21–24.

57. Murray Edelman, *Constructing the Political Spectacle* (Chicago: University of Chicago Press, 1988).

58. Russell Baker, "Meanwhile, in Zanzibar," *New York Times Magazine*, February 6, 1977, 12.

59. Reported in Stuart Schear, "Covering Health Care: Politics or People?," *Columbia Journalism Review*, May/June 1994, 36–37.

60. Wendy Gross, Tobias H. Stark, Jon Krosnick, Josh Pasek, Gaurav Sood, Trevor Tompson, Jennifer Agiesta, Dennis Junius, "Americans' Attitudes toward the Affordable Care Act: Would Better Public Understanding Increase or Decrease Favorability," Stanford University, 2013, accessed March 16, 2014, https://pprg.stanford.edu/wp-content/uploads/Health-Care-2012-Knowledge-and-Favorability.pdf.

61. See John Zaller, *The Nature and Origins of Mass Opinion* (New York: Cambridge University Press, 1992). See also John Zaller, "Elite Leadership of Mass Opinion: New Evidence from the Gulf War," in *Taken by Storm: The Media, Public Opinion, and U.S. Foreign Policy in the Gulf War*, ed. W. Lance Bennett and David L. Paletz (Chicago: University of Chicago Press, 1994), 186–209.

62. Dunaway and Lawrence, "What Predicts the Game Frame?"

63. Lawrence, "Game-Framing the Issues."

64. Ibid., 110.

65. Patterson, *Informing the News*.

66. Michael Wolff, "The Importance of 'Controlling the Narrative,'" *USA Today*, December 29, 2013, accessed March 1, 2015, http://www.usatoday.com/story/money/columnist/2013/12 /29/mayor-elect-de-blasio-controls-his-daughters-story/4220773/.

67. Horowitz, "Obama 'Narrative.'"

68. "Gallup: Obama Job Approval," accessed August 10, 2010, www.gallup.com/poll/113980 /gallup-daily-obama-job-approval.aspx.

69. Horowitz, "Obama 'Narrative.'"

70. David Remnick, "Annals of the Presidency: Going the Distance," *New Yorker*, January 27, 2014, accessed March 17, 2014, http://www.newyorker.com/reporting/2014/01/27/140127fa _fact_remnick?currentPage=all.

71. For an exploration of the news as popular spectacle, see Edelman, *Constructing the Political Spectacle*.

72. Charlotte Grimes, "Whither the Civic Journalism Bandwagon?" (discussion paper, Joan Shorenstein Center, Harvard University, February 1999), 3.

73. Free Press, http://www.freepress.net (accessed March 17, 2014).

CHAPTER THREE

1. Benjamin I. Page, *Who Deliberates? Mass Media in Modern Democracy* (Chicago: University of Chicago Press, 1996), 1.

2. Robert M. Entman, *Projections of Power: Framing News, Public Opinion, and U.S. Foreign Policy* (Chicago: University of Chicago Press, 2004), 126.

3. Quoted in Tony Schwartz, "Struggling to Disconnect from Our Digital Lives," *New York Times*, July 31, 2015, accessed August 3, 2015, http://www.nytimes.com/2015/08/01/business /dealbook/struggling-to-disconnect-from-our-digital-lives.html?mabReward=CTM& moduleDetail=recommendations-0&action=click&contentCollection=Politics&region=Footer &module=WhatsNext&version=WhatsNext&contentID=WhatsNext&src=recg&pgtype=article.

4. Stuart Ewen, *PR! A Social History of Spin* (New York: Basic Books, 1996).

5. Walter Lippmann, *Public Opinion* (New York: The Free Press, 1922).

6. John Zaller, *The Nature and Origins of Mass Opinion* (Cambridge: Cambridge University Press, 1992).

7. Maxwell E. McCombs and Donald L. Shaw, "The Agenda-Setting Function of Mass Media," *Public Opinion Quarterly* 36, 2 (1972): 176–87.

8. Eric Lichtblau, "F.E.C. Can't Curb 2016 Election Abuse, Commission Chief Says," *New York Times*, May 2, 2015, accessed May 3, 2015, http://www.nytimes.com/2015/05/03/us/poli tics/fec-cant-curb-2016-election-abuse-commission-chief-says.html?emc=eta1&_r=0.

9. Bruce Drake, "More Americans Say U.S. Failed to Achieve Its Goals in Iraq," Pew Research Center, June 12, 2014, accessed May 3, 2015, http://www.pewresearch.org/fact-tank/2014 /06/12/more-americans-say-us-failed-to-achieve-its-goals-in-iraq/.

10. Kathleen Hall Jamieson and Joseph Cappella, *The Echo Chamber: Rush Limbaugh and the Conservative Media Establishment* (Oxford: Oxford University Press, 2008).

11. David Moore, *The Opinion Makers: When Media Polls Undermine Democracy* (Boston: Beacon, 2008).

12. David W. Moore and Jeffrey M. Jones, "Directive vs. Permissive Public Opinion" (paper presented at the Annual Meeting of the American Association for Public Opinion Research, St. Petersburg, Florida, May 16–19, 2002).

13. Morris P. Fiorina, *Culture War? The Myth of a Polarized America* (New York: Pearson/ Longman, 2005).

14. Murray Edelman, *The Symbolic Uses of Politics* (Urbana: University of Illinois Press, 1964).

15. Robert M. Entman and Andrew Rojecki, *The Black Image in the White Mind: Media and Race in America* (Chicago: University of Chicago Press, 2000).

16. Jennifer L. Hochschild, "Affirmative Action as Culture War," in *The Cultural Territories of Race*, ed. Michele Lamont (Chicago: University of Chicago Press, 1999), 343–70.

17. Entman and Rojecki, *Black Image in the White Mind*, 110.

18. Ibid.

19. Results posted at www.pollingreport.com/immigration.htm (accessed August 16, 2010).

20. Results posted at www.pollingreport.com/immigration.htm (accessed August 16, 2010).

21. Walter Lippmann, *Public Opinion* (New York: Macmillan, 1922).

22. Edelman, *Symbolic Uses of Politics*.

23. Murray Edelman, *Constructing the Political Spectacle* (Chicago: University of Chicago Press).

24. Robert M. Entman, *Democracy without Citizens: Media and the Decay of American Politics* (New York: Oxford University Press, 1989).

25. Susan Herbst, *Reading Public Opinion: How Political Actors View the Democratic Process* (Chicago: University of Chicago Press, 1998).

26. Paul Gronke and Timothy E. Cook. "Disdaining the Media: The American Public's Changing Attitudes toward the News," *Political Communication* 24, 3 (2007): 259–81.

27. See Shanto Iyengar and Donald Kinder, *News That Matters: Television and American Opinion* (Chicago: University of Chicago Press, 1987).

28. Reported in Barton Gellman and Walter Pincus, "Errors and Exaggerations: Prewar Depictions of Iraq's Nuclear Threat Outweighed the Evidence," *Washington Post National Weekly Edition*, August 18–24, 2003, 6.

29. Tom Zeller, "The Iraq-Qaeda Link: A Short Story," Week in Review, *New York Times*, June 20, 2004, 4.

30. Mira Sotirovic, "How Individuals Explain Social Problems: The Influences of Media Use," *Journal of Communication* 53 (2003): 122–37.

31. See Moore, *Opinion Makers*, ch. 1.

32. See Robert Putnam, *Bowling Alone: The Collapse and Revival of American Community* (New York: Simon and Schuster, 2000).

33. See Joseph Turow, *Breaking Up America: Advertisers and the New Media World* (Chicago: University of Chicago Press, 1997).

34. Todd Spangler, "CNN to Push 'Political Prophecy' Game for 2016 Elections," *Variety*, May 8, 2015, accessed May 11, 2015, http://variety.com/2015/digital/news/cnn-political -prophecy-predictive-market-2016-elections-1201490747/.

35. National Center for Biotechnology Information, reported in "Attention Span Statistics," accessed March 15, 2015, http://www.statisticbrain.com/attention-span-statistics/. I've concluded that the sources behind this shocking claim, which appeared in many news sites and blogs, including the venerable BBC, are a bit dodgy, which illustrates the echo chamber effect of the web in which news sites cite each other without checking the original source. In other words, this was a story "too good to fact-check." However, the general decline of attention has been documented in numerous studies of multitasking involving digital media.

36. Markus Prior, *Post-Broadcast Democracy: How Media Choice Increases Inequality in Political Involvement and Polarizes Elections* (New York: Cambridge University Press, 2007).

37. Charles M. Blow, "Lost in Translation," *New York Times*, January 29, 2010, accessed August 11, 2010, www.nytimes.com/2010/01/30/opinion/30blow.html.

38. George Will, "The Price of Political Ignorance," *Washington Post*, January 1, 2014, accessed March 15, 2015, http://www.washingtonpost.com/opinions/george-will-the-price-of -political-ignorance/2014/01/01/7dbe2936-7311-11e3-9389-09ef9944065e_story.html.

39. James Hamilton, *All the News That's Fit to Sell: How the Market Transforms Information into News* (Princeton, NJ: Princeton University Press, 2003), 262.

40. Zaller, *Nature and Origins of Mass Opinion*.

41. See David Domke, *God Willing? Political Fundamentalism in the White House, the "War on Terror," and the Echoing Press* (London: Pluto Press, 2004).

42. W. Russell Neuman, Marion R. Just, and Ann N. Crigler, *Common Knowledge: News and the Construction of Political Meaning* (Chicago: University of Chicago Press, 1992), 8.

43. Thomas Patterson and Philip Seib, "Informing the Public" (report to the Press Commission, Institutions of Democracy Project of the Annenberg Foundation Trust, commission meeting at Rancho Mirage, CA, February 5–8, 2004).

44. Doris A. Graber, *Processing Politics: Learning from Television in the Internet Age* (Chicago: University of Chicago Press, 2001); see also Doris A. Graber, *Processing the News: How People Tame the Information Tide*, 2nd ed. (New York: Longman, 1988).

45. John Fiske, *Television Culture* (London: Methuen, 1987).

46. William Gamson, *Talking Politics* (New York: Cambridge University Press, 1992), 179.

47. Neuman, Just, and Crigler, *Common Knowledge*, ch. 7, esp. p. 111.

48. Ibid., ch. 5. See also Graber, *Processing the News*.

49. Kenneth Olmstead, Mark Jurkowitz, Amy Mitchell, and Jody Enda, "How Americans Get TV News at Home," Pew Research Center, October 11, 2013, accessed May 10, 2015, http:// www.journalism.org/2013/10/11/how-americans-get-tv-news-at-home/. Monica Anderson and Andrea Caumont, "How Social Media Is Reshaping News," Pew Research Center, September 24, 2014, accessed May 10, 2015, http://www.pewresearch.org/fact-tank/2014/09/24/how -social-media-is-reshaping-news/.

50. Doyle Murphy, "Americans Prefer Smartphones to Sex, Study Finds," *New York Daily News*, February 9, 2014, accessed January 16, 2016, http://www.nydailynews.com/news/na tional/americans-prefer-smartphones-sex-study-finds-article-1.1607822. Harris Interactive, January 29, 2014, accessed May 10, 2015, http://www.harrisinteractive.com/NewsRoom /HarrisPolls/tabid/447/ctl/ReadCustom%20Default/mid/1508/ArticleId/1373/Default.aspx.

51. Charles Winick, "The Function of Television: Life without the Big Box," in *Television as Social Issue*, ed. Stuart Oskamp (Newbury Park, CA: Sage, 1988), 217–37.

52. Graber, *Processing Politics*.

53. Zaller, *Nature and Origins of Mass Opinion*.

54. For the magnitude of this information campaign, see "Well-Heeled" (report published by the Center for Public Integrity, Washington, DC, 1994).

55. *Newsweek* poll reported in Steven Waldman, Bob Cohn, and Eleanor Clift, "How Clinton Blew It," *Newsweek*, June 27, 1994, 28.

56. Polls reported in Melinda Beck, "Rationing Health Care," *Newsweek*, June 27, 1994, 30.

57. Quoted in Maureen Dowd, "Bush's Top Strategists: Smooth Poll-Taker and Hard Driving Manager," *New York Times*, May 30, 1988, 11.

58. George E. Marcus, W. Russell Neuman, and Michael MacKuen, *Affective Intelligence and Political Judgement* (Chicago: University of Chicago Press, 2000). See also W. Russell Neuman, Michael B. MacKuen, George E. Marcus, and Joanne Miller, "Affective Choice and Rational Choice" (paper presented at the Annual Meeting of the American Political Science Association, Washington, DC, September 1997).

59. See the more detailed discussions in W. Lance Bennett, *The Governing Crisis: Media, Money and Marketing in American Elections* (New York: St Martin's, 1992), esp. chs. 1 and 4.

60. Barbara G. Farah and Ethel Klein, "Public Opinion Trends," in *The Election of 1988: Reports and Interpretations*, ed. Gerald M. Pomper (Chatham, NJ: Chatham House, 1989), 103.

61. Arthur Lupia and Matthew McCubbins, *The Democratic Dilemma: Can Citizens Learn What They Need to Know?* (New York: Cambridge University Press, 1998).

62. See Samuel Popkin, *The Reasoning Voter: Communication and Persuasion in Presidential Campaigns*, 2nd ed. (Chicago: University of Chicago Press, 1994).

63. Iyengar and Kinder, *News That Matters*.

64. Shanto Iyengar, *Is Anyone Responsible? How Television Frames Political Issues* (Chicago: University of Chicago Press, 1991).

65. For an overview of trends in the field, see Elihu Katz, "Communications Research since Lazarsfeld," *Public Opinion Quarterly* 51 (1987): 25–45. For an introduction to the "uses and gratification" concept, see Jay G. Blumler and Denis McQuail, *Television in Politics: Its Uses and Influences* (Chicago: University of Chicago Press, 1969). Also, Lee B. Becker, "Two Tests of Media Gratification: Watergate and the 1974 Elections," *Journalism Quarterly* 53 (1976): 26–31.

66. See, for example, Tamar Liebes, "Cultural Differences in the Retelling of Television Fiction," *Critical Studies in Mass Communication* 5 (1986): 277–92.

67. Roderick Hart, *Seducing America: How Television Charms the Modern Voter* (New York: Oxford University Press, 1994), 22.

68. Putnam, *Bowling Alone*, 36.

69. Ibid.

70. See Hamilton, *All the News That's Fit to Sell*, ch. 3.

71. See, for example, Michael X. Delli Carpini and Scott Keeter, *What Americans Know about Politics and Why It Matters* (New Haven, CT: Yale University Press, 1996), 21.

72. Graber, *Processing Politics*.

73. Michael J. Robinson, "The News Interest Index, 1986–2007," Pew Research Center Database, updated 2007, http://pewresearch.org/assets/pdf/NewsInterest1986-2007.pdf.

74. Gamson, *Talking Politics*.

75. See W. Lance Bennett and Alexandra Segerberg, *The Logic of Connective Action: Digital Media and the Personalization of Contentious Politics* (New York: Cambridge University Press, 2013).

CHAPTER FOUR

1. Announcement accompanying the signing of Executive Order 11652 expediting the declassification of national security documents, March 1972, in "Richard M. Nixon," accessed July 3, 2015, http://www.sourcewatch.org/index.php/Richard_M._Nixon.

2. Dick Morris, *The New Prince: Machiavelli Updated for the Twenty-First Century* (New York: St. Martin's Press, 1999), 178.

3. Walter Pincus, "Newspaper Narcissism: Our Pursuit of Glory Led Us Away from Readers," *Columbia Journalism Review*, May/June 2009, 54.

4. William Comcowich, "Is Public Relations the New Journalism?," CyberAlert, February

19, 2015, accessed July 3, 2015, http://www.cyberalert.com/blog/index.php/is-public-relations -the-new-journalism/.

5. Robert W. McChesney and John Nichols, *The Death and Life of American Journalism: The Media Revolution That Will Begin the World Again* (New York: Nation Books, 2010), 49.

6. See, for example, Lawrence Lessig, *Republic, Lost: How Money Corrupts Congress—and a Plan to Stop It* (New York: Hachette, 2011); Martin Gillens, *Affluence & Influence: Economic Inequality and Political Power* (Princeton, NJ: Princeton University Press, 2012).

7. Dana Milbank, "Obama's Disregard for Media Reaches New Heights at Nuclear Summit," *Washington Post*, April 14, 2010, accessed August 22, 2010, www.washingtonpost.com/wp-dyn /content/article/2010/04/13/AR2010041303067.html.

8. Kendra Marr, "White House Photos Irk Press Corps," *Politico*, March 24, 2010, accessed August 22, 2010, www.politico.com/news/stories/0310/34972.html.

9. Santiago Lyon, "Obama's Orwellian Image Control," *New York Times*, December 11, 2013, accessed July 4, 2015, http://www.nytimes.com/2013/12/12/opinion/obamas-orwellian-image -control.html?smid=fb-nytimes&WT.z_sma=OP_OOI_20131211&bicmp=AD&bicmlukp=WT .mc_id&bicmst=1385874000000&bicmet=1388638800000&fblinkge0&_r=2&.

10. Susan Milligan, "The President and the Press," *Columbia Journalism Review*, March/ April 2015, 22 27 (quotations at 23 24).

11. Nicholas Johnson and Edwin Chen, "Obama Answers Questions on YouTube in Voter Outreach," *Bloomberg Businessweek*, February 1, 2010, accessed August 22, 2010, www.busi nessweek.com/news/2010-02-01/obama-hits-youtube-to-answer-questions-in-outreach-to -voters.html.

12. Reported in Howard Kurtz, "White House Press Corps Feels Bypassed by Obama in Favor of TV Shows, YouTube," *Washington Post*, February 8, 2010, accessed August 22, 2010, www.washingtonpost.com/wp-dyn/content/article/2010/02/07/AR2010020702693.html. Kurtz's ellipsis.

13. Lloyd Grove, "The Death of the White House Press Corps," *Daily Beast*, April 3, 2010, accessed August 22, 2010, www.thedailybeast.com/blogs-and-stories/2010-04-03/death-of-the -white-house-press-corps/2/.

14. Reported in ibid.

15. Peter Hamby, "Did Twitter Kill the Boys on the Bus? Searching for a Better Way to Cover a Campaign" (Joan Shorenstein Center on the Press, Politics, and Public Policy, Discussion Paper D-80, September 2013), accessed July 3, 2015, http://shorensteincenter.org/wp-content /uploads/2013/08/d80_hamby.pdf.

16. Ibid., 15.

17. Timothy Crouse, *The Boys on the Bus* (New York: Random House, 1972).

18. Daniel Kreiss, "Seizing the Moment: The Presidential Campaigns' Use of Twitter during the 2012 Election Cycle," *New Media & Society*, online December 5, 2014, doi:10.1177 /1461444814562445.

19. Peter Hamby, "Did Twitter Kill the Boys on the Bus? Searching for a Better Way to Cover a Campaign" (Harvard University Shorenstein Center, August 23, 2013), http://shorensteincen ter.org/d80-hamby/.

20. Mark Coddington, Logan Molyneaux, and Regina G. Lawrence, "Fact Checking the Campaign: How Political Reporters Use Twitter to Set the Record Straight (or Not)," *International Journal of Press Politics* 19 (October 2014): 391–409.

21. Frank Luntz, *Words That Work: It's Not What You Say, It's What People Hear* (New York: Hyperion, 2007), xiii.

22. Reported in Sam Stein, "Frank Luntz Pens Memo to Kill Financial Regulatory Reform," *Huffington Post*, February 1, 2010, accessed August 19, 2010, www.huffingtonpost.com/2010/02/01/frank-luntz-pens-memo-to_n_444332.html.

23. Luntz Research Companies, "Straight Talk: The Environment: A Cleaner, Safer, Healthier America," p. 132, accessed August 18, 2010, www.ewg.org/files/LuntzResearch_environment.pdf.

24. Ibid., 131.

25. Frank Luntz, interview by PBS *Frontline*, November 13, 2006, accessed August 18, 2010, www.pbs.org/wgbh/pages/frontline/hotpolitics/interviews/luntz.html.

26. I am indebted to Leah Ceccarelli, a colleague in the Department of Communication at the University of Washington, for her helpful analysis of how the political attack on science has been so effective.

27. Luntz Research Companies, "Straight Talk," 138.

28. Leah Ceccarelli suggests that scientists should engage more positively with political challenges to their work in order to gain the attention of audiences and show them in direct language why the challenges are not credible.

29. Maxwell T. Boykoff and Jules M. Boykoff, "Balance as Bias: Global Warming and the US Prestige Press," *Global Environmental Change* 14 (2004): 125–36.

30. Pew Research Center for the People and the Press, "Global Warming: A Divide on Causes and Solutions," January 24, 2007, accessed December 10, 2010, http://pewresearch.org/pubs/282/global-warming-a-divide-on-causes-and-solutions.

31. Matthew C. Nisbet and Chris Mooney, "Framing Science," *Science* 316 (April 6, 2007): 56.

32. Luntz, interview by PBS *Frontline*. First ellipsis in transcript.

33. Poll commissioned by the Yale Project on Climate Change, accessed August 19, 2010, http://environment.yale.edu/climate/publications/americans-global-warming-beliefs-and-attitudes-2010/.

34. *Wikipedia*, s.v. "Frank Luntz," accessed August 19, 2010, http://en.wikipedia.org/wiki/Frank_Luntz.

35. Gallup polls, 2014, 2015, reported in Justin McCarthy, "In U.S., Worries about Terrorism, Race Relations Up Sharply," March 17, 2015, accessed July 5, 2015, http://www.gallup.com/poll/182018/worries-terrorism-race-relations-sharply.aspx?utm_source=americans%20level%20of%20worry%202015&utm_medium=search&utm_campaign=tiles.

36. Dean Acheson, *Present at the Creation: My Years in the State Department* (New York: Norton, 1969), 375.

37. Leon V. Sigal, *Reporters and Officials: The Organization and Politics of News Reporting* (Lexington, MA: Heath, 1973), 122–24.

38. See, for example, Daniel C. Hallin, Robert Karl Manoff, and Judy K. Weddle, "Sourcing Patterns of National Security Reporters" (paper presented at the Annual Meeting of the American Political Science Association, San Francisco, August 30–September 2, 1990); and Jane Delano Brown, Carl R. Bybee, Stanley T. Wearden, and Dulcie Murdock, "Invisible Power: Newspaper Sources and the Limits of Diversity," *Journalism Quarterly* 64 (1987): 45–54. More recently, see W. Lance Bennett, Regina G. Lawrence, and Steven Livingston, *When the Press Fails: Political Power and the News Media from Iraq to Katrina* (Chicago: University of Chicago Press, 2007).

39. Thomas E. Patterson, "Doing Well and Doing Good: How Soft News and Critical Journalism Are Shrinking the News Audience and Weakening Democracy—and What News Outlets Can Do about It" (Working paper, Joan Shorenstein Center on the Press, Politics and Public

Policy, John F. Kennedy School of Government, Harvard University, 2000), http://shor ensteincenter.org/wp-content/uploads/2012/03/soft_news_and_critical_journalism_2000 .pdf.

40. Steven Livingston and W. Lance Bennett, "Gatekeeping, Indexing, and Live Event News: Is Technology Altering the Construction of News?," *Political Communication* 20, no. 4 (October/December 2003): 363–80.

41. W. Lance Bennett, "Toward a Theory of Press-State Relations in the United States," *Journal of Communication* 40, no. 2 (1990): 103–27.

42. Walter Lippmann, *Public Opinion* (New York: Free Press, 1922), 9.

43. Acheson, *Present at the Creation*.

44. See Murray Edelman, *Political Language: Words That Succeed, Policies That Fail* (New York: Academic Press, 1977).

45. Ibid.

46. See David L. Altheide and Robert P. Snow, *Media Logic* (Beverly Hills, CA: Sage, 1979).

47. See, for example, Mark Hertsgaard, *On Bended Knee: The Press and the Reagan Presidency* (New York: Shocken, 1989); also Jarol B. Manheim, *All of the People, All the Time: Strategic Communication and American Politics* (Armonk, NY: M. E. Sharpe, 1991).

48. Quoted by F. Christopher Arterton, "Campaign Organizations Face the Mass Media in the 1976 Presidential Nomination Process" (paper presented at the Annual Meeting of the American Political Science Association, Washington, DC, September 1977), 4.

49. NBC News, "White Paper on the Reagan Presidency," December 30, 1981.

50. For the classic discussion of symbols in politics, see Murray Edelman, *The Symbolic Uses of Politics* (Urbana: University of Illinois Press, 1964).

51. Elahe Izadi and Abby Phillip, "South Carolina House Votes to Remove Confederate Flag from Statehouse Grounds," *Washington Post*, July 9, 2015, accessed July 10, 2015, http://www .washingtonpost.com/news/post-nation/wp/2015/07/09/south-carolina-house-votes-to -remove-confederate-flag-from-statehouse-grounds/.

52. Manheim, *All of the People, All the Time*.

53. Martha Joynt Kumar, *Managing the President's Message: The White House Communications Operation* (Baltimore: Johns Hopkins University Press, 2007).

54. David R. Mayhew, *Congress: The Electoral Connection* (New Haven, CT: Yale University Press, 1974).

55. See J. William Fulbright, *The Pentagon Propaganda Machine* (New York: Vintage, 1970); also Richard Barnet, *Roots of War* (Baltimore: Penguin, 1973).

56. David Wise, *The Politics of Lying: Government Deception, Secrecy and Power* (New York: Vintage Books, 1973), 270–74.

57. Ibid., 273.

58. Quoted in Hertsgaard, *On Bended Knee*, 33.

59. The following overview of Hertsgaard's analysis, from *On Bended Knee*, is organized along the lines suggested by Steven Livingston of George Washington University.

60. Hertsgaard, *On Bended Knee*, 35.

61. Ibid., 48.

62. Ibid., 49.

63. Ibid., 36.

64. Ibid.

65. Jack Honomichl, "Richard Wirthlin, Advertising Man of the Year," *Advertising Age*, January 23, 1989.

66. Quoted in Hedrick Smith, *The Power Game: How Washington Works* (New York: Ballantine, 1988).

67. Quoted ibid., 409.

68. Quoted in ibid., 407.

69. Luntz, *Words That Work*, 4–5.

70. See Doris A. Graber, *Processing the News: How People Tame the Information Tide*, 2nd ed. (New York: Longman, 1988); Russell Neuman, Marion Just, and Ann Crigler, *Common Knowledge* (Chicago: University of Chicago Press, 1993); and Michael Delli Carpini and Bruce Williams, "Television in Political Discourse" (paper presented at the Annual Meeting of the American Political Science Association, Washington, DC, September 1991).

71. For a detailed discussion of how this worked, see Joe McGinniss, *The Selling of the President* (New York: Pocket Books, 1969).

72. Luntz, *Words That Work*, 22.

73. See Susan Herbst, *Reading Public Opinion: How Political Actors View the Democratic Process* (Chicago: University of Chicago Press, 1998); and Robert M. Entman, *Democracy without Citizens* (New York: Oxford University Press, 1989).

74. Daniel Boorstin, *The Image: A Guide to Pseudo-events in America* (New York: Atheneum, 1961).

75. Ibid., 11–12.

76. See W. Lance Bennett, Regina G. Lawrence, and Steven Livingston, *When the Press Fails: Political Power and the News Media from Iraq to Katrina* (Chicago: University of Chicago Press, 2007).

77. Robert M. Entman, *Scandal and Silence: Media Responses to Presidential Misconduct* (Cambridge: Polity Press, 2012).

78. Based on data compiled by John Woolley and Gerhard Peters, The American Presidency Project, accessed July 7, 2015, http://www.presidency.ucsb.edu/data/newsconferences.php.

79. Ken Auletta, "Fortress Bush," *New Yorker*, January 19, 2004, accessed January 16, 2016, http://www.newyorker.com/magazine/2004/01/19/fortress-bush.

80. Mark Knoller, "Obama's First Year: By the Numbers," CBS News, January 20, 2010, accessed August 22, 2010, www.cbsnews.com/8301-503544_162-6119525-503544.html.

81. Mark Knoller, "Knoller's Numbers: President Obama's Late Night TV Appearances," CBS News, March 12, 2015, accessed July 7, 2015, http://www.cbsnews.com/news/knollers-numbers-president-obamas-late-night-tv-appearances/.

82. Kurtz, "White House Press Corps Feels Bypassed."

83. Joe Foote, "The Network Economic Imperative and Political Access," *Political Communication Review* 10 (1985): 2.

84. AP wire story, *Seattle Times*, February 8, 1982, A3.

85. John Anthony Maltese, *Spin Control: The White House Office of Communications and the Management of Presidential News* (Chapel Hill: University of North Carolina Press, 1992).

86. An excellent, richly documented account of the Snowden case can be found in *Wikipedia*, s.v. "Edward Snowden," accessed July 8, 2015, https://en.wikipedia.org/wiki/Edward_Snowden.

87. Andrew Collins, "The Obama Administration and Its War on Whistleblowers," Watchdog .org, September 29, 2014, accessed July 9, 2015, http://watchdog.org/173721/obama-adminis tration-whistleblowers/.

88. Leonard Downie Jr., "In Obama's War on Leaks, Reporters Fight Back," *Washington Post*, October 4, 2013, accessed July 8, 2015, http://www.washingtonpost.com/opinions/in-obamas

-war-on-leaks-reporters-fight-back/2013/10/04/70231e1c-2aeb-11e3-b139-029811dbb57f
_story.html.

89. Karen McVeigh, "Obama's Efforts to Control Leaks Most Aggressive since Nixon, Report Finds," *Guardian*, October 10, 2013, accessed July 8, 2015, http://www.theguardian.com
/world/2013/oct/10/obama-leaks-aggressive-nixon-report-prosecution. A PolitiFact investigation supported this claim also: Jon Greenberg, "CNN's Tapper: Obama Has Used Espionage Act More than All Previous Administrations," PolitiFact, January 10, 2014, accessed July 9,
2015, http://www.politifact.com/punditfact/statements/2014/jan/10/jake-tapper/cnns-tapper
-obama-has-used-espionage-act-more-all-/.

90. Matt Apuzzo, "Condoleezza Rice Testifies on Urging The Times to Not Run Article," *New York Times*, January 15, 2015, accessed July 9, 2015, http://www.nytimes.com/2015/01/16/us/
politics/condoleezza-rice-testifies-on-urging-the-times-to-suppress-leak.html?_r=0.

91. James Risen, *State of War: The Secret History of the CIA and the Bush Administration*
(New York: The Free Press, 2006).

92. Richard Morin, "Budget Czars for a Day," *Washington Post National Weekly Edition*,
November 23–29, 1992, 36.

93. Murray Edelman, *Constructing the Political Spectacle* (Chicago: University of Chicago
Press, 1988).

CHAPTER FIVE

1. "Is Glenn Greenwald the Future of News?" [exchange between Bill Keller and Glenn
Greenwald], *New York Times*, October 27, 2013, accessed July 24, 2015, http://www.nytimes.com
/2013/10/28/opinion/a-conversation-in-lieu-of-a-column.html.

2. Ibid.

3. Robert Entman, *Scandal and Silence: Media Responses to Presidential Misconduct* (Cambridge: Polity Press, 2012).

4. Reported in Sally Kohn, "Trump's Outrageous Mexico Remarks," CNN, June 18, 2015,
accessed July 25, 2015, http://edition.cnn.com/2015/06/17/opinions/kohn-donald-trump
-announcement/.

5. Quoted in Ben Schreckinger, "Trump Attacks McCain: 'I like people who weren't captured,'" *Politico*, July 18, 2015, accessed July 25, 2015, http://www.politico.com/story/2015/07
/trump-attacks-mccain-i-like-people-who-werent-captured-120317.html.

6. James Hohmann, "The Donald: Almost Half of All Conversation Last Week on Social
and Regular Media Was about Him," *Washington Post*, July 9, 2015, accessed July 25, 2015,
http://www.washingtonpost.com/news/powerpost/wp/2015/07/09/trump-dominates-social
-media/.

7. Quoted in Michael Massing, "The Press: The Enemy Within," *New York Review of Books*
52, no. 20 (December 15, 2005).

8. Charles Bierbauer, remarks at the conference "Politics and the Media in the New Millennium," hosted by the Annette Strauss Institute, University of Texas, Austin, held at Belo Mansion, Dallas, Texas, February 18, 2006.

9. See, for example, Jay G. Blumler and Michael Gurevitch, "Politicians and the Press: An
Essay in Role Relationships," in *Handbook of Political Communication*, ed. Dan Nimmo and
Keith Sanders (Newbury Park, CA: Sage, 1981), 467–93.

10. Herbert J. Gans, *Deciding What's News* (New York: Pantheon, 1979); and Gaye Tuchman,
Making News (New York: Free Press, 1978).

11. Bernard C. Cohen, *The Press and Foreign Policy* (Princeton, NJ: Princeton University

Press, 1963); and Timothy Cook, *Governing with the News* (Chicago: University of Chicago Press, 1998).

12. Thomas E. Patterson, "Doing Well and Doing Good: How Soft News and Critical Journalism Are Shrinking the News Audience and Weakening Democracy—and What News Outlets Can Do about It" (Working paper, Joan Shorenstein Center on the Press, Politics and Public Policy, John F. Kennedy School of Government, Harvard University, 2000), http://shorensteincenter.org/wp-content/uploads/2012/03/soft_news_and_critical_journalism_2000 .pdf.

13. See the argument in Robert W. McChesney, *The Problem of the Media: U.S. Communication Politics in the Twenty-First Century* (New York: Monthly Review Press, 2004).

14. Thomas E. Patterson, "Irony of a Free Press: Professional Journalism and News Diversity" (paper prepared for the Annual Meeting of the American Political Science Association, Chicago, September 3–6, 1992). See also Thomas E. Patterson, *Out of Order* (New York: Knopf, 1993; New York: Vintage Books, 1994).

15. Timothy Cook, "Domesticating a Crisis: Washington Newsbeats and Network News after the Iraq Invasion of Kuwait," in *Taken by Storm: The Media, Public Opinion, and U.S. Foreign Policy in the Gulf War*, ed. W. Lance Bennett and David L. Paletz (Chicago: University of Chicago Press, 1994), 105–30.

16. See, for example, the numerous accounts of reporters, including Lou Cannon, *Reporting: An Inside View* (Sacramento: California Journal Press, 1977); Robert Darnton, "Writing News and Telling Stories," *Daedalus* 104 (Spring 1975): 175–94; and Lewis Lapham, "Gilding the News," *Harper's*, July 1981, 31–39.

17. For an excellent discussion of this syndrome, see Tuchman, *Making News*.

18. Robert Scholes, "Double Perspective on Hysteria," *Saturday Review*, August 24, 1968, 37.

19. For a detailed analysis of how this pattern occurs, see Leon Sigal, *Reporters and Officials* (Lexington, MA: Heath, 1973).

20. Tom Bethell, "The Myth of an Adversary Press," *Harper's*, January 1977, 36.

21. Reported in Steve Goldstein, "How about Term Limits for the Unelected Elite," *Columbia Journalism Review*, May/June 1994, 35.

22. Ibid.

23. See, for example, Warren Breed's classic study, "Social Control in the Newsroom," *Social Forces* 33 (May 1955): 326–35.

24. Edward Jay Epstein, *News from Nowhere* (New York: Vintage, 1973).

25. Ibid.

26. See Timothy Crouse, *The Boys on the Bus* (New York: Ballantine, 1973).

27. Mark Fishman, *Manufacturing the News* (Austin: University of Texas Press, 1980), 80–81.

28. Ibid., 81.

29. Stephen Hess, *The Washington Reporters* (Washington, DC: Brookings Institution, 1981), 130.

30. See Larry Sabato, *Feeding Frenzy* (New York: Free Press, 1991).

31. See W. Lance Bennett, "The Cueless Public: Bill Clinton Meets the New American Voter in Campaign '92," in *The Clinton Presidency*, ed. Stanley Renshon (Boulder, CO: Westview Press, 1995).

32. Quoted in Maureen Dowd, "How a Battered Clinton Has Stayed Alive," *New York Times*, March 16, 1992, 1.

33. David Shaw, "Dire Judgments on Clinton Started Just Days into Term," *Los Angeles Times*, September 16, 1993, A1.

34. Jacob Weisberg, "The White House Beast," *Vanity Fair*, September 1993, 169.

35. Maureen Dowd, "Beached," *New York Times Magazine*, June 19, 1994, 18.

36. Tom Howell Jr., "Donald Trump Accuses Hillary Clinton of 'Criminal Activity' in Email Scandal," *Washington Times*, July 26, 2015, accessed July 28, 2015, http://www.washingtontimes .com/news/2015/jul/26/donald-trump-accuses-hillary-clinton-of-criminal-a/.

37. Michael E. Schmidt and Mike Apuzzo, "Inquiry Sought in Hillary Clinton's Use of Email," *New York Times*, July 23, 2015, accessed July 31, 2015, http://www.nytimes.com/2015/07/24/us /politics/inquiry-is-sought-in-hillary-clinton-email-account.html.

38. Kurt Eichenwald, "How 'The New York Times' Bungled the Hillary Clinton Emails Story," *Newsweek*, July 24, 2015, accessed July 31, 2015, http://www.newsweek.com/hillary-clinton-new -york-times-emails-357246.

39. Margaret Sullivan, "A Clinton Story Fraught with Inaccuracies: How It Happened and What Next?," *New York Times*, July 27, 2015, accessed July 31, 2015, http://publiceditor.blogs .nytimes.com/2015/07/27/a-clinton-story-fraught-with-inaccuracies-how-it-happened-and -what-next/.

40. See, for example, Philip Meyer's criticism of market research and defense of more reliable social science investigations in his article "In Defense of the Marketing Approach," *Columbia Journalism Review*, January/February 1978, 61.

41. Bruce A. Williams and Michael X. Delli Carpini, *After Broadcast News: Media Regimes and the New Information Environment* (Cambridge University Press, 2011).

42. Ibid., 10.

43. Glenn Greenwald, "The Spirit of Judy Miller Is Alive and Well at the NYT, and It Does Great Damage," *The Intercept*, July 21, 2015, accessed July 29, 2015, https://firstlook.org/ theintercept/2015/07/21/spirit-judy-miller-alive-well-nyt-great-damage/.

44. "Nonprofit News Outlets," Pew Research, accessed July 31, 2015, http://features.journal ism.org/nonprofit-news-outlets/.

45. "About Us," ProPublica, accessed July 30, 2015, https://www.propublica.org/about/.

46. "Editorial Mission," *The Intercept*, accessed July 30, 2015, https://firstlook.org/theinter cept/staff/.

47. Adrienne Russell, "Hacking the News: Journalism, Activism, and Media Sensibilities" (paper presented at the conference "Protest Participation in Variable Communication Ecolo- gies," Alghero, Italy, June 24–27, 2015), accessed July 25, 2015, http://protestcommunication ecologies.com.

48. Carey Shenkman, "Whistleblowers Have a Human Right to a Public Interest Defense, and Hactivists Do, Too," *Huffington Post*, May 20, 2015, accessed July 25, 2015, http://www.huff ingtonpost.com/carey-shenkman/whistleblowers-have-a-hum_b_6903544.html.

49. Russell, "Hacking the News."

50. Andrew Chadwick and Simon Colister, "Boundary-Drawing Power and the Renewal of Professional News Organizations: The Case of the Guardian and the Release of the Edward Snowden NSA Leak," *International Journal of Communication* 8, 2 (2014): 2420–41.

51. Michael Sontheimer, "Spiegel Interview with Julian Assange: We Are Drowning in Ma- terial," *Der Spiegel*, July 20, 2015, accessed July 31 2015, http://www.spiegel.de/international /world/spiegel-interview-with-wikileaks-head-julian-assange-a-1044399.html.

52. Robert M. Entman, *Democracy without Citizens: Media and the Decay of American Poli- tics* (New York: Oxford University Press, 1989).

53. Dan Nimmo and James E. Coombs, *Mediated Political Realities*, 2nd ed. (New York: Longman, 1989).

CHAPTER SIX

1. Alex S. Jones, *Losing the News*, excerpted in "An Argument Why Journalists Should Not Abandon Objectivity," *Nieman Reports*, n.d., accessed August 2, 2015, http://niemanreports.org /articles/an-argument-why-journalists-should-not-abandon-objectivity/.

2. Ben Bagdikian, *The Media Monopoly* (Boston: Beacon Press, 1997), excerpted at Third World Traveler, accessed August 2, 2015, http://www.thirdworldtraveler.com/Media/Demo Media_Bagdikian.html.

3. Hunter S. Thompson, *Fear and Loathing on the Campaign Trail '72* (New York: Simon & Schuster, 1973), excerpted at Goodreads, accessed August 2, 2015, http://www.goodreads.com /quotes/145766-so-much-for-objective-journalism-don-t-bother-to-look-for.

4. Joan Didion, *Political Fictions* (New York: Alfred A. Knopf, 2001). The quote is from Joseph Lelyveld, "Another Country," *New York Review of Books*, December 20, 2001, 10.

5. David T. Z. Mindich, *Just the Facts: How "Objectivity" Came to Define American Journalism* (New York: New York University Press, 1998), 5–6.

6. Pew Research Center for the People and the Press survey, March 1999, www.people-press .org/press99sec1.htm.

7. Gerald J. Baldasty, *The Commercialization of News in the Nineteenth Century* (Madison: University of Wisconsin Press, 1992).

8. Ibid., ch. 2.

9. For discussions of the origins and impact of the wire services, see Bernard Roscho, *Newsmaking* (Chicago: University of Chicago Press, 1975); Frank L. Mott, *The News in America* (Cambridge, MA: Harvard University Press, 1952); and Edwin Emery and Henry Ladd Smith, *The Press in America* (New York: Prentice-Hall, 1954).

10. See Mindich, *Just the Facts*.

11. Ibid.

12. Michael Schudson, *Discovering the News* (New York: Basic Books, 1978), ch. 3.

13. Upton Sinclair, *The Brass Check* (Pasadena, CA: Author, 1920); see also Meyer Berger, *The Story of the New York Times* (New York: Simon & Schuster, 1951); and John Tebbell, *The Media in America* (New York: Mentor, 1974).

14. For a history of this period and its ideas, see, among others, Harold J. Laski, "The Present Position of Representative Democracy," *American Political Science Review* 26 (August 1932): 629–41; John Diggins, *Mussolini and Fascism: The View from America* (Princeton, NJ: Princeton University Press, 1972); and Schudson, *Discovering the News*.

15. See the following books by Walter Lippmann: *Drift and Mastery* (New York: Kennerly, 1914), *Liberty and the News* (New York: Harcourt Brace, 1920), *Public Opinion* (New York: Free Press, 1922), and *The Phantom Public* (New York: Harcourt Brace, 1925).

16. For supporting evidence for this claim, see, among others, Berger, *Story of the New York Times*; Mott, *News in America*; Emery and Smith, *Press in America*; Tebbell, *Media in America*; and Schudson, *Discovering the News*.

17. Tebbell, *Media in America*, ch. 12.

18. Lou Cannon, *Reporting: An Inside View* (Sacramento: California Journal Press, 1977), 35.

19. Mindich, *Just the Facts*, 8.

20. For a review of these professional norms, see Tebbell, *Media in America*; John W. C. Johnstone, Edward J. Slawski, and William W. Bowman, *The News People: A Sociological Portrait of American Journalists and Their Work* (Urbana: University of Illinois Press, 1976); Gaye Tuchman, *Making News: A Study in the Construction of Reality* (New York: Free Press, 1978); and Schudson, *Discovering the News*.

21. In recent years, the much-touted specialist has entered the reporting ranks. However, the use of specialists continues to be restricted to a few subject areas, such as science and economics. Also, specialists are employed by a relatively small number of big news organizations. Because the bulk of political reporting continues to be done by generalists who rotate assignments periodically and who refrain from introducing technical or theoretical perspectives in their reports, the practice of generalism merits inclusion here.

22. See Timothy Cook, *Governing with the News: The News Media as a Political Institution* (Chicago: University of Chicago Press, 1998); Bartholomew Sparrow, *Uncertain Guardians: The News Media as a Political Institution* (Baltimore: Johns Hopkins University Press, 1999); Rodney Benson, "News Media as a 'Journalistic Field': What Bordieu Adds to New Institutionalism, and Vice Versa," *Political Communication* 23 (2006): 187–202.

23. Tuchman, *Making News*, 87.

24. See, for example, Murray Edelman, *The Symbolic Uses of Politics* (Urbana: University of Illinois Press, 1964); Peter L. Berger and Thomas Luckmann, *The Social Construction of Reality* (New York: Anchor, 1966); and W. Lance Bennett, *Public Opinion in American Politics* (New York: Harcourt Brace Jovanovich, 1980), chs. 13 and 14.

25. C. Jack Orr, "Reporters Confront the President: Sustaining a Counterpoised Situation," *Quarterly Journal of Speech* 66 (February 1980): 17–32.

26. Ibid., 22.

27. See, for example, Harvey Molotch and Marilyn Lester, "Accidents, Scandals, and Routines: Resources for Insurgent Methodology," *Insurgent Sociologist* 3 (1973): 1–12; Harvey Molotch and Marilyn Lester, "News as Purposive Behavior: On the Strategic Use of Routine Events, Accidents, and Scandals," *American Sociological Review* 39 (February 1974): 101–12; Murray Edelman, *Political Language* (New York: Academic Press, 1977), ch. 3; Todd Gitlin, *The Whole World Is Watching* (Berkeley: University of California Press, 1980), chs. 2 and 7; and Doris A. Graber, *Mass Media and American Politics*, 3rd ed. (Washington, DC: Congressional Quarterly Press, 1989), ch. 8.

28. David L. Altheide and Robert P. Snow, *Media Logic* (Beverly Hills, CA: Sage, 1979), chs. 3 and 4.

29. See, for example, Howard Simmons and Joseph A. Califano Jr., eds., *The Media and Business* (New York: Vintage, 1979).

30. Henry Beck, "Attentional Struggles and Silencing Strategies in a Human Political Conflict: The Case of the Vietnam Moratoria," in *The Structure of Social Attention: Ethological Studies*, ed. M. R. A. Chanu and R. R. Larson (New York: Wiley, 1976).

31. Jan S. Wenner and William Greider, "The Rolling Stone Interview: Bill Clinton," *Rolling Stone*, December 9, 1993, 40–45.

32. For a fascinating look at Richard Nixon's ins and outs with the press, see Marvin Kalb, *The Nixon Memo* (Chicago: University of Chicago Press, 1995).

33. For a more detailed analysis of the spoon-fed aspects of Watergate investigative reporting, see Gladys Engel Lang and Kurt Lang, *The Battle for Public Opinion: The President, the Press, and the Polls during Watergate* (New York: Columbia University Press, 1983). The Langs also provide extensive documentation on the overwhelming emphasis, both in the White House and among the press, on Nixon's personal image and popularity during the Watergate saga.

34. Lisa Leff and Jonathan Adolph, "AIDS and the Family Paper," *Columbia Journalism Review*, March/April 1986, 11.

35. Quoted in David Walker, "The War Photo That Nobody Wanted to See," *Photo District News*, August 1991, 16.

36. Quoted in ibid.

37. See, for example, Brian Stelter, "James Foley Beheading Video: Would You Watch It?," CNN, August 21, 2014, accessed August 5, 2015, http://edition.cnn.com/2014/08/20/us/isis-beheading-social-media/.

38. Daniel Boorstin, *The Image* (New York: Atheneum, 1961).

39. See W. Lance Bennett, "Storytelling in Criminal Trials: A Model of Social Judgment," *Quarterly Journal of Speech* 64 (February 1978): 1–22; and W. Lance Bennett and Martha S. Feldman, *Reconstructing Reality in the Courtroom* (New Brunswick, NJ: Rutgers University Press, 1981).

40. Bennett and Feldman, *Reconstructing Reality in the Courtroom*, ch. 4.

41. James David Barber, "Characters in the Campaign: The Literary Problem," in *Race for the Presidency: The Media and the Nominating Process*, ed. John Barber (Englewood Cliffs, NJ: Prentice-Hall, 1978).

42. Edward Jay Epstein, *News from Nowhere* (New York: Vintage, 1973), 4–5.

43. Herbert Gans, *Deciding What's News* (New York: Vintage, 1979), 173.

44. Ibid., 171.

45. Bennett, "Storytelling in Criminal Trials"; and Bennett and Feldman, *Reconstructing Reality in the Courtroom*.

46. See Edelman, *Political Language*; and Bennett, *Public Opinion in American Politics*.

47. Gans, *Deciding What's News*, ch. 2.

48. See Tuchman, *Making News*; and Mark Fishman, *Manufacturing the News* (Austin: University of Texas Press, 1980).

49. Robert Darnton, "Writing News and Telling Stories," *Daedalus* 104 (Spring 1975): 189.

50. Edward Jay Epstein, "The Grand Cover-Up," *Wall Street Journal*, April 19, 1976, 10.

51. Johnstone, Slawski, and Bowman, *News People*.

52. Gans, *Deciding What's News*, 143.

53. Epstein, *News from Nowhere*, 137.

54. Gans, *Deciding What's News*, 143.

55. Ibid.

56. Ibid.; also Timothy Crouse, *Boys on the Bus* (New York: Ballantine, 1973).

57. Gans, *Deciding What's News*, 142.

58. A summary of remarks by Diana Henriques at a seminar titled "Corporate Power: You Can Run, but You Can't Hide," Shorenstein Center, Kennedy School of Government, Harvard University, October 12, 1999.

59. See, for example, Warren L. Breed, "Social Control in the Newsroom," *Social Forces* 33 (May 1955): 326–35; Walter Geiber, "Across the Desk: A Study of 16 Telegraph Editors," *Journalism Quarterly* 33 (Fall 1956): 423–32; Epstein, *News from Nowhere*; Crouse, *Boys on the Bus*; and Gans, *Deciding What's News*.

60. For discussion of the impact of wire services on newspaper coverage, see Crouse, *Boys on the Bus*; and Leon Sigal, *Reporters and Officials* (Lexington, MA: D. C. Heath, 1975). The impact of the "wires" on television news is discussed extensively in Epstein, *News from Nowhere*; and Gans, *Deciding What's News*.

61. Edwin Diamond, *Good News, Bad News* (Cambridge, MA: MIT Press, 1980) 228.

62. "Last Week Tonight with John Oliver: Climate Change Debate (HBO)," May 11, 2014, accessed August 3, 2015, https://www.youtube.com/watch?v=cjuGCJJUGsg&feature=youtu.be.

63. Dan Balz and Scott Clement, "Poll: Major Damage to GOP after Shutdown, and Broad Dissatisfaction with Government," *Washington Post*, October 22, 2013, https://www .washingtonpost.com/politics/poll-major-damage-to-gop-after-shutdown-and-broad -dissatisfaction-with-government/2013/10/21/dae5c062-3a84-11e3-b7ba-503fb5822c3e_story .html.

64. *Wikipedia*, s.v. "False balance," accessed August 3, 2015, https://en.wikipedia.org/wiki /False_balance.

65. Margaret Sullivan, "Another Outbreak of 'False Balance'?," *New York Times*, February 7, 2015, accessed August 3, 2015, http://www.nytimes.com/2015/02/08/opinion/sunday/another -outbreak-of-false-balance.html.

66. Katherine Trendacosta, "BBC Institutes Changes to Prevent 'False Balance' in Science Reporting," *io9*, April 7, 2014, accessed August 3, 2015, http://io9.com/bbc-institutes-changes -to-prevent-false-balance-in-sc-1600207025.

67. John Vidal, "MPs Criticize BBC for 'False Balance' in Climate Change Coverage," *Guardian*, April 2, 2014, accessed August 3, 2015, http://www.theguardian.com/environment /2014/apr/02/mps-criticise-bbc-false-balance-climate-change-coverage. Vidal's ellipsis and brackets.

68. Katrina vanden Heuvel, "The Distorting Reality of 'False Balance' in the Media," *Washington Post*, July 15, 2014, accessed August 3, 2015, https://www.washingtonpost.com/opinions /katrina-vanden-heuvel-the-distorting-reality-of-false-balance-in-the-media/2014/07/14 /6def5706-0b81-11e4-b8e5-d0de80767fc2_story.html.

69. Johnstone, Slawski, and Bowman, *News People*; see also Charles J. Brown, Trevor R. Brown, and William L. Rivers, *The Media and People* (New York: Holt, Rinehart and Winston, 1978); and Stephen Hess, *The Washington Reporters* (Washington, DC: Brookings Institution, 1981).

70. Tuchman, *Making News*.

71. Gaye Tuchman, "Objectivity as Strategic Ritual: An Examination of Newsmen's Notions of Objectivity," *American Journal of Sociology* 77 (1972): 660–79.

CHAPTER SEVEN

1. Victor Pickard, "Can Government Support the Press? Historicizing and Internationalizing a Policy Approach to the Journalism Crisis," *Communication Review* 14 (2011): 73.

2. Robert W. McChesney, *Rich Media, Poor Democracy: Communication Politics in Dubious Times* (New York: The New Press, 2015), i.

3. Mark Jurkowitz, "The Growth of Digital Reporting," Pew Research Center, March 26, 2014, accessed August 9, 2015, http://www.journalism.org/2014/03/26/the-growth-in-digital -reporting/. For the figures up to 2015, see Ken Doctor, "Newsonomics: The Halving of America's Daily Newsrooms," *Nieman Lab*, July 28, 2015, http://www.niemanlab.org/2015/07 /newsonomics-the-halving-of-americas-daily-newsrooms/.

4. Google DE, "18 Hacks You Didn't Realize You Could Do with Google," BuzzFeed, July 5, 2015, accessed August 14, 2015, http://www.buzzfeed.com/googlede/life-hacks-you -didnt-realise-you-could-do-with-625#.eyxlYLoakY.

5. Frederic Fillous, "Legacy Media: The Lost Decade in Six Charts," *Monday Note*, August 31, 2014, accessed August 12, 2015, http://www.mondaynote.com/2014/08/31/legacy-media-the -lost-decade-in-six-charts/.

6. Michael Barthel, "Newspapers: Fact Sheet," Pew Research Center, April 29, 2015, accessed August 11, 2015, http://www.journalism.org/2015/04/29/newspapers-fact-sheet/.

7. Robert G. Kaiser, "The Bad News about the News," Brookings Report, October 16, 2014, accessed August 11, 2015, http://www.brookings.edu/research/essays/2014/bad-news.

8. "Facebook and Google Are about to Overtake All of TV in Audience Size," *Business Insider*, November 25, 2013, accessed August 11, 2015, http://www.businessinsider.com/facebook-and-google-to-overtake-tv-in-reach-2013-11?IR=T.

9. Kaiser, "Bad News."

10. Victor Pickard and Alex T. Williams, "Salvation or Folly? The Promises and Perils of Digital Paywalls," *Digital Journalism* 2 (2014): 195–213.

11. Vindu Goal and Ravi Somaiya, "Facebook Begins Testing Instant Articles from News Publishers," *New York Times*, May 13, 2015, accessed August 9, 2015, http://www.nytimes.com/2015/05/13/technology/facebook-media-venture-to-include-nbc-buzzfeed-and-new-york-times.html.

12. David Segal, "Ariana Huffington's Improbable, Insatiable Content Machine," *New York Times*, June 30, 2015, accessed August 12, 2015, http://www.nytimes.com/2015/07/05/magazine/arianna-huffingtons-improbable-insatiable-content-machine.html?_r=0.

13. Quoted in Erik Wemple, "Ezra Klein's Vox.com: Precious, in More Ways than One," *Washington Post*, April 7, 2014, accessed August 13, 2015, https://www.washingtonpost.com/blogs/erik-wemple/wp/2014/04/07/ezra-kleins-vox-com-precious-in-more-than-one-way/.

14. Eric Eldon, "A Closer Look at Chorus, the Next Generation Platform That Runs Vox Media," *TechCrunch*, May 7, 2012, accessed August 13, 2015, http://techcrunch.com/2012/05/07/a-closer-look-at-chorus-the-next-generation-publishing-platform-that-runs-vox-media/.

15. Frédéric Filloux, "Hard Comparison: Legacy Media vs. Digital Native," *Monday Note*, November 24, 2014, accessed August 14, 2015, http://www.mondaynote.com/2014/11/24/hard-comparison-legacy-media-vs-digital-native/.

16. Michael Massing. "Digital Journalism: The Next Generation," *New York Review of Books*, June 25, 2015, accessed August 12, 2015, http://www.nybooks.com/articles/archives/2015/jun/25/digital-journalism-next-generation/.

17. Pablo Boczkowski, *News at Work: Imitation in an Age of Information Abundance* (Chicago: University of Chicago Press, 2011).

18. Dean Starkman, "The Hamster Wheel: Why Running as Fast as We Can Is Getting Us Nowhere," *Columbia Journalism Review*, September/October 2010, 24–28.

19. Ibid., 28.

20. From Neil Hickey, "So Big: The Telecommunications Act at Year One," *Columbia Journalism Review*, January/February 1997, 23.

21. Quoted in Dante Toza, "Clear Channel Rewrites Rules of Radio Broadcasting," CorpWatch, October 8, 2003, accessed January 13, 2016, www.corpwatch.org/article.php?id=8728.

22. Christine Chen, "The Bad Boys of Radio," *Fortune*, May 3, 2003, http://money.cnn.com/magazines/fortune/fortune_archive/2003/03/03/338343/.

23. Ibid., 23.

24. Bill Carter, "Chief of ABC News Is Resigning," *New York Times*, September 6, 2010, accessed September 6, 2010, www.nytimes.com/2010/09/07/business/media/07abc.html?_r=3&hp.

25. See Neil Hickey, "Money Lust: How Pressure for Profit Is Perverting Journalism," *Columbia Journalism Review*, July/August 1998, 28.

26. Amy Mitchell, "State of the News Media 2015," Pew Research Center, April 29, 2015,

accessed August 17, 2015, http://www.journalism.org/2015/04/29/state-of-the-news-media
-2015/.

27. Gene Roberts, "Drowning in Shallow Waters," *Columbia Journalism Review* (May/June 1996): 55.

28. Doug Underwood, *When MBAs Rule the Newsroom* (New York: Columbia University Press, 1993).

29. Ibid., xii.

30. Quoted in Ken Auletta, "Look What They've Done to the News," *TV Guide*, November 9, 1991, 5.

31. Alessandra Stanley, "How to Persuade the Young to Watch the News? Program It, Executives Say," *New York Times*, January 15, 2000, C6.

32. David Laventhol, "Profit Pressures," *Columbia Journalism Review*, May/June 2001, 19.

33. Craig Flournoy and Tracy Everbach, "Damage Report," *Columbia Journalism Review*, July/August 2007, 33.

34. Ibid., 35, 37.

35. Ibid., 36.

36. Quoted in ibid.

37. Matthew A. Baum, *Soft News Goes to War: Public Opinion and American Foreign Policy in the New Media Age* (Princeton, NJ: Princeton University Press, 2003).

38. Robert W. McChesney and John Nichols, "Up in Flames," *Nation*, October 17, 2003, www .thenation.com/doc.mhtml?i=20031117s=mcchesney&c51.

39. "Net Neutrality: What You Need to Know," Free Press, 2015, accessed August 17, 2015, http://www.savetheinternet.com/net-neutrality-what-you-need-know-now.

40. See Richard Kielbowicz, *News in the Mail: The Press, Post Office and Public Information, 1700–1860s* (Westport, CT: Greenwood Press, 1989).

41. Jochai Benkler, *The Wealth of Networks* (New Haven, CT: Yale University Press, 2006).

42. McChesney, *Rich Media, Poor Democracy.*

CHAPTER EIGHT

1. Thomas Jefferson to Charles Yancy, 1816, Colonial Williamsburg, accessed August 18, 2015, http://www.history.org/foundation/journal/winter11/literacy.cfm.

2. Graham Murdock and Peter Golding, "Information Poverty and Political Inequality: Citizenship in the Age of Privatized Communications," *Journal of Communication* 39 (1989): 180.

3. Henry Jenkins, *Confronting the Challenges of Participatory Culture: Media Education for the 21st Century*, with Ravi Purushotma, Margaret Weigel, Katie Clinton, and Alice J. Robinson (Cambridge, MA: MIT Press, 2009), xi.

4. Walter Pincus, "Newspaper Narcissism: Our Pursuit of Glory Led Us Away from Readers," *Columbia Journalism Review*, May/June 2009, 55.

5. Steven Livingston, "The 'Nokia Effect': The Reemergence of Amateur Journalism and What It Means for International Affairs," in *From Pigeons to News Portals: Foreign Reporting and the Challenge of New Technology*, ed. David Perlmutter and John Hamilton (Baton Rouge: Louisiana State University Press, 2007), 47–69.

6. Quoted in Jake Batsell, "Lone Star Trailblazer: Will the Texas Tribune Transform Texas Journalism?," *Columbia Journalism Review*, July/August 2010, 40.

7. "About Us," *Texas Tribune*, accessed September 25, 2010, www.texastribune.org/about/.

8. James S. Fishkin, *The Voice of the People* (New Haven, CT: Yale University Press, 1995).

9. John Gastil, *By Popular Demand: Revitalizing Representative Democracy through Deliberative Election* (Berkeley: University of California Press, 2000).

10. Ibid. See also Fishkin, *Voice of the People*; and Fishkin, *Democracy and Deliberation* (New Haven, CT: Yale University Press, 1991).

11. Mark E. Kann, "More or Less Democracy in the Internet Age?," *networked publics* (blog), USC Annenberg School for Communication, October 6, 2005. http://networkedpublics.org/digital_democracy/more_or_less_democracy_in_the_internet_age.html.

12. Diana Mutz, *Hearing the Other Side: Deliberative vs. Participatory Democracy* (New York: Cambridge University Press, 2006).

13. See Anthony Giddens, *Modernity and Self-Identity: Self and Society in the Late Modern Age* (Stanford, CA: Stanford University Press, 1991).

14. Jürgen Habermas, *Structural Transformation of the Public Sphere: An Inquiry into a Category of Bourgeois Society* (Cambridge, MA: MIT Press, 1989).

15. Todd Gitlin, lecture, University of Washington, May 20, 1999.

16. Nina Eliasoph, *Avoiding Politics: How Americans Produce Apathy in Everyday Life* (New York: Cambridge University Press, 1998).

17. Michael Schudson, *The Good Citizen: A History of American Civic Life* (New York: The Free Press, 1998).

18. For an extended discussion of these ideas, see W. Lance Bennett, "The UnCivic Culture: Communication, Identity, and the Rise of Lifestyle Politics," *P.S.: Political Science and Politics* 31, no. 4 (December 1998): 41–61.

19. See Erik Asard and W. Lance Bennett, *Democracy and the Marketplace of Ideas: Communication and Government in Sweden and the United States* (Cambridge: Cambridge University Press, 1997).

20. Robert W. McChesney, *Telecommunications, Mass Media & Democracy: The Battle for Control of U.S. Broadcasting, 1928–1935* (New York: Oxford University Press, 1993).

21. Robert W. McChesney and John Nichols, *The Death and Life of American Journalism: The Media Revolution That Will Begin the World Again* (New York: Nation Books, 2010).

22. See Paul Farhi, "PBS Scrutiny Raises Political Antennas," *Washington Post*, April 22, 2005, accessed January 2, 2016, http://www.washingtonpost.com/wp-dyn/articles/A8067-2005 Apr21.html.

23. Thomas E. Patterson, "Irony of the Free Press: Professional Journalism and News Diversity" (paper presented at the annual meeting of the American Political Science Association, Chicago, September 3–6, 1992), 2.

24. Ibid.

25. Quoted in Frank L. Mott, *The News in America* (Cambridge, MA: Harvard University Press, 1952), 5.

26. "Weighing Anchor: At the Start of His Final Year, Tom Brokaw Takes Stock and Looks Ahead," interview by Jane Hall, *Columbia Journalism Review*, January/February 2004, 19.

27. Brent Cunningham, "Re-thinking Objectivity," *Columbia Journalism Review*, July/August 2003, 24.

28. Steven Livingston, *The Terrorism Spectacle* (Boulder, CO: Westview, 1994).

29. Douglas M. McLeod and Dhavan V. Shah, *News Frames and National Security: Covering Big Brother* (New York: Cambridge University Press, 2015).

30. Dannegal G. Young, "The Daily Show as New Journalism," in *Laughing Matters: Humor and American Politics in the Media Age*, ed. J. S. Morris and J. C. Baumgartner (New York: Routledge, 2007), 241–59.

31. Shanto Iyengar, *Is Anyone Responsible?* (Chicago: University of Chicago Press, 1993).

32. Reported in Cunningham, "Re-thinking Objectivity," 27.

33. Mark R. Levy and John P. Robinson, "The 'Huh?' Factor: Untangling TV News," *Columbia Journalism Review*, July/August 1986, 50.

34. Regina G. Lawrence, "Game-Framing the Issues: Tracking the Strategy Frame in Public Policy News," *Political Communication* 17, no. 2 (April/June 2000): 93–114.

35. Levy and Robinson, "'Huh?' Factor," 48.

36. Lawrence Lessig, *Republic, Lost: How Money Corrupts Congress—and a Plan to Stop It* (New York: Hachette, 2011).

37. Ken Klukowski, "Founding Fathers Smiling after Supreme Court Campaign Finance Ruling," January 22, 2010, accessed September 27, 2010, http://www.foxnews.com/opinion/2010/01/22/ken-klukowski-supreme-court-amendment-mccain-feingold/.

38. Quoted in Warren Richey, "Supreme Court: Campaign Finance Limits Violate Free Speech," *Christian Science Monitor*, January 21. 2010, accessed September 27, 2010, www.csmonitor.com/USA/Justice/2010/0121/Supreme-Court-Campaign-finance-limits-violate-free-speech.

39. Amie Parness and Kevin Cirilli, "The $5 Billion Presidential Campaign?," *The Hill*, January 21, 2015, accessed August 28, 2015, http://thehill.com/blogs/ballot-box/presidential-races/230318-the-5-billion-campaign.

40. Quoted in Michael Hiltzik, "Five Years after Citizens United Ruling, Big Money Reigns," *Los Angeles Times*, August 28, 2015, accessed August 28, 2015, http://www.latimes.com/business/hiltzik/la-fi-hiltzik-20150125-column.html.

41. See, for example, Harris Poll, February 16–21, 2010, reported at www.pollingreport.com/politics.htm (accessed September 28, 2010). See also Gallup 2014 survey, reported in Jon Clifton, "Americans Less Satisfied with Freedom," July 1, 2014, accessed August 28, 2014, http://www.gallup.com/poll/172019/americans-less-satisfied-freedom.aspx.

42. Tim Mak, "Poll: Corruption is No. 2 Issue," *Politico*, July 30, 2012, accessed August 28, 2012, http://www.politico.com/story/2012/07/poll-corruption-is-no-2-issue-079109.

43. Reported in "Americans' Views on Money in Politics," *New York Times*, June 2, 2015, accessed August 26, 2015, http://www.nytimes.com/interactive/2015/06/02/us/politics/money-in-politics-poll.html?_r=0.

44. Maureen Dowd, "Bush and Clinton Dynasties Hit Trump Bump," *New York Times*, August 29, 2015, accessed August 30, 2015, http://www.nytimes.com/2015/08/30/opinion/sunday/maureen-dowd-bush-and-clinton-dynasties-hit-trump-bump.html?&moduleDetail=section-news-4&action=click&contentCollection=Opinion&region=Footer&module=MoreInSection&version=WhatsNext&contentID=WhatsNext&pgtype=article.

45. Reported in Ibid.

46. McChesney, *Telecommunications*.

47. Stephen Coleman and Jay Blumler, *The Internet and Democratic Citizenship* (New York: Cambridge University Press, 2009).

48. Report of the Hutchins Commission on Freedom of the Press, quoted in *A Free and Responsible Press*, ed. Robert D. Leigh (Chicago: University of Chicago Press, 1947), 15.

49. Victor Pickard, *America's Battle for Media Democracy: The Triumph of Libertarianism and the Future of Media Reform* (New York: Cambridge University Press, 2015).

50. Amanda Zamora, "ProPublica's 'Get Involved' Aims to Inspire More Crowd-Powered News," ProPublica, August 20, 2015, accessed September 3, 2015, http://www.propublica.org/article/propublicas-aims-to-spur-more-crowd-powered-news.

51. Geoff Livingston, "Jodi Gersh on Social Media-Driven Journalism," *Geoff Livingston* (blog), August 19, 2015, accessed September 3, 2015, http://geofflivingston.com/2015/08/19/jodi-gersch-on-social-media-driven-journalism/.

52. Elia Powers, "The Rise of Engagement Editors and What It Means," MediaShift, August 19, 2015, accessed September 3, 2015, http://mediashift.org/2015/08/the-rise-of-the-engagement-editor-and-what-it-means/.

53. Leonard Downie Jr. and Michael Schudson, "The Reconstruction of American Journalism," *Columbia Journalism Review*, November/December 2009, 28–29.

54. Ibid., 45–51.

55. McChesney and Nichols, *Death and Life of American Journalism.*

56. Peter Hamilton, "Public Television Funding: Comparison across 18 Western Countries," December 10, 2014, accessed September 6, 2015, http://www.documentarytelevision.com/public-television/public-television-funding-compared-across-18-western-countries/. See also McChesney and Nichols, *Death and Life of American Journalism*, 192.

57. Reported in M. G. Siegler, "Every 2 Days We Create as Much Information as We Did up to 2003," *TechCrunch*, August 4, 2010, http://techcrunch.com/2010/08/04/schmidt-data/.

58. Quoted in Bree Nordenson, "Overload: Journalism's Battle for Relevance in an Age of Too Much Information," *Columbia Journalism Review*, November/December 2008, 30.

59. Quoted in Tony Schwartz, "Struggling to Disconnect from Our Digital Lives," *New York Times*, July 31, 2015, accessed August 27, 2015, http://www.nytimes.com/2015/08/01/business/dealbook/struggling-to-disconnect-from-our-digital-lives.html.

60. Ibid.

INDEX

Baker, Russell, 49

balance: bias and, 97, 132, 155; broadcast licenses and, 26; climate change and, 97; criticism of, 176–77; versus due weight, 178; ethics and, 178; fairness and, 129, 190; false, 176–78; forced, 176, 178; governing with the news and, 15; government shutdown over the budget and, 176–77; "he said, she said" journalism and, 178; Hutchins Commission and, 234; impartiality tradition in journalism and, 124; indexing and, 15–16, 125, 155, 176; journalistic passivity and, 156; objectivity and, 156–57, 161, 176–78; political comedy and, 176, 177; spin and, 128–29; when one side is not true, 15–16, 111, 124, 176–77, 216

Baldasty, Gerald, 158

Baltimore Sun, 5

Bartlett, Dan, 115

Baum, Matthew, 202

BBC, 177–78, 184, 237

Belo, Alfred Horatio, 201

Belo Corporation, 193, 201

Benghazi, Libya, embassy attack, 142–43

Benson, Rodney, 162

Bernstein, Carl, 165, 171

Bethell, Tom, 134

Bezos, Jeff, 1, 182

bias: acknowledged, 158; balance and, 97, 132, 155; toward the bizarre and sensational, 73; cheapening of news content and, 202; complexity versus simplicity and, 50; against complex underlying realities, 33; confirmation bias and, 72; culture of journalism and, 185–86; debate over, 33, 36; episodic versus thematic news and, 35; extreme versus representative cases and, 48; fact versus fiction and, 48–49; journalists' avoidance of, 226–27; media logic and, 102; myths about, 213; narratives and drama and, 40; news-gathering routines and, 131, 132–33; objectivity and, 125, 128–29, 131, 148–49, 154, 156, 175, 178–79, 218; perception of, 30–31, 32–33; profitable production and, 56; public

attention and, 74; public broadcasting and, 215–16; reporters' personal politics and, 250nn11–12; scripted events and, 39; spin and, 128–29; stereotyping and, 174–75; TV versus print news sources and, 69; types of, xi–xii. *See also* dramatization; fragmentation; framing; personalization

Bierbauer, Charles, 129

Bild, 184

Bimber, Bruce, 24

bin Laden, Osama, 68, 69

bloggers and blogging: activism and, 153; audience participation and, 228, 237; feeding frenzies and, 126; formation of publics and, 60; *Huffington Post* and, 185, 235; hybrid media and, ix, 125, 128; innovation in news formats and, 238; investigative journalism and, 148; in legacy and digital media, 188; Obama administration press strategy and, 91, 94; stories planted with, 126

Blow, Charles, 72

Blumler, Jay, 130

Boczkowski, Pablo, 188

Boehner, John, 12, 41

Boorstin, Daniel, 114, 168–69

Boston Globe, 182

Boykoff, Jules, 97

Boykoff, Maxwell, 97

Brecht, Bertolt, 203

Brooks, David, 12

Bush, George H. W., and G. H. W. Bush administration, 82, 130, 140

Bush, George W., and G. W. Bush administration: Axis of Evil and, 109; climate change and, 15, 95–96; Corporation for Public Broadcasting and, 215; energy policy of, 173; Enron Corporation and, 173; feeding frenzies and, 140; governing with the news and, 14, 16; Hurricane Katrina and, 32, 40; media consolidation and, 203; "mission accomplished" and, 32, 34–35, 114–15; NSA spying scandal and, 32; press conferences and, 115; press management and, 32, 34–35. *See also* Iraq War

Business Insider, 181
BuzzFeed, ix, 92, 181, 182, 184

campaign finance, 61, 90, 229–31
Cannon, Lou, 160
Cap Cities, 193
Cappella, Joseph, 39, 56
Card, Andrew, 68
Carter, Jimmy, and Carter administration, 45–46, 130, 140, 164
CBS: buyout of, 193; CBS News and, 199; Walter Cronkite and, 146, 199; Iraq War coverage and, 17; media consolidation and, 194, 199; Edward R. Murrow and, 199; profitability of news and, 199
Ceccarelli, Leah, 258n28
Center for Investigative Reporting, 235
Center for Public Integrity, 235
Chadwick, Andrew, 151
Charleston, South Carolina, shootings, 104
Charter Communications, 195
Cheney, Dick, 68
Chorus technology platform, 186
Churchill, Winston, 72
Citizen Four (film), 118
Citizens United ruling, 230
Clapper, James, 119
class warfare, 55
Clear Channel, 192
climate change: balance in reporting and, 97, 176, 177–78; as campaign issue, 97–98; corporate interests and, 97; debate on *Last Week Tonight* and, 176, 177; framing and, 33–34, 95–96; global concern about, 98, 97–98; versus global warming, 96; as partisan news story, 95–98; spin and, 15; 2009 Copenhagen climate summit and, 98
Clinton, Bill, and Bill Clinton administration: campaigning for other candidates and, 10; as car crash dummy, 141; corporate concentration of ownership in media and, 191; feeding frenzies and, 140–42; game-framing during, 52; health care reform and, 50–51, 79–80; media treatment of, 31, 130; negativity

in election campaigns and, 82; New Beginnings and, 109; personalization of the presidency and, 43–44; personal scandals and, 37, 110, 140–41; press management and, 31–32, 98, 115, 141–42, 164; Republican criticisms of, 28; Telecommunications Act of 1996 and, 193, 194; uncontrolled news situations and, 142; welfare reform and, 42–43; Whitewater scandal and, 164
Clinton, Hillary: health care reform and, 80; political scandals and, 142–44, 147, 164; 2008 election and, 54; 2016 election and, 28, 127, 142–44
CNBC, 195
CNN: international bureaus of, 138; Iraq War coverage and, 17; legacy press and, ix; Political Prophecy game and, 70–71; polls and, 44, 65, 71; speed of publication and, 92
Coddington, Mark, 93–94
Cohen, Bernard, 130
Colbert, Stephen, 17–18, 20–22, 44
Colbert Report, The, 18
Collister, Simon, 151
Columbia Journalism Review, 221
Comcast, 194–96, 199, 203
Comedy Central, 18
comedy news. *See* political comedy
Commission on Freedom of the Press, 234–35
Confederate flag, 104
Congress and the legislative process: declining confidence in, 162; dramatization of news and, 46–47, 48; emotion provoked by, 103; government shutdown over the budget and, 176–77; negative coverage of, 130; Obama-era obstructionism and, 142; poison pills in legislation and, 41; reelection concerns and, 105; Republicans as "party of No" and, 72; veto blocks and, 97
Cook, Timothy, 9–10, 47, 130, 132–33, 162
Corporation for Public Broadcasting, 215
Couric, Katie, 18, 116, 146
Creative Commons, 149, 205
Crigler, Ann, 74, 76, 109–10

crime and criminal justice, 49
Cronkite, Walter, 146, 199
Crouse, Timothy, 93, 139
Curbed, 186
cynicism: crisis of credibility and, 179–80; versus critical analysis, 225; game-framing and, 169, 179–80; among journalists, 93; myth of the free press and, 220; political communication process and, 85; strategic communication and, 123

Daily Beast, 137, 148
Daily Show, The, 18, 20, 22
Dallas Morning News, 201
Darnton, Robert, 47, 170
Dateline, 73
Deaver, Michael, 106
de Blasio, Bill, 53
de Blasio, Chiara, 53
Deepwater Horizon oil spill, 40, 54–55
DeLillo, Don, 48
Delli Carpini, Michael X., 1, 4, 86, 109–10, 146
democracy and governance: activism and, 67, 75–76, 87–88; Arab Spring and, 228; big government and, 80, 95, 101, 223, 229, 239; with or without citizens, 152–53; effective narrative and, 30; fragile link between news and, 25–27; history of journalism and, 160; ill-informed voters and, 72; independent thought and, xiv; journalists holding politicians accountable and, 89; marketplace of ideas for, 214; media reform and, 181; media regulation and, 232; myth of open government and, 163; news and quality of, 24; news as essential to, xiii, 121, 189; news management and, 9–11; public deliberation and, 56; public opinion as engine of, 59; public protests and, 217–18; public sphere and, 211; reinvention of government and, 241; shaping of political behavior and, 60; social media for campaigns versus governing and, 142; technology and, 205–6; vicious politi-

cal cycle and, 121–22. *See also* politics; public policy
Dennis, Everette, 31, 33
Department of Homeland Security, 41
Der Spiegel, 118, 152. See also *Spiegel Online*
Diamond, Edwin, 174–75
Didion, Joan, 156
digital media: activism and, 87–88, 237; adapt or die and, 184–88; advertising and, 197; audience-driven, 182, 188; citizen-produced information and, 23–24, 209; click-through rates and, 113; culture of journalism and, 185–88; The Daily Me and, x, 1, 3; data mining and, 61–62; delivering consumers to advertisers and, 6; digital natives and, ix, 1; ease of public access and, 149; echo chamber effect and, 62; emerging content trends and, 181–82; experimentation in, 182, 187; fragmentation and, 9, 24; free internet and, 150; future of news and, 206; global trends and, 188; history of journalism and, 233–34; information overload and, 75, 239–41; innovation in news formats and, 235–36, 237–38; legacy media as source for, 181; native digital organizations and, ix, 181; net neutrality and, 57; new business models and, xiii; nonprofit status and, 238; number of outlets launched and, 148; Obama administration public relations and, 91; online communities and discussion boards and, 210–11; participatory culture of, xi, 2–3, 7, 208, 236–37; profitability and, 188–89; revenue for, 187, 236; speed of publication and, 92–93. *See also* investigative journalism; social media
Disney, 193, 194, 196–97
Donaldson, Sam, 141
Donsbach, Wolfgang, 250n12
Dowd, Maureen, 17–18, 30, 141, 231
Downie, Leonard, 232–33, 238
dramatization: adversarial reporting and, 159, 161; advertising and, 73; bias and, 33–34, 37–38, 40, 45–50, 62, 74, 252n46;

conflict among officials and, 101–2; distracted public and, 71, 74; dramatic elements of news stories and, 169–70; journalists' avoidance of, 226–27; journalists' preference for, 170; news-gathering routines, 133; politics as a spectacle and, 66; public opinion and, 64, 66–67, 69; reasons people follow the news and, 84; self-fulfilling news realities and, 69; Watergate and, 165

Dukakis, Michael, 82

Dunaway, Johanna, 51–52

Eater, The, 186

economics of journalism. *See* political economy of the news

Edelman, Murray, 49, 57, 64, 66, 101, 123

Eichenwald, Kurt, 143–44

election campaigns: campaign slogans and, 109; daily public relations battle in, 79; Electoral College and, 39; history of, 158; horse race narrative and, 39, 52–53; journalists ignoring policy-oriented content during, 29; legacy versus digital media and, 93; market research and, 61; negativity in, 28–29, 82; obsession with campaign narratives and, 29; polling and, 39, 64; press pack following candidates and, 93; spending on, 71; swing voters and, 71; war rooms and, 93. *See also* campaign finance

election of 1988, 82

election of 1992, 82

election of 2008, 54, 91, 97–98

election of 2012, 28, 43, 55, 91, 126, 188

election of 2014, 55

election of 2016, 28, 45, 61, 126–27, 142–44, 231

Ellsberg, Daniel, 118

emotions: campaign slogans and, 109–10; public opinion and, 77, 81, 95, 100; versus reason, 94–95, 103; symbols and, 103

Encyclopedia Britannica, 208

Enron Corporation, 173

Entman, Robert: on democracy without citizens, 67, 152; on dramatization of news, 32, 45, 48; on escalation of scan-dals, 115; feeding frenzies and, 125–26; on framing, 33–34; on leaders' access to public opinion, 59; on media logic, 23; on personalization of the presidency, 43, 45; racial conflict in polls and the news and, 64–65

environment, 151

Epstein, Edward Jay, 138, 169, 171, 172

Espionage Act, 119, 120, 261n89

evolution, 177

Exxon, 97

Facebook, 3, 87, 183–85, 188, 237

FactCheck.org, 43

fairness. *See* balance

Fairness and Accuracy in Reporting (FAIR), 33

Farah, Barbara, 82

FCC. *See* Federal Communications Commission

Federal Communications Commission (FCC), 26, 190, 202–4, 233, 238

feeding frenzies: appearance of press in-dependence and, 129–30; George W. Bush and, 140; Bill Clinton and, 140–42; Hillary Clinton and, 142–43; competi-tion among journalists and, 129; con-flict between press and politicians and, 129, 130; gotcha journalism and, 129–30; Obama and, 142; presidents from Lyndon Johnson to George H. W. Bush and, 140; press-politics and, 82, 99, 113, 125–27, 129

Fey, Tina, 146

Filloux, Frédéric, 187

Fiorina, Morris, 63–64

First Amendment, 25–26, 119, 121, 206

Fishkin, James, 210

Fishman, Mark, 139

Fiske, John, 75

FlipBoard, 182

Foley, James, 168

Foote, Joe, 116

foreign policy: dramatization of news and, 48; officials' domination of news coverage and, 100; polling and public opinion and, 64

Fortune, 237

Fox, buyout of, 193

Fox News: brand identity of journalists and, 41; on *Citizens United* ruling, 230; Stephen Colbert's commentary on, 21; Iraq War coverage and, 17; Obama administration and, 120; partisan nature of, 10, 31, 129; popularity of, 41; similarity across news sources and, 128; staged politics and, 100

fragmentation: of audience into communities of interest, 209, 210, 212; bias and, 33, 34, 38–39, 49–51; cheapening of news content and, 202; content inside Facebook and, 184; journalists' avoidance of, 226–27; low-information consumers and, 202; news-gathering routines and, 133; of political experience, 211; public opinion and, 69; of social institutions, 212

framing: big government and, 95; climate change and, 33–34, 95–96; declining confidence in the press and, 162; *Deepwater Horizon* oil spill and, 40; engagement of multiple mental activities and, 112; episodic, 35, 83; meaning organizers and, 112; people influenced by, 76; politics as a game and, 33, 35, 39–41, 44, 51–53, 169, 179–80, 226–28; scripted events and, 34–35; strategic communication and, 109, 111–12; winners and losers and, 130

Freedom Forum, 250n11

Free Press, 57, 202, 203, 220, 232

future of news: activism and, 237; alternative publications and, 224–25; buzz building and, 237; campaign finance reform and, 229–30; chaotic transitional period and, 235; citizen news voucher system and, 238–39; citizens as reporters and, 209; civic journalism and, 57; critical analysis of the news and, 223–24, 227; data mining and, 209–10, 211; improving audience understanding and, 227–28; information overload and, 239–41; innovation in news formats and, 235–39; interactive databases and,

228–29, 238; media monopolies and, 231–32, 233; net neutrality and, 220, 233, 235; new information order and, 206; news and power and, 217–18, 219; participatory culture and, 207, 208, 228, 236–37; partnerships and, 236; political comedy and, 225; proposals for citizens and, 222–26; proposals for journalists and, 226–28; proposals for politicians and government and, 229–33; public broadcasting and, 232, 238; public discussion on role of the press and, 233–35; public responsibility standards and, 231–33; public sphere and, 211–12; self-critical audiences and, 225–26

game framing. *See* framing

Gamson, William, 87

Gannett, 182–83, 193, 201

Gans, Herbert, 130, 169, 170, 171, 172

Garfield, Bob, 176

Garnson, William, 75–76

Gastil, John, 210

Gates, Bill, 172

Gawker, 181

gay rights, 188

General Electric (GE), 193, 199

Gergen, David, 106, 117

Gibson, Charlie, 116

Ginsburg, Ruth Bader, 230

Gitlin, Todd, 211

global financial crisis, 87, 173, 231

GlobalPost, 182

global warming. *See* climate change

Golding, Peter, 207

Goldstein, Steve, 135

Google, 183, 187, 204

Gore, Al, 97

gotcha journalism. *See* feeding frenzies

Graber, Doris, 25, 75, 77, 86, 109–10

Great Recession, 197

Great Society, 109

Greenwald, Glenn: career of, 151; as critic of *New York Times*, 22; on deference to official spin, 147; on impartiality in journalism, 124, 147, 148–49, 154; independent media and, 130; *The Intercept* and,

Kurtz, Howard, 116
Kuwait, 68, 132

Lady Gaga, 188
Lang, Gladys Engel, 265n33
Lang, Kurt, 265n33
Lapham, Lewis, 47
Last Week Tonight, 176, 177
LA Times, 189
Lawrence, Regina: on game-framing, 33–34, 39, 51–52, 169, 227–28; on journalists' use of Twitter, 93–94; negativity of politics and, 56
Lay, Kenneth, 173
leaks and leakers: digital watchdog journalism and, 182; future of news and, 206; intimidation and prosecution of, 119–21, 150; news authority and, 169; strategic communication and, 117–21; Watergate and, 165, 171
legacy media: adapt or die and, 184–85; agenda-setting function of, 60, 94; aging audience of, 1–2, 3; as arbiter of what is important, 145; bureaus and, 137–38; captive audience and, ix–x, 3, 9, 60–61, 71–72; continued dominance of, 58, 62, 94, 127–28, 183–84, 188; Walter Cronkite's tag line and, 146; culture of journalism and, 185–86; The Daily Us and, 1–2; declining confidence in, 30, 162; declining quality of, x, 4–5, 25–27, 144, 197; digital content of, 181–82; evolution of, 27; failing business model of, 147; feeding frenzies and, 125–26, 127–28; gatekeeping and, 145, 146; hamster wheel of, 189; illusion of independence and, 163–64; inflexibility of, 187; influence of, on public opinion, 74–75; journalists as gatekeepers and, 25; niche for, 188; 1980s as height of mass media era and, 71–72; Obama administration public relations and, 91, 92; origins of, xiii; other outlets' reliance on, 181; partnerships and, 153; paywalls and, 5, 184; press conferences and speeches and, 116; public service standards for license renewal and, 189, 192, 232–33;

revenue for, x, 2, 5, 183, 187; speed of publication and, 92–93; staffing cuts and, 149, 153, 181, 183, 189; standardized reporting and, 180; survival strategies of, 188–90; valuation of companies and, 182–83
legislatures. *See* Congress and the legislative process
Le Monde, 118, 152
Lessig, Lawrence, 229–30
Levy, Mark, 227
Lewinsky, Monica, 110, 166
libel, 36
Liddy, G. Gordon, 165
Limbaugh, Rush, 12, 79
Lippmann, Walter, 60, 66, 100, 160
Livingston, Steven, 46, 224
Los Angeles Times, 97, 128–29
Luce, Henry, 234
Luntz, Frank, 94–98, 104, 109–12
Lyon, Santiago, 90–91

MacKuen, Michael, 81
Maltese, John Anthony, 117
Manheim, Jarol, 104
Manning, Chelsea, 120, 150
Marcus, George, 81, 141
mass media. *See* legacy media
Mays, Lowry, 192
McCain, John, 54, 127
McCarthyism, 164
McChesney, Robert: on allocation of broadcast bandwidth, 232–33; on big business versus the public interest and, 206; on citizen news voucher system and, 238–39; on media consolidation and, 203; on media reform, 181; on public broadcasting and, 214–15; on public subsidies for journalism, 6
McClatchy, 183
McHugh, Philip, 41–42
McKibben, Bill, 151
McLeod, Douglas, 224
media logic, 23, 101–2, 126, 208, 236
Media Watch, 26
Mencken, H. L., 72
Merkel, Angela, 118

140; investigative journalism and, x; leakers and whistleblowers and, 119; new Nixon and, 110; resignation of, 165; Watergate and, 118, 140, 165, 265n33; White House Plumbers unit and, 118, 119; on withholding information from the public, 89

Noah, Trevor, 22, 225

North Korea, 109

NPR. *See* National Public Radio

NSA. *See* National Security Agency

Nye, Bill, 176

Obama, Barack, and Obama administration: Affordable Care Act and, 50–51, 80, 142; birther movement and, 44–45, 54, 80, 126, 142, 164; campaign advertising and, 70; campaign slogans of, 109; control of the news narrative and, 29–30, 40, 54–55, 94, 140, 142; *Deepwater Horizon* oil spill and, 40, 54–55; deportations and, 41, 65; Espionage Act and, 120, 261n89; FCC and, 203, 204; feeding frenzies and, 142; interviews and television appearances and, 115–16; leakers and whistleblowers and, 119–21; media treatment of, 32; NSA spying scandal and, 32; personal attacks against, 44–45, 54, 80; political style of, 72; popularity levels and, 10; press relations and, 90–92, 98–99, 115–16, 119–21; religious beliefs of, 164; Republican opposition and, 32, 72; Senate filibusters and, 142; Edward Snowden leaks and, 117, 119; as a socialist, 223; social media and, 91–92, 142; 2008 election and, 54; 2012 election and, 28, 55; wars in Iraq and Afghanistan and, 14, 61; welfare reform and, 43

Obamacare. *See* Affordable Care Act

objectivity: adversarial role of the press and, 162–65, 179; balance and, 156–57, 161, 176–78; bias and, 125, 128–29, 148–49, 154, 156, 175, 178–79, 218; business reporting and, 172–73; decency and good taste and, 161, 166–68; as defense mechanism for journalists, 180; de-

fining elements of, 161; documentary reporting practices and, 168–69; editorial review and, 174–75; exhaustive representations of reality and, 170–71; formulaic stories and, 169–71, 174–75; as illusion, 162–63, 180; impossibility of, 154, 179, 180; independent journalism and, 178–79; myth of the free press and, 213, 216–17, 220–21; origins of, 157–60; power inequalities and, 219; professional norms of journalism and, 124, 131, 140, 148–49, 155–57, 178–79; reporters' dependence on sources they cover and, 133–34, 154, 155, 172, 179; in Society of Professional Journalists code of ethics, 157; spin and, 155, 179, 216, 221; staged events and, 168, 170; truth and, 154, 156–57, 169, 221

Occupy Wall Street, 67, 87–88, 150

O Globo, 118, 152

Oliver, John, 18, 176, 177

Omidyar, Pierre, 125, 149

O'Reilly, Bill, 18, 21, 41

O'Reilly Factor, 18

Organizing for Action, 92

Orr, C. Jack, 163–64

Page, Benjamin, 59

Paletz, David, 43, 45, 48

Paley, William S., 199

Palin, Sarah, 12

Patterson, Thomas: on attracting citizen attention, 75; on core values of journalism, 5–6; on game-framing, 169; on government-generated distortions in the news and, 15; on homogenization of US journalism, 132; on irony of free press and, 216; on journalistic bias, 250n12; on negativity in politics, 56, 130; on political fog of war, 29; on politics as a game, 39; on spin versus truth, 28

Paul, Rand, 28

PayPal, 120

PBS. *See* Public Broadcasting Service

personalization: bias and, 34, 36–37, 40–46, 74; cheapening of news content

personalization (*continued*)
and, 202; digital media and, 62; dramatization and, 48–49; fragmentation and, 50; framing and, 83; of information delivery system, 209–10; journalists' avoidance of, 226–27; low-information consumers and, 202; news-gathering routines and, 133; of political experience, 211; public opinion and, 69

Petraeus, David, 121

Pew Research, 65–66, 72, 227–28

Pfeiffer, Dan, 91

Philadelphia Inquirer, 200–201

Phillips, Macon, 91

photojournalism and images, 167–68

Pickard, Victor, 181, 235

Pincus, Walter, 89, 207

Plante, Bill, 92

Poitras, Laura, 118, 124–25, 149, 151

polarization. *See* public opinion

political comedy: ability to point out deception and, 20; balance and, 176, 177; challenges to legacy media and, 147; climate change debate and, 176, 177; conformist reporting and, 129; credibility of, 18; future of news and, 225; gotcha journalism and, 129; hard and soft news and, 202; informed audience of, 20; infotainment and, 12; Iraq War and, 14; low-information consumers and, 202; as primary information source, 146; ratings for, 18; relief from spin and, 58; shortcomings of "real news" and, 17; versus traditional journalism, 20

political economy of the news: adapt or die and, 184–88; big business versus the public interest and, 196–202, 206; changing audience habits and, 183–84; cheapening the product and, 199–202; citizen movement for media reform and, 202–5; collapsed business model and, 183, 190, 207–8; corporate concentration of ownership in, 190–91; corporate influence on content and, 198–99, 200–201; corporate ownership of public information and, 213–14; Creative Com-

mons and, 149, 205; culture of journalism and, 185–88; decline of legacy media and, 181, 183; delivery of prime demographics to advertisers and, 197; end of local programming and, 192–93; executive pay and, 201; free markets and free press and, 219–20; hamster wheel of legacy media and, 189, 190; legacy media survival strategies and, 188–90; media monopolies and, 194–96, 213, 231–32, 233; mergers and breakups and, 190–96, 200, 203, 232; more with less and, 189; net neutrality and, 204; ownership deregulation and, 190–94, 199; paywalls and, 184; profitability and, 42, 52, 56, 138, 189, 197, 199, 200; profit squeezing and, 201, 208–9; profits subsidizing public good and, 208–9; public interest journalism and, 197, 198, 199; social responsibility standards and, 190–94, 199, 206, 214, 231–33; synergy and, 194, 196, 204; valuation of media companies and, 182–83

Political Prophecy game, 70–71

Politico, 181

politics: abandonment of, 85–86; angry voters and, 122; controlling political images and, 105; corruption and, 5, 229–30; fog of war in, 29; as a game, 33–35, 39–40, 51–53, 169, 179–80, 228; generational differences in engagement and, 85–86; generation gap in knowledge about, 8–9; negativity and, 4, 56, 130, 229; of newsmaking, 121–23; obstacles to creative action and, 229; political images and resulting actions and, 101, 103; political narratives and, 29–30; political reality versus news reality and, 102; popular lack of interest in, 72; post-truth age of, 22; as a spectacle, 66; spin versus truth and, 28; symbolic uses of, 102–5. *See also* campaign finance; democracy and governance

PolitiFact, 12, 261n89

polling: Arizona immigration law and, 65–66; campaign finance and, 230–

31; don't knows and don't cares and, 63–64; influence of, on outcomes, 64; Iraq War and, 63; market research and, 61, 73–74; phrasing of poll questions and, 62–63; polarized framing of, 64–66; public quiescence and, 64; pushing publics into opinions and, 63–64; race and immigration and, 64–66; spin and, 62–63; in strategic communication, 105, 107

Polygon, 186

Pool, Tim, 150–51

Popkin, Samuel, 83

Portland Afoot, 148

Powell, Michael, 203

PR. *See* public relations

presidency, 43–45, 46, 117, 141, 163–64

press-politics: adversarial relationship between politicians and the press and, 164–65; antigovernment politicians and, 12; Beltway versus the rest of the country and, xii; code of secrecy and, 90; controlling the news narrative and, 29–30, 40, 53–56, 94; cynicism and, 85; difficulty correcting politicians' assertions and, 19–20, 22; discipline of reporters and politicians and, 113; dissatisfaction with, 56; editions of this book and, ix–x, 20; feeding frenzies and, 82, 99, 113, 125–27; feeding the beast and, 98–100; governing with the news and, 9–11, 14, 106; images and, 100–101; information for decision making and, 4; meaning of, 10; misinforming the public and, 16–17; oversimplified storytelling and, 56; politics of newsmaking and, 121–23; power versus credibility and, 19; press as fourth branch of government and, 11; self-fulfilling messages and, 101; spin versus truth and, 28; symbiotic press-politician relationship and, 112–13; withdrawal from politics and, 56, 57

priming, 68–69

Prior, Markus, 71–72

professional norms of journalism: ad-versarial role of the press and, 161; anonymity of sources and, 147; core values and, 5–6; culture of journalism and, 185–86; decency and good taste and, 161, 166–68; deferential press and, 131–32, 164; economic changes in news industry and, 131; editorial review and, 162, 174–75; evolution of, 157–60, 185; fact checking and, 254n35; game-framing and, 130; gatekeeping and, 146; generalists versus specialists and, 162, 171, 265n21; house style and, 135, 136; interpretation of the news and, 227; journalists' commitment to, 147, 157; morality code and, 168; pressure to standardize and, 135–36, 139–40; public service and, 189–90, 192; reform and, 145; reporting versus issue advocacy and, 57; socialization of reporters and, 135–36; training of journalists and, 160–62. *See also* objectivity

Prometheus Radio Project, 191

ProPublica, ix, xii, 148–49, 182, 236–37

public broadcasting, 213–16, 232, 238–39

Public Broadcasting Service (PBS), 17, 33, 145, 215

public interest journalism. *See* investigative journalism

public opinion: anchoring mediated information and, 82–83; bolstering positions and, 79–81; citizen's dilemma and, 84–87; on climate change, 97–98; construction of, 66, 69, 81, 83, 86; cueing and, 78–79, 80; don't knows and don't cares and, 63–64; emotions and, 81–82, 95, 100; as engine of democracy, 59; late 1980s as turning point in, 67; media's influence on, 60, 62–66, 74–75; negative messages and, 82; news as stand-in for, 67; polarization in, 64–66, 72, 102; polls pushing publics into opinions and, 63–64; poverty of attention and, 59, 71–74, 254n35; processing the news and, 74–84; public policy at odds with, 231; quiescence and, 64, 66; selling of the Iraq War and, 67–70; strength of,

public opinion (*continued*)
exaggerated, 63–64, 69–70; TV versus print news sources and, 76–77, 81. *See also* polling

public policy: game-framing versus policy focus and, 52; interpretation of news and, 227–28; at odds with public opinion, 231

public relations: Affordable Care Act and, 72, 94; climate change and, 95–96, 97; control of the news and, 102; countering negative messages and, 82; daily news menu and, 89–90; desired public actions and, 73, 75; emotions versus reason and, 94–95; feeding frenzies and, 126; filling the news hole and, 137; honesty and dishonesty in, 70; Iraq War and, 13, 16, 61, 147; news events and, 105, 106; planting stories with friendly bloggers and, 126; public attention and, 61, 70–71, 73; self-fulfilling messages and, 101; simplification and, 67; social media and, 84, 91; spending on, 61; TV versus print news sources and, 69. *See also* spin

Putnam, Robert, 85–86

Quinnipiac University Poll, 65–66

race and racial conflict, 64–66, 104
Racked, 186
Reagan, Ronald, and Reagan administration: end of fairness doctrine and, 190; federal budget and, 116–17; Great Communicator and, 107; media treatment of, 31; negative coverage of, 130; New Federalism and, 109; news leaks and, 116–17; political reality versus news reality and, 102; press criticism and, 107–8; press management and, 31, 106, 115, 116; strategic communication and, 106–8; Teflon president and, 107; welfare and, 42
Re/code, 186
reform of journalism: citizen movement for, 202–5; end of gatekeeping and, 146–47; net neutrality and, 203, 204–5; new

investigative journalism and, 147–48; partnerships between investigative and conventional media organizations and, 153; potential of electronic technology and, 152–53. *See also* future of news

Rice, Condoleezza, 68, 121
Rich, Frank, 21
Risen, James, 120–21
Roberts, Cokie, 43–44
Robinson, John, 227
Rockefeller, Jay, 122
Rojecki, Andrew, 64–65
Rolling Stone, 164
Romney, Mitt, 28, 43, 55
Roof, Dylann, 104
Roosevelt, Franklin, 109
Rosen, Jay, 4, 22
Rotich, Juliana, 151
Roussef, Dilma, 118
Rubio, Marco, 13
Rumsfeld, Donald, 68
Russell, Adrienne, 150

Saddam Hussein, 68, 69, 224–25
Saturday Night Live, 18
Sawyer, Diane, 116
SB Nation, 186
Scahill, Jeremy, 149
scandals: adversarial role of the press and, 164; Bill Clinton's personal scandals and, 37, 110, 140–41, 166; Hillary Clinton's political scandals and, 142–44, 147; escalation of, 115; NSA spying scandal and, 32, 124–25; rising volume of sex scandals and, 166; Whitewater scandal and, 164
Schmidt, Eric, 239
Schneider, William, 10
Scholes, Robert, 134
Schudson, Michael, 212, 232–33, 238
Schwartz, Tony, 241
science, 96, 258n28
Seattle Post Intelligencer, 236
Seib, Philip, 75
September 11 attacks: civil liberties and, 224; Iraq War and, 13–14, 16, 67–69, 221, 224–25; lack of local news and, 192–93;

spin and, 32; US security and intelligence operations since, 121

Shah, Dhavan, 224

Shirky, Clay, 7, 22

Sidorsky, David, 47

Sigal, Leon, 99

Silverstein, Ken, 128–29

Simon, Herbert A., 59, 240–41

Slate, 185

Snow, Robert, 23, 101, 164

Snowden, Edward, 117–20, 125, 149–52, 188

social media: activism and, 87–88; buzz building and, 237; for campaigns versus governing, 142; direct outlets for politicians' messages and, 90; echo chamber effect and, 62; emotion and opinion formation and, 81; feeding frenzies and, 125; future of news and, 206; global financial crisis and, 87; journalists' use of, 92; legacy media and, 87; many-to-many communication logic and, 3; as news feed, 3, 7, 57, 184; as news filter, 23; Obama and Obama administration and, 91–92; press replaced by, 92–94; public relations and, 84; Donald Trump's 2016 candidacy and, 126–27; Brian Williams's fake war story and, 17–18. *See also* digital media

Society of Professional Journalists, 157

Sparrow, Bartholomew, 162

Spiegel Online, 184

spin: versus analysis and accountability, 226–27; blurred boundary between reporting and, 29; climate change and, 15; controlling the news narrative and, 53; corruption of news and, 81; distorted policy agendas and, 231; failure to hold officials accountable and, 149; formulaic stories and, 134, 135; government control of the news and, 11; how it works, 128–31; Hurricane Katrina and, 32, 100; indexing and, 15–16, 176; Iraq War and, 13–15, 32, 67; market research and, 61; misinforming the public and, 16–17; myth of the free press and, 216–17; news authority and, 169; 9/11 attacks and, 32; objectivity and, 128–29,

155, 179, 216, 221; politicians' logic and, 56; polling and, 62–63; power versus credibility and, 19; press pack and, 140; press's dependence on, 128, 130, 133–34, 147; public opinion and, 59–60, 66–67; versus reality, 28, 67, 69, 117; reasons for effectiveness of, 112–13; saturation of daily life with, 71; spin control and, 107; symbiosis between journalists and politicians and, 20, 22–23, 133–34; timing of, 68; truthiness and, 17. *See also* bias; public relations

Stahl, Lesley, 107–8

Stanton, Edwin, 159

Starkman, Dean, 189, 190

Starr, Kenneth, 166

Starr, Paul, 5

Stephanopoulos, George, 116, 141

Sterling, Jeffrey, 120–21, 150

Stevens, John Paul, 230

Stevenson, Richard, 29

Stewart, Jon, 18–22, 115, 225

strategic communication: aspirational language and, 112; consistent messaging and, 106, 110; controlling the news narrative and, 113–19; coordinated communication and, 106–7; cynical use of, 123; escalation of scandals and, 115; frame of mind and, 106; goals of, 105; interviews with ground rules and, 115; limited scope of news and, 123; managing the message and, 108–12; news as an event in its own right and, 122; news leaks and, 116, 117–19; pictures versus words and, 108; planning and, 106; political problems as communication problems and, 105; press conferences and, 115–16; press releases and, 116; propaganda and, 168–69; Ronald Reagan and, 106–8; repetition and, 106; spin control and, 107; staged events and, 113–15, 133, 168, 170; symbiotic press-politician relationship and, 112–13; symbolic politics and, 104–5; whistleblowers and, 117–21

Sullivan, Margaret, 177

Supreme Court, 46, 66, 118, 121, 230

Survivor, 199